18/5/23

Revolution of the Ordinary

Revolution of the Ordinary

LITERARY STUDIES AFTER
WITTGENSTEIN, AUSTIN, AND CAVELL

Toril Moi

The University of Chicago Press   CHICAGO AND LONDON

The University of Chicago Press, Chicago 60637
The University of Chicago Press, Ltd., London
© 2017 by Toril Moi
Published 2017

26 25 24 23 22 21 20 19 18 17   1 2 3 4 5

ISBN-13: 978-0-226-46430-5 (cloth)
ISBN-13: 978-0-226-46444-2 (paper)
ISBN-13: 978-0-226-46458-9 (e-book)
DOI: 10.7208/chicago/9780226464589.001.0001

Library of Congress Control Number: 2017005407

For Stanley Cavell
and
for David, as always

A *picture* held us captive. And we couldn't get outside it, for it lay in our language, and language seemed only to repeat it to us inexorably.

WITTGENSTEIN

Contents

Acknowledgments

I began work on this book in March 2009, at the Camargo Foundation in Cassis. I came to Cassis intending to work on a quite different project. But the stunning views of the Mediterranean cleared my mind. Although I was daunted by the difficulty and scope of the project, I really wanted to write about the philosophers who had changed my own intellectual life. I wanted to show that ordinary language philosophy—the philosophy of Ludwig Wittgenstein, J. L. Austin, and Stanley Cavell—can transform literary studies. In Cassis I wrote a paper on Cavell and Derrida, parts of which are included in chapter 3. I am grateful to the resident directors, Connie Higginson and Leon Selig, for making my semester in Cassis so delightful. In May and June 2012 I spent six weeks in residence at the House of Literature in Oslo, on the invitation of Aslak Sira Myhre, and with much support from Silje Riise Næss. The first version of chapter 10 was written there. In April and May 2014, the Bogliasco Foundation offered inspiring views and fabulous walks along the Ligurian coast. The first full draft of chapter 5 was written there. I am grateful for the hospitality of these institutions.

Yet this project has older roots. I spent a year at the National Humanities Center (NHC) here in North Carolina, from 1994 to 1995. At the NHC I joined a reading group on the everyday, where I began to read Wittgenstein and Austin in the company of the philosophers George Wilson and Richard Moran. Without their presence in that reading group, I might never have grasped the appeal of this radically different way of thinking about language and philosophy.

That same year I also met Stanley Cavell. Stanley's help and support over many years have been invaluable. He gave patient feedback on drafts from my book *What Is a Woman?* (1999) and even more on *Henrik Ibsen and the Birth of Modernism* (2006). His intellectual generosity and kindness were only matched by his ear for the slightest "off" tone in a draft.

I am also grateful for Cathleen Cavell's friendship and hospitality. I will never forget Stanley and Cathleen's visit to Duke University in the fall of 2009, when Stanley graciously agreed to inaugurate Duke's Center for Philosophy, Arts, and Literature (PAL).

Richard Fleming is my other teacher of ordinary language philosophy. In 2008/9 my colleague Sarah Beckwith and I obtained funds from Duke's Department of English to run an interdisciplinary working group. We wanted to read Wittgenstein systematically and invited Richard Fleming to guide the group's work. That academic year he flew down from Bucknell University for three intense weekends in which we read *Philosophical Investigations* remark by remark. My understanding of Wittgenstein owes an enormous amount to him. Richard also read a draft of this manuscript, rescuing me from many unfortunate formulations.

I also received much intellectual inspiration and support after I began working on this project. The "OLP and Feminism" group began to meet in 2011, in order to explore what ordinary language philosophy can bring to feminist theory. My fellow feminist investigators were Nancy Bauer, Sarah Beckwith, Alice Crary, Sandra Laugier, and Linda Zerilli. The intellectual power and brilliance of this group was (and remains!) awe-inspiring. To support the group's work, Nancy Bauer and I applied for, and received, a grant to run a Radcliffe Institute Exploratory Seminar, which met in Cambridge in April 2013. Eventually, the result of our labors turned into a cluster of articles, published under the title "Feminist Investigations" in *New Literary History* in Spring 2015. Chapter 4 in this book was originally written for that issue. But here I must acknowledge that I might never have been able to write chapter 4 if Yolonda Wilson hadn't taken the time to read intersectionality articles with me in 2012, and if Salla Peltonen hadn't done the same in 2013.

As the editor of *New Literary History*, Rita Felski welcomed and edited the articles in "Feminist Investigations." She also persuaded me to write a paper on the hermeneutics of suspicion for the Modern Language Association's convention in Vancouver in January 2015. Chapter 8 would not exist without her. I am grateful to Elizabeth Anker, Rita Felski, Niklas Forsberg, and Hugo Strandberg for useful feed-back on various versions of that chapter. Rita has been more than an editor. She has been a fine reader of drafts, a generous sharer of her own work, and a stalwart friend. Working with Rita is a privilege and a pleasure.

Chapter 10 is a much transformed version of an essay that began life in Norwegian as a pamphlet called *Språk og oppmerksomhet* (*Language and Attention*). I first began to think about language and attention in May and June 2012, as I attended parts of the trial of the terrorist of July 22, 2011 at

Oslo District Court. I am grateful to Åsne Seierstad, who inspired me to do this. Without the enthusiasm and encouragement of Trygve Åslund, Nora Campbell and Nazneen Khan Østrem at Aschehoug Publishers, I might never have begun work on this chapter. Finally, I must thank Ane Farsethås who commented on a very early draft on an hour's notice.

Over the years, I have presented material from this project in more places than I can mention. But two "sister-institutions" must be singled out. First, the Humanities Center at Johns Hopkins University. I have enjoyed the friendship and support of Ruth Leys and Michael Fried, and of Stephen Nichols for twenty years. I presented the very first version of my efforts to read Derrida from an ordinary language philosophy point of view at Johns Hopkins in November 2008. This spring I presented a version of chapter 9 there, at the conference held to celebrate the fiftieth anniversary of the Humanities Center. I also owe much to the Program in Philosophy and Literature at Stanford University, run by Joshua Landy and R. Lanier Anderson. Our collaboration has been a source of all kinds of ideas, not just for intellectual work, but for teaching and programs on our respective campuses.

Duke University funded the Center for Philosophy, Arts, and Literature (PAL) in 2009. PAL has become a hub of ordinary language philosophy activities at Duke. Without it, I might have lost courage. Duke also granted me two years of leave (2008/9 and 2013/14) for which I am deeply grateful. The Franklin Humanities Institute (FHI) at Duke gave me the opportunity to present an early draft of the book at an FHI Manuscript Workshop in November 2014. I am grateful to Josh Landy, Magdalena Ostas, and Ken Wissoker for their detailed feedback at that memorable occasion. The workshop wouldn't have happened without the hard work of Chris Chia and Beth Perry.

Over the years, two young women philosophers, Leonore Fleming and Heather Wallace, have helped me run PAL. Their enthusiasm and commitment have brightened my life and inspired my work. I am grateful to Shahrazad Shareef for her attentive proofreading of the manuscript and to Casey Williams for reading the typeset proofs. Finally, I want to thank the many graduate students who have taken my seminar on "Wittgenstein and Literary Theory" over the years. Their responses and suggestions to draft chapters have improved this book.

I also want to thank my "OLP friends": Anna-Klara Bojö, Christine Hamm, Yi-Ping Ong, Magdalena Ostas, Salla Peltonen, and Bernie Rhie for always being ready to discuss, comment, and support.

Sarah Beckwith has been there from the start. She was in that reading group at the NHC in 1994. At Duke, she and I read *The Claim of Reason* together. She co-organized our Wittgenstein seminars with Richard Fleming. She was a stalwart member of the "OLP and Feminism" group. Sarah is my brilliant friend. Without her company and conversation, both I and the book would be the poorer.

My two American stepchildren, Gabriel M. Paletz and Susannah B. F. Paletz, have been encouraging, witty, and full of ideas. My dear father, Seval Moi, and my loving brother, Geir Arne Moi, have always had total faith in me and my writing. My mother, Nora Moi, died on New Year's Eve in 2013. I miss her more than I can say.

My beloved husband, David L. Paletz, has lived with me and this book since the beginning. He was there in Cassis, in Oslo, and in Bogliasco. He participated in the manuscript workshop in 2014. He hosted meetings of the "OLP and Feminism" group at our house. For years, on our daily walks, he let me hold forth about my struggles with this project. He helped me figure out what I really wanted to say. He strengthened my voice. David is my advisor, my friend, and my heart's companion.

* * *

I gratefully acknowledge permission to reprint previously published material from the following publications and publishers. I have substantially edited and rewritten most of the material listed. Chapter 3 includes key parts of "'They Practice Their Trades in Different Worlds': Concepts in Poststructuralism and Ordinary Language Philosophy," *New Literary History* 40, no. 4 (2009): 801–24. (A few pages also appear in the introduction.) Chapter 4 includes almost all of "Thinking through Examples: What Ordinary Language Philosophy Can Do for Feminist Theory," *New Literary History* 46, no. 2 (2015): 191–216. Chapter 8 is an expanded version of "'Nothing Is Hidden': From Confusion to Clarity, or Wittgenstein on Critique," an essay published in *Rethinking Critique*, edited by Elizabeth S. Anker and Rita Felski (Durham, NC: Duke University Press, 2017). Chapter 9 contains brief, much edited excerpts from "The Adventure of Reading: Literature and Philosophy, Cavell and Beauvoir," *Literature and Theology* 25, no. 2 (2011): 125–40. This text was republished in *Stanley Cavell and Literary Studies: Consequences of Skepticism*, edited by Richard Eldridge and Bernard Rhie (New York: Continuum, 2011), 17–29.

Abbreviations

References to the following works are given in the text,
preceded by the relevant sign or abbreviation:

§   Ludwig Wittgenstein, *Philosophical Investigations*. The German text, with an English translation. 1953. Rev. 4th ed. Translated by G. E. M. Anscombe, P. M. S. Hacker, and Joachim Schulte. Edited by P. M. S. Hacker and Joachim Schulte. Oxford: Wiley-Blackwell, 2009.

BB   Ludwig Wittgenstein, *The Blue and Brown Books: Preliminary Studies for the "Philosophical Investigations"* (1958). 2nd ed. New York: Harper Torchbooks, 1965.

CG   Ferdinand de Saussure, *Course in General Linguistics* (1916). Translated by Wade Baskin; edited by Perry Meisel and Haun Saussy. New York: Columbia University Press, 2011.

CR   Stanley Cavell, *The Claim of Reason: Wittgenstein, Skepticism, Morality, and Tragedy* (1979). New York: Oxford University Press, 1999.

KA   Stanley Cavell, "Knowing and Acknowledging." In Cavell, *Must We Mean What We Say? A Book of Essays*, 238–66. Cambridge: Cambridge University Press, 2002.

MM   Stanley Cavell, "A Matter of Meaning It." In Cavell, *Must We Mean What We Say? A Book of Essays*, 213–37. Cambridge: Cambridge University Press, 2002.

OD   Jonathan Culler, *On Deconstruction: Theory and Criticism after Structuralism*. Ithaca, NY: Cornell University Press, 1982.

OM   Herbert Marcuse, *One-Dimensional Man: Studies in the Ideology of Advanced Industrial Society*. Boston: Beacon Press, 1964.

PPF   Ludwig Wittgenstein, "Philosophy of Psychology—A Fragment" (previously known as 'Part II'), in *Philosophical Investigations*.

SEC   Jacques Derrida. "Signature Event Context." In *Limited Inc*, 1–23. Evanston, IL: Northwestern University Press, 1988.

SR   Paul de Man. "Semiology and Rhetoric." In *Allegories of Reading: Figural Language in Rousseau, Nietzsche, Rilke and Proust*, 3–19. New Haven, CT: Yale University Press, 1979. Originally published as "Semiology and Rhetoric," *Diacritics* 3, no. 3 (Autumn 1973): 27–33.

TNY Stanley Cavell, *This New Yet Unapproachable America: Lectures after Emerson after Wittgenstein*. Albuquerque, NM: Living Batch Press, 1989.

Introduction

In this book I show that ordinary language philosophy has the power to transform the prevailing understanding of language, theory, and reading in literary studies today. By "ordinary language philosophy" I understand the philosophical tradition after Ludwig Wittgenstein, J. L. Austin, as constituted and extended by Stanley Cavell, specifically through his reading of Wittgenstein's *Philosophical Investigations*. This book, then, takes as its starting point the later Wittgenstein's vision of language and theory.

Wittgenstein is one of the twentieth century's most influential and most difficult thinkers. Naturally, his work has been interpreted in conflicting ways. I make no attempt to compare different readings of Wittgenstein (surely a life's work in itself); I read Wittgenstein as ordinary language philosophers read him. Fundamentally formed by Cavell, my understanding of Wittgenstein is also deeply inspired by the teaching of Richard Fleming, and by the work of Cora Diamond. From now on, I shall simply call this tradition the "ordinary" reading of later Wittgenstein.[1]

It is difficult to write about Wittgenstein's philosophy. It is even more difficult to convey why his thinking should matter to literary scholars. His vision of language runs so profoundly counter to the dominant tradition in literary studies today that even the most motivated readers find it difficult to "get" his concerns. Wittgenstein gives us no theory that can be summarized and used, but rather gives us a radical alternative to theory. He teaches us to give up theory's craving for generality and instead look to examples. He insists that the old scientistic way of "doing theory" simply won't work. And once we have swept away the old cobwebs, we're on our own. All Wittgenstein leaves us with is a certain spirit or attitude in which to go about our investigations. Here the word "spirit" stands in opposition to "approach," or "method," or "theory," for ordinary language philosophy proposes no such thing. By "spirit" I mean something like the unmistakable tone, or aura, or atmosphere that characterizes ordinary language philosophy. (In a similar vein, Rita Felski speaks of the "thought style" or the "mood" uniting otherwise different kinds of critique.) In relation to this philosophy, the word seems to impose itself: Cora Diamond calls her collection of essays *The Realistic Spirit*; Richard Fleming has a whole chapter called "The Spirit of *The Claim of Reason*."[2]

Radical challenges breed radical misreadings, as Wittgenstein well knew. It is no coincidence that scenes of understanding and misunderstanding are everywhere in *Philosophical Investigations*. For an admirer of ordinary language philosophy, the result has often been dispiriting: while ordinary language philosophy sees itself as announcing a philosophical revolution, its readers have mostly failed to notice the revolution. In this situation I can only have modest hopes of making myself understood. Yet, for me, the rewards of reading ordinary language philosophy have been so great that it seems only natural to want to make its characteristic spirit—the spirit of the ordinary—available to others. The question is how to go about it.

I have decided to focus on Wittgenstein's vision of language, and of philosophy, for these are the areas of his thought that most fundamentally challenge prevailing views in literary studies today. I make no attempt to introduce or present Wittgenstein's full range of concerns or the full breadth of ordinary language philosophy. Even Cavell's epochal investigation of skepticism is almost absent from this book, not because I don't appreciate its importance but because it requires its readers to understand Cavell's own analysis of Wittgenstein's vision of language to make full sense. And while there are a number of books introducing Cavell's thought, there is no book that returns to Wittgenstein to show how ordinary language philosophy can make a radical, innovative, and distinctive contribution to literary studies.[3]

Recently, the distinguished Wittgenstein scholar P. M. S. Hacker lamented the decline of interest in Wittgenstein that began in the 1980s. "Wittgenstein's ideas," he writes, "are at odds with the spirit of the times. We live in a culture dominated by science and technology. We are prone to think that all serious questions can be answered by the natural sciences. . . . In such a cultural context, Wittgenstein's ideas are even more difficult to understand than they were fifty years ago."[4] He is right. We live in an age when even humanists appear to have embarked on a quest to substitute measurement for judgment in every human practice. Wittgenstein's vision of language, and of philosophy, reminds us why this is a doomed project. This is one reason why his thought is of vital importance to the humanities today.

Hacker points out that the "rejection of Wittgenstein's philosophy and methodology has not been the result of the refutation of his ideas and the proven inadequacy of his methods. Indeed, it has not even rested on comprehension of his ideas." To counter such neglect, he argues, we need to show how the power of Wittgenstein's thought can illuminate "new domains."[5] Hacker would probably not appreciate the "ordinary" reading of Wittgenstein that I favor. Nevertheless, this book is an attempt to do precisely what he is calling for, namely use Wittgenstein's thought to do original work in the "new domain" of literary studies.

In this introduction I'll first draw up a brief overview of the book. Then I'll turn to some general questions arising in relation to this project. First, I'll consider the name "ordinary language philosophy," which can easily be misleading. I'll also show that this tradition has largely been absent from literary theory. Second, I'll focus on the question of misreading and misunderstanding that always comes up in relation to this philosophy. Is there something about ordinary language philosophy that makes it particularly easy to misunderstand? Why do its practitioners so often feel radically misunderstood, while its critics often appear to think that they have understood it only too well? Third, I'll explain why I return to Saussure and the post-Saussureans. Finally, I'll say something about why I write in the way I do.

Overview

Here's the road map. I have divided the book in three parts. The first, "Wittgenstein," deals with Wittgenstein's vision of language and theory. The second, "Differences," turns to some dominant strands of contemporary thought to explain how they clash with ordinary language philosophy, namely the vision of language in Saussure and the post-Saussurean tradition, and the vision of philosophy and politics that makes Marcuse and other partisans of "critical theory" or "critique" viscerally hostile to Wittgenstein. When one looks at ordinary language philosophy through the lens offered by these traditions, misunderstandings usually arise. This section can be read as an attempt to revise recent intellectual history, to deepen the understanding of ordinary language philosophy's originality, and prepare the ground for a creative use of its insights. In part 3, "Reading," I draw on the "spirit of the ordinary" to investigate fundamental questions concerning texts, and reading and writing.

I begin, then, by setting out Wittgenstein's vision of language. Readers already familiar with the "ordinary" reading of Wittgenstein will recognize my reading of the beginning of *Philosophical Investigations*. Yet they may still enjoy my efforts to make this material come alive in new ways, as when I try to re-imagine the scene in which a man wants to buy five red apples, or discover an utterly Wittgensteinian view of dictionaries (and bullfighting) in a short story by Julio Cortázar. The two first chapters focus entirely on what it means to claim that the "meaning of a word is its use in the language" (§43). I show how "use" is illuminated by terms such as "language-games," "grammar," and "forms of life," and how Wittgenstein's analysis intertwines language and the world. In these chapters I bring out Wittgenstein's radical rejection of the idea that language is fundamentally a matter of naming (representation) and show that much of the force of his argument comes from his refusal to attribute "meaning" to individual words, "as if the meaning were an aura the word brings along with it and retains in every kind of use" (§116). I also show that Wittgenstein's "forms of life" are not synonymous with "social conventions," and consider Wittgenstein's "realistic spirit." Chapters 1 and 2 provide the foundations for the rest of the book.

In chapters 3 and 4 I turn to Wittgenstein's critique of theory. Focusing on the intellectual power of examples, both chapters stress the fundamental importance of paying attention to the particular case. I first examine the contrast between Derrida's classical understanding of concepts (and thus of theory), and Wittgenstein's radical undoing of the very notion of what a concept is. I then turn to Wittgenstein's critique of our "craving for generality," which is intertwined with his critique of traditional notions of concepts, and show that it helps us to diagnose what goes wrong in the particular kind of feminist identity theory called "intersectionality theory."

In part 2 I return to some of Saussure's most fundamental concepts, in order to show how they come across to an admirer of ordinary language philosophy (chapter 5). I contrast my own reading of key passages in Saussure's text with the way the post-Saussurean tradition has understood them. I focus on the arbitrariness of the sign, the split sign and the materiality of the signifier, and the idea that language is a closed system. Above all I draw attention to various recent efforts to use Saussure as a starting point for a new "materialist" understanding of language.

In chapter 6 I turn to two classic texts in literary theory, Steven Knapp and Walter Benn Michaels's "Against Theory" and Paul de Man's "Semiology and Rhetoric," in order to analyze salient assumptions about language and literature in the post-Saussurean tradition. This chapter focuses on the "empty signifier" or the "mark," and on the assumption that language itself somehow has agency. This leads me to consider not just language, but the marriage of Archie and Edith Bunker, and what is at stake when we fail to find someone else's joke funny.

In chapter 7 I examine the claim that ordinary language philosophy is inherently conservative, or even reactionary. Was Wittgenstein recommending quietism? Forbidding us from wishing to change the world? Although I begin by taking a brief look at Ernest Gellner's attack on Austin and Wittgenstein in *Words and Things*, I focus most closely on Herbert Marcuse's influential denunciation of Wittgenstein and Austin in *One-Dimensional Man*. Marcuse's attitude toward ordinary language philosophy has been accepted by generations of radical literary critics. I show that Marcuse's misreadings reveal a mandarin disdain for the ordinary. Some of the questions that emerge from Marcuse's critique are nevertheless fascinating. What exactly is ordinary language? Is it possible to write in something other than ordinary language? Is common sense always reactionary? And is it really true that in order to break the stranglehold of ideology, intellectuals must use a special, philosophical vocabulary? And how about writing? What are we to make of conservative attacks on obscure theory writing? Or the left-wing defenses of the same obscurity? Should we lay down requirements for how to write theory?

I begin part 3 by investigating the hermeneutics of suspicion, by which I mean the belief that the text hides its own ("underlying") meanings. I provide a new perspective on the recent debates about surface and depth reading by showing that adherents of the hermeneutics of suspicion don't read differently from other readers. Talk about texts having "depths" and "surfaces," and ideas about uncovering hidden ideologies, or psychological investments "beneath the textual surface" are empty. The only thing the hermeneutics of suspicion makes us do is read texts in a spirit of suspicion. While that spirit may sometimes be justified, it is not always helpful, or even interesting. By turning to Søren Kierkegaard's struggles to understand the story of Abraham, I show that suspicion is certainly not required to produce subtle, complex, critical, and far-reaching readings. I don't propose a competing "method." In my view, literary criticism has no method other than reading. There is nothing special about our reading, except the attention, judgment, and knowledge we bring to the task.

To get away from the belief that suspicion is the only possible attitude for a serious literary critic, we need to break with the picture of texts as objects with surface and depth. In chapter 9 I propose that we picture texts as action and expression, and reading as a practice of acknowledgment. This will allow us to lift the taboo on the author's intentions, a taboo that depends on the idea that texts are objects. We should also give up hopes of defining "literature," or "literariness," once and for all. Literature isn't one thing, but a loosely configured network of texts and practices. What a work of literature does to a particular reader will depend on the text, on the reader, and on the circumstances of the reading. By picturing reading as a practice of acknowledgment, we will avoid the temptation to treat texts as illustrations of our own pre-existing theories. Rather, we place ourselves in a position in which to learn from the text. In this way, reading can become an adventure, an exploration of the unknown.

Acknowledgment requires attention, which Iris Murdoch defines as a "just and loving gaze." "Attention to particulars!" could be Wittgenstein's slogan. In chapter 10 I show that ordinary language philosophy allows us to connect the ethics of attention developed by three women philosophers—Simone Weil, Iris Murdoch, and Cora Diamond—to questions of language and writing. When we lose our sense of the meaning of words, we lose our sense of reality. In a world in which politicians have long since begun openly to exhibit their disdain for the "reality-based community," in which "truthiness" constantly threatens to take the place of truth, it is crucial to recover a sense of the value of words.[6] The philosopher and the writer both use a sharpened sense of words to hone a sharpened sense of reality. The best writing helps us to deal with what Diamond calls the "difficulty of reality," experiences in which "we take something in reality to be resistant to our thinking it."[7] It is no coincidence that I began to write this chapter in the aftermath of the massacre at Utøya in Norway on July 22, 2011. In this last chapter, I show, through brief examples from Henrik Ibsen, Rainer Maria Rilke, Virginia Woolf, and Vigdis Hjorth, that writers too investigate language and attention, and set out to teach us how to see.

Ordinary Language Philosophy and Literary Studies

"Ordinary language philosophy" is a tricky term. It can easily lead to misunderstandings, not least among philosophers, who often take it to mean either a certain Oxford-based postwar linguistic philosophy centered on Austin or certain contemporary analytic continuations of that linguistic philosophy. Mainstream analytic philosophers, Richard Fleming notes, often "take the 'ordinary' to mean unreflective, conventional common sense," whereas ordinary language philosophers mean by it the exemplary, the public, the shared, or what Fleming calls the "necessary order of our common existence."[8] The term also tends to exclude Cora Diamond's pathbreaking work on Wittgenstein, which is a fundamental source of inspiration for this book.[9]

Cavell constantly expresses misgivings about the term, but nevertheless continues to use it.[10] Throughout his career, Cavell also uses other terms: "post-positivism," the "philosopher appealing to ordinary language," or simply "the ordinary," as in the "creation and conflict of skepticism and the ordinary" (CR, xii).[11] Tempted to name this tradition the "philosophy of Constraints and Entanglements," or "First Word Philosophy," Richard

Fleming also ends up sticking with "ordinary language philosophy."[12] To me, a huge disadvantage of the term is that it makes most people think that there are (at least) two kinds of language: ordinary and extraordinary; ordinary and literary; or ordinary and philosophical language. As I shall show (in chapter 7), this is not the case. Yet, the term does have the advantage of emphasizing the importance of the ordinary. Since I can't think of a better one, I'll stick with it.

The name certainly raises the question of what "ordinary language" actually is, and why the ordinary and the everyday matter so much to these philosophers. Why does Cavell identify with "Emerson's and Thoreau's emphasis on the common, the near, and the low"?[13] Why is Austin convinced that only a philosopher who proceeds from ordinary language—someone who "examin[es] what we should say when"—will be able to unsettle the foundations of traditional philosophy?[14] And why does Wittgenstein insist that "what *we* do is to bring words back from their metaphysical to their everyday use"? (§116). By the end of this book, I hope to have conveyed some sense of what's at stake in the return to the ordinary and the everyday.

The "ordinary" reading of Wittgenstein differs significantly from other well-known readings. It rejects the idea that Wittgenstein was a postmodern relativist, a social constructionist *avant la lettre*, an idea nourished by Saul Kripke's "skeptical" account of Wittgenstein.[15] Because it also rejects attempts to read Wittgenstein as someone who offers a *theory* of something (language, rule-following, the mind), the ordinary reading also differs radically from scientistic and positivistic interpretations of Wittgenstein. In the same way, the "ordinary" reading of Austin is at odds both with John Searle's understanding of him as a systematic theorist of speech acts, and with poststructuralist attempts to turn him into a theorist of performatives and performativity.

Ordinary language philosophy remains marginal to literary studies. I don't mean to say that the names Wittgenstein, Austin, and Cavell are absent from the discipline. I mean to say that the "ordinary" understanding of these philosophers is absent. There simply is no book that attempts to do what I do here: to make the "ordinary" reading of Wittgenstein available to literary studies and show what difference it can make to our work.

This may sound surprising. Austin in particular has held a central place in literary studies ever since Jacques Derrida formulated his famous critique of Austin in "Signature Event Context" in 1971.[16] Literary theorists regularly draw on Austin to bolster theories of performatives and performativity.[17] But such readings of Austin differ markedly from the "ordinary" reading, in ways I cannot begin to detail here.[18]

Literary scholars have long read Wittgenstein in relation to Derrida. Already in 1976, Charles Altieri argued that Wittgenstein provides a serious challenge to Derrida.[19] In 1984 Henry Staten's *Wittgenstein and Derrida* attempted to show that Wittgenstein's philosophical project is compatible with Derrida's. Staten's effort was followed by a number of books and articles that sought to show that Wittgenstein either supports or subverts deconstruction.[20] But until Cavell himself intervened in the discussion, in his 1994 essay on Derrida and Austin, none of the participants in these debates argued from the point of view of the "ordinary" reading of Wittgenstein and Austin.[21]

A number of literary critics have turned to Wittgenstein to illuminate literary modernism. Marjorie Perloff's *Wittgenstein's Ladder* (1996) casts Wittgenstein as a modernist, but without engaging with Wittgenstein's philosophy.[22] Altieri often writes on Wittgenstein and literature, but he does so, as he himself often stresses, in a spirit radically different from Cavell's.[23] As far as I can tell, Altieri takes Wittgenstein to be a theorist (rather than a radical subverter of theory) and actively sets out to turn his writing "into abstract arguments."[24] I can hardly imagine a procedure more alien to the "ordinary" reading of Wittgenstein.

There are a few exceptions to the rule of "non-ordinary" readings of Wittgenstein in literary studies. In his recent *Dialectic of the Ladder*, Ben Ware returns to the question of Wittgenstein and modernism.[25] Drawing on Cora Diamond's and James Conant's "resolute" reading of the *Tractatus*, Ware provides a fine analysis of nonsense and the question of the limits of language, largely in the spirit of ordinary language philosophy. But Ware doesn't engage with *Philosophical Investigations*, and his focus is modernism, not literary theory.

Michael Fischer's genuinely pioneering *Stanley Cavell and Literary Skepticism*, published in 1989, is another exception. Deeply congenial to my own work, Fischer's book was the first to make a persuasive case for Cavell's place in literary studies.[26] Fischer and I discuss some of the same topics, notably Paul de Man's account of a scene from *All in the Family*, and Cavell's response to that account. We agree that the flight from the ordinary and the turn to skepticism characterize much literary theory. Yet, as his title declares, Fischer's major concern is skepticism, which is not my focus at all.

Finally, since the early 2000s, Cavell's work has had a relatively large uptake among literary critics, particularly within Shakespeare studies and with reference to theater.[27] Cavell has also inspired an increasingly rich body of work in film studies, which I shall not go into here. So far, however, the conversation between ordinary language philosophy and literary theory has been almost nonexistent.

I just used the terms "philosophy" and "theory." For experimental scientists, the difference between a theory and a philosophy is obvious. But in the humanities today (with the significant exception of philosophy departments), the terms are used in relatively unsystematic ways. In literary studies we tend to call French structuralists or poststructuralists such as Barthes, Lacan, Derrida, and Foucault "theorists." But we also call the last two "philosophers." "Theory" is routinely taken to include the critical philosophy of the Frankfurt School: Walter Benjamin, Theodor Adorno, Herbert Marcuse. Certain kinds of psychoanalytic writing (Freud, Lacan, Kristeva) count as "theory," other kinds (Donald Winnicott, Nina Coltart, Adam Phillips) do not. Judith Butler is a "theorist," Simone de Beauvoir is not. But both are "philosophers." In this book I make no attempt to impose new, stringent definitions of "theory" and "philosophy." I simply fall in with current usage.[28] The current fluidity of these terms hasn't been a problem for me in writing this book, and I hope it won't be for the reader either.

Missing the Revolution: Misunderstandings and Intimate Conflicts

"The feature of ordinary language philosophy which seems to me of the greatest significance is the *pervasiveness* of its conflict with accepted philosophical opinion," Cavell writes.[29] He calls such conflicts "intimate conflicts." I'll show why "intimate conflicts" are likely to be particularly confusing to new readers.

But let's begin with the revolution. Austin calls the event of ordinary language philosophy a "revolution in philosophy."[30] Cavell refers to ordinary language philosophy as a revolution and speaks of Wittgenstein's and Austin's "revolutionary tasks."[31] Yet, when Derrida picked up *How to Do Things with Words*, he didn't notice the revolution at all. Cavell read Derrida's attack on Austin's understanding of speech acts "with disheartenment." Derrida, he felt, was "denying the event of ordinary language philosophy, . . . seeing it as, after all, a continuation of the old questions, the old answers."[32] Where Austin and Cavell see a revolution, Derrida only sees more of the same. How can that be? How can anyone *miss* a revolution?[33]

The answer has to do with ordinary language philosophy's refusal to conform to traditional philosophy's understanding of concepts and theory. If readers trained in the classical tradition simply project that tradition's understanding of concepts and theory onto ordinary language philosophy, they will miss the difference. This is particularly easy to do when the traditions share many of the same concerns.

I have sometimes felt that it is simply impossible to convey a position inspired by ordinary language philosophy to an audience steeped in the post-Saussurean tradition. The experience makes me feel helpless, as if I suddenly were speaking a foreign language. Everyone I know who works on ordinary language philosophy has similar tales to tell. Why is this experience so common?

Cavell noted the problem already in the 1960s when he wrote about the "misunderstanding and bitterness" between positivists and philosophers proceeding from ordinary language. Confronted with the analytic philosopher's objections, he writes, "the philosopher who proceeds from everyday language stares back helplessly, asking, 'Don't you feel the difference? Listen, you *must* see it.' Surely, both know what the other knows, and each thinks the other is perverse, or irrelevant, or worse."[34] Cavell's "both know what the other knows" tells us that the bitterness arises because the two philosophies see exactly the same things, yet somehow they don't seem able to communicate their different visions to each other. Wittgenstein's duck-rabbit comes to mind, and so does Thomas Kuhn's "paradigm-shift," a concept built on the duck-rabbit: "The proponents of competing paradigms," Kuhn writes, "practice their trades in different worlds. [They] see different things when they look from the same point in the same direction.... That is why a law that cannot even be demonstrated to one group of scientists may occasionally seem intuitively obvious to another."[35]

Kuhn catches with almost uncanny accuracy Cavell's experience of the frustration arising in the encounter between ordinary language philosophy and the analytic tradition. This is no coincidence. In spirit and argumentation, the *Structure of Scientific Revolutions* is deeply Wittgensteinian, not to say Cavellian. In the 1950s, when Kuhn was writing his classic book, he and Cavell were colleagues and friends at Berkeley, "at times almost in possession of something you might call an intellectual community," Cavell writes.[36] Kuhn for his part calls Cavell his "creative sounding board," and the "only person with whom I have ever been able to explore my ideas in incomplete sentences."[37] (I don't mean to say that Kuhn's "paradigm" fits all historical developments in the humanities. I am just saying that it fits *this* case.)

Kuhn describes a situation in which a scientific law that seems intuitively obvious to one group of scientists "cannot even be demonstrated" to another. This explains why Cavell and Austin's revolution appeared to Derrida simply as business as usual. They all see and know the same things

yet slot them into radically different frameworks for how to make sense
of them. In his critique of Derrida's reading of Austin, Cavell emphasizes
both the closeness of the quarrel, and the difficulty of assessing it:

> Each pivotal concept at issue between Derrida and Austin—presence,
> writing, voice, word, sign, language, context, intention, force, commu-
> nication, concept, performance, signature; not to mention, of course,
> consequent ideas of philosophy, of the ordinary, of analysis, of the end
> of philosophy, of work, of fun—is turned by their differences. I know
> of no position from which to *settle* this systematic turning.[38]

The same concepts figure both in Austin and in Derrida, but are given
different weight, placed in different contexts, given different work to do.
Evidently, these traditions don't stand in a relationship of straightforward
opposition, for it is simply not the case that what the one asserts, the other
denies.[39] Yet local agreement cannot be trusted, for it often masks deep
divergence.[40] The relationship between ordinary language philosophy
and deconstruction is an example of what Cavell calls an *intimate conflict*:
"What a philosopher finds wrong with philosophy is an intimate measure
of what he thinks right, and important to say," he notes.[41] The closer the
overlap in interests, the more likely it is that the differences will be difficult to gauge, and easy to either exaggerate or overlook.

Wittgenstein, Cavell notes, was caught in precisely such an intimate
conflict with empiricism: "although [his] immediate audience was the
empiricist tradition of philosophy, his views are going, or ought, to of-
fend an empiricist sensibility at *every* point—which is only to say that
this conflict is an intimate one" (CR, 17–18). Cavell himself has always
felt himself to be involved in precisely such an intimate quarrel with analytic philosophy.[42]

Ordinary language philosophy, then, entertains intimate conflicts with
deconstruction, empiricism, and analytical philosophy. No wonder its
practitioners sometimes despair of ever being understood. How, then,
can anyone begin this philosophy? The question of how to begin—in this
case, how to begin reading Wittgenstein—makes up the beginning of *The
Claim of Reason*.[43] There is no "approach" to guide us safely inside *Philosophical Investigations*. We simply have to throw ourselves into it, begin,
as Cavell does, "without an approach," begin by finding a "blur or block
from which to start" (CR, 6). We begin as best we can. The challenge is
to figure out how to go on.

In his memoir, *Little Did I Know*, Cavell asks how or when to fit Austin and Wittgenstein into a philosophical curriculum. If it is done too

soon, the students may never feel the validity or weight of the traditional questions or "recognize the incessant force of philosophical 'mistakes' in themselves." But if it is done too late, when the students already have developed substantial philosophical investments of their own, then it may be "too much to ask," for then we are asking them "to be willing to take [themselves] apart."[44]

To engage seriously with ordinary language philosophy is a little like undergoing psychoanalysis. Wittgenstein assumes that we don't begin doing philosophy just for the sake of it, but because something is making us feel confused, as if we had lost our way. Who wants to undergo philosophical therapy if they feel that everything in their intellectual life is just fine as it is? Paradoxically, then, the best readers of the reputedly "conservative" Wittgenstein might be those who genuinely feel a need for change.

Looking in the Wrong Place

If Cavell is right about the nature of ordinary language philosophy's intimate conflicts, and if I am right that the conflicts sometimes seem to go as deep as a Kuhnian paradigm, then I have a problem. How to convey this philosophy in such circumstances? When we feel confused, Wittgenstein writes, what we need is *eine übersichtliche Darstellung*—a "surveyable representation," a "clear view," an "overview" (§122). To me, that means trying to *lay bare the picture*—to spell out the presuppositions and assumptions underpinning characteristic responses and reactions to Wittgenstein's texts, in order to see where the fundamental disagreement actually is. My aim is to make it possible to follow the logic of Wittgenstein's thought as ordinary language philosophy sees it.

In that spirit, I want to look at one particular reason why conversations between ordinary language philosophers and (conventional) theorists quickly come to feel frustrating. I have in mind the Wittgensteinian habit of rejecting both the assertion and denial of a claim as being based on the "wrong picture." Cora Diamond writes that her project is to "show how the laying down of metaphysical requirements is connected with our thinking that what we want lies somewhere, while it in fact lies somewhere else." In other words: we get stuck because we believe that our question is "dependent on something which it is not dependent on."[45] We look in the wrong place. We have the wrong picture of how the phenomenon works. Once we realize our mistake, the original problem disappears. (New ones may of course arise.)

This may all sound a bit abstract. It is difficult to give examples without working in depth and in detail, but it is worth trying to convey, however roughly, how this works. Let's say that I am invited to agree that Wittgenstein held that the "relation between words and objects is mediated by social praxis," as Ewa Ziarek puts it.[46] If I deny it, the theorist will most likely cast me as some kind of Platonist (if it's not "social praxis," then surely it must be "essences," or "ideas," or "universals"). Then I will feel misunderstood, for nothing could be further from Wittgenstein's view. Yet it doesn't follow that I can agree with Ziarek's formulation.

Wittgenstein certainly thinks that "forms of life" affect the meaning of our words. But not in the way Ziarek thinks. If *Philosophical Investigations* has one ambition, it is to make us *stop* believing that *the* problem of language is to figure out how words get connected to objects, to make us *give up* the picture that posits a gap between a word and its meaning, a gap that we will then rush in to fill with, for example, a theory of "social praxis," or of "essences," or "universals," or with a blanket denial that there *is* a connection between words and things. The problem here, in other words, is the picture of meaning underlying Ziarek's formulation. She is looking for a theory of *the* connection between object and word, whereas Wittgenstein offers no such thing, but rather challenges the very picture of language that gives rise to her question.

Another example. Assume that a theorist wants to "get beyond representation." Maybe she wants to be able to deal with matter, affects, things, without having to assume that they are "representations" or "linguistic constructs." Usually (but remember, this is rough), the theorist tries to solve the problem by finding ways to bypass language (and therefore human subjectivity) altogether. For the ordinary language philosopher, however, this very strategy shows that she actually begins by accepting the underlying picture, namely the idea that "language is representation"; otherwise she wouldn't work so hard to get out of that straitjacket. She is looking in the wrong place.

If this theorist starts a conversation with the ordinary language philosopher, it can quickly go wrong. The theorist says she wants to get "beyond representation." The ordinary language philosopher asks why she wants to do that. The theorist might then leap to the conclusion that the ordinary language philosopher sees *no* problem with the idea that language is representation and slot her into the box marked "traditional representationalists." But Wittgenstein begins *Philosophical Investigations* by *challenging* representation. Yet he neither asserts nor denies that "language is representation." Rather he shows that "language as such" can't be brought under a single concept or theory. To claim that "language as such" is this or that (representation or the failure of representation), is to set oneself up to prove the unprovable. At the same time, Wittgenstein fully acknowledges that representation—naming—is one of the many things we do with language. After all, it makes no sense to *deny* that we sometimes name things. But there are so many other language-games, so many other things we do with words that have nothing to do with representation. Shouting "Help!" for example.

Instead of being for or against representation, and instead of thinking of representation as the essence or purpose of language, Wittgenstein offers an alternative analysis, one that gives representation its place but never considers it paradigmatic of "language as such." It might be tempting to claim that Wittgenstein is already "beyond representation." This, in fact, is roughly the argument made by Susan Hekman, who claims that the "new materialists" would profit from returning to Wittgenstein.[47]

Unfortunately, unlike Hekman, I doubt that there can be a harmonious union between new materialism and Wittgenstein. For once ordinary language philosophy has finished its analysis, we no longer have any reason to construct an elaborate theory of how to avoid or get past representation. In other words: When representation loses its status as *the* definition of "language as such," it no longer seems urgent to elaborate complex theories to find a way around it, and the theory formation itself loses its allure.

This, roughly, is what it means to say that after ordinary language philosophy much theoretical work comes to seem pointless, for reasons that are hard to convey neatly and quickly, since they emerge only after detailed investigation of the fundamental assumptions—the picture of how things must be—underlying the original project. The ordinary language philosopher wants to learn *why* the theorist cares about affects, matter, or things; find out *why* she thinks that "representation" blocks her from doing what she wants to do; and, above all, get clear on what problem the theorist believes she can solve if she could just get rid of the idea that language is representation. If we could have *those* conversations, we might well find common ground, and even discover new and unexpected ways of moving past the original problem.

This brings me to the question of "theoreticism," namely the belief that "theoretical correctness somehow guarantees political correctness."[48] In *What Is a Woman?* I show that the sex/gender distinction does less work than it has generally been taken to do and that, in most cases, radical feminist politics doesn't depend on having the correct anti-essentialist position. It certainly does not depend on avoiding the word "woman" in the belief that this word is essentially essentialist. In this book I don't explicitly discuss theoreticism. Yet a number of the positions I challenge in this book are taken to be utterly necessary for some radical political projects: for example, the belief that the ordinary is the home of common sense, which must always be wedded to the status quo. Or the belief that the mere mention of human agency (or speakers, or authors, or intentions and motivations, or expression) must be complicit with the most antediluvian humanism. I won't go into such debates. I'll simply say that in my view, nothing I say in this book is incompatible with radical politics.[49]

Why Return to Saussure and the Post-Saussureans?

In 1948 Wittgenstein's friend, the psychiatrist Maurice O'Connor Drury, asked him about Hegel. Wittgenstein replied: "Hegel seems to me to be always wanting to say that things which look different are really the same. Whereas my interest is in shewing that things which look the same are really different. I was thinking of using as a motto for my book a quotation from *King Lear*: 'I'll teach you differences.'"[50] He didn't, but differences are still a crucial preoccupation in *Philosophical Investigations*. Throughout his book, Wittgenstein is trying to show that we get stuck in our conviction of how things *must* be precisely because "only the one case and no other occurred to us" (§140). Only when we are able to describe the picture that held us captive in the first place will we realize that it is no longer compulsory, no longer the only option. Then we will be able to see differences—to see more than one case.

Ordinary language philosophy challenges views of language, meaning, and theory currently taken for granted. Insofar as these views go without saying, they make up the *doxa*: the dominant, never challenged, presuppositions of a theory or critical practice. To loosen its grip, one must bring out its unspoken assumptions, lay bare the picture that holds us captive, to quote Wittgenstein loosely (see §115).

In the humanities today, the *doxa* concerning language and meaning remains Saussurean or, rather, post-Saussurean. Although this appears quite obvious to me, I have discovered that it is in fact a contentious claim. My colleagues tell me that nobody reads Saussure anymore. They say that there is no point in returning to Paul de Man, or in mentioning Jonathan Culler's name, for they are yesterday's theorists, and unless I address the latest theories to enter the scene my views are uninteresting. For me this is a little like saying that someone interested in psychoanalysis should not bother with Freud, or that someone who wants to understand Marxism should skip Marx in favor of his latest avatars.

I am certainly not saying that every literary scholar today is a card-carrying Saussurean. On the contrary: I agree that most of us hardly mention his name anymore. But his views on language are still with us. Again and again, I note that when questions of language, meaning, and reference surface in discussions, the Saussurean or post-Saussurean vision of language turns out to be the only one in play. In contemporary theory I constantly come across the following Saussurean assumptions: that language is a closed system; that the sign must be split into a signified and a signifier; that Saussure's most important discovery was the "materiality of the signifier"; that it makes sense to speak of the "empty signifier" or the "mark"; that it is crucial to stress that the sign is arbitrary; that language is a system of differences with no positive terms; and that when one discusses language and meaning there is no need to invoke speakers ("subjects"), for it is enough to speak of "language" itself, as in "language represents" or "language fails to represent." It also used to be generally accepted that Saussure thought that talk about a "referent" was meaningless, but this view has come under pressure in recent years.[51] All these assumptions are open to challenge. In so far as contemporary theorists draw on such Saussurean assumptions—and they do—they need to understand and deal with Wittgenstein's challenge to this vision of language.

In general, the Saussure we encounter in literary studies today is post-Saussurean. In this book a "post-Saussurean" is anyone in literary studies who draws on Saussure's linguistics, particularly after World War II. The term includes both structuralists and poststructuralists. It also includes anyone else who builds on signature Saussurean concepts. "Post-Saussurean" is not a new term. Catherine Belsey used it in 1980 in much the same way as I do here.[52] My use of the term includes scholars who vociferously deny that they *are* post-Saussureans. In chapter 6, for example, I show that even the staunch neopragmatists Stephen Knapp and Walter Benn Michaels require the post-Saussurean concept of the "mark"—a concept they detest—to get their own arguments off the ground.

The famous "linguistic turn" in the humanities "philosophized" Saussure by turning his linguistic theory into a philosophy of language, a philosophy with explicit views on the relationship between the sign and the world. In my view the "philosophical Saussure" is a product of the post-Saussurean generation.[53] So is the "political Saussure." In *Course of General Linguistics* Saussure appears to be no more interested in politics than Wittgenstein in *Philosophical Investigations*. Yet that never stopped radical literary scholars from appropriating Saussure for their own political purposes. This is not a problem for me, for I am not trying to argue for a return to a "pure" Saussure. Nor am I opposed to political appropriations of classic texts. I just think it is important to realize that the postwar "philosophizing" and "politicizing" of Saussure took place, mostly because it helps us to understand the difference between Saussure and his post-Saussurean followers.

Sometime in the 1990s many theorists came to feel that the then well-established post-Saussurean tradition was exhausted. A new generation of post-Saussureans began to emerge. A number of new theory formations—affect theory, new materialism, posthumanism, and so on—began their struggle to throw off the yoke of the "linguistic turn," which had become irksome because of its apparent neglect of matter. Partisans of such theories often believe that they have left the post-Saussurean tradition behind. But they have not. Here, for example, is Karen Barad, one of the leading voices in "new materialism":

> Language has been granted too much power. The linguistic turn, the semiotic turn, the interpretative turn, the cultural turn: it seems that at every turn lately every "thing"—even materiality—is turned into a matter of language or some other form of cultural representation. [We need] a rethinking of the key concepts (materiality and signification) and the relationship between them.[54]

Barad's starting point is the post-Saussurean tradition, which she feels has turned everything into language. Setting out to rethink "materiality and signification," Barad returns to Saussure, via Vicki Kirby's "materialist" account.[55] Even for Barad herself, then, the return to a genuine appreciation of matter and materiality passes through a rereading of Saussure. And Barad is not alone: I think one could show, had one but time enough, that all recent theory formations that seek to get past subjectivity and language still work with the Saussurean and post-Saussurean picture of language, even if only implicitly and for lack of other alternatives.

I agree that the Saussurean and post-Saussurean picture of language is implausible and constraining. I just think that Wittgenstein's vision of language is a far more radical and liberating alternative than yet another attempt to redefine the "materiality of the signifier." This is not to say that Wittgenstein and Saussure are always at loggerheads. The relationship between these two visions of language is complex, and difficult to disentangle, mostly because they arise from radically different projects: Saussure wants to found a science; Wittgenstein wants to understand how language works in our lives.

Writing in Search of Reason

Our words express and reveal us. They tell others who we are (at least if they pay attention.) The choice of style is as revealing for an academic as for a literary writer. Faced with the daunting difficulty of my material, I had a hard time finding my own voice. I often felt as if I were drowning in the sea of philosophy. In the end I realized that I sounded more like myself when I try to write as clearly and as concretely as I can, not as a master (or should that be mistress?) of the field, but as someone who says what she sees, while also giving voice (in asides or in counterarguments) to her own questions and her own confusion. This has not been easy. While I strive to make the arguments as accessible as I possibly can, the project of this book—to rethink fundamental issues in literary theory in the light of the "ordinary" reading of Wittgenstein—is challenging. Wittgenstein once wrote, as if in chastisement of himself: "Are you a bad philosopher then, if what you write is hard to understand? If you were better you would make what is difficult easy to understand.—But who says that's possible?! [Tolstoy]."[56] Wittgenstein's kind of clarity is at once a philosophical and a stylistic achievement. "Philosophical clarity," Drury writes, "puts a full-stop to our enquiry and restlessness by showing us that our quest is in one sense mistaken."[57] Such clarity is surely beyond our reach, since even Wittgenstein thought he failed to achieve it most of the time. Yet we can always try.

I just said "we." The word has a bad reputation, for it is often taken to be inherently "exclusionary." But "we" can be used in myriad ways, and only a few of those ways are objectionable. Ordinary language philosophy often talks about "what we should say." The usual rejoinder is to reject the "we" as normative, as an attempt to tell others what they *must* say. But this "we" is neither an order nor an empirical claim. It is, rather, an *invitation* to the reader to test something for herself, to see if she can see what I see. If she can't, we can try to figure out why. The claims of ordinary language philosophy are invitations to a conversation, invitations to do philosophy together.[58]

"We" and "I" make a sentence personal and avoid the kind of passive formulations that obscure agency and responsibility. Because the first-person stresses the personal and existential aspects of a claim, it often turns up in Sartre's and Beauvoir's prose. In his famous analysis of shame, Sartre imagines a jealous lover looking through a keyhole in an empty hotel corridor: "But all of a sudden I hear footsteps in the hall. Someone is looking at me!"[59] Sartre's "I" isn't autobiographical or empirical. Sartre isn't confessing that he himself ever spied on a lover in this way (although I am pretty sure he once did). His "I" is *exemplary*. It encourages us, Sartre's readers, to see the scene from the "I"'s point of view, to think with and through the example, to imagine what *we* would feel in the same situation. Would *I* freeze in shame if I heard footsteps in a similar situation?

The power of the example depends on our answer. In this sense, Sartre's "I" is dialogic, *open to response.*

"The philosophical appeal to what we say," Cavell writes, "[is a claim] to community" (CR, 20). It isn't an attempt to speak for others, an attempt to express or represent a pre-existing community, but an attempt to *find* an audience, to discover with whom one is in community: "I have nothing more to go on than my conviction that I make sense," Cavell writes. "It may prove to be the case that I am wrong, that my conviction isolates me, from all others, from myself. That will not be the same as a discovery that I am dogmatic or egomaniacal. The wish and search for community are the wish and search for reason" (20). Our expressions are at once acts of self-revelation and an appeal to others. (Silence is also a form of expression. In some situations, silence may be the only possible course of action.)[60] If I don't speak up, I will never discover whether there can be a community that includes me. Maybe there isn't, at least not right now. To write is to risk rebuff. But to give up the search for the right words is to give up the search for reason.

PART I

Wittgenstein

1

"Five Red Apples"

MEANING AND USE

Five Red Apples: From Naming to Use

To understand ordinary language philosophy one must read Wittgenstein.[1] Cavell suggests that to understand his work it is essential to "spend the two dozen hours it would take to go sensibly over the opening half-dozen pages of the *Philosophical Investigations* and come to an end somewhere."[2] Reading Wittgenstein closely is challenging, but it is also exhilarating, for Wittgenstein's text is an invitation to immerse oneself in a way of thinking that is utterly different from the dominant traditions of thought in literary studies. Wittgenstein's style—his mode of writing—challenges all established assumptions about how to write philosophy. Reading about Wittgenstein can't substitute for actually reading his work. Let's begin, then, by reading the first paragraph in *Philosophical Investigations*:

> When grown-ups named some object and at the same time turned towards it, I perceived this, and I grasped that the thing was signified by the sound they uttered, since they meant to point *it* out. This, however, I gathered from their gestures, the natural language of all peoples, the language that by means of facial expression and the play of eyes, of the movements of the limbs and the tone of voice, indicates the affections of the soul when it desires, or clings to, or rejects, or recoils from, something. In this way, little by little, I learnt to understand what things the words, which I heard uttered in their respective places in various sentences, signified. And once I got my tongue around these signs, I used them to express my wishes (Augustine, *Confessions*, I.8).[3]
>
> These words, it seems to me, give us a particular picture of the essence of human language. It is this: the words in language name objects—sentences are combinations of such names.—In this picture of language we find the roots of the following idea: Every word has a meaning. This meaning is correlated with the word. It is the object for which the word stands.

Augustine does not mention any difference between kinds of word. Someone who describes the learning of language in this way is, I believe, thinking primarily of nouns like "table," "chair," "bread," and of people's names, and only secondarily of the names of certain actions and properties; and of the remaining kinds of words as something that will take care of itself.

Now think of the following use of language: I send someone shopping. I give him a slip of paper marked "five red apples." He takes the slip to the shopkeeper, who opens the drawer marked "apples"; then he looks up the word "red" in a chart and finds a colour sample next to it; then he says the series of elementary number-words—I assume that he knows them by heart—up to the word "five," and for each number-word he takes an apple of the same colour as the sample out of the drawer.—It is in this and similar ways that one operates with words.— "But how does he know where and how he is to look up the word 'red' and what he is to do with the word 'five'?"—Well, I assume that he *acts* as I have described. Explanations come to an end somewhere.—But what is the meaning of the word "five"?—No such thing was in question here, only how the word "five" is used. (§1)[4]

In the last paragraph, a taciturn man hands a slip marked "five red apples" to an errand-boy. When he gets to the store, an old-fashioned shop with deep wooden drawers, the boy gives the slip to the shopkeeper. Maybe the boy can't read. But the shopkeeper can, for he does not hesitate to open the drawer marked "apples." This shopkeeper is a bit odd, though, for he takes out a color chart to make sure he gets the color of the apples right. Doesn't he know what red is? (Or what red means? Should I worry about the difference?) At least he can't be color-blind. Once he has the right color, he counts out the apples aloud (so he is not mute). While the shopkeeper consults his charts and counts his goods, the errand-boy politely waits in front of the counter.

What kind of scene is this? It could be the opening of a prewar Hollywood movie. Maybe the beginning of a heartwarming family film, featuring the young Jimmy Stewart as the shopkeeper with a strange relationship to colors. Or maybe we are dealing with a postwar thriller: Robert Mitchum would be terrific as the brooding, taciturn man in need of apples. But this seems too dark. Doesn't the very ordinariness of the scene point towards romantic comedy? We never find out, for the story ends here. We don't even learn whether the apples are handed over, let alone whether they ever make their way back to the man who wanted them in the first place.

Is this modernism? The mid-twentieth-century setting suggests it might be. The story certainly leaves the reader feeling challenged, maybe a little annoyed. What's the point of telling us a story about someone who goes to the store and buys five red apples for someone else? Why dwell on something so desperately banal? Is this supposed to be a parable of human existence? But nothing here points towards Beckett or Adorno. The story is so clearly not about life and death, or the meaning of life. Nobody is making dramatic choices, nobody is complaining that nothing makes any difference anyway. Nor is there a palpable sense of distress and despair. Perhaps the shopkeeper's need for the color chart is intended to reveal some kind of disability, yet even that is represented as perfectly ordinary. Maybe there is a slight homoerotic subtext in the idea of five apples circulating among three males? But here I must confess that I invented the errand-boy. The story itself just has "someone" (*jemand*). For all I know, the someone could be a little girl, or a grown woman (although I find that implausible).

Although this is a story about shopping, it is hard to see it as an allegory of commercialization, or the commodification of culture. The five red apples don't seem to represent anything but themselves. Maybe the storyteller has Cézanne's painting *Five Apples* in mind.[5] But the apples in that painting are not red. And Cézanne painted so many apples! I can find no subtle point about painting here. But the intense attention Cézanne pays to his apples may be relevant. His painting shows us how to look at apples as if for the first time. By resisting our efforts to turn the buying or the apples into metaphors for something else, this story does something similar. It forces us to look closely at the simple action of buying five red apples. But why should we focus on such a banal transaction? Well, the author tells us that if we do, we will understand how "one operates with words." But what does this explain? How *do* we "operate with words"? Wittgenstein imagines a quizzical interlocutor who has the same question:

> —"But how does he know where and how he is to look up the word 'red' and what he is to do with the word 'five'?"—Well, I assume that he *acts* as I have described. Explanations come to an end somewhere.— But what is the meaning of the word "five"?—No such thing was in question here, only how the word "five" is used.

In this case explanations come to an end rather quickly. Wittgenstein has a short fuse. Why does his interlocutor try his patience so fast? The story says that the shopkeeper looks up the color sample to find out what red is.

But how did he learn to do that? Where do the color samples come from? It is not obviously pointless to ask, just as it is not obviously pointless to wonder how the shopkeeper knows that "five" is a number-word, that he is to count it out, not look for a drawer labeled "five." We should also wonder why the interlocutor finds "red" quite problematic, takes "five" to be a mystery, yet takes for granted that "apples" goes without saying.

Wittgenstein brushes off the question about the "meaning of the word five." He is only interested in one thing, namely "how the word 'five' is used." Does he think that use is more important than meaning? But he doesn't say that. He says, rather, that "no such thing was in question here." It is as if the interlocutor is asking for the wrong thing, as if he were wrong to bring up "meaning" at all. But why is that? By now I have begun to parrot the interlocutor. Like him, I have turned into a child who can't stop asking "why?" This may be an unavoidable effect of reading Wittgenstein's prose. It turns us into children endlessly wondering about reasons and causes. But then he also turns us into philosophers, for Plato writes that philosophy begins in wonder, and Descartes concurred, for he thought that wonder (*admiration*) was the most philosophical passion of the soul.[6]

Why doesn't the interlocutor ask how the shopkeeper knows he is to look for the drawer marked "apples"? Why does he think this particular feat goes without saying? The assumption that the word "apples" requires no further explanation marks him out as a member of the "Augustinians," the large and varied group of philosophers who believe in some version or other of the "Augustinian picture of language" described at the very beginning of §1: "The words in language name objects—sentences are combinations of such names.—In this picture of language we find the roots of the following idea: Every word has a meaning. This meaning is correlated with the word. It is the object for which the word stands."[7]

James Wetzel reminds us that Wittgenstein profoundly admired Augustine. He is not using *Confessions* as an example of mindless philosophical error, but rather as a reminder that even the greatest minds may yield to this particular philosophical temptation.[8] To Wittgenstein, the trouble with the Augustinian picture of language is the prominence it gives to representation, to the idea that if we just can understand how names or naming works, then we will have captured the essence of language. Someone in the grip of the Augustinian picture of language may, for example, think that the word gets connected with the meaning when we point at the object and say "apples!" or otherwise present it in some explicit way, for example by saying "this is an apple!" (Philosophers call this "ostension," and talk about "ostensive definitions.") Wittgenstein has no patience with this theory: "An ostensive definition," he writes, "can be variously interpreted in *any* case" (§28).

Shouldn't the next step then be to figure out a *better* theory of how the word gets connected to the thing? Wittgenstein is quite funny about what happens to philosophers who take this route. Such philosophers, he writes, think of naming as an occult process. To them, "naming seems to be a *strange* connection of a word with an object" (§38). A misguided philosopher—someone who tries to "sublimate [*sublimieren*] the logic of our language," he writes, will try to "fathom the relation between name and what is named by staring at an object in front of him and repeating a name, or even the word 'this,' innumerable times. For philosophical problems arise when language goes on holiday. And then we may indeed imagine naming to be some remarkable mental act, as it were the baptism of the object" (§38).

This kind of philosopher wants to be *deep*. He will not be satisfied with Wittgenstein's exhortation to lighten up a little and remember that "when philosophizing, it will often prove useful to say to ourselves: naming something is rather like attaching a name tag to a thing" (§15). The deep philosopher doesn't think that sticking labels on jars or tying tags to teddy bears is a dignified, let alone philosophical, explanation of what naming is.[9] If he can't establish the connection between the word and the object in some deep way, he will declare that there is no connection, that words simply have no relationship at all with the things they name. This is skepticism. Or at least a form of it. If Augustine claims that there is a connection between name and word, the skeptic will deny it. Yet this move will not save him from Wittgenstein's scorn, for the deep philosopher has done nothing to unsettle the fundamental framework of Augustine's picture, namely that the key thing we have to understand about language is the relationship between words and things. The Platonist and the deconstructionist are closer to each other than they think.[10]

This is why the Augustinian does not feel the need to ask how the shopkeeper knows what drawer to look in. To him, it is self-evident that the meaning of "apples" must be the actual objects contained in the drawer. He also takes for granted that words—all words—work exactly like names. When Wittgenstein confronts him with something other than names of concrete objects, the Augustinian is in trouble, for he thinks of "the remaining kinds of words as something that will take care of itself." No wonder that numerals and words for sensations confuse him.

The Augustinian may have a theory of certain nouns, but he does not have a theory of language—unless, of course, we imagine a language consisting exclusively of concrete nouns. (This is precisely what Wittgenstein goes on to do in §2, when he imagines a tribe of builders sharing a language consisting of only four nouns.) Augustine's picture of language, then, is not so much wrong, as too simple and too circumscribed. He does "describe a system of communication; only not everything that we call language is this system" (§3).

The strategy of §1 is now clear: Wittgenstein's story is intended to make us wonder about Augustine's. Augustine shows us a child who learns to express his wishes simply by naming things; Wittgenstein responds by drawing our attention to a man who expresses his simple wish for five red apples, only to provoke a barrage of puzzled questions.

But why *do* explanations come to an end, and so suddenly? It helps to know that Wittgenstein thinks that an "explanation serves to remove or prevent a misunderstanding—one, that is, that would arise if not for the explanation, but not every misunderstanding that I can imagine" (§87). An explanation is meant to clear up a specific problem, not every conceivable problem. But if this is what an explanation is, then *no* explanation would ever satisfy the interlocutor, for what he wants to know is how words like "red" and "five" can have meaning at all, quite outside any specific context of use. Moreover, explanations are given in words. They are useless to someone who hasn't already learned the language. We don't teach a little child to speak by *explaining* how words are used. We *train* the child until he or she becomes adept enough to understand explanations (cf. §5).

The distinction between *training* and *explaining* is crucial. Training is constant practice; explaining is giving reasons. Augustine underestimates how much we have to learn in order to learn to do the simplest things—naming, explaining—with language: "[He] describes the learning of human language as if the child came into a foreign country and did not understand the language of the country; that is, as if he already had a language, only not this one" (§32).

The interlocutor is not asking for explanations because he is genuinely puzzled. To me, the question "But what is the meaning of the word 'five'?" is in bad faith. He *obviously* knows what "five" means. His problem is not the meaning of "five," but that he can no longer explain to himself why the word means what he knows it means. He wants Wittgenstein to supply a different ground of meaning, a new story about what connects the word with the thing.

It may look as if Wittgenstein fails to reply properly. For all he does is to draw attention to two features: how the shopkeeper acts, and how the word "five" is used. It would be easy to conclude that we are to attend to what we do with words rather than what they mean. But if that were our conclusion, we wouldn't be getting the point after all, for here the word "rather" gives us the wrong idea. Wittgenstein does not think of use as something like the "ground" of meaning, as many critics believe.[11] He thinks of it as use, as he says in §43: "the meaning of a word is its use in the language."

Use is not a ground. Use is a practice grounded on nothing. Use is simply what we do. Nothing—no essences, no built-in referential power—obliges us to continue using language as we do now. In fact, we don't always continue: language is a constantly changing practice. But as long as we are willing to continue to speak to each other, use creates a semblance of ground, what Cavell calls "a thin net over the abyss" (CR, 178).

The Augustinian interlocutor will most certainly think that Wittgenstein is begging the question: for how can we use words without first knowing what they mean? But as soon as we divide the matter up in that way (use here, meaning over there) we miss Wittgenstein's radical point: there is no meaning "behind" the use (for if there were, what kind of thing would it be? A mental [psychological] entity? A real thing in the real world?—I shall return to this), there is only meaning in use.

For all his brusqueness, Wittgenstein actually told the interlocutor what he wanted to know. What makes "five red apples" mean "five red apples"? What we do, what we say, the fact that we use those words in precisely that way. In use they live. But this is also why explanations must come to an end. There really is no *reason* why apples are called "apples," or why "five" means five. The questioner is rebuffed because he is asking for a ground. Or for an explanation of what he takes to be the self-evident gap between name and thing. He has the wrong picture of how language works. He is asking for something Wittgenstein neither can nor will provide.

Wittgenstein's revolution, then, begins right here, in §1, when he tells us not to ask about naming, but to look at the use. In the next forty-two paragraphs of *Philosophical Investigations* he takes us on a dazzling tour of a previously undiscovered philosophical landscape dotted with signposts directing us to significant places: "use," "language-games," "forms of life," "examples." Wittgenstein shows us toddlers just learning to talk, children playing ring-a-ring-a-roses, and two different tribes of builders. The members of the first tribe possess only four words between them ("block," "pillar," "slab," "beam"); the members of the second also have "there" and "this," number-words, and color samples like those used by the shopkeeper in §1. The children and the builders spend much time pointing to things. Sometimes the pointing works fine, other times it appears to produce quite a muddle.

The country's philosophers are of no help, for they spend their time muttering "this, this, this" while staring intensely at ordinary objects. The capital of this strange yet familiar land is the ancient city of language with its "maze of little streets and squares," surrounded by a "multitude of new suburbs with straight and regular streets and uniform houses" (§18). If we are willing to move slowly through this landscape—like Rousseau's Émile and his mentor, we should travel on foot—the voyage will transform us. By the time we reach §43, we will understand what Wittgenstein means when he writes that the "meaning of a word is its use in the language" (§43).[12]

Lucas and His Spanish Classes

In the Argentine writer Julio Cortázar's 1979 book *A Certain Lucas* (*Un tal Lucas*), the protagonist gets a job as a Spanish teacher at the Berlitz language school in Paris. The director, a bully from Castile, insists that Lucas teach only proper (*castizo*) Spanish without the slightest trace of Argentinianisms. He is to bear in mind that his students are there because they want to learn the sort of Spanish tourists need to get around. In his first class, Lucas hands out photocopies of a passage from a newspaper article on bullfighting: "note how modern and how, by his lights, it should be the quintessence of the proper [*castizo*] and the practical since it deals with bullfighting." The passage drives the students to despair. Increasingly distressed, they feverishly consult their dictionaries, throw their hands up, pull their hair out. In the end, they leave in disgust, "after letting it be known in French what they think of Spanish and especially of dictionaries that have cost them their good francs."[13]

The passage that caused Lucas's students to hurl their dictionaries across the room was not fiction. Cortázar inserted a paragraph from a real bullfight review by the legendary Spanish bullfighting critic Joaquín Vidal, which appeared in *El País* on September 17, 1978, just as the story has it.[14] In Cortázar's story, the joke is that when the director comes to inspect Lucas's class, only one nerdy student is left, and he wants to know whether the reference to "el maestro salmantino"— the master from Salamanca— could be an allusion to the mystical poet Fray Luís de León. (In fact it refers to the great bullfighter El Viti, who also came from Salamanca.) When the student leaves, the director tells Lucas that "there's no need to start with classical poetry, of course Fray Luís and all that, but try to find something simpler, let's say something bloody typical like a visit by tourists to a restaurant or a bullring, you'll soon see how they'll get interested and learn overnight."[15]

It is tempting to reproduce here the passage that caused such consternation to Lucas's students. But if I were to quote it in English, most of the point would be lost, for English doesn't truly have a bullfighting language. In the Spanish text the transition from Cortázar's to Vidal's style is stunning. For even in Spanish, Vidal's language appears quite alien.[16] Of course, Lucas must have known this: his assignment of the bullfighting text to a class of language learners is a subtle revolt against the tyranny of the school's director. The effect is to make the reader of Cortázar's original text feel she is reading a foreign language although she is still reading Spanish. In translation, this effect is partly lost. But here we should not blame the translator. Anyone who has tried translating bullfighting Spanish knows that it is extraordinarily difficult, that it always leads to frantic and frustrating consultation of dictionaries in just the way Cortázar describes it.

I remember endlessly looking up the word *soso*, only to find, every time, that it means "bland, insipid, tasteless." But I kept looking it up, for what on earth is an "insipid" bull? What's the difference between a bull said to be *manso*, which the dictionaries translate as "gentle," "docile," or "tame," and one said to be *flojo*, which is supposed to mean "slack," "lazy," or "cowardly"? However many times I looked them up, the dictionary failed to tell me what I needed to know about these words. Reading bullfighting reviews, one gets the sense that fighting bulls aren't supposed to be either *soso* or *flojo*, but this insight is of little help to the translator, who needs to find just the right word. Terms of praise are no easier: for what is it for a bull to be, as in Vidal's review, *encastado* and *noble*? The dictionaries tell us to translate "thoroughbred" and "noble." But aren't all fighting bulls thoroughbred? And how can it be that only some of those thoroughbred bulls are said to be noble?

A few lines further down, Lucas's students had to deal with a sentence in which Vidal praises El Viti's *naturales, de pecho,* and *ayudados por alto y por bajo.* The published English translation has: "There were incomparable naturals and tremendous chest passes, and the help of two-handed ups and downs."[17] Even in Spanish *ayudados por alto y por bajo* is meaningless unless we know that an *ayudado* is a pass in which the bullfighter uses the sword to extend and support the muleta. This can be done *por bajo,* which means near the ground, right in front of the bull's head, or *por alto,* which means that the sword-extended muleta is held up high so that the bull passes right under it. True aficionados consider the former to be more courageous and skillful than the latter.

In the same way, it is perfectly fine to translate *naturales* as "naturals." But what good does it do me if I don't know that a *natural* is a pass carried out with the left hand? Or that because it exposes more of the bullfighter's body to the bull, a left-handed pass is more dangerous than a right-handed one? The obligatory pass marking the end of a series, the "chest pass" (*pase de pecho*) is, as it were, the semicolon of bullfights. Must I know this to understand the text? But even this may be to take too much for granted. For if I don't know what a "pass" is, and can't really explain the difference between a "cape" and a "muleta" (after all, they are both reddish pieces of cloth), then where do I begin?

"Lucas and His Classes" is brilliant not just because it wittily captures the spirit of a rather stupid bully running an authoritarian institution, but because it makes us think about what it is to learn a language. Cortázar shows that dictionaries only get us so far. In certain cases, they can utterly fail to convey what we need to know to make our way with a particular kind of language. To understand the language of bullfights, one must understand the corrida, be able to appreciate the art of the bullfighter, and be knowledgeable about bulls in the way breeders of fighting bulls are. It is impossible to learn this language without understanding the practices that give rise to it. Many—maybe most—Spaniards never learn it. Some find the very thought of doing what it takes to learn it morally offensive.

Among those who do know the language of bullfighting, some complain that reporters covering the corridas are increasingly incapable of writing with the precision and elegance of Joaquín Vidal, that instead of accurately conveying the nuances of the bullfight they rely on vastly overgeneralizing stock phrases. The question is whether journalists who can't mobilize the full resources of bullfighting language are in fact seeing the bullfight properly. (What would we say about a food critic who can't tell the difference between *en croûte* and *en papillote*, or a car mechanic who can't explain the difference between a carburetor and a single-point fuel-injection system?)

What it takes to learn bullfighting language is exactly what it takes to learn any language, including our first language. It takes training: training of our attention as much as of our vocabulary and syntax. To learn the language of bullfighting is to learn to *see* the bullfight, just as learning the language of sewing is to learn to see stitches and seams with the proper attention. If I am using the language of bullfighting as an example, it is because it gives me a chance to write about Cortázar's brilliant short story. But I could have made the same kind of points about the language of cricket or football (by which I mean "soccer"), *haute couture*, or software engineering.

When we learn to speak, we do not simply learn names, we are initiated into practices of every kind, into a form of life. Cavell writes brilliantly about how children learn to speak from us. When they start to utter language-like sounds, we smile and nod, and encourage them to leap ahead in their use of words: "We initiate them, into the relevant forms of life held in language and gathered around the objects and persons of our world" (CR, 178). Augustine's picture of how he learned language as a child is not so much wrong as premature: only someone who already knows what it means to point, and what it is to name something, will be able to follow such instructions (cf. §32).

Once we know what words are, and what it means to name something, dictionaries can be quite useful. A dictionary is, as it were, a snapshot of our speaking and writing practices—our use—at a given historical moment. But the less we know about a certain region of practice (cooking, sewing, car mechanics, bullfighting), the less we will get out of the dictionary's presentation of its terms.

Words and practices are intertwined. To find out what a word means is to discover something about the world. Learning the word is learning to see. Learning to see is learning the word. It is impossible to draw a strict distinction between investigating the world and investigating language. Cavell asks us to imagine that we are "reading a book of reminiscences and come across the word 'umiak.' You reach for your dictionary and look it up. Now what did you do? Find out what 'umiak' means, or find out what an umiak is? ... We forget," he continues, "that we learn language and learn the world *together*, that they become elaborated and distorted together, and in the same places."[18] When we discover that "umiak" means a "large Eskimo boat, consisting of a wooden frame with skins drawn over it, and propelled by paddles," we have enlarged our world; our world now contains umiaks. Yet until the moment we came across that umiak in the book, we had no idea that our world was lacking in umiaks.

We may go about this in the opposite direction and bring the dictionary to the world. Imagine that you are in Alaska and keep seeing a certain kind of boat that you haven't seen before. Or that you are at the bullfights and keep noticing that the bullfighter seems to pass the red cloth along the spine of the bull from front to back just before he turns his back to the animal and slowly walks away, right in front of its head. You turn to your companions and ask ... what exactly?

Cavell wants us to pause and think about what we would say in such a situation. Would we ask what the thing or behavior is or what it is called? It doesn't much matter: "In either case," Cavell writes, "the learning is a question of aligning language and the world. What you need to learn will depend on what specifically it is you want to know; and how you can find out will depend specifically on what you already command."[19] Your needs may not be my needs. I may have grown up on a bull-breeding farm, or in Alaska. But more crucially: even when we ask about the same word, the same action, or the same thing, the kind of explanation we each need and want may be different. I may be an expert boat builder, so what I really am asking for is a detailed account of how to build an umiak. You may be more than satisfied with learning its name. If, in response to your simple question, I launch into a long explanation of umiak building, you may decide that I am a crushing bore. Such things—how we perceive, how we feel about one another—are also part of what we learn when we learn to speak, part of our *training*. We don't just learn to speak, we learn to speak *together*, which means that to learn to speak is also to learn to recognize kindred spirits, or to discover that our passions for certain things (boat building, bullfights) doom us to isolation.

To learn a language is to acquire a world. When the practices that give rise to that language die, the language will die, too. Bullfighting language will be doomed the day the bullfights become unacceptable to the Spanish, and the Mexicans, and the other Latin American countries that still practice bullfighting. What dies with a language, however, are not just words, but practices, and the forms of praise and criticism that go with those practices: the capacity to see, and to appreciate, certain distinctions, certain moments of beauty and courage. This is what it means to say that world and word are intertwined, or as Wittgenstein puts it: "To imagine a language means to imagine a form of life" (§19).

Use

"Meaning is use" sounds simple enough. Maybe that's why the phrase has become a veritable mantra for people who want to encapsulate Wittgenstein's vision of language in three words. Yet Wittgenstein's ideas about use are often misunderstood. I take him to mean that there is no "meaning"— no "it" that a word means, no "something" that adheres to words in isolation from their use. Words get their meaning from the sentences they appear in. But those sentences also stand in need of determination. We can't understand what work a sentence does, or what work a word does in a sentence, until we understand the work the sentence does in the specific circumstances in which it has been uttered. Austin's method for understanding the work of words—to "examine what we should say when, what words we should use in what situations"—is compatible with Wittgenstein's view of meaning.[20]

In my experience, the apparently simple slogan "meaning is use" is truly difficult to grasp, and even when we do grasp it, it is hard to keep hold of the vision contained in it without backsliding. We are constantly tempted to fall back on the understanding of meaning that Wittgenstein is at extreme pains to undo, namely that meaning is like an essence or entity that adheres to individual words—a view Wittgenstein dismisses with a curt "as if meaning were an aura the word brings along with it and retains in every kind of use" (§117).

Wittgenstein's insistence on use makes his vision of language profoundly different from all kinds of "Augustinian" views of language. On one Augustinian view, words simply have a given meaning, and to use a word is to insert that pre-existing meaning in a new context. The context may perhaps shape and stretch the meaning a little, but that's all. This view takes for granted that the meaning is something other than the word. The perennial problem for this kind of view of language is to figure out how to connect the meaning to the word, for now the word itself becomes an empty shell (this is where theories of the "mark," or the "empty signifier" take off), and the meaning something separate from that shell—a thing, a psychological process, a concept or a signified, *différance*, "iterability." But must we not already know what these "marks" mean in order to connect them to the relevant signified, the relevant meaning? (I'll discuss this problem in chapters 5 and 6.)

For Wittgenstein, the "general concept of the meaning of a word surrounds the working of language with a haze which makes clear vision impossible" (§5). "Use" provides a clearer view. Yet Wittgenstein's concept of "use" is hard to grasp, first of all, because it requires us to relinquish the ingrained idea that meaning is *elsewhere*, in some third realm, somewhere *between* the words and our understanding of them, as if there were a gap or a "relationship" between words and their meaning. But we also have trouble understanding him because (as he emphasizes in §1), we simply don't accept that "use" explains anything. Use seems so flimsy. We don't pay attention to use, because we keep looking for something firmer, deeper, something that can *ground* use itself, something like the ultimate explanation of meaning as such. Wittgenstein's most fundamental conviction—and the hardest to follow—is that the request for such an ultimate explanation is meaningless precisely because it presupposes a picture in which meaning, or use, has a ground. Because he considers that picture to be profoundly misguided, no answer offered in response to questions based on it will make sense.

Why does Wittgenstein want us to stop at use, to realize that no further explanations of meaning are necessary? To grasp what's at stake, it helps to turn to something he says in the *Tractatus* about how we use the term "laws of nature":

> 6.371 The whole modern conception of the world is founded on the illusion that the so-called laws of nature are the explanation of natural phenomena.

> 6.372 Thus people today stop at the laws of nature, treating them as something inviolable, just as God and Fate were treated in past ages.[21]

When a child asks "Why do apples fall from trees?" we may answer by saying something about Newton and the law of gravity. If the child then asks, "Why is there a law of gravity?" we may reach for Einstein's theory of relativity. But explanations come to an end. As Wittgenstein's student and friend Maurice O'Connor Drury writes, "Ultimately we will have to accept some facts as unexplained and say, 'Well that is just how it is.'"[22] If instead of saying "that's just how it is," we say, "well, that's the laws of nature," the "laws of nature" here isn't a "deeper" explanation than "that's just how it is"; it's just a fancier name for the same thing. Wittgenstein's point is that in some contexts, these utterances do the same work as talk about God and Fate. Explanations only take us so far. This is why Wittgenstein thinks that the task of philosophy is to provide not explanations, but descriptions.

The case of "use" is like this. We (literary theorists, for example) keep pressing for something *more*, something that will *explain* use more fundamentally than Wittgenstein's simple exhortation to look and see. "Use" alone doesn't seem to be an explanation of anything. What grounds use? Nowadays, answers such as the "essence" or the "Idea" won't get us far in intellectual company. "God" or "Fate" won't get much of a hearing either. But literary theorists are still quite likely to accept something like "iterability" or "interpretive communities" or "social conventions" as perfectly satisfying explanations of how meaning gets attached to words.

Such answers satisfy "our craving for generality," which usually takes the form of trying to find something all the relevant phenomena have in common. We never entertain the thought that they may share no common features at all.[23] "Use" is not a common feature shared by all words and utterances. It is rather the condition of possibility of having words and utterances in the first place. It's because there is use that there is meaning. And to figure out what the meaning is we have to look at the use—the specific use in the particular case. There is no one way or one method for analyzing use. As we have seen, Wittgenstein is at pains to show us that to find the meaning of "five" is not the same thing as to find the meaning of "red," which again is different from finding the meaning of "apples." Why do we persist in thinking that "social convention" or "iterability" tell us more about the meaning of "five red apples" than Wittgenstein's suggestion that we look at the use? Because we cling to the idea that the meaning must be separate from the word.

Meaning and Use

Misunderstandings of Wittgenstein's "use" abound. Some readers imagine that "the meaning is the use" is shorthand for a distinction between semantics (meaning) and pragmatics (use). Others conclude that Wittgenstein is trying to distinguish between "speaker's meaning" (what I have in mind when I utter something), and what the words generally mean in the language. Such theories rest on the idea that use simply mobilizes and modifies an underlying core of meaning, which exists apart from the use. For Wittgenstein, this is precisely the wrong picture of meaning: "Here the word, there the meaning. The money, and the cow one can buy with it" (§120).

Deconstructionists have been quick to assume that "use" is the "ground" of meaning, that is, that "use" functions as a kind of stabilizing limit to meaning. They conclude that Wittgenstein's understanding of meaning really is a theory of context, a theory that is bound to fail, since "context is boundless," as Jonathan Culler puts it, and thus can provide no stabilizing of meaning at all.[24] But "use" doesn't mean "context." Use is what we *do* with words. If we do nothing with them, they remain dead:

§431. "There is a gap between an order and its execution. It has to be closed by the process of understanding [*durch das Verstehen*]."

"Only in the process of understanding [*im Verstehen*] does the order mean that we are to do THIS. The *order*—why, that is nothing but sounds, ink-marks.—

§432. Every sign by *itself* seems dead. *What* gives it life?—In use it *lives*. Is it there that it has living breath within it?—Or is the *use* its breath?

Wittgenstein's distinction between dead signs (sounds, ink-marks) and living signs (signs in use) may look like Saussure's famous distinction between signifier and signified, but Wittgenstein's point is existential, not formal. How is it that words come alive for us? What makes us experience certain sounds as meaningful? Giving voice to the view Wittgenstein opposes, sections 431 and 432 show why we are so quick to accept the picture of a gulf between word and meaning. It seems to make sense to think that *first* we hear utterly meaningless sounds—"shut the door"—and *then* "a process of understanding" intervenes, so that I *now* realize that your words *mean* "shut the door."

How we imagine "understanding" is not important here: maybe we label it "interpretation" and think of it as a mental act or process. Maybe we imagine mechanical wheels turning, synapses firing, MRI scans lighting up. Wittgenstein, of course, does not deny that something happens in the brain when we speak and understand language. Exactly what goes on in the brain would be a matter for biology or neuroscience to figure out. Regardless of what the sciences come up with concerning the brain, the Wittgensteinian point would remain the same: that those firing synapses, the bright colors on the scan, are not the *meaning* of our words. To stare at a scan of someone's brain when he is thinking about "tea" is (obviously) not the same thing as to understand the word "tea." In fact, scientists staring at the scan take for granted that they already know what "tea" means, or they wouldn't know where to begin. And to know what "tea" means is to know what we do with the word, the drink, the meal.

Wittgenstein begins *Philosophical Investigations* by stressing that we can't understand words or sentences unless we place them in a context of significant use. This is why he begins by showing us language at work in simple practices (children playing ring-a-ring-a-roses; laborers working on a building site). As James Conant explains: if we persist in thinking of meaning as an "it" that a sentence (or word) means, quite "apart from any consideration of the context of significant use, . . . then we will unwittingly end up seeking its meaning in the realm of the psychological."[25] But to make meaning psychological is no better than making it purely referential.

In my experience it is really hard truly to hang on to the simple idea that meaning isn't an "it" separate from use. (Conant reminds us that this is the case for sentences as well as for words. There simply is no such thing as "*the* thought which *the sentence itself* expresses."[26]) Even if I keep repeating to myself that use isn't a ground, but a practice, something we *do*, the example of concrete nouns (five red apples) always returns to haunt me. What about the brilliant red, white, and black bird pecking away at a tree outside my window? Am I wrong to name it a "pileated woodpecker" and think that the meaning of that name is the thing, the bird itself? Or the image of it in my head? And if I am not wrong about this, doesn't that make the meaning an "it," separate from its use?

Wittgenstein himself raises the same question: "What is the relation between name and thing named?—Well, what *is* it?" (§37). He answers by telling us to look at the language-game where the name occurs: "Among other things, this relation may also consist in the fact that hearing a name calls before our mind the picture of what is named; and sometimes in the name's being written on the thing named or in its being uttered when the thing named is pointed at" (§37). This is exactly what happens with my pileated woodpecker! So Wittgenstein obviously doesn't deny that some words are names, or that certain names call to mind certain pictures. (Say "Pyramiden" to me and I instantly see before me the haunting vistas of an abandoned Soviet model city in a spectacular Arctic landscape.) This is what we do in the language-game—the specific practice—called "naming." The trouble is that we take this one language-game to represent all language. So we forget about examples like "Help!" or "Bingo!"

To bring out Wittgenstein's understanding of meaning and use more fully, I'll now look at two particularly hard cases—proper names, and ostensive definitions. I call them hard cases because both have a tendency to make us fall back on the idea that meaning is an "it" existing apart from use. Drawing on Frege, Conant compares the rather poetic sentence "Trieste is no Vienna" to the more prosaic "Vienna is the capital of Austria." The temptation is to think that there has to be some kind of "core" or "essence" to the meaning of, say, "Vienna," something we can call the "literal" or "basic" meaning (so that all other meanings become "metaphorical").[27] Conant calls this the "tendency to think that one already knows what 'Vienna' means taken all by itself outside the context of the proposition—it means one presumes roughly what it means in a sentence like 'Vienna is the capital of Austria.'"[28]

But knowing that Vienna is the capital of Austria doesn't really help us to grasp what "Trieste is no Vienna" actually means. As a teenager in Norway, I would have been utterly incapable of explaining the meaning of "Trieste is no Vienna," even though I knew perfectly well that we were talking about the names of two different European cities. It's a little like knowing perfectly well that *soso* means "bland, insipid, tasteless" and still have no clue what it means when applied to a fighting bull.

In the first sentence, Conant points out, "Vienna" is what Frege would call a "concept-expression"; in the second, it is an "object-expression." In other words, in the first case "Vienna" means something like a "metropolis" or a "refined and elegant cultural capital." In the second it just defines the capital of Austria. In these two sentences, Conant notes, the same word simply doesn't have the same meaning, to the point that Frege uses a completely different logical symbol for the two occurrences of the "same word." The logical difference, we might say, is the different *work* the word

"Vienna" does in the sentence.[29] Note that Frege's logical analysis presupposes that we *already* know the difference between the two uses of "Vienna." This difference arises from a whole world of practices and experiences with European cities.

When I sigh, "Trieste is no Vienna," the sentence itself stands in need of further determination. Or rather: its meaning will depend on the specific circumstances in which I utter it. Maybe I feel exiled in Trieste in 1900 and long for the cosmopolitan life of Vienna. Maybe I miss the rays of the afternoon sun falling across my Sachertorte. Maybe I miss the art museums, or the opera. But in other circumstances such nostalgic, bourgeois interpretations, turning on culture and the good life, may become completely irrelevant. Let us imagine a discussion, in 2016, of anti-Semitism in European cities during World War II, in the course of which a Jewish participant declares that "Vienna was no Copenhagen." How does this compare to "Trieste is no Vienna," spoken in 1900? Does "Vienna" really reduce to the same fundamental thing (the same "it") in these two utterances?

In his discussion of "ostensive definitions"—definitions given by showing or pointing to a thing—Wittgenstein tries to help us escape from the idea that words (names) simply *have* a given, core meaning (see §§27–43). I hold up an apple and say: "This is an apple." I point through the plane window and say: "The city you see down by the river over there is called Vienna." Surely, we think, an ostensive definition simply gives *the* meaning of the word, in isolation from any specific use. But then we forget that an ostensive definition itself is a specific language-game, a particular kind of use. (The same is true for dictionary definitions.) Again, Wittgenstein wants us to resist the temptation to generalize about "language as such" from the particular case.

Wittgenstein notes that we can only ostensively define certain kinds of words: "a person's name, the name of a colour, the name of a material, a number-word, the name of a point of the compass, and so on" (§28). This leaves other words ("notwithstanding," or "Help!") to fend for themselves. What happens if I point to two nuts and say, "That is called 'two'" (§28)? The sentence is perfectly open to misunderstanding. My interlocutor may think I am telling him the name of this specific group of nuts. If I say, "this person is called Hans," he may still get it wrong. Maybe he will take Hans to be the name of a "colour, of a race, or even of a point of the compass." Even in these cases, then, the "core" meaning theory doesn't hold. Wittgenstein's conclusion is clear: "an ostensive definition can be variously interpreted in *any* case" (§28).

Wittgenstein considers definition or explanation to be an exchange, an interaction between interlocutors. My definition fails if the other's "uptake" (to invoke an Austinian term) fails. But if the other gets it wrong, it is not necessarily because I explained it badly: "Any explanation can be misunderstood" (note to §28). If my interlocutor doesn't already know how to play the language-game of "definitions" or "naming," she won't have the slightest idea what to do with my ostensive definitions: "So, one could say: an ostensive definition explains the use—the meaning—of a word if the role the word is supposed to play in the language is already clear.... One has already to know (or be able to do) something before one can ask what something is called. But what does one have to know?" (§30).

The trouble, then, is not with ostensive definitions, or definitions per se. Dictionary definitions are perfectly all right, too. The trouble is that we can't *use* even the clearest definition if we don't already know how to do things with words. (That's Cortázar's point in "Lucas and His Classes.") If I don't know anything about the fate of Austrian as opposed to Danish Jews in World War II, "Vienna is no Copenhagen" will make no sense to me.

There is so much we need to know before we can understand the simplest explanations! That's precisely Wittgenstein's point:

> And now, I think, we can say: Augustine describes the learning of human language as if the child came into a foreign country and did not understand the language of the country; that is, as if he already had a language, only not this one. Or again, as if the child could already think, only not yet speak. And "think" would here mean something like "talk to himself." (§32)

To learn language is to learn how to *use* words and sentences. And to learn that is to learn practices, the language-games that go with them, and to be initiated into the relevant forms of life.

Definitions, or dictionary meanings, then, aren't the ground of use, they are handy snapshots of the most common uses of individual words at a given time. Dictionaries struggle to keep up with use, not the other way around: "To understand a sentence means to understand a language. To understand a language means to have mastered a technique" (§199). When we teach a child how to use the phrase "turn down," Cavell notes, she has to learn, somehow, the difference between "turn down the phonograph," "turn down the bed," and "turn down the offer," but on what grounds? There are none. This is why Cavell calls language a "thin net over an abyss" (CR, 178): nothing but our willingness to continue talking holds it together.

Dictionary definitions, then, presuppose use. If I come to the dictionary without the necessary pre-existing knowledge of use, I won't be able to make sense of its definitions and explanations. Dictionaries failed Lucas's students because Vidal was drawing on a world of practices unknown to them. The language of bullfights is just an extreme example: anyone who has tried to learn a foreign language, will know the feeling.

If a word (or a sentence) has no use, it will have no meaning. In a note appended to §38, Wittgenstein writes: "Can I say 'bububu' and mean 'if it doesn't rain, I shall go for a walk'? — It is only in a language that I can mean something by something." Culler takes Wittgenstein to *deny* that one can give "bububu" this specific meaning.[30] But this is too quick. Wittgenstein isn't denying anything. He is simply saying that as it stands, "bububu" has no use in English (or German), and therefore no meaning either.

To say "bububu" and attach a specific mental content, or a specific intention to the sound, is simply to give it a private meaning — a psychological content or association. If I share that association with you, we will now have a secret code we can use when the occasion calls for it. But this still doesn't give "bububu" a use in the language, a meaning in English, or German, for we still haven't found a place for it in our language-games: the phrase has no *grammar*, Wittgenstein might say. "Bububu" may of course acquire a use at some point in the future. In *The Blue Book*, Wittgenstein uses the example of a "man who tells us he feels the visual image two inches behind the bridge of his nose." We don't understand what the man means, but it doesn't follow that we never could: "The grammar of this phrase has yet to be explained to us" (BB, 10).

Wittgenstein explains use through examples in which one person is trying to understand another. This is no coincidence. Cavell puts it this way: "The meaning is the use" calls attention to the fact that what an expression means is a function of what it is used to mean or to say on specific occasions by human beings" (CR, 206). Without human beings there is no use, and no meaning either. This may sound so banal as to go without saying. Unfortunately, Cavell notes, the history of philosophy is full of attempts to explain the meaning of a word "in isolation from a systematic attention to their concrete uses," for example by "searching for the meaning of a word in various realms of objects," or by setting up an "idea of perfect understanding as being achievable only through the construction of a perfect language" (206–7). If we wrote the history of such attempts, Cavell suggests, it could be called "Philosophy and the Rejection of the Human" (207). Some recent interpretations of Saussure attempt to reinscribe meaning in an object-world without speakers in exactly such ways.[31] Any such attempt is bound to find itself on the see-saw between positivism and skepticism that characterizes the post-Saussurean heritage.[32]

"The meaning of a word is its use in the language": it sounds so simple.

It *is* simple. Yet the insight is momentous. This claim binds us to the world, binds us to other users of the language, speakers who share our practices and perceptions, share our sense of when to use this, rather than that word or expression.

We have seen that Wittgenstein's understanding of use is based on the idea that to learn a language is to be trained in a practice, to be initiated into a form of life. ("And to imagine a language means to imagine a form of life" [§19].) In this chapter I have tried to convey the excitement — and challenge — of reading Wittgenstein, by focusing closely on the beginning of *Philosophical Investigations*. My main concern has been to convey Wittgenstein's radical challenge to "Augustinian" theories of language by focusing on what he means by saying "meaning is use in the language." Later, I shall show that the whole post-Saussurean tradition is a form of "Augustinianism." But first I'll deepen my account of Wittgenstein's vision of the interconnection between word and world by examining three crucial terms: *language-games*, *grammar*, and *forms of life*.

2

Our Lives in Language

LANGUAGE-GAMES, GRAMMAR, FORMS OF LIFE

Wittgenstein's understanding of meaning as use unfolds into a deeply original vision of the intertwinement of world and word, and of our lives in language. Ultimately, he proposes a new kind of realism—not a theory, but rather an attitude. Cora Diamond calls it the "realistic spirit." Wittgenstein's vision is sustained by three terms of art: *language-games, grammar,* and *forms of life*. As he elaborates these terms, Wittgenstein constantly returns to scenes of conversation, of ordinary understanding and misunderstanding to show that language binds us together even in our differences and disagreements. Such scenes exemplify our "agreement in judgments" (§242), which means our "agreement[s] not in opinions, but rather in form of life" (§241).[1]

Language-Games

In German the word for language-game is *Sprachspiel*. A *Spiel* is a game. The verb *spielen* means to play, in contexts such as "play with toys," "play the piano," "play poker," and "play Hedda in *Hedda Gabler*." But the word "play" may lead us astray. We shouldn't conclude that only playful (fun, lightweight, amusing, "nonserious") activities are language-games. "Praying" (§23) intertwines language and practice just as much as "playing." So does "giving orders, and acting on them" (§23). In general, Wittgenstein uses "language-game" to mean something like "language-practice." The point of the term is to draw attention to the intertwinement of words and practices, to show us that we can't understand a word or an utterance unless we understand the practice it is a part of. The concept of "language-game" tells us that to learn a language is not to learn a set of names, but to be trained in—to learn to recognize and participate in—a vast number of human practices.

In §2 of *Philosophical Investigations* we encounter a tribe of builders whose language consists of only four nouns ("block," "pillar," "slab," and "beam"). When one builder calls out one of those words, another brings the appropriate stone. Wittgenstein says that we can call this a language-game. He likens it to "one of those games by means of which children learn their native language.... Think of certain uses that are made of words in games like ring-a-ring-a-roses [*Reigenspielen*]" (§7). This is the first occurrence of the word "language-game" in *Philosophical Investigations*. Ring-a-ring-a-roses is a lovely example of a simple attunement between words and action. A common English version of the words used in this game goes like this:

> Ring-a-ring-a-roses,
> A pocket full of posies;
> ashes! ashes!
> we all fall down.

The children sing the words while dancing in a ring, and when they get to the last line, they fall down. (Some folklorists connect ring-a-ring-a-roses to the Black Death.) While the game has innumerable variations in different languages, the children always perform some kind of action alongside the singing. Learning the language of the builders is like learning to play ring-a-ring-a-roses: it is to learn that words and action, talking and doing, are intertwined: "We learn language and learn the world *together*."[2] Without the practice of building, it would make no sense to call out "Slab!" To understand use is to understand such things.

Wittgenstein pushes the example further, by giving the builders a few more words, namely some color samples, number-words, and the words "there" and "this" used with a pointing gesture (see §8). To learn this language, a child needs to be trained: she must memorize the number-words and learn how to use them. Maybe the teacher uses ostensive definitions to help the child learn the names of numbers and of the different stones. The teaching of "this" and "there" is done by pointing, but Wittgenstein stresses that "the pointing occurs in the *use* of the words too and not merely in learning the use" (§9). To learn "this" and "that" is not to learn a metalinguistic activity. We learn such words in ordinary practices.

At this point Wittgenstein imagines someone who *still* wants to ask: "Now what do the words of this language *signify* [*bezeichnen*]?" Wittgenstein thinks he has explained this. But the interlocutor thinks he hasn't, for he assumes that meaning can only be explained through conventional definitions that always take the same form: "the word ... signifies ..." Wittgenstein reacts impatiently: "How is what they signify supposed to come out other than in the kind of use they have? And we have already described that" (§10). Definitions are themselves examples of a specific kind of language-game. They come in handy in the language-game we can call "removing misunderstandings." If you realize that I am taking "slab" to mean "block," you may correct me by saying "this is a slab." But such explanations presuppose that I already understand the role these words play in the language (if I take them to function as number-words, I simply won't understand even the most ostensive definition). In short, "making the descriptions of the uses of these words similar in this way cannot make the uses themselves any more like one another! For, as we see, they are absolutely unlike" (§10).

To learn to recognize and practice language-games, then, is to learn to recognize and practice *differences*. To be able to distinguish between language-games is also to be able to tell the difference between the use of the *same* word in different language-games. No wonder Wittgenstein considered using King Lear's "I'll teach you differences" as a motto for *Philosophical Investigations*.[3] In §23 Wittgenstein lists a number of different language-games:

> Giving orders, and acting on them—
> Describing an object by its appearance, or by its measurements—
> Constructing an object from a description (a drawing)—
> Reporting an event—
> Speculating about the event—
> Forming and testing a hypothesis—
> Presenting the results of an experiment in tables and diagrams—
> Making up a story; and reading one—
> Acting in a play—
> Singing rounds—
> Guessing riddles—
> Cracking a joke; telling one—
> Solving a problem in applied arithmetic—
> Translating from one language into another—
> Requesting, thanking, cursing, greeting, praying

The list appears quite random. It includes things that require extensive nonlinguistic action (obeying an order, constructing objects, acting in a play), and things that don't even seem to require us to speak (praying, speculating about an event). Wittgenstein makes no attempt to be exhaustive, to set up a systematic inventory of language games. On the contrary: he declares that any such attempt would be impossible: "But how many kinds of sentences are there?... There are *countless* kinds; countless different kinds of use of all the things we call 'signs,' 'words,' 'sentences.' And this diversity is not something fixed, given once for all; but new types of language, new language-games, as we may say, come into existence, and others become obsolete and get forgotten" (§23). Use is open-ended, in constant transformation, always responding to new circumstances.

If you tried to develop a definition of "game," you would fail.[4] While some language-games appear to be related (maybe: requesting, begging, demanding), others have nothing in common ("singing rounds" vs. "forming and testing a hypothesis"). There can be no *one* theory, no *one* definition, to hold such different practices together. To try to find such a theory would be like trying to find one definition for all past and future human actions.

Whenever we try to posit something as the common essence of all language-games, we will fail. One literary scholar proposes that all language-games are "agonistic" and therefore always produce "wins and losses as well as draws and exchanges."[5] But nobody wins at ring-a-ring-a-roses. If I fail at the language-games of cursing or thanking or praying, I haven't lost a game, I haven't cursed or thanked or prayed at all. On the other hand, winning and losing are intrinsic to the language-game of betting. Here I am tempted, for a second, to divorce the language from the practice: maybe "betting" simply is the *name* of the right words, uttered in the right circumstances? But would I really be playing the language-game of betting if I were uttering the right words, for example, "I bet you five dollars," without having any notion that real-life winning or losing was involved? That would be like saying that you could play ring-a-ring-a-roses without singing, dancing or falling down. If I think of betting as simply a matter of uttering the right words, without any understanding of risks, gains, stakes, and so on, I turn "betting" into a kind of description or representation—that is, I fail to grasp what a language-game is, and therefore also fail to grasp what Wittgenstein calls the "grammar" of betting.

Freeing us from the stranglehold of "representation," the concept of language-games helps us to see that there are many different tools in the toolbox of language (see §11). To speak or write is never just to represent something, but to do something: "Talking together is acting together, not making motions and noises at one another, nor transferring unspeakable messages or essences from the inside of one closed chamber to the inside of another," Cavell writes.[6]

Words and world can be intertwined—or come apart—in any number of different ways. Language-games are so diverse, so manifold, that even a fairly simple one, like "description," has different rules for different purposes: "Remember how many different kinds of things are called 'description': description of a body's position by means of its co-ordinates, description of a facial expression, description of a sensation of touch, of a mood" (§24). Wittgenstein's reminder helps us to realize how crude the notion of "representation" is when it is used to cover all the things we do with words, whether in everyday life or in writing.

A language-game does something reasonably specific. It is an action. It can be described by a verb. "Describing or analyzing a poem" strikes me as a language-game; "literary studies" does not. An academic discipline may be a "discourse" in Foucault's sense, but hardly a language-game. Wittgenstein never calls philosophy a "language-game." On the contrary, he complains that philosophers have a terrible tendency to use words *outside* the language-games in which they are usually "at home," that is, outside "their everyday use" (§116).

What is this "speaking outside language-games"? Cavell writes: "When we speak outside language-games our words are 'deprived of their ordinary criteria of employment'" (CR, 226). In such cases, our words don't exactly lose all meaning (for they are still trading on the meanings they have in their ordinary language-games), but they are left stranded "without relation to the world" (226). To remove words from use is to place them in a position in which they are no longer responsive to the world, which means they no longer carry out any *work*.

"Work" is a key concept here: "For philosophical problems arise when language *goes on holiday*" (§38). "The confusions which occupy us arise when language is, as it were, idling, not when it is doing work" (§132). When language is "idling," its gears and levers aren't connecting with anything. The words come out, but they make no difference. We think we are saying something meaningful, but we are not. When this happens, we are using words "absolutely," or "outside language-games." Literary critics inspired by theories of the sublime have tried to make the idea of speaking outside language games into a "particularly literary gesture."[7] I certainly agree that literature can be a site for experiments in meaninglessness. But there is nothing specifically literary—and certainly nothing sublime— about speaking outside language-games.

Words used outside the language-games where they are at home stand in need of philosophical therapy: "What *we* do is to bring words back from their metaphysical to their everyday use" (§116). Here we may be tempted to think that Wittgenstein is setting up a distinction between "metaphysical uses" and "everyday uses." But this is not the case.[8] To speak "outside language-games" is not just another kind of "use." (If it were, then such language would actually *do* something; it would no longer be "on holiday.") Rather, the distinction is between language that fails to make sense because it does no work and language that works. When language fails to make sense, the problem isn't the *words*, but our "failure to specify a meaning for them," as Ed Witherspoon puts it.[9] To think of language as use is to realize that language isn't the problem. The problem is always *us*.

Grammar

A simple definition of Wittgenstein's concept of grammar is "rules for how we use language." The concept tells us that use is not random, but systematic. Conant notes that "what early Wittgenstein calls *the logic of our language* ... later Wittgenstein calls grammar."[10] This isn't hard to understand, yet I have always found Wittgenstein's "grammar" far more puzzling than "language-games." It certainly took me a long time to get clear on what Wittgenstein is doing with the term. Maybe I was being particularly obtuse because I have spent so much time studying grammar in the usual sense of the word, namely in learning foreign languages. In my mind, "grammar" always conjures up something like the rules for how to use the subjunctive in French or Latin. But then Wittgenstein writes something like "Grammar tells what kind of object anything is" (§373) or "Essence is expressed by grammar" (§371). What is this "grammar"? How can it have such powers of revelation?

In *Philosophical Investigations* Wittgenstein uses grammar to investigate different scenarios of understanding and misunderstanding in philosophy and life. Wittgenstein's way of doing philosophy is a practice of "grammatical investigation." In everyday life, Wittgenstein invokes the notion of grammar to explain how it can be that meaning is public and shared. Wittgenstein's famous discussion of rule-following is an investigation of what it means to share a sense of when (under what circumstances) to say what. Here I will not discuss rule-following as such. I'll simply begin with Wittgenstein's "'Following a rule' is a practice" (§202). We are trained to follow rules, just as we are trained to speak our mother tongue. If someone fails to understand the training, explanations will quickly come to an end. I tell you to "add two" to every number; you do it fine until you get to 1,000. But then you continue by adding four. You nevertheless insist— and truly believe—that you are doing exactly the same thing as before, firmly following the rule of adding two (see §185). What can I say to make you realize your mistake?

In §206, which is part of the rule-following discussion, Wittgenstein shows why any of this matters to our efforts to live with others:

Following a rule is analogous to obeying an order. One is trained to do so, and one reacts to an order in a particular way. But what if one person reacts to the order and training *thus*, and another *otherwise*? Who is right, then?

Suppose you came as an explorer to an unknown country with a language quite unknown to you. In what circumstances would you say that the people there gave orders, understood them, obeyed them, rebelled against them, and so on?

Shared human behavior is the system of reference by means of which we interpret an unknown language. (§206)

This paragraph deals with life. It connects language to behavior (action, practices). By conjuring up the image of the explorer, it also draws on the idea of "forms of life" (which I shall discuss below). It foregrounds the challenges involved in interacting with others. If I can't connect the others' words to their practices, I will not understand them. The idea of "grammar" surfaces in the observation that all I have to go on in my attempts to learn their language is an assumption of "shared human behavior." But maybe there is no such shared behavior. Then my attempts at understanding will fail. The notion of "shared behavior" isn't normative. Wittgenstein isn't saying that we must, or always will, share behavior. He is saying that if we really don't share any practices, we will find it difficult, even impossible, to understand why these strangers do what they do. Our judgments are not in "attunement" (*Übereinsstimmung*, §242). This is not a value judgment, but rather a reminder of the challenges involved in learning any language, including our own.

In his discussion of how to do and not do philosophy, Wittgenstein says that we can suffer from "grammatical illusions" (§110). He complains that "our grammar is deficient in surveyability" and that we therefore "don't have *an overview* of the use of our words." To solve philosophical problems—to get past our "failure to understand"—we need to get clear on—gain an overview of—the *grammar* of our words. When we feel lost, confused, bewildered, when we suffer from a lack of understanding, we undertake a "grammatical investigation." It is a therapy for our own words, as it were. The aim is to reach a "surveyable representation" (*übersichtliche Darstellung*), a concept that goes to the very heart of Wittgenstein's philosophy: "The concept of surveyable representation," he writes, "is of fundamental significance for us. It characterizes the way we represent things, how we look at matters. (Is this a 'Weltanschauung'?)" (§122).

Wittgenstein prizes the "surveyable representation"—a phrase earlier translations rendered as a "clear view"—because he sees it as the very essence of his work: Philosophy—his kind of philosophy—should be a therapy for (our own) confusion. Like psychoanalytic therapy it should loosen our mental shackles and make us freer in our responses to the world: "A *picture* held us captive. And we couldn't get outside it, for it lay in our language, and language seemed only to repeat it to us inexorably" (§115). To see our "real need" (§108), we must escape from the fog of misunderstanding. But we can't do that unless we are willing to admit that we feel lost: "A philosophical problem has the form: 'I don't know my way about'" (§123).

Wittgenstein's therapeutic method is simple: we must "bring words back from their metaphysical to their everyday use" (§116). To do so, we engage in grammatical analysis, which Wittgenstein describes in one sentence: "he should ask himself in what special circumstances this sentence is actually used. There it does make sense" (§117). To gain clarity we must remind ourselves of what we already know, namely how the word is used. We must remind ourselves of the obvious, the ordinary, that which we so often take for granted.

Imagine a drawing of a machine, or a diagram explaining how to put together IKEA furniture, in which the wrong parts are connected. The picture makes it impossible for us to get that engine to work, or that chair to stand up. As long as we fail to question the picture, we will keep coming up with all kinds of clever solutions to make the engine work, or the chair stick together, but we will never succeed. Only a "clear view"—one that shows us where the old picture goes wrong—will enable us to stop banging our head against the wall of our prison cell: "The results of philosophy are the discovery of some piece of plain nonsense and the bumps that the understanding has got by running up against the limits of language. They—these bumps—make us see the value of that discovery" (§119). The discovery sets us free, enables us to move on.

To benefit from Wittgenstein's therapy, we must feel lost in the fog of language, suffer the pain from the bumps on our understanding. Only then will we want to undertake the necessary investigation in order to reach the longed-for *übersichtliche Darstellung*—the surveyable representation that makes me feel the pleasure and relaxation that comes with clarity: oh, so *that's* how it all fits together. (I am tempted to posit a connection between Wittgenstein's longing for a clear view and his passion for detective novels.[11])

How exactly do we carry out a "grammatical investigation," then? To echo Austin: We look at what we should say when. This can't be done in the abstract. To get going, we need examples of language use. We are looking for—or rather: trying to remember, trying to get clear on—our *criteria* for using words in particular ways. Conant defines a grammatical investigation as "a convening of our criteria for the employment of a particular concept."[12] To use criteria is to exercise *judgment*, the judgment that *this* is the word to use, the sentence to utter in *these* specific circumstances. "Criteria are criteria of judgment; the underlying idea is one of discriminating or separating cases, of identifying by means of differences," Cavell writes (CR, 17). He goes on to give a brilliant overview of what a "grammatical investigation" is:

> These investigations seem to describe three main steps: (1) We find ourselves wanting to know something about a phenomenon, e.g., pain, expecting, knowledge, understanding, being of an opinion.... (2) We remind ourselves of the kinds of statement we make about it. (3) We ask ourselves what criteria we have for (what we go on in) saying what we say....
>
> There are two general or background claims about what we say which Wittgenstein summarizes with the idea of grammar: that language is shared, that the forms I rely upon in making sense are human forms, that they impose human limits upon me, that when I say what we "can" and "cannot" say I am indeed voicing necessities which others recognize, i.e., obey (consciously or not); and that our uses of language are pervasively, almost unimaginably, *systematic*. (CR, 29)

We want to know something—usually because something confuses us. Or maybe because it fills us with wonder: How can *this* be? To carry out a grammatical investigation we simply ask: "under what circumstances, in what particular cases, do we say ...?" (CR 30). The answers we come up with are our *criteria* for using the word or phrase.

Criteria are shared—they govern the use. They tell us that we can say "feed the cat," "feed the machine," and "feed the meter," but not "feed the phone" or "feed the table." As the examples show, convening criteria is not the same thing as appealing to "received" or "standard" rules for "good" English. You are free to say "feed the table" as much as you like. The point is that if you do, other speakers of the language won't get what you are saying. You will have to struggle to make yourself understood. Of course, "feed the table" may well make full sense in specific circumstances. If a furniture maker says "I am feeding the table," as he is oiling a table he has just made, we won't have any trouble understanding him. For all we know, "feed the table" will become a widely used expression in the future. It's just that, like "bububu," right now the phrase has no (Wittgensteinian) grammar in the language (see §37).

A grammatical investigation investigates whatever it is that makes us puzzled and confused. In such an enterprise it would be absurd to imply that only upper-class or "standard" phrases count. (Sociolinguistics explores the systematicity of use in specific social groups. There is no conflict between that enterprise and Wittgenstein's philosophical project.)

The appeal to criteria reveals that language arises from a "background of pervasive and systematic agreements among us, which we had not realized, or had not known we realize," says Cavell. We also discover the "astonishing fact of the astonishing extent to which we *do* agree in judgment; eliciting criteria goes to show therefore that our judgments *are* public, that is, shared" (CR, 30, 31).

For Wittgenstein, Cavell, and Austin, human knowledge is the "human capacity for applying the concepts of a language to the things of a world" (CR, 17). "Grammar tells what kind of object anything is" (§373) because we have criteria of judgment for when to apply *this* rather than *that* word or expression. This means that if I systematically say "toffee" in situations where everyone else says "coffee," you would be justified in wondering whether I really know what either toffee or coffee is. In other words, I seem not to know the grammar of coffee. The result will be misunderstanding. (If I say "toffee" for "coffee" just once, chances are you will think it was a slip of the tongue.)

Wittgenstein thinks that grammatical investigations are particularly useful to philosophers, who often land themselves in deep metaphysical trouble because they have, without noticing it, removed words from the language-games in which they are ordinarily at home. But, as we have now seen, to carry out a grammatical investigation is to investigate *use*. And to investigate use is to look at our lives: "The rules of grammar," Rush Rhees writes, "are rules of the lives in which there is language."[13]

Cora Diamond provides some illuminating examples of the role of grammar in our lives. If we want to understand the grammar of "fear," Diamond writes, we must understand "how the commerce with the word 'fear' is interwoven with the rest of the lives of the people who use the word."[14] In the 1920s, she writes, Soviet linguists interviewed Kashgar villagers who simply did not play the same language-games with descriptions as speakers of Russian, or English:

> If these people are told "Bears in the Far North, where it snows, are white; Novaya Zemlya is in the Far North, and has lots of snow; what colour are the bears there?", they will say "I can't say, I have never been there." ... These are people who are perfectly capable of drawing conclusions about things familiar in their own experience. But their replies

to the investigators who are pushing them to draw conclusions ... function like grammatical reminders: "We always speak only of what we see; we don't talk about what we haven't seen."[15]

This example shows that to establish the grammar of a specific use is a descriptive, not a normative activity. This is one reason why Wittgenstein insists that "philosophy must not interfere in any way with the actual use of language, so it can in the end only describe it" (§124). For what authorizes a philosopher to tell the Kashgars that they must deal with descriptions the way he does?[16]

The example shows that it makes no sense to declare one set of (Wittgensteinian) grammatical rules superior to another. That would be like declaring that Latin is superior to English because it has more cases. To understand use is to understand the place a specific language-game has in the lives of the speakers. This is also why grammar tells what something is: "How do I know that this colour is red? — It would be an answer to say: 'I have learnt English'" (§381). "You learned the concept 'pain' when you learned language" (§384).

Forms of Life

"Grammar is to be seen in how we live," Cora Diamond notes.[17] Wittgenstein famously declares that "to imagine a language means to imagine a form of life" (§19). "Form of life" (*Lebensform*—life-form) is one of Wittgenstein's most famous concepts and one of the most misunderstood. Literary critics who align it with Stanley Fish's "interpretive communities" have been quick to assume that "forms of life" means "social conventions" or "social norms."[18] Ernest Gellner and Herbert Marcuse, who make the same assumption, subject the concept to blistering political critique without asking whether their conventionalist understanding of the term is correct, or even plausible.[19]

To take "forms of life" to mean "social conventions" is to turn the concept into a mere shadow of itself. In reality, Wittgenstein's "forms of life" invites us to rethink the role conventions play in our lives, and to consider afresh what we share (and don't share) with others. In fact, once I grasped what Wittgenstein wanted from this concept, I began to wonder what the routine invocations of "social construction" in literary studies actually explain.

Post-Saussurean critics are apt to say things like "The arbitrariness of the sign ... points to the fact that language is a matter of convention. The linguistic community 'agrees' to attach a specific signified to a specific signifier.... In other words, meaning is socially constructed."[20] The quotation marks around "agrees" shows the critic's own discomfort with the term. In any case, I don't so much disagree with such claims as wonder what exactly the critic is saying. "Socially constructed" as opposed to what?[21] Usually, such critics embrace "social construction" (or similar terms) because they think of "conventions" as historical, social, political, and therefore open to change. They usually think of "social construction" as the opposite of "essence" or, in some cases, of "biological essentialism." I won't start discussing essences here.[22] But how easy do such critics think it is to change a "convention"? How do they imagine the "agreement" about attaching signifiers to signifieds to come about? Case by case? Or in some global or universal way?

A convention, Cavell notes, is always in the "service of some project." That it can be changed is internal to what a convention is. ("Changeability" is part of its grammar.) If a convention no longer serves the original purpose, we change or discard it. To think of language-games as conventional is to imagine that they "may as well be changed as not, depending upon some individual or other's [or some group or other's] taste or decision" (CR, 120). In most cases, however, this is not the way it is with language.[23]

The social dimension of "form of life" is obvious. The concept steers our attention away from the inner and the individual and toward the outer, toward practices and conventions. To say that language is a social phenomenon is hardly original, however: Rousseau certainly thought of language as social, and Saussure calls language a "social fact" (*le fait social*; CG, 6). But the social dimension does not exhaust Wittgenstein's concept. In some passages it is obvious that he thinks of "forms of life" as something all human beings share. He connects the idea of language-games to the "natural history" of humankind: "Giving orders, asking questions, telling stories, having a chat, are as much a part of our natural history as walking, eating, drinking, playing" (§25).[24]

"Forms of life" means both our cultural practices *and* their connectedness to the natural conditions of our lives. Cavell conveys the point by saying that "forms of life" has two dimensions: one "ethnological or horizontal" dimension, and one "biological or vertical."[25] The stress is always on *life*. Obviously, all human practices presuppose the human form of life (this is a tautology). But some practices are more intrinsically connected to our biology or anatomy, to the very shape of our bodies, than others. Cavell writes: "Here the romance of the hand and its opposable thumb comes into play, and of the upright posture and of the eyes set for heaven; but also the specific strength and scale of the human body and of the human senses and of the human voice" (TNY, 42).

Cutting across the nature/culture divide, the concept of "forms of life" is elastic enough to range from the purely biological to the completely cultural, to encompass the human body as well as the finest distinctions of the practices in a specific culture. To learn to speak is to be initiated into all this, or rather into the version of all these practices that apply in our family, our society, our version of human forms of life. When we learn to speak, we learn at once the shared criteria for the meaning of words, and the personal nuances those meanings will have for us: "In 'learning language' you learn not merely what the names of things are, but what a name is; not merely what the form of expression is for expressing a wish, but what expressing a wish is; not merely what the word for 'father' is, but what a father is; not merely what the word for 'love' is, but what love is" (CR, 177). To learn what to call a thing (father, love) is to learn what it is (cf. the example of the umiak again). I learn what love is by noticing how my parents use the word. (For some, that lesson may require years of psychoanalysis to undo.) To learn a language is not usually to learn all there is to know about a phenomenon. I think I know what "heat" is, but a physicist will explain it in ways I can't even begin to formulate. In the same way, I learn some version of love as a child. If I grow up to become a Christian theologian, I will learn a lot more.

All this means that we grow up to share with others, Cavell writes, "routes of interest and feeling, modes of response, senses of humor and of significance and of fulfilment, of what is outrageous, of what is similar to what else, what a rebuke, what forgiveness, of when an utterance is an assertion, when an appeal, when an explanation...."[26] These things are deeply social. Some are quirkily personal. None is easy to change. How do I change my sense of humor, or the lack of it?

Cavell often uses the word "natural" about forms of life. For this he has been criticized by critics who think of "natural" as a synonym for unchanging, immutable, untainted by social and cultural forces. But the term "natural" doesn't always mean "rooted in biological essences." We often use the word about things we do without thinking, what Daniel Kahneman would call "System 1" behavior, which includes the meaning of common expressions in our native tongue.[27] To say that a behavior is "natural" doesn't always mean that it is inborn. It means that it is something that goes without saying in our specific culture. Many of those behaviors and reactions are behaviors we learn when we learn language.

I stress that "forms of life" encompass natural and biological facts, not to raise the ghost of "biologism" or "essentialism," but to remind us that the human body is a fundamental condition of possibility for our behavior, for the way we see the world, for what we do and say and think. The fact that we point as we do, for example, is determined by the anatomy of the human hand and arm. Yet we also rightly consider "pointing" to be a cultural practice. In his discussion of rule-following, Wittgenstein asks us to imagine that "it comes naturally to a person to react to the gesture of pointing with the hand by looking in the direction from fingertip to wrist, rather than from wrist to fingertip" (§185). We can easily imagine such a person. But can we easily imagine how she came to be this way? What the world looks like to her? Understand why she can't simply change her ways so as to fall in with *our* practice of pointing? Wittgenstein isn't saying anything normative here. He is not saying that "our" way of pointing is superior. He is simply asking whether we are able to *understand* the person who relates to "pointing" in this way.

Many literary critics react to the word "natural" as if it were a red cloth. Ewa Ziarek, for example, concludes that Cavell's understanding of the relationship between natural and conventional somehow makes him "eliminate altogether the possibility of change or of critical intervention into the patterns of communal life."[28] But Cavell's discussions of forms of life and grammar have nothing to do with denying change or denying the possibility of critical interventions. This isn't a matter for abstract discussion, though. Precisely what concrete "critical interventions" does *The Claim of Reason* rule out?

For Wittgenstein and Cavell, as for Beauvoir and Merleau-Ponty, it is impossible to divide human characteristics and behavior into a purely biological and a purely cultural part. "Man is a historical idea," Merleau-Ponty writes: "It is impossible to superimpose on man a lower layer of behaviour which one chooses to call 'natural,' followed by a manufactured cultural or spiritual world. Everything is both manufactured and natural in man."[29] Cavell notes that "forms of life" conveys a "vision ... of the social as natural to the human" (TNY, 42). Elsewhere he spells out the point:

> Wittgenstein's discovery, or rediscovery, is of the depth of convention in human life; a discovery which insists not only on the conventionality of human society but, we could say, on the conventionality of human nature itself, on what Pascal meant when he said "Custom is our nature" (*Pensées*, §89); perhaps on what an existentialist means by saying that man has no nature. (CR, 111)

Wittgenstein's friend Maurice O'Connor Drury gives an example of Wittgenstein's non-normative attitude toward different practices. At one time, Drury was reading the opening chapters of Frazer's *Golden Bough* aloud to Wittgenstein:

Frazer thinks he can make *clear* the origin of the rites and ceremonies he describes by regarding them as primitive and erroneous scientific beliefs.... Now Wittgenstein made it clear to me that on the contrary the people who practised these rites already possessed a considerable scientific achievement: agriculture, metalworking, building, etc. etc.; and the ceremonies existed alongside these sober techniques. They were not mistaken beliefs that produced the rites but the need to *express* something; the ceremonies were a form of language, a form of life.[30]

This example tells us, first, that in talking about forms of life Wittgenstein, as always, is concerned with understanding—*acknowledging*—the practices of others, not with censoring or criticizing them from a preestablished normative position. Second, it illuminates the difference between a "social convention" and a form of life. Forms of life (the rites and ceremonies described by Frazer) have a strong social dimension. They are arbitrary, but only in the sense that they probably could have evolved differently. However, once they exist, they are meaningful (they express something), they tell us something about a community's shared way of life.

Daniel Everett, who with Keren Everett spent thirty years studying the language and culture of the Pirahã, a small tribe in the Amazonian jungle, reports that the Pirahã language has no number-words at all, nor does it distinguish between singular and plural forms of nouns or verbs. The Pirahã's form of life simply doesn't include counting:

In 1980, at the Pirahã's urging, Keren and I began a series of evening classes in counting and literacy.... Each evening for eight months we tried to teach Pirahã men and women to count to ten in Portuguese. They wanted to learn this because they knew that they did not understand money and wanted to be able to tell whether they were being cheated (or so they told us) by the river traders. After eight months of daily efforts, without ever needing to call the Pirahãs to come for class (all meetings were started by them with much enthusiasm), the people concluded that they could not learn this material and classes were abandoned. Not one Pirahã learned to count to ten in eight months.[31]

If we want to call counting or not-counting a social practice, we must simultaneously take measures to avoid implying that it is *therefore* easily open to change. The concept of form of life reminds us that many cultural practices are so fundamental to our ways of being in the world—so *natural* to us—that we can't change them at will, however much we want to.

Certain kinds of forms of life can and do change. The point is that they usually don't change by individual or collective *decision*. They may change as a result of technological innovations (agriculture, industrialization, the high-tech revolution), as a result of religious developments (the Vikings' conversion from the old Norse faith to Christianity, the Reformation), or they may be abolished by violence and war. Colonizers and invaders brutally change traditional forms of life. If the Pirahã lose their language to the encroachment of Portuguese, they will surely learn to count, but at what cost?

When we emphasize the social to the point of eclipsing the natural aspect of forms of life, we get a skewed picture of Wittgenstein's philosophy: "The partial eclipse of the natural makes the teaching of the *Investigations* much too, let me say, conventionalist," Cavell writes, "as if when Wittgenstein says that human beings 'agree in the language they use' he imagines that we have between us some kind of contract or an implicitly or explicitly agreed upon set of rules. A conventionalized sense of form of life will support a conventionalized, or contractual, sense of agreement" (TNY, 41).

Wittgenstein famously (or infamously) claims that forms of life simply have to be accepted: "What has to be accepted, the given, is—one might say—forms of life" (PPF, §345).[32] If we take "forms of life" to mean "social conventions," this makes little sense. When we see it as a concept in which the natural and the social "mutually absorb" each other, as Cavell puts it, the claim looks different:

> In being asked to accept this [the human form of life] or suffer it, as given for ourselves, we are not asked to accept, let us say, private property, but separateness; not a particular fact of power but the fact that I am a man, therefore of *this* (range or scale of) capacity for work, for pleasure, for endurance, for appeal, for command, for understanding, for wish, for will, for teaching, for suffering. The precise range or scale is not knowable a priori, any more than the precise range or scale of a word is to be known a priori. (TNY, 44)

Cavell rightly draws attention to the biological, anthropological, and existential aspect of "form of life." What has to be accepted is, first and foremost, our finitude, our mortality, our separation from each other. But this is not all. If I am trying to understand why you say what you say and do what you do, I can't just will away your form of life. On the contrary, I must accept it as the conditions of possibility for your words and acts. This is not a normative point: we are not talking about "agreement ... in opinions" (§241) here. (I am still free to judge your form of life to be racist or sexist, exploitative or plain evil. Or to admire it as the perfect realization of Utopia. The point is that I can't even make such judgments unless I acknowledge it as the condition of possibility for your use of language.) Wittgenstein continues by asking what it would be like if we found ourselves with a tribe who used color-words entirely differently from us:

> —One man would say that a flower was red, which another called blue; and so on.—But with what right could one then call these people's words "red" and "blue" *our* "colour-words"?—
>
> How would they learn to use these words? And is the language-game which they learn still the one we call the use of "colour names"? There are evidently differences of degree here. (PPF, §346)

There is no normativity implied here. To accept or acknowledge isn't the same thing as to admire or approve. But if we are to understand these people's use of color-words we can't wish their form of life away or make it other than what it is.

As Cavell rightly points out, some aspects of our form of life aren't open to change (our mortality; the way we point; the opposable thumb). Others are more purely social: footbinding, sati, limiting marriage to heterosexuals only. But what should we say about the Pirahã's relationship to counting? The point here is to resist the urge to provide a *theory* of "forms of life," a theory that somehow lays out in advance how social or how biological, how rigid or how malleable, a form of life must be to qualify for the concept. We will never know this a priori: it has to be made out in each case.

Cavell contrasts Wittgenstein's emphasis on accepting the given with *Philosophical Investigations'* intense call for change: "The inquiry must be turned around, but on the pivot of our real need" (§108; see TNY, 43–44). The need to free ourselves from illusions is as strong in Wittgenstein as it is in Marx and Freud: "A *picture* held us captive. And we couldn't get outside it, for it lay in our language, and language seemed only to repeat it to us inexorably" (§115). Wittgenstein, Cavell notes, sees humanity as "a form of life … standing in need of something like transfiguration—some radical change" (TNY, 44).

Now we are in a position to look more closely at Wittgenstein's understanding of the role of *agreement* in our form of life:

> "So you are saying that human agreement decides what is true and what is false?"—What is true or false is what human beings *say*; and it is in their *language* that human beings agree. This is agreement not in opinions, but rather in form of life. (§241)

Nothing Wittgenstein says about forms of life implies that we will agree in *opinion*. On the contrary, an ideological disagreement *presupposes* a shared form of life. The agreement at stake in §241 is something like the conditions of possibility for us to be able to actually *have* disagreements—to play the language-games of disagreement, opposition, objection, and so on—in the first place. Unless I share your language, share your judgments about what counts as a disagreement, as a devastating reply, I can neither tell you how abominable your opinions are nor subject your views to meticulous ideological critique.

To share a language is to make the same judgments concerning grammar, criteria, and language-games. We can only mark our differences, realize our disagreements, puzzlement, confusion—against the background of a shared understanding. The Pirahã don't *disagree* with Portuguese-speaking Brazilians over the language-games they play with number-words. They find them utterly baffling. However hard they try, they can't get those language-games to make sense. This is the difference between (dis)agreement in opinion and in form of life.

Voice, World, Realism

The very idea of *use* focuses the attention on *us*, the speakers of the language. Yet ordinary language philosophy offers nothing we can call a "theory of the subject." In literary studies, the term is often used to designate Marxist, psychoanalytic, or Foucauldian ideas about how a human being's consciousness is constituted. Various postmodern theories insist that "the subject" has no essence, that it is socially constructed, always bound up with power, and that it comes into being through language itself. Such theories often take themselves to be arguing against something we used to call the "liberal humanist subject," defined as the belief in an essential self, understood as a self-enclosed, fundamentally rational, and fundamentally autonomous consciousness, independent of the social and linguistic structures that surround it. When some theorists speak of the "death of the subject," they usually mean the death of this liberal humanist picture of the self.

As far as I know, neither Wittgenstein nor Austin ever discusses the "subject." They certainly don't require us to hold a specific theory of what a "speaking subject" must be like. To follow their discussions, you simply need to agree that human beings use language. Rather than offering a "theory of the subject," Cavell provides a magnificent exploration of *voice*, in philosophy and in our lives. By looking in detail at use, language-games, grammar, forms of life, Cavell offers magisterial explorations of muteness and silence; listening and hearing; finding or failing to find a voice; the joy of finding the words for a conversation; the pain of being forced to speak, or of being forced to remain silent; the risk of speaking; the desire for understanding and the experience of misunderstanding; the fear of being unknown and the fear of becoming known; the search for attunement with other voices; speaking for oneself and speaking for others; our responsibility for what we say and for the way we listen to others; acknowledgment and avoidance; and love.[33]

Just as ordinary language philosophy offers no "theory of the subject," it offers no theory of how language connects to the world.[34] The reason is obvious: Wittgenstein's understanding of use, language-games, grammar, and forms of life provides an alternative picture, one which doesn't posit a gap between a word and its meaning, or between language and the world. Wittgenstein's "agreement in language," then, is not offered as a response to the question of how words and world are connected, or how I can be sure that I am correctly describing reality with my words, for such questions presuppose the picture Wittgenstein refuses to accept, namely the idea that words are here, the world there, so that the two must be connected by "agreement."

For Wittgenstein, our words don't stop short of the facts: "When we say, *mean*, that such-and-such is the case, then, with what we mean, we do not stop anywhere short of the fact, but mean: *such-and-such—is—thus-and-so*" (§95). In "A Plea for Excuses," Austin says something similar: "When we examine what we should say when, what words we should use in what situations, we are looking again not merely at words (or 'meanings,' whatever they may be) but also at the realities we use the words to talk about."[35] This runs counter to the idea that Austin thinks that performatives (or all speech acts, since all speech act has a performative—illocutionary—aspect) have no relationship to reality at all.[36] In fact, Austin is at pains to show that performatives are responsive to reality in all kinds of ways. The dimension of true/false is not the *only* one that applies to the relationship between words and world.[37]

Both Cora Diamond and Sandra Laugier return to Wittgenstein's remark: "Not empiricism and yet realism in philosophy, that is the hardest thing."[38] Both conclude that Wittgenstein offers us a new kind of realism. Laugier uses the word "realism," while Diamond speaks of Wittgenstein's "realistic spirit."[39] I like Diamond's term. The realistic spirit, she notes, is a particular *Einstellung zur Wirklichkeit*—attitude toward reality.[40] The term echoes Wittgenstein's: "My attitude towards him is an attitude towards a soul [*eine Einstellung zur Seele*]. I am not of the *opinion* that he has a soul" (PPF, §22).

A spirit—an attitude—is not an opinion, and certainly not a philo-sophical position, a doctrine, or a theory. The realistic spirit is ordinary. It pays "certain kinds of attention to reality: to detail and particularity," Diamond writes. Attention—the willingness to look and see—is the very hallmark of the realistic spirit.[41] Diamond draws attention to a passage in which Wittgenstein's—ordinary language philosophy's—challenge to traditional philosophy is expressed in one of the "banal" examples that irritate many scholars:

> If I am inclined to suppose that a mouse comes into being by sponta-neous generation out of grey rags and dust, it's a good idea to examine those rags very closely to see how a mouse could have hidden in them, how it could have got there, and so on. But if I am convinced that a mouse cannot come into being from these things, then this investiga-tion will perhaps be superfluous.
>
> But what it is in philosophy that resists such an examination of de-tails, we have yet to come to understand. (§52)[42]

"Philosophy" (which Wittgenstein here, as so often, uses pejoratively) re-sists the turn to particulars. Instead of examining the details, it clings to its theories. The realistic spirit encourages us to root around in the dusty rags of our lives. We are to look and see. Pay attention to particulars. Even if I am convinced that mice don't emerge by spontaneous generation, I may gain from looking at the rags and the dust: "The realistic spirit does not then know so well that you cannot get a mouse from rags that it will not *look at* the rags," Diamond notes.[43] Maybe I'll finally discover where the mice in my study actually come from. Philosophical insight can arise in the most unlikely places.

The key to Wittgenstein's realism is his commitment to the ordinary (to ordinary language, to what we say, to the everyday), his refusal to set up an ideal language, to countenance any idea of a "beyond" of language, and his refusal to posit a gap between word and world. For him, to exam-ine what we say, how we use words, is to examine our lives in the world, our lives in language. This is certainly not empiricism. Nor is it realism as traditionally conceived. This kind of realism—the realistic spirit—is not above examining dusty rags. It assumes that philosophical insight will arise from attentive investigation of the ordinary and the everyday. Most cru-cially, it gives up the quest for ultimate explanations and grand theories. Exactly how Wittgenstein does that, and why this matters for contempo-rary theory, will be the topic of the next two chapters.

3

Concepts

WITTGENSTEIN AND DECONSTRUCTION

Ordinary language philosophy challenges the "theory project" that has dominated much of the humanities since the 1970s. In so doing it clears the ground for ways of thinking that are more attentive to particulars, to individual experience, more attuned to the ways we actually use language, more open to the questions thrown up by actual human lives, than the standard attempts to "do theory." In this chapter I begin to bring out the difference between "theory as usual"—the traditional concept of what philosophy is—and ordinary language philosophy. This chapter, then, should help us to see why Cavell thinks of ordinary language philosophy as a revolution in philosophy.[1] But I shall also show that if philosophers and theorists miss that revolution, it is usually because they fail to realize that Wittgenstein (and Austin and Cavell) isn't working with the same idea of what philosophy (or theory) is. This appears most clearly in their different ways of thinking about concepts.

In this chapter, then, I'll first compare Derrida's and Wittgenstein's understanding of concepts and theory. Then I'll examine some passages in *On Deconstruction* in which Jonathan Culler—whose writing I always return to for its exceptional clarity—shows how he reads Wittgenstein and Austin. I turn to Culler because his response to ordinary language philosophy exemplifies a certain skepticism connected to his understanding of theory, an understanding he shares with theorists beyond the confines of the tradition of deconstruction. The aim is always to bring out differences and thus help to deepen the understanding of ordinary language philosophy.

Wittgenstein's, Austin's, and Cavell's critique of traditional theory or philosophy should not be confused with the neopragmatist critique of theory. Literary critics such as Knapp and Michaels, and Fish, take "theory" to mean something like a meta-language laying down rules for a specific practice ("an effort to govern practice," Fish writes), and vigorously deny that there can be any such thing.[2] Anything that aspires to the status of theory, they claim, never influences the practice it pretends to govern; "theory" is simply another practice. But such criticisms leave the nature of "theory" intact. The neopragmatists aren't challenging the theoretical enterprise as such, they are simply saying that whatever theory is, it's not going to make any difference to other practices.

Literary neopragmatists have mostly been interested in the relationship between literary theory and the practice of reading. According to them, our beliefs about meaning and intention have no effect on what we actually do with texts; our reading practices remain unaffected by the "theory" (deconstruction, Marxism, feminism, and so on) we espouse. In some ways they are right: most theory-inspired readings presuppose the same "suspicious" attitude toward the text, and most of them also inherit the New Critics' obsession with irony and ambiguity.[3] But such arguments pay no attention to the critics' thematic interests. The result is a curious formalism, as if it makes no difference whether a critic writes about women's oppression, alienation under capitalism, or the self-undoing structures of the text.

Derrida's "Rigorous and Scientific" Concepts

I'll compare Derrida's view of concepts in "Signature Event Context" to Wittgenstein's. Any comparison between Wittgenstein and Derrida is difficult. Everyone who reads the two philosophers agree that their views overlap on a number of points.[4] The question is what follows from such apparent agreement. Henry Staten's pioneering book *Wittgenstein and Derrida* (1984) essentially argues that Wittgenstein was a deconstructionist *avant la lettre*.[5] Against this, one can read Martin Stone's essay "Wittgenstein on Deconstruction," which argues that Derrida in fact shares the picture of philosophy that has dominated the philosophical tradition from Plato onward, a tradition Wittgenstein challenges far more profoundly.[6]

As we saw in the introduction, Cavell brings out the simultaneous closeness and difference between the two by speaking of the "systematic turning" of shared concepts between Derrida and Wittgenstein.[7] Whatever we make of their overlapping concerns, Derrrida and Wittgenstein exhibit startlingly different attitudes toward philosophy, language, and human experience. They don't seem to have the same sense of what counts as philosophically and humanly interesting questions. Their writing styles are strikingly different. Even when they do say almost the same thing, they do so in a different spirit, a spirit that reveals their profoundly different attitudes toward theory, and toward the ordinary and the everyday.

Derrida's first words in "Signature Event Context" strike me as melodramatic, for they are too insistent, too absolute: "Is it certain that to the word *communication* corresponds a concept that is unique, univocal, rigorously controllable, and transmittable: in a word, communicable? Thus in accordance with a strange figure of discourse, one must first of all ask oneself whether or not the word or signifier 'communication' communicates a determinate content, an identifiable meaning, or a describable value" (SEC, 1). Some might see humor, or irony, in this language, but even if they are right, Derrida is deadly serious about his philosophical point.

Cavell finds Derrida's opening lines philosophically bizarre: "How many things are wrong with that remark?," he asks, quoting Austin. Derrida's question ("Is it certain that . . .") implies that someone has been saying that it *is* certain. Yet that someone was not Austin: "It is a problem for me to understand how Derrida imagines Austin to be captured in these questions," Cavell writes. "Austin must take the opening question of 'Signature Event Context' as a certain instance of what he calls 'a quite unreal question.'"[8] An unreal question is a "question that *has* no answer." The only philosophically reputable way to deal with an unanswerable question, Austin notes, is "not to get bamboozled into asking it at all."[9]

Apparently, then, the immediate response of ordinary language philosophy to Derrida's question is to imply that it is meaningless, and to say straight out that he would be better off never asking it in the first place. A Derridean will find this as baffling and unphilosophical as Cavell finds Derrida's opening lines. I shall now try to explain why Cavell reacts as he does to Derrida's question. Why is it impossible for an ordinary language philosopher to enter into this conversation on the terms Derrida offers?

Derrida begins "Signature Event Context" twice. In the first sentence he asks whether we can be certain that concepts "correspond" to words. Here Derrida uses *word* to mean "signifier," and *concept* to mean "signified" (see also CG, 67). The question is whether we can be certain that one signifier has only one rigorously controllable signified attached to it. In other words: can we be sure that a given word (in this case "communication") has only one, strictly defined meaning? It is hard for me to conceive that anyone would answer "yes!" to this. Surely Derrida can't be serious?[10]

Serious or not, Derrida's whole argument takes off from this extreme demand for "univocal" meaning. The implication is that if words don't have one "unified" and "rigorously controllable" meaning, then they either don't have any meaning at all or become so "polysemic" that we can never tell what they mean (SEC, 1). How then is it possible to understand words at all? The usual explanation, which Derrida invokes, is that context can "massively reduc[e]" the ambiguities of words (2).[11]

This gets us to the principal subject and second beginning of "Signature

Event Context": "But are the conditions [*les réquisits*] of a context ever absolutely determinable? This is, fundamentally, the most general question that I shall endeavor to elaborate. Is there a rigorous and scientific concept of context?... Stating it in the most summary manner possible, I shall try to demonstrate why a context is never absolutely determinable, or rather, why its determination can never be entirely certain or saturated. This structural non-saturation would ... mark the theoretical inadequacy *of the current concept of context*" (SEC, 2–3). Again, we are confronted with a demand for *absolute* determination and total certainty. Yet the terms of the argument have changed. In this passage "concept" no longer means "signified," but rather a "rigorously scientific" term, of the kind required to ground a theory. Derrida is getting ready to show that because it is impossible to give a context an "absolutely determinable" definition, there can be no theory, and therefore no "rigorous and scientific" concept of context. According to Derrida, if he is right, context cannot be a serious subject for philosophy, and Austin's whole understanding of speech acts falls flat. (But Derrida never pauses to ask himself whether Austin's project really is to produce a *theory*, in Derrida's understanding of the term.)

The two beginnings have a parallel structure: both set up a demand for absolute certainty and rigor, and both build toward the conclusion that such certainty, such rigor, cannot be had. Yet Derrida's argument concerning concepts in the sense of "signifieds" and concepts in the sense of "scientifically rigorous terms" is quite different. In the first case, the absence of "unique, univocal" signifieds leads to the idea that meaning is plural and multiple, which Derrida develops (here and elsewhere) through concepts such as *différance*, trace, mark, and others. In the second, the lack of a rigorously scientific concept of context leads to an attempt to provide a new concept that actually is "rigorous and scientific," namely *iterability*.

What does Derrida want from concepts? Since there is no evidence that he ever read, let alone responded to, Cavell's defense of Austin, we must look for an explanation in his response to John Searle's critique of "Signature Event Context."[12] Here I must stress that Searle's critique of Derrida is quite alien to ordinary language philosophy, which is why I don't discuss it here.[13] Yet Searle raises one question about concepts that ordinary language philosophers also find relevant, namely when he accuses Derrida of believing that "unless a distinction can be made rigorous and precise it isn't really a distinction at all."[14] Derrida reacts with fury: "Among all the accusations that shocked me coming from his pen, and which I will not even try to enumerate, why is it that this one is without a doubt the most stupefying, the most unbelievable? And, I must confess, also the most incomprehensible to me" ("Afterword," 123).

Is Derrida furious because Searle has failed to realize that he is not interested in establishing rigorous concepts, but in deconstructing them?
Not at all. He is shocked because he can't fathom how *anyone* could possibly take such a notion of concepts to be a *problem*. For Derrida, "rigorous
and precise" distinctions are the very foundation of philosophy: "What
philosopher ever since there were philosophers, what logician ever since
there were logicians, what theoretician ever renounced this axiom: in the
order of concepts (for we are speaking of concepts and not of the colors
of clouds or the taste of certain chewing gums), when a distinction cannot be rigorous or precise, it is not a distinction at all" ("Afterword," 123).

Ordinary language philosophers will react with dismay, or even rage,
to Derrida's casual exclusion of color and taste, and clouds and chewing
gum, from the field of philosophy (from the "order of concepts"), for they
will hear in his words contempt for the ordinary and the everyday, for the
very things that they value most. For an ordinary language philosopher,
the taste of Canary wine, and the difficulty of pointing to the color blue,
occupy a happy and honored place among the concerns of philosophy,
as do impertinent questions ("Do you dress that way voluntarily?") and
stories about shooting donkeys by accident or by mistake.[15] That Derrida
so casually, and with such condescension, excludes such things from philosophy dramatizes the radical difference in *spirit* between the two traditions' understanding of the task of philosophy.

What is at stake in Derrida's commitment to "rigorous and scientific"
concepts? Everything, I am tempted to say. Rigorous concepts are the very
hallmark of "theory." They are required for deconstruction to get off the
ground. A characteristic deconstructive analysis begins by showing that a
key conceptual opposition breaks down under pressure, usually because
it has to exclude features that actually are central to its operation. The deconstruction brings out the incoherence, or self-contradiction, of the original concepts, and shows that they are, in fact, "incapable of describing or
accounting for anything whatsoever" ("Afterword," 126).

One example is Derrida's famous deconstruction, in *On Grammatology*,
of Saussure's distinction between writing and speech. Famously claiming
that Saussure privileges speech over writing, Derrida easily deconstructs
Saussure's concept of language. In fact, he shows, the repressed concept
of writing returns to destroy the coherence of Saussure's notion of speech.
Derrida concludes that speech was always a form of writing; writing itself
is the repressed origin of language.

The new concept of writing, however, is not the same as the old one.
Derrida calls it *archi-écriture*, or "arche-writing." "Arche-writing" is not
writing at all, but rather something like the condition of all language,

whether written or spoken. For my argument, however, it doesn't matter what "arche-writing" is; what matters is its structural function as a concept capable of generating (subsuming under itself) *both* speech and writing, both the traditional concept and the exception that destroyed it. Derrida continues to call the new concept "writing" because it "essentially communicates with the vulgar [*vulgaire*] concept of writing."[16] (In Derrida's derogatory use of "vulgar" for "ordinary," I see another sign of the difference in spirit between him and Wittgenstein, who recommends that theorists spend some time rooting around in filthy mouse-ridden corners.[17]) Derrida's genius shows itself precisely in such moves, in his capacity for creating new, previously unheard-of concepts, which all conform to the requirements of the standard notion of theory: that they should be able to predict future cases, and have explanatory power.

After deconstruction comes construction. New concepts, like "arche-writing," must be found to replace the old: "Instead of excluding 'marginal' or 'parasitical' cases, what must be recognized is how a structure called normal or ideal can render possible or necessary all these phenomena, all these 'accidents.' And to accomplish this task, other concepts must be formed, the habitual logical space transformed (others will say, deformed), etc." ("Afterword," 127). For Derrida, then, a concept is a "structure called normal or ideal," and his project is to produce them. This gives rise to the long series of Derridean concepts: *différance*, mark, supplement, iterability, trace, pharmakon, hymen, parergon, and many others.[18] These all function like "arche-writing" in that they all occupy a higher level of generality than the concepts they replace.

A Derridean concept also has to account for all possible *future* mishaps: "Inasmuch as it does not integrate the *possibility* of borderline cases, the essential possibility of those cases called 'marginal,' of accidents, anomalies, contaminations, parasitism, inasmuch as it does not account for how, in the ideal concept of a structure said to be 'normal,' 'standard,' etc. (for example, that of a promise), such a divergence is *possible*, it may be said that the formation of a general theory or of an ideal concept remains insufficient, weak, or empirical ("Afterword," 118). There are Husserlian overtones here: concepts and the theories based on them belong in the realm of the ideal; the rest is merely empirical, and as such has no philosophical interest. In his understanding of concepts Derrida is, as he stresses in his reply to Searle, a perfectly traditional philosopher. (In contrast, Wittgenstein offers a truly radical critique of the traditional notion of concepts, and the notion of "theory" they support.[19])

Derrida's view of concepts explains why he accuses Austin of having failed to "ponder" the fact that "a possibility—a possible risk—is *always* possible, and is in some sense a necessary possibility" (SEC, 15). For ordinary language philosophers, this is an almost incomprehensible critique of Austin, who constantly stresses that the performative (or any other speech act) may "misfire," be "infelicitous," or in some other way go wrong. Cavell rightly complains that Derrida fails to acknowledge that Austin "affirms in every sentence" precisely what Derrida criticizes him for denying, namely that "failure is an essential risk of the operations under consideration."[20]

Since Austin so fully and freely acknowledges this, as Stone points out, Derrida's requirement can't just be that Austin should *say* that failures will always happen. What, then, is Derrida asking Austin to do? Stone answers: "What is needed beyond Austin's acknowledgment of the possibility of accidents, is an *account* of this possibility. 'Anomalies' ... must be represented as not anomalous at all, as falling, rather, under an integrating 'law.'" Simon Glendinning reaches the same conclusion: Derrida, he writes, "wishes to stress that 'impurity' is an irreducible structural or 'original' feature of all locutionary acts, and so it is not conceived, as it is for Austin, as something that just typically comes to pass."[21]

A *theoretical* account of the possibility of mishaps isn't the same thing, then, as explaining how one or more of them came about. Theory isn't interested in the specific circumstances of a particular case, but in a general account that can predict all anomalies, mistakes, misunderstandings in advance. Derrida thus requires concepts that build an account of possible mishaps into their very being: any other form of acknowledgment of mishaps and accidents simply will not suffice. At this point, the two traditions are at loggerheads. Ordinary language philosophers see this requirement as a misguided demand (an "unanswerable question") first, for something language neither can nor should deliver, namely *absolutely* rigorous concepts (I shall return to this), and, second, for an attempt to provide *a general account of meaning as such.*

The second point requires clarification. Why do I say that Derrida's understanding of concepts, and the critique of Austin based on it, amount to a demand for a general account of meaning as such? To answer, we must first return to Austin, who constantly reminds us that the meaning of an utterance depends on who says what to whom under what circumstances. ("What we should say when, what words we should use in what situation.")[22] For Austin, there can be no higher order account of meaning than a precise accounting for (a "recounting," Cavell might say) the specific words used in a specific situation. This is why Austin shows by example that the same words often mean something different in new situations; that a phrase that works in one case may "misfire," come off all wrong, in another. But Austin's case-by-case acknowledgment of mishaps is exactly what Derrida objects to. Paradoxically, his critique of Austin parallels the logical positivists' critique of Wittgenstein's talk about *countless* language-games, and his refusal to account for language in general (see §65).

Derrida's alternative to Austin's procedures is to propose exactly what Wittgenstein considers a completely senseless idea, namely a general account of how words come to mean anything at all regardless of any specific context. This is what the concept of *iterability* is supposed to provide: "For, ultimately, isn't it true that what Austin excludes as anomaly, exception, 'non-serious' citation . . . is the determined modification of a general citationality—or rather, a general iterability—without which there would not even be a 'successful' performative?" (SEC, 17). Thus, on an extraordinarily high level of generality, *iterability* is supposed to account for the way any specific utterance, past, present, and future, gets meaning. Derrida speaks, quite seriously, of a "*general* iterability which constitutes a violation of the allegedly rigorous purity of *every* event of discourse or *every* speech act" (18; my emphases).

To an ordinary language philosopher, "iterability" as Derrida defines it is an attempt to totalize all possible, past, present, and future speech acts in one concept. Since the task is plainly impossible, such a concept can't mean anything at all; it is a perfect example of language "on holiday" (§38), language that does no work, that is, language that means nothing. This is what Cavell has in mind when he warns that "it *makes no sense* at all to give a general explanation for the generality of language" (CR, 188).[23] It is hard to imagine a greater clash between philosophical visions.

This difference cannot be bridged, for it arises from the respective traditions' most fundamental understanding of meaning: for the post-Saussurean Derrida meaning is an effect of a *system*; for the Wittgensteinian Cavell it is *use*. A system can in principle be accounted for by a general theory; use—understood as the countless ways in which human beings use, have used and will use language every day—cannot.

Both traditions agree that mishaps, mistakes, misunderstandings, and accidents will arise in human communication. But deconstruction draws the skeptical conclusion, namely that this means that we can *never* really be sure that we know what a word or sentence means. Ordinary language philosophers respond by pointing out that we are often quite sure about meaning, and that even severe mistakes and misunderstandings, as well as plain puzzlement, don't change our usual understanding of the relevant concepts. ("The signpost is in order—if, under normal circumstances, it fulfils its purpose" [§87].) This kind of reasoning, however, holds no sway over the deconstructionist, who is convinced that such local or individual experiences of certainty amount to a kind of empiricist forgetting of the structural conditions of meaning as such. Since the ordinary language philosopher is convinced that there can be no such thing as the "structural conditions of meaning as such" (and thus no such thing as "iterability"), further conversation becomes impossible.

As we have seen, Derrida refers to concepts, including his deconstructive ones, as "ideal." "Classical theory," he writes, engages in "necessary idealizations" ("Afterword," 118). Derrida's deconstructive concepts at once enact and deconstruct such ideality.[24] Here, for example, is Derrida's account of the powers of "iterability": "The concept of iterability itself, like all the concepts that form or deform themselves in its wake, is an ideal concept, to be sure, but also the concept that marks the essential and ideal limit of all pure idealization, the ideal concept of the limit of all idealization, and not the concept of nonideality (since it is also the concept of the possibility of ideality).... [Iterability] entails the necessity of thinking at once both the rule and the event, concept and singularity" (119). All strong theoretical concepts, including the deconstructive concepts Derrida develops in order to construct a "different 'logic,' a different 'general theory'" (117), are idealizations. I assume Derrida thinks of an "idealization" as something we strive for, but don't quite reach.

In fact, Derrida's work presupposes the very understanding of concepts (Frege's) that Wittgenstein explicitly argues against. I don't mean to say that Derrida simply *is* a traditional philosopher, and that Wittgenstein simply is *not*. Such an opposition would be too simplistic.[25] Both philosophers stand in a complex relationship to their traditions, and, as many philosophers, including Cavell, have shown, their thought overlaps in many specific places. But I think it is fair to say that Derrida's deconstruction of the tradition is more closely intertwined with the tradition than Wittgenstein's attempts to get us to give up asking Big Questions.[26]

Wittgenstein: "Back to the Rough Ground!"

Like Husserl and Derrida, Wittgenstein uses the word "ideal" about "rigorous and scientific" concepts (SEC, 3). But for Wittgenstein, this is criticism, not praise. The quest for absolutely rigorous concepts is a hopeless enterprise, caused by our fatal commitment to the ideal: "we are dazzled by the ideal, and therefore fail to see the actual application of the word 'game' clearly" (§100).

Wittgenstein also describes the "ideal" as "the purest crystal" (§97). The quest for "crystalline purity" (§107 and §108) will lead to nothing but clownish pratfalls: "We have got on to slippery ice where there is no friction, and so, in a certain sense, the conditions are ideal; but also, just because of that, we are unable to walk. We want to walk: so we need *friction*. Back to the rough ground!" (§107). Why does Wittgenstein think that we can't walk, can't think, can't do anything useful at all, if we succumb to the temptation to look for absolutely rigorous concepts? The answer can be found in his critique of Frege, who famously claims that philosophical concepts must be absolutely sharply defined: "The concept must have a sharp boundary.... [A] concept that is not sharply defined is wrongly termed a concept."[27] The parallel to Derrida's "when a distinction cannot be rigorous or precise, it is not a distinction at all," is striking ("Afterword," 123).[28]

To convey why he thinks that Frege's demand for sharp concepts is disastrous for philosophy, Wittgenstein uses the example of the word "game." He begins by pointing out that sometimes blurred concepts work just fine:

> One can say that the concept of a game is a concept with blurred edges. — "But is a blurred concept a *concept* at all?" — Is a photograph that is not sharp a picture of a person at all? Is it even always an advantage to replace a picture that is not sharp by one that is? Isn't one that isn't sharp often just what we need?
>
> Frege compares a concept to a region, and says that a region without clear boundaries can't be called a region at all. This presumably means that we can't do anything with it. — But is it senseless to say "Stay roughly here"? (§71).

Here we may be tempted to conclude that although rough concepts work just fine in many situations, sharp ones will always work even better. Wittgenstein is at pains to stress that this is not the case. Often the blurred concept is exactly what we want: "If someone were to draw a sharp boundary, I couldn't acknowledge it as the one that I too always wanted to draw, or had drawn in my mind. For I didn't want to draw one at all. It can then be said: his concept is not the same as mine, but akin to it" (§76).

In many cases, then, it is useless to spend time and energy trying to produce a sharp concept. To avoid meaningless work, we need to understand the situation we are dealing with. If I want to take a picture of you in front of the Eiffel Tower, surely "stand roughly there" is all I need to say. I could get out the satellite navigation system and geocode your position, but unless there is some reason why I must take a picture of you on an exact spot defined by longitude and latitude, it would be pointless to go to so much trouble.

Wittgenstein, who trained as an engineer, is not *against* precise concepts and *for* rough ones. It takes extremely precise concepts to solve mathematical problems, for example. But such concepts are neither superior to nor "more philosophical" than ordinary ones. Extremely precise technical languages such as infinitesimal calculus are simply "new suburbs" of the "ancient city" of language (§18). Just as a city has different neighborhoods, language has many regions. Any field of human practice—car mechanics, botany, bullfighting, *haute couture*—develops the specialized concepts it needs, and they all belong to ordinary language.[29]

For Derrida, concepts are specialist philosophical tools (rigorous, pure, absolutely determinable); for Wittgenstein, concepts are ordinary words doing ordinary work. Just like any other concept, theoretical or philosophical concepts must do useful work, or they will be meaningless. The difference between the precise concepts of a car mechanic and the ideal concepts of a (confused) philosopher is that the car mechanic's concepts are not "on holiday" (§38). Working concepts teach us differences; idle ones draw no distinctions. A concept that is "like an engine idling" no longer means anything at all (§132). We can't do anything with it: "On the one hand, it is clear that every sentence in our language 'is in order as it is.' That is to say, we are not *striving after* an ideal, as if our ordinary vague sentences had not yet got a quite unexceptionable sense, and a perfect language still had to be constructed by us.—On the other hand, it seems clear that where there is sense, there must be perfect order.—So there must be perfect order even in the vaguest sentence" (§98).

In §98 there are a number of claims. Most important is the idea that the quest for rigorous concepts reveals the belief that ordinary language lacks something that only philosophy can supply. Against this, Wittgenstein insists that ordinary language is in "order as it is." This means that philosophy has no business trying to "fix" or "improve" ordinary language, for ordinary language already provides us with all the distinctions we need to express ourselves as well and as precisely as human beings can ever hope to do.[30] Wittgenstein, in short, is trying to get us to respect the powers of discrimination and expression of ordinary language. This is why a Wittgensteinian can find no common ground with a Derridean, or anyone else who shares the view that ordinary language must be left behind for philosophy to begin.

In *Philosophical Investigations*, Wittgenstein distinguishes between the kind of philosophy that leads us away from the ordinary and the kind that leads us back to it. The former is what Wittgenstein calls metaphysics; the latter is "what *we* do." Metaphysics requires therapy (see §133); the task of the kind of philosophy that "*we* do" is to clear up the confusions produced by philosophy. "What *we* do" is to "bring words back from their metaphysical to their everyday use." This can be done by reminding us of something we already know, namely how we use words in the "language in which it is at home" (§116). Cavell notes that "metaphysics" in Witt-genstein's sense arises from our wish for "super-concepts joined by super-connections in a super-order," and this wish itself expresses the "human restlessness in the ordinary and its attraction to the beyond."[31]

But isn't there a different sense in which ordinary language cannot pos-sibly be "in order as it is"? Isn't ordinary language the medium in which dominant ideology is expressed? Isn't a defense of ordinary language also a defense of common sense, which many theorists take to be inherently conservative? — These questions are so important to literary scholars that I shall devote a whole chapter to them (see chapter 7). Here I just want to say that Wittgenstein is obviously not defending every single utterance ever made or ever to be made in ordinary language: how could he be? Calls for uprising and revolution are also made in ordinary language. By considering language as use, as a practice, as an act, he places the burden of responsibility on us: you are responsible for your words, I for mine.

Here it seems justified to ask whether *everything* is ordinary language. What is *not* ordinary?[32] Fundamentally, there is just ordinary language, language that *works*, and thus helps us to draw distinctions, to see the world more clearly. As we have seen, the opposite of this is not a different, non-ordinary language, but language that *idles*. In philosophy, this leads to metaphysics. Metaphysics arises when we give in to the "tendency to sub-limate the logic of our language" (§38). To sublimate a demand for preci-sion (for example) is to strip off the specific reasons we had for wanting precision in the first place, so that we are left with a general demand for a "state of complete exactness" (§91). In *Sense and Sensibilia* Austin provides a fine account of the madness this provokes. All we can ever do, he notes, is to determine whether a concept is precise enough *for a particular pur-pose*: "There is no terminus to the business of making ever finer divisions and discriminations, [for] what is precise (enough) for some purposes will be much too rough and crude for others. A description, for example, can no more be absolutely, finally, and ultimately precise than it can be abso-lutely *full* or *complete*."[33] To ask a question in general, without bearing in mind the reasons we have for asking it, is the beginning of the process of "sublimating" our words.

Ordinary language, however, gives us no protection against skepticism, or indeed against metaphysics. The picture that holds us captive *lies in our language*, Wittgenstein writes (§115): this means not just that the language of metaphysics holds us captive, but, far more disturbingly, that there is something about ordinary language itself—and something about us— that will always make it possible for us to turn away from the ordinary.[34] If Derrida sees ordinary language as an "effect" of a general writing, Cavell sees metaphysics as an effect of ordinary language.[35] The questions that arise here—questions of criteria, skepticism, attunement, acknowledgment, responsibility, ethics—are at the very heart of Cavell's philosophy. Nothing short of a full account of *The Claim of Reason* could begin to do justice to them. Here I shall stick to the question of theory and concepts.

Returning to the Ordinary: From Concepts to Examples

I just quoted the beginning of Wittgenstein's §71. To see what he proposes instead of "rigorously scientific" concepts, we must read the rest of the paragraph:

> —But is it senseless to say "Stay roughly here"? Imagine that I were standing with someone in a city square and said that. As I say it, I do not bother drawing any boundary, but just make a pointing gesture—as if I were indicating a particular spot. And this is just how one might explain what a game is. One gives examples and intends them to be taken in a particular way.—I do not mean by this expression, however, that he is supposed to see in those examples that common feature which I—for some reason—was unable to formulate, but that he is now to employ those examples in a particular way. Here giving examples is not an *indirect* way of explaining—in default of a better one. For any general explanation may be misunderstood too. *This*, after all, is how we play the game. (I mean the language-game with the word "game.") (§71)

To my knowledge, the only deconstructionist to comment on §71 is the distinguished Derrida scholar Geoffrey Bennington, who concludes that Wittgenstein must mean that the "actual nature of concepts [is] constitutively to be blurred."[36] That this is a severe misreading cannot be in doubt. It is interesting here because it shows what goes wrong when Derrida's understanding of concepts—that is, the standard understanding of what theory is—is applied to Wittgenstein. Bennington, who here stands for the theoretical spirit, reasons as follows: Since Wittgenstein freely admits that misunderstandings will arise, he must want to integrate this insight into a new general ("structural") account of concepts, which can only be that they are blurred. This makes it look as if Wittgenstein's blurred boundaries occupy the same conceptual ground as Frege's sharp boundaries: as if "blurred" boundaries were intended to stand as the alternative to "sharp" boundaries. But this is not the case.

In §71 Wittgenstein moves from blurred concepts, to "stay roughly here," to examples. The turn to examples is particularly puzzling to Bennington. If concepts can have blurred boundaries, and therefore must be established through examples, and if we are not supposed to look for what the examples have in common (Bennington thinks this *must* mean look for their essence), then what makes words mean anything at all? Bennington's picture of concepts forces him to turn to mysticism: the answer must be, he writes, that for Wittgenstein the "identity of any concept is not to be secured definitionally at all, but by a process of exemplification which, insofar as it does not function in view of an essence (of which the examples would be examples), necessarily implies an irreducible *this*." Bennington's "necessarily" arises from his traditional (Derridean) view of concepts. (For Wittgenstein there is no such necessity). This leads Bennington to formulate a perfectly absurd theory of Wittgenstein's commitment to a "mystical unnamable 'this,'" which includes the claim that Wittgenstein takes all language-games to have a "nucleus of opacity and inexplicability."[37] My point is that this outlandish idea follows logically from the assumption that Wittgenstein must agree that the task of philosophy is to produce "ideal concepts."

Bennington's commitment to "theory" blinds him to Wittgenstein's own explanation of why he moves from concepts to examples. In §71 Wittgenstein's "Here giving examples is not an *indirect* way of explaining—in default of a better one" means that examples *are* the explanation. Examples neither *represent* nor *hide* essences; they *teach* (*show, instruct*) us how to *use* words; examples *teach* us *how to go on*: Wittgenstein is simply reminding us what we do when we learn to speak. Knowing how to go on, how to use words in ever new contexts is what Cavell calls *projecting* a word.[38] By turning from concepts to examples, Wittgenstein opens up a vast new field of inquiry: an investigation of what it is to learn a word. That investigation will show that we "learn language and learn the world *together*, that they become elaborated and distorted together, and in the same places."[39]

This move is based on solid arguments. For however precise our concepts may be, they will still need to be taught, and learned. Cavell points out that every time we use a word in a new situation (every time we "project" a word), every time we show some creativity in our use of language, we will need to explain what we mean:

> Once we see ... that concepts do not usually have, and do not need "rigid limits," [and once we see that] a new application of a word or a concept will still have to be *made out, explained*, in the particular case ... and see, finally that I *know* no more about the application of a word or concept than the explanations I can give, so that no universal or definition would, as it were, *represent* my knowledge (cf. §73)—once we

see all this, the idea of a universal no longer has its *obvious* appeal, it no longer carries a sense of explaining something profound.[40]

In short, concepts are not superior to examples. On the contrary, if we are to learn how to use them, even the most rigid concepts *require* examples.

Wittgenstein's shift from concepts to examples leads us away from metaphysics and back to the ordinary and the everyday. It makes him ask how we grow into a life in language, and what it means to live in a world of language. Much of *Philosophical Investigations* is about learning, finding out, wanting to find out, knowing how to do something, knowing how to go on.[41] It is no coincidence that Wittgenstein begins by quoting Augustine's account of how *he* learned to speak. As Cavell has shown in many different ways, scenes of instruction, education, teaching, and learning lie at the very heart of ordinary language philosophy, for it is by understanding what happens in such circumstances that we will discover how we become creatures of language in the first place.[42]

This is where the real adventure of ordinary language philosophy begins: the story it has to tell about how "we talk and act," and about how "in 'learning language' [we] learn not merely what the names of things are, but what a name is; not merely what the form of expression is for expressing a wish, but what expressing a wish is; not merely what the word for 'father' is, but what a father is; not merely what the word for 'love' is, but what love is."[43] Because ordinary language philosophy pictures the connection between world and word as one of growing into a world, into a form of life, because it investigates the many ways that words are "worldbound" ("Counter-Philosophy," 116, 118), it posits no gap between the order of language and the order of history, between language and other kinds of human practices.

Because it grasps language as a human practice, ordinary language philosophy cannot think about language without immediately also thinking about the other, about the human body and the human mind, about existence, morality, and politics. It immerses us in a world of learning and teaching, of understanding and misunderstanding, madness and skepticism, isolation and solidarity, in short, in the ordinary and everyday world in which we all live. This world is the world of language: "we learn language and learn the world *together*."[44]

Bububu, or How to Misread Wittgenstein

In chapter 2 I briefly discussed Culler's reaction to Wittgenstein's "bububu." I now want to examine Culler's response to this passage more closely since it demonstrates with exceptional clarity how a certain conception of theory will produce misunderstandings of Wittgenstein. Wittgenstein writes: "Can I say 'bububu' and mean 'If it doesn't rain, I shall go for a walk'? — It is only in a language that I can mean something by something" (§38, box). Culler mistakenly takes Wittgenstein to lay down an arbitrary limit for the meaning of "bububu," that is, to have declared that there is at least *one* thing ("if it doesn't rain," etc.) that it can *never* mean (OD, 124). I now want to show that this misreading of Wittgenstein is produced by Culler's concept of theory, which he shares with Derrida and more generally with most traditional theorists.

For Culler, Wittgenstein's "closing down" of meaning of "bububu" is just a particularly clear case of what we all do in everyday life: we "[make] determinations of meaning and [halt] *for practical reasons*, the investigation and redescription of context" (OD, 130; my italics). Culler here sounds just like the traditional epistemologists mentioned by Cavell, those who declare that "our common view and capacity of certainty is all right 'for practical purposes,'" but not for their own "theoretical" investigations (CR, 145).[45] For such theorists, practice lacks the dignity of theory. Whatever we do with language in everyday life may well *work* — the meanings we arrive at are "generally sufficient for our purposes," as Culler acknowledges (OD, 130) — but serious reflection will soon reveal that our ordinary practices have no *theoretical* significance. At this point the difference between "theory as usual" and ordinary language philosophy becomes acute. For such a picture — a picture of a distinction between the ordinary and the theoretical — is *precisely* what ordinary language philosophy refuses to accept.

What would count as a proper theory of meaning or language for Culler? Taking for granted that Austin — the subject of the discussion in which "bububu" suddenly turns up — is attempting to produce a theory of speech acts, Culler argues that no such thing can be had. In so doing, he usefully spells out his criteria for what a theory is: "A theory of speech acts must in principle be able to specify every feature of context that might affect the success or failure of a given speech act or that might affect what particular speech act an utterance effectively performed" (OD, 123). As far as I know, Culler's definition is uncontroversial. I would assume that most literary critics today would agree that a theory must have explanatory power and be capable of predicting future occurrences.[46]

We can't have a *theory* of speech acts, Culler notes, because context is infinite, always "open to further description," always "unmasterable," and "boundless" (OD, 123, 124, 128). Therefore, the only theoretically serious attitude is to acknowledge that there can be no theory of meaning. Now,

Culler, Derrida, Wittgenstein, Austin and Cavell actually all *agree* on this point. None of them believes that there can be a general theory of meaning. On closer inspection, however, it is obvious that they radically disagree on what it means to say this. Cavell writes: "I think that what Wittgenstein ultimately wishes to show is that it *makes no sense* at all to give a general explanation for the generality of language" (CR, 187). Or in other words: for Cavell, *denials* and *assertions* of the possibility of a general explanation of language are equally meaningless.

Culler (and Derrida) sees the question quite differently. The best way of putting this is to say that they *assert the absence* of a general theory of language. For them, only the presence of such a theory would provide the necessary "ground" of meaning, the ground that would secure the meaning of our words once and for all. Since there is no such ground, they draw the skeptical conclusion: because we can't theorize the infinity of possible speech acts, the meaning of our words is always infinitely open, unstable, ultimately undecidable. No theory of language, no determinate meanings. They subscribe, I want to say, to a theory of the *absence* of a theory. It is because he takes the "theory of no theory" for granted, that Culler (and many others) feels entitled to accuse anyone who resists skepticism, anyone who thinks that meaning is *not* always undecidable, of positing a general "ground" of meaning.

Against this, we should consider Wittgenstein's: "All that philosophy can do is to destroy idols. And that means not creating a new one—for instance as in "absence of an idol."[47] As Stone points out, the "negation of a metaphysical notion of presence has the form of a representation of absence. It is what Wittgenstein calls the 'absence of an idol.'"[48] In this case, the idol is the "theory of language as such" or the "ground" of meaning. The negation still preserves the assertion or, in other words, the very act of negating it implies that the assertion itself is meaningful.

Cavell and Wittgenstein, on the other hand, consider the assertion and the denial to be equally meaningless. Not only can there be no general theory of meaning as such, the fact that we can't have one doesn't change anything, for the picture that made us think we could were simply "buildings of air" (*Luftgebaüde*), which Elizabeth Anscombe translates as "houses of cards" (§118). To destroy a building made of air has no consequences whatsoever. In short: To fetishize the *absence* of a theory of meaning—to claim that because we don't have one, all meanings are free-floating—is exactly as theory-ridden as to posit the *presence* of a theory of meaning.

To understand "bububu," or any other utterance, we don't need a theory of language. We simply need to establish its context of significant use, that is, we need to grasp what language-game it participates in, understand what *work* "bububu" is doing. To establish this requires us to engage in a form of description. We look and see, and try to establish the grammar of the utterance, for example by calling for the criteria we go on when we use it. In the case of "bububu," we will discover that it doesn't mean anything because it has not (yet) received a place in our language-games. It doesn't follow that it couldn't one day be given such a place.[49]

Obviously, this kind of work can't be done in advance (i.e., before the utterance even exists); it can only be done once a problem has arisen, and even then it can only be done case by case. (We need cases of significant use to work with.) To carry out a Wittgensteinian investigation, in short, is not to "do theory." On Culler's view of theory, however, we don't have to wait for specific questions to arise. A theory is *always* required: it provides the necessary intellectual backdrop for activities we may otherwise take for granted. (This view can lead to a great deal of condescension toward people who fail to be sufficiently suspicious of their ordinary practices. Paul de Man's attitude towards Archie Bunker exemplifies the point, as we shall see in chapter 6.) On this view, to "do theory" can be imagined as a heroic activity, for the successful theorist now appears as someone who manages to explain the hidden principles or forces that account for even our most mundane activities. This is the belief that fuels not just the hermeneutics of suspicion, but most versions of critique.[50]

Instead of giving in to such cravings for generality, we should consider when (under what circumstances) an occurrence or phenomenon requires an explanation, and how far those explanations need to go. If we pay attention to the specific reasons why doubts and questions arise, then the questions of meaning that arise are no longer general and abstract, but concrete and specific: "A rule stands there like a signpost. —Does the signpost leave no doubt about the way I have to go? ... It sometimes leaves room for doubt, and sometimes not. And now this is no longer a philosophical proposition, but an empirical one" (§85). The problem has left the realm of theory and returned to the ordinary. We have brought our "words back from their metaphysical to their everyday use" (§116).

Skepticism, or the Ghost of Uncertainty

The connection between the "absence of an idol" and skepticism is fundamental to the post-Saussurean tradition. Culler's brief discussion of the "grounds" of language-games brings this out: "Wittgenstein asserts that 'the language game is so to say something unpredictable. I mean, it is not based on grounds. It is not reasonable (or unreasonable). It is there—

like our life.' His admirers speak as though the language game were itself a ground—a true presence which determined meaning" (OD, 130).[51]

Culler, who quotes *On Certainty* rather than *Philosophical Investigations*, sets up a distinction between Wittgenstein, who declares that "the language-game ... is not based on grounds," and Wittgenstein's followers, who are said to think that "the language-game" *is* a ground. I am not denying that some readers of Wittgenstein may have drawn that conclusion. But for ordinary language philosophy, the distinction between ground and not-ground does not make sense in relation to Wittgenstein's concept of language-games. On the contrary: Wittgenstein is trying to get us to see that *any* talk about the grounds of language—about some general features (a theory) that secures meaning as such, or simply the meaning of a particular language-game—is nonsensical. Nothing grounds language. But we must also guard against the temptation to view this as an absence or negation. As we saw in chapter 1, language is use, and use is neither a ground nor a lack or an absence. In short, to understand Wittgenstein, we need to give up the usual picture of theory.

Although Culler does quote Wittgenstein, my first reaction is that his wording sounds odd. I don't really believe that Wittgenstein would speak of "the" language-game in this way, as if there were only one. After all, Wittgenstein is the philosopher who declares that there are "countless kinds" of sentences and confidently proclaims that that "new types of language, new language-games ... come into existence" all the time (§23). (I shall return to this.) To my ears, the oddness is exacerbated when Culler formulates the Derridean perspective on "the" language-game:

> A Derridean would agree that the language game is played but might go on to point out that one can never be quite certain who is playing, or playing "seriously," what the rules are, or which game is being played. Nor is this uncertainty accidental or external. Those who cite Wittgenstein are inclined to adduce the language game and its rules as a simple given.... It is always possible, though, that redescription will alter rules or place an utterance in a different language game. Discussing a sentence that appears in quotation marks in Nietzsche's *Nachlass*, "I have forgotten my umbrella," Derrida writes, "a thousand possibilities will always remain open." They remain open ... because other specifications of context or interpretations of the "general text" are always possible. (OD, 130–31)

Here Culler confidently declares his generalized doubt about the power of language to mean anything. For him, the skeptical perspective is an inevitable consequence of the absence of a ground of meaning: "one can never be quite certain who is playing, or playing 'seriously,' what the rules are, or which game is being played."

That uncertainty can arise is true. But is it really true that we can *never* know who is playing (etc.)? Wittgenstein, Austin, Culler, and Derrida all agree that doubts and misunderstandings can and do arise. But Culler considers this to be a significant point about meaning *as such*: "this uncertainty [is not] accidental or external," he writes. "Not accidental" means necessary. Since the uncertainty Culler has in mind can't have anything to do with specific situations (situations are merely "practical" circumstances we navigate as best we can), he must mean that the uncertainty is built into language as such. (We have returned to the idea that there is such a thing as "language as such.")

Wittgenstein reminds us that there is a difference between being able to imagine a doubt and actually having one: "But that is not to say that we are in doubt because it is possible for us to *imagine* a doubt" (§84). He supplies the following example: "I can easily imagine someone always doubting before he opened his front door whether an abyss did not yawn behind it, and making sure about it before he went through the door (and he might on some occasion prove to be right)—but for all that, I do not doubt in such a case" (§84). The skeptic is like the man who checks for an abyss every time he steps outside his front door. Wittgenstein's point is not that no abyss could ever open up (that would be like declaring that "bububu" could *never* mean "If it rains ..."), but rather that, even as he fully acknowledges the possibility, he *still* wouldn't be able to manufacture the doubt that drives the unfortunate man to fear the abyss every day.

Why does Culler think that the step from *sometimes* to *always* being in doubt about meaning is compulsory? Well, he begins by taking any given utterance—any given string of words—to be a tiny part of an untheorizable infinity called the "general text." Infinite and inexhaustible, the "general text" is a metaphor for *everything*: "History is not a privileged authority but part of what Derrida calls ... the general text, which has no boundaries," Culler writes (OD, 130). The "general text" is the total context of everything, and, as we have seen, "A total context is unmasterable, both in principle and in practice" (123).

On this view, meaning is a function of an inexhaustible context, pictured as an atemporal, synchronic structure. Whatever meaning we think we have grasped can always be redescribed in the light of some other part of that "general text." In its synchronous infinity, the general text is ever-present, all meanings are potentially available all the time; interpretation can in principle go on forever; stopping the process of interpretation is never *theoretically* justified.

One of the most fascinating differences between the post-Saussurean tradition and ordinary language philosophy is the radically different *temporal* perspectives they take on language. Culler justifies his sense of general skepticism about meaning by constantly gesturing toward the radically uncertain, always open *future*, towards possibilities of doubt that, while they may not yet be present, may be realized any minute now. (The abyss may always open up in front of my doorstep.)

For ordinary language philosophy, on the other hand, any language-game I might want to investigate is already *over*. An utterance is an action: like all other actions, it takes place in time. It has a beginning and an end. Like all actions, it can have unexpected repercussions and ramifications. It can land me in or get me out of trouble. But whatever I say, once I've said it, it's done. No logical necessity compels me to continue, to say more. The continuation that makes up language rests on nothing but our willingness to go on, to go on talking together, go on acting together. Or in other words: it rests on use.[52]

The theorists' constant gesturing toward future mishaps appears plausible only because such theorists, in true post-Saussurean fashion, genuinely don't consider speakers to be relevant to questions of language and meaning. For them, language exists as a self-contained, atemporal structure. In Culler's account, the generalized doubt, the insecurity about future meanings, aren't actually experienced by anyone. Or rather: it is indifferent whether anyone actually feels this doubt or not. The very possibility of doubt is enough. We are to imagine the presence of a doubt on principle, as it were. If we don't, we are simply theoretically naive.

Culler takes for granted that a proper theory of language does not need to pay attention to the actual lives of speakers: "What we call our experience is scarcely a reliable guide in these matters" (OD, 132). Culler is positing, in other words, that regardless of whether anyone actually experiences any doubt, the ghost of uncertainty will always hover over the plainest meanings, the most anodyne sentences, including "I have forgotten my umbrella."

The infinite synchronicity of the "general text" makes Nietzsche's "I have forgotten my umbrella" open to any conceivable interpretation. Wittgenstein and Cavell would agree that the phrase is open, but they would also point out that it is open because it has come down to us on a loose piece of paper, divorced from any particular language-game. As a result, we don't know what context to give it. *Any* utterance quoted in the absolute, cut loose from any conceivable human situation, adrift outside all language-games, will come across as equally mysterious.

Usually the questions we ask in order to figure out what something means will vary with the kind of puzzlement we experience. But in the case of Nietzsche's note, we have nothing to go on. The horizon of potentially relevant questions is infinite: Was he reminding himself to buy an umbrella? Did he jot down the sentence to remind himself of a comic scene that arose because of the forgetting? Is "umbrella" code for something personal that had nothing to do with either forgetting or umbrellas? Or is it a reminder to add a discussion of that umbrella to something he was writing? My point is that such questions aren't philosophical, but practical, or empirical. If some scholar in the future uncovers the exact situation in which Nietzsche wrote down his sentence, we may all learn what he meant. No general theory of meaning, no philosophical problem is at stake here.

Now we can see why Culler misreads Wittgenstein's "the language-game is so to say something unpredictable. I mean, it is not based on grounds. It is not reasonable (or unreasonable). It is there—like our life." He reads Wittgenstein's passage as a theorist, by which I mean that he projects the traditional notion of what a theory is on to Wittgenstein. He confidently takes Wittgenstein to share that notion, and therefore to have a general theory of "grounds" or, failing that, of the "absence of grounds." Culler's logic is of the all-or-nothing variety, as if we only had two options: to deny or to assert the metaphysical concept of "ground of meaning." But, as we have seen, to deny a metaphysical picture is still to imply that it is meaningful. It may be "placed under erasure," but it is still there: no alternative has been proposed.

To establish an "ordinary" alternative to Culler's reading, we need to return to Wittgenstein's words and consider what work they do in their original context. When I went back to the text Culler quotes, namely *On Certainty*, I discover that the passage doesn't deal with language-games in general. (I was right in hearing something slightly amiss in Culler's generalization of "the" language-game.) The passage only deals with certain language-games we play with expressions of knowledge (so it's perfect for the topic of skepticism). It appears in the course of a discussion concerning the difference between saying that we *know, believe,* or *assume* something.

It makes sense, Wittgenstein writes, to ask whether someone's *beliefs* are reasonable or unreasonable given the specific circumstances, but it doesn't make sense to ask whether someone's *knowledge* is reasonable or unreasonable: "We say we know that water boils when it is put over a fire. How do we know? Experience has *taught* us.... We are *in a position to know* every time."[53] When I say that I *know* that "water boils and does not freeze under such-and-such circumstances," I simply can't conceive of being wrong:

> §558. Whatever may happen in the future, however water may behave in the future, we *know* that up to now it has behaved *thus* in innumerable instances.
>
> This fact is fused into the foundations [*das Fundament*] of our language-game.

> §559. You must bear in mind that the language-game is so to say something unpredictable. I mean: it is not based on grounds [*Es ist nicht begründet.*] It is not reasonable (or unreasonable).
>
> It is there—like our life.[54]

Experience is rooted in the past, but holds no guarantees for the future. The laws of nature have worked like this until now, but nothing guarantees that they won't change tomorrow. Yet—and this is the point—we still claim, and *rightly so*, that we *know* when water boils. There is no need to hedge this claim in any way.

When we speak of knowing something about physical facts (e.g., what happens when we heat water), we base our claims on experience, not reason. "Explanations come to an end somewhere" (§1). Why is Wittgenstein saying this? Because he wants to show that when I say, "I know when water boils," then the facts of the matter are *part of the language-game* we play with "I know." This is one of the myriad ways in which world and word come together in use.

Word and world are intertwined. If you come over to my house for tea, and I tell you, with some excitement, that I have just worked out that there are good reasons to believe that if I put the kettle on the stove, and turn on the gas, the water will boil, you may wonder whether I am in my right mind. If I don't know how to play the language-game concerning knowledge about boiling water, it is not just my knowledge, but my grasp of reality that is in doubt.

Wittgenstein, then, is not writing about *all* language-games. And he certainly isn't addressing the question of whether all language-games presuppose a metaphysical ground of meaning. The last line, "It is there—like our life," doesn't mean "our life is the ground of meaning." Nor does it mean "our life is *not* the ground of meaning." The Derridean concept of "ground of meaning" simply does not apply. The line means that *this* specific language-game—the one about knowledge of physical facts like the boiling point of water—goes as deep as our life. Lose hold of that game, and you will lose hold of your sense of reality. The line is not a theory. It is not about uncertainty but about sanity, not about epistemology but about our life in language.

4

Thinking through Examples

THE CASE OF INTERSECTIONALITY

By now it should be clear that Wittgenstein's understanding of theory, concepts, and examples in *Philosophical Investigations* is at odds with traditional philosophy, and with the prevailing understanding of theory in literary studies today. It is time to analyze a particular case, namely feminist intersectionality theory. After all, the only way to bring out the spirit of Wittgenstein's understanding of theory and philosophy, is through the close examination of specific cases. If Wittgenstein teaches us anything, he teaches us *how to think through examples*. In so doing, he shows us how to escape from the logic of representation—the logic of inclusion/exclusion—that dominates so much theory today.[1]

The purpose of my analysis is to make Wittgenstein's critique of theory available to new readers, and to show its power. In this case, ordinary language philosophy helps us to see why feminist identity theory—and any other theory-formation obsessed with "exclusionary" concepts—is bound to be self-defeating. The very idea of "exclusionary" concepts is based on a wrong-headed and counterproductive picture of concepts and theory, a picture that in fact presupposes the very "exclusionariness" or "boundedness" that feminist theorists are eager to undo. The effect is to render feminist theorists unable to pay attention to the particular case, and thus unable to provide the kind of concrete, feminist analysis that helps to make women's lives intelligible.

Finally: in the current theoretical climate I may have to explain why I still use words such as "women" and "feminism." Like all politically radical movements, feminism combines critique and utopia. Feminism names both the critique of the oppression and exploitation of women and a vision of freedom, justice, and equality for women. At this point someone will always remind me, first, that there are many other kinds of oppression and exploitation, and, second, that there are many people in the world who don't fit in the conventional category of "women." I agree, of course.

But, as I argue in *What Is a Woman?*, it doesn't follow that all uses of words such as "feminism" and "women" are doomed to be "exclusionary."[2] And although it is true that women aren't oppressed solely because of their sex or gender, and that many women also suffer from other forms of oppression and exploitation, for a feminist it remains necessary to analyze women's specific experiences in all their complexity.

Why Bring Ordinary Language Philosophy to Feminist Theory?

At first blush, ordinary language philosophy is not a promising starting point for someone interested in doing feminist theory. This philosophy doesn't offer a theory of sex, or gender, or sexuality. Nor does it claim that power is an intrinsic part of language as such. It doesn't even believe in "language as such." While it does have things to say about what it means to be an embodied creature sharing a world with others, it tends to connect the body to the soul, and many feminists would scoff at the very notion that they should take an interest in something called the "soul." Ordinary language philosophy, moreover, has nothing to say about the gendered organization of society. There is nothing in Wittgenstein, Austin, or Cavell about the experience of being a woman in the world. Apart from Cavell's discussions of female characters in film and theater, which have been heavily criticized by some feminists, there is not even that much about women.[3]

In short, it may seem perverse to insist, as I do, that ordinary language philosophy offers feminism a revolution in theory. But I persist. Ordinary language philosophy challenges, profoundly, the "theory project" that has dominated feminist theory and much of the humanities too since the 1970s. Ordinary language philosophy clears the ground for ways of thinking that are more attentive to particulars, to individual experience, more attuned to the ways we actually use language, more open to the questions that arise in actual human lives, than the standard attempts to "do theory."

Ordinary language philosophy doesn't set out to provide a theory of anything. I am not writing to recommend that we "use" or "apply" ordinary language philosophy as one "uses "or "applies" Marxist or psychoanalytic theory. The work of ordinary language philosophy is to help us reach a clear view of problems we find confusing. "A philosophical problem has the form: "I don't know my way about," Wittgenstein writes (§123). Genuine philosophical work begins with one's own sense of lostness. Thus, right from the start, ordinary language philosophy encourages us to begin where feminist thought has always begun: with a woman's own experience of pain and confusion.

In its commitment to the common and the everyday, the spirit of ordinary language philosophy contrasts sharply with the atmosphere of skepticism and suspicion that pervades so much of contemporary theory.[4] Ordinary language philosophy also helps us to think seriously about the particular case, about the ordinary, the common and the low, in ways that are helpful to feminism.[5] But my focus in this chapter will be on ordinary language philosophy's most radical contribution to theory, namely its capacity to name and diagnose the reason why so much theory simply cannot deal with the particular case other than as an illustration of previously existing theoretical commitments. Ordinary language philosophy teaches us how to think from within. It teaches us to think through examples.

Feminist Theory and the Power of the Particular Case

Why does feminist theory need a revolution? Because it has become abstract and overgeneralizing, operating at a vast remove from women's concrete experiences. The rebarbative prose style cultivated by so many theorists doesn't help. Many feminist theorists appear to share the widespread belief that only a certain kind of difficulty of concepts and style can save us from the tyranny of the given, and from subjection to ideology and common sense.[6] But my topic in this chapter is not writing. Rather, I want to get clear on the philosophical reasons why feminist theory has become so abstract, so removed from women's ordinary lives.[7]

We appear to have come a long way from Marilyn Frye's conviction that the task of feminism is to "mak[e] the experiences and lives of women intelligible" and to identify the "forces which maintain the subordination of women to men." I like Frye's emphasis on both the individual and the systemic aspects of women's oppression. I also like her idea that the "measure of the success of the theory is just how much sense it makes of what did not make sense before."[8] In this respect, Frye reminds me of Simone de Beauvoir, who also stressed the connection between personal experience and philosophy: "In truth, there is no divorce between philosophy and life," Beauvoir noted when she was working on *The Second Sex*.[9] The result was a pathbreaking work that consistently invests women's most ordinary and everyday experiences with the dignity of philosophy, at the same time as it sets out to force philosophy finally to take note of the existence of women.

Maybe Frye's insistence that feminist theory should illuminate women's experience disappeared from view because the category of experience itself became so contentious for feminists. In the 1970s and 1980s feminists regularly appealed to women's experience. A popular anthology of feminist literary criticism was called *The Authority of Experience*.[10] By the end of the 1980s, however, we had become properly skeptical toward the category. For many feminists, Joan Scott's powerful 1991 essay, "The Evidence of Experience," settled the case. Opposing the tendency among feminist historians to "appeal to experience as uncontestable evidence and as an originary point of explanation," Scott reminded us that "experience is at once always already an interpretation *and* something that needs to be interpreted. What counts as experience is neither self-evident nor straightforward; it is always contested, and always therefore political."[11]

If Scott means that we often miss the adventure of our own existence, often fail to understand our own experience, and often pay no attention to the experience of others, I certainly agree. I disagree with her extreme emphasis on interpretation, which reveals a skeptical epistemological agenda. However, I largely agree with Scott's conclusion that "experience is ... not the origin of our explanation, but that which we want to explain."[12] At least on certain readings, Scott's view is perfectly compatible with Frye's wish to make women's experiences intelligible.

To take an interest in one's own or someone else's experience is not to assume that a woman's, or man's, account of his or her experience is infallible, or unbiased, or beyond politics.[13] Nor is it to assume that individual experience is unaffected by larger social and historical conditions, or to deny that our very categories of understanding are historical through and through. But agreeing with all this doesn't prevent us from recognizing that individual experience matters, and that it remains uniquely important to feminist theory.

In this chapter I take most of my examples of the feminist attitude toward concepts and theory from intersectionality theory. I have (of course) nothing against the fundamental project of intersectionality theory, which I'll preliminarily define as the attempt to understand the experience of complex forms of oppression, the identities formed under such conditions, and the power structures that produce them. My general argument is simply that the very notion of theory, as currently understood in the field, blocks the important and necessary project at stake.

I turn to intersectionality theory for three reasons: first, because the field itself worries intensely about concepts, including the concept of "intersectionality"; and, second, because intersectionality theorists explicitly discuss the dangers of using "exclusionary" concepts. Such discussions offer particularly rich material for my investigation of the picture of concepts in feminist theory. Finally, I personally find intersectionality theory unusually knotty and difficult to read. For me, this kind of writing expresses the abstraction and distance from the particular case that bothers me in so much contemporary theory.

I am not claiming that intersectionality theory *stands for* (*represents*) all other forms of feminist theory. Nor am I reading it as an *allegory* of feminist theory. I see it rather as an *exemplary* case: a case that is good to think with. To the extent that it is well chosen, it will illuminate other cases. But I am not claiming that my analysis holds for every conceivable example of intersectionality theory, let alone feminist theory in general. For reasons that will become clear, I doubt that *any* analysis could ever achieve such a lofty goal. I also think that such a goal expresses a misguided—and impossible—dream of completion.

Whatever I say about intersectionality theory, or contemporary feminist theory, there will always be exceptions, different examples, different ways with concepts, and theory, both in feminist theory in general, and within intersectionality theory. The question is what such exceptions mean, what (if anything) they change in the original analysis. It is not enough just to mention different examples. New examples are invitations to further analysis. Philosophy begins when we realize that your examples vie with mine. Then our task is to get clear on what the new examples imply; how or whether they affect the analysis of the old ones; what zones of agreement and disagreement they help us to outline. "Disagreement is not disconfirming," Cavell writes, "it is as much a datum for philosophizing as agreement is."[14]

To think through examples is to appeal to the reader's experience. The ordinary language philosopher, Cavell writes, attempts to get the reader to *test* something against her own experience. She is saying: "Look and find out whether you can see what I see, wish to say what I wish to say."[15] This is not an order, but an invitation, what Simone de Beauvoir would call an appeal to the other's freedom.[16]

The Craving for Generality

In *The Blue Book* Wittgenstein provides a perspicacious diagnosis of the ills besetting theory today. (I occasionally return to a few passages in *The Blue Book* because they help to deepen the understanding of theory and concepts in *Philosophical Investigations* that I discuss in chapter 3. They also fit the case of intersectionality theory particularly well.) His name for the problem is "our craving for generality" (BB, 17). Wittgenstein explains: "Instead of 'craving for generality' I could also have said 'the contemptuous attitude towards the particular case'" (18). "Contempt" is a strong word, but I share Wittgenstein's view. Theorists in the grip of the "craving for generality" are interested in the general concept, not the particular case. For them, the particular case is not *theoretically* interesting; it remains a mere illustration of the general claim. This is also true for intersectionality theorists. Even when the theorists' whole project is fueled by a desire to understand the infinite differences among women in all their particularity, they set out to do so by producing a general theory (of difference, identity, language, power, and so on) that they hope will generate the appropriate understanding of the particular case. My argument is that such efforts to reach the particular through the general will always fail. A theory fueled by the craving for generality will always reproduce that hallmark distance from actual human experience, the contempt for the particular case, that Wittgenstein warns us against.

The "craving for generality" is an often-unacknowledged intellectual attitude that governs our thinking. It is a picture that holds us captive (cf. §115). I'll now focus on three features of this craving that I take to be particularly relevant both for feminist theory and for literary studies: (1) the tendency to require concepts to have clear boundaries; (2) the wish to emulate the natural sciences' understanding of what an explanation is; and (3) the demand for completeness. I shall now show what is at stake in each of these features.

(1) *Wittgenstein challenges the belief that concepts must have clear boundaries* (this is a point he returns to, with renewed energy, in *Philosophical Investigations*).[17] The craving for generality begins with the "tendency to look for something in common to all the entities which we commonly subsume under a general term" (BB, 17). This seems innocuous enough. Yet it is fundamental: unless we give up this belief, we will never escape the craving for generality.

The belief that all the instances that fall under a concept must have something in common is usually called essentialism. Wittgenstein's radical critique of essentialism appears to align him with contemporary forms of anti-essentialism. But there is a difference, for, unlike Wittgenstein, contemporary anti-essentialists propose no alternative view: they remain trapped in negation. This may sound cryptic. I mean, simply, that current anti-essentialisms usually only give us two options, namely to assert or negate the essentialist view. Nowadays, there are few, if any, defenders of essentialism in feminist theory. But to negate essentialism is not to escape its grip. Whether we deconstruct, undo, critique, or displace the original concept, whether we put it in motion or demonstrate that what appears to be an essence in fact is an effect of performativity, we remain captives of our original picture of concepts. (We can't begin the work of deconstruction unless we have something to deconstruct.) This is why so many contemporary theorists assert that we can only undermine, subvert, or ironically mimic traditional concepts ("woman," for example). To them, concepts are prison-houses: we can register our protest against our imprisonment, but we can't escape. One of the most liberating achievements of ordinary language philosophy is to free us from this picture.

Wittgenstein doesn't enter into the logic of assertion and negation. He takes the more radical route, namely proposing a different idea of how concepts work (see §§65–71). In his famous discussion of the word "game," he shows that as we move from board-games to card-games to ball-games, similarities and differences crop up and disappear, yet we find no feature shared by all the things we call games: "And the upshot of these considerations is: we see a complicated network of similarities overlapping and criss-crossing: similarities in the large and in the small" (§66).[18]

The craving for generality relies on the belief that the different instances of a concept must share common features. This isn't just a belief about concepts, it is also a belief about theory. Here is an example of how this attitude surfaces in fairly ordinary discussions. Over the years, I have found that if I use the word "poststructuralist" in even a faintly critical way, someone with allegiances to that tradition will immediately deny that whatever I said tells us anything about poststructuralism, either because it doesn't hold for every member of the group ("But what about Derrida [or Lacan, or Foucault]?" Or: "So-and-so never used the term about herself!"), or because there is no such thing as "poststructuralism." In other words: my interlocutors deny that my example is representative of poststructuralism. But since I don't think of examples as representations (or as attempts to form a general concept), but as descriptions of a particular case, I fail to see the force of that particular objection. At this point, the conversation usually grinds to a halt.

My interlocutors take for granted that the very existence of *other* and *different* particular cases that fall under the same concept automatically invalidates anything I can say about one specific case. To my interlocutors, even the most concrete, specific, well-documented example has no standing—no claim to theoretical significance—unless I can somehow prove that everyone else who might fall under the same concept shares exactly the same beliefs. This is of course impossible, for in any intellectual movement there will always be exceptions and outliers. The underlying assumption—the unspoken picture of concepts—is that all "poststructuralists" must have something—the same something—in common. Either poststructuralism is an essentialist concept, or it doesn't exist. To me, this is like saying that I can't call chess a game, just because it has nothing in common with tennis, or with ring-a-ring-a-roses. Or that a thoughtful analysis of tennis tells us nothing about the nature of games, just because other games also exist.

Such disagreements turn on different notions of what a word (concept) is. When I say something about a given poststructuralist, my interlocutors take it as a (doomed) attempt to say something that would hold for all possible cases falling under the name. (They slot it into a logic of representation.) For me, the specific analysis of one example is an invitation to *"look and see"* (§65). If a concept is a criss-crossing network of similarities, as Wittgenstein suggests, then we can't proceed in any other way: any investigation must begin with the particular case (see §66). To understand how one game relates to another, there is no alternative to examining their *use*, their place in the grammar that connects world and word.[19]

As we have seen in chapter 3, Wittgenstein isn't against sharp definitions or crisply defined concepts. He thinks that we can always give a concept a highly specific definition, *for a particular purpose*. Our mistake is to assume that this is *always* necessary, for then we assume that we always use the same word for the same purpose, always insert it in the same language-game. We don't always need the sharpest and most precise concepts to convey our experience with perfect accuracy. As Austin reminds us, there is no logical end to the potential refinements and further precisions, for "what is precise (enough) for some purposes will be much too rough and crude for others."[20] Think of the difference between saying, "I live around forty kilometers outside Oslo," and saying, "I live 42,195 meters from Oslo City Hall." Each sentence can be perfectly precise for its purpose. Am I trying to convey how long it will take you to drive out to see me? Or convince you to start a marathon race right outside my house? To master the language-games we play with distances is to know when to say the one and when to say the other. In particular, it is to know that if we *always* gave the exact distance to the last meter, we would come across as rather peculiar, as if we weren't fully at home in this region of our life in the language.

For Wittgenstein, words only gain meaning in use. Use is infinite, open-ended, and fundamentally untheorizable. Use, Wittgenstein writes, "is not everywhere bounded by rules" (§68). No theory can predict all future uses of a word. On this view, there can be no general theory of the generality of language (see CR, 188). Since use is always specific and concrete, we can establish and respond to specific "exclusionary" uses without first providing an account of what "woman" must mean in general, as if it were possible to divorce the meaning from the use.[21] It is quite sufficient to establish that the word was used in demeaning or exclusionary ways in *this* case. The problem isn't the *word*, but the *use*.

We can't solve problems of political inclusion and exclusion by laying down requirements for what a word must or must not mean in advance of its utterance. Such requirements have no force: all they reveal is what I, or you, *wish* the word to mean. But meaning in the language cannot be decided by individuals or by committees. Meaning is revealed in use. The attempt to lay down requirements for what a word must mean is an expression of the craving for generality. Instead of taking up the invitation to "look and see," to investigate further the differences between different examples, different cases of use, we try to generalize. This is why the idea that concepts must have clear boundaries is a fundamental part of the craving for generality.

(2) *Wittgenstein claims that philosophers who crave generality are seduced by the methods of science*: "Philosophers constantly see the method of science before their eyes, and are irresistibly tempted to ask and answer questions in the way science does. This tendency is the real source of metaphysics, and leads the philosopher into complete darkness." As examples, he mentions "reducing the explanation of natural phenomena to the smallest possible number of primitive natural laws" and "unifying the treatment of different topics by using a generalization" (BB, 18). These are fighting words. For Wittgenstein, "complete darkness" represents the antithesis of what philosophy is supposed to do, namely help us escape confusion and get to a clear view.

But this may seem irrelevant to contemporary theory. While most contemporary theorists give in to the temptation to generalize, they don't show much interest in "primitive natural laws." Nor do they, as a rule, explicitly set out to emulate the natural sciences. But Wittgenstein's point is not that philosophers—or scholars in the humanities more generally—actually talk about natural laws. Rather, he is targeting a specific intellectual *attitude*, namely the constant search for the kind of explanation that brings all particular cases under *one* concept or *one* theory.

A scientific theory must have explanatory power and be capable of predicting future occurrences. Insofar as feminist theorists treat their own concepts this way, they end up "unifying the treatment of different topics by using a generalization." In my view, the concept "intersectionality" itself is precisely such a generalization (I shall return to this). That this attitude is at work in much contemporary theory, inside and outside feminism, is beyond doubt. In chapter 3 I showed what work it does in Jonathan Culler's requirements for a theory of speech acts. Theorists lay down the same requirements for a "theory of intersectionality." The theorist will set out to specify the concept of intersectionality in the hope that the concept so defined will subsume all past, present, and future cases under itself. This project inevitably pushes the theorist away from the particular case and toward abstraction. In this way, theory itself becomes an attempt to produce rigidly bounded concepts. To some, this—the production of concepts—is the very goal of philosophy, and thus also for feminist theory.[22] To ordinary language philosophy, this is conventional philosophy's greatest problem.

(3) *The craving for generality is driven by a dream of completeness.* This is yet another variation of the search for the common element that unites all the instances of a term or concept. We should note that Wittgenstein has nothing against completion in the case of a treatise on apples, for example, for here there is no problem about what would count as complete ("Here we have a standard of completeness in nature," he notes). But how about a game? "Supposing ... there was a game resembling that of chess but simpler, no pawns being used in it. Should we call this game incomplete?" (BB, 19). The question is unanswerable, for in such cases we have no idea what the standard of completion would be. The demand amounts to an impossible, metaphysical requirement. Concepts and expressions of a "grammatical" kind, Wittgenstein writes, can't meaningfully be subjected to the demand for completion:

> If we study the grammar, say, of the words "wishing," "thinking," "understanding," "meaning," we shall not be dissatisfied when we have described various cases of wishing, thinking, etc. If someone said, "surely this is not all that one calls 'wishing,'" we should answer: "certainly not, but you can build up more complicated cases if you like." And after all, there is not one definite class of features which characterize all cases of wishing. (BB, 19)

By "grammar" Wittgenstein means the criteria, rules, or conditions of use for a word or a phrase. (As we have seen in chapter 2, Wittgenstein's "grammar" is bound up with our forms of life.) His point—that there isn't a specific set of features that make up the concept, a set of features that will account for all possible cases of use now and in the future—is the same whether he is talking about "thinking" and "wishing" or about "games." All we ever have and will have are examples of use. No attempt at generalization (attempts at theory) will exhaust the concept or catch all its nuances. We get clear on specific *regions* of use by examining specific cases. (This is what Wittgenstein calls a "grammatical" investigation.)

In a particularly important passage, Wittgenstein spells out the reasons why the craving for generality breeds contempt for the particular case: "The idea that in order to get clear about the meaning of a general term one had to find the common element in all its applications has shackled philosophical investigation; for it has not only led to no result, but also made the philosopher dismiss as irrelevant the concrete cases, which alone could have helped him to understand the usage of the general term" (BB, 19–20). Note the strong language here. Wittgenstein says that this way of establishing the "common term" shackles philosophy, precisely because it makes us overlook the lessons to be learned from investigations of the particular case.

Some years ago I wrote a paper in Norwegian about what I consider the wrongheaded vision of language in poststructuralist gender theory.[23] Although I often used the example "woman," I also deliberately used what I took to be the uncontroversial case of "water," mostly because I had discussed "woman" at great length in previous work. The case of "water," I argued, shows that linguistic meaning simply doesn't always arise from binary oppositions. I thought we could learn something about the limited reach of binary oppositions from pondering the different meaning of water if we place it alongside fire, earth, and air, or engage in a discussion of Evian, Perrier, and Badoit. The immediate response was: but what about "woman"?

I learn from Wittgenstein that the only possible response to such objections is to say: of course "woman" has its own specific uses, and of course human beings have quite different interests in relation to women and water, so I urge you to "build up more complicated cases if you like" (BB, 19). An analysis—description—of the particular case can only ever be an invitation to look and see, to consider whether, or how far, you can use it for your own purposes. But this is where philosophical (theoretical) discussion *begins*, not where it ends. By discussing the new example, we can work out why you can't see what I say I see. Maybe I unwittingly placed some restrictions on the situation. Maybe I overlooked an obvious feature, or a particularly crucial case of use. By engaging in concrete discussion of particular cases we begin the philosophical work of building up a clear understanding of the problem at stake. (Another implication of this view is that philosophical discussions of this kind always require us to *stake ourselves* in them: to stake our own experience, perceptions, judgments.)

This notion of what it is to do theoretical work is neither new nor unknown. On the contrary, it is well established in many branches of the humanities, not least in literary studies, art history, and intellectual history. Literary critics often reach new insights about general categories—

"modernism," "realism"—by examining relatively few works in great detail. But nowadays we often withhold the term "theory" from such efforts, just because they deal in particulars. The craving for generality prevents us from appreciating the full power of some of the best thought in the humanities. (By the way: the very term "humanities" is a classic example of a criss-crossing network of similarities.)

Much of the humanities deals in particulars. The critic's love for the particular case—the specific poem, novel, or film, the specific artist, painting, composition—fuels her work. When we internalize the craving for generality, we may become contaminated by contempt for our own work, for it can make us feel that there is something inferior, something unsatisfying about the attentive reading of *one* novel (or even four or five), the biography of *one* historical figure, the results from the excavation of *one* archeological site, the close examination of *one* painting or *one* sculpture, as if this is no contribution to serious thinking about painting, and sculpture, or ancient Greek culture, and so on.

When claims about a specific case are met not with an effort to test the case against one's own convictions, perceptions, and experiences, but with a wholesale dismissal on the grounds that it is either not locating the essence of the concept (i.e., it is not pinpointing what *all* instances in the relevant family of cases have in common), or that it fails to cover all conceivable cases of the concept, the effect is to shackle further investigation. This is what it means to have a contemptuous attitude toward the particular case. Insofar as feminist theorists crave generality, that craving blocks them from paying close attention to the specific experiences they wish to illuminate.

Identity Theory as an Expression of the Craving for Generality

Feminist theorists routinely subject the word "woman" to the craving for generality. They begin with the assumption that all the cases that fall under the concept must have some common features. But it is pretty clear that no one feature is shared by all women. In the same way, it is pretty clear that no definition—or theory—of what a woman is will cover all possible relevant instances. The usual conclusion is that the word itself is "exclusionary." The claim that "woman can't be defined" is the recoil from the belief in common features. So is the attempt to avoid the word completely, for example by suggesting that feminists say "individuals with feminine body signs" rather than "women."[24] But if the use is the same, the meaning of "individuals with feminine body signs" will be the same, too. Other identity-words (Black women, Chicana women, disabled women, and so on) get the same treatment. The result is a hopeless double-bind in which we desperately need precisely the words we consider poisoned to the core.

At this point, ordinary language philosophy offers a genuinely liberating vision. For if Wittgenstein is right, there is no need to assume that the concept "woman" or "women" must have a common essence. Rather, we can think of the word as a network of criss-crossing similarities, constantly established and extended in concrete use. This is not at all the same thing as to suggest that "woman" now *means* "criss-crossing network of similarities."

My claim is not that Wittgenstein proposes a new, standard definition of "concept," namely as "criss-crossing." He is clearly not suggesting that this is the essence shared by all instances of "concept." If a concept such as "game" turns out to be a criss-crossing network of similarities, it is because of the way we use it. Use establishes meaning in each particular case. Use is infinitely varied precisely because it is always bound up with our infinitely varied actions and purposes. Nothing prevents us from imposing strong boundaries on a concept, *for particular purposes*. Think of mathematical concepts, for example. My argument is simply that it doesn't serve any feminist purposes to impose strongly defined boundaries on the concept of "woman." And that the common practice today, which is to impose such boundaries only to lament their existence and mount a hugely abstract theoretical machinery to undo them, is profoundly wrong-headed. Anyone who wants to get clear on what "woman" means must investigate specific cases. If we turn our backs on the individual case, we shackle the inquiry, for it will lead to no result (cf. BB, 19).

The irony is that many feminist theorists want to attend to the particular, to specific situations and cases. But they also think they need to build a general theory of identity, gender, or femininity (or language, or power, or affects, or matter) to get there. Usually the purpose is to establish a complex understanding of identity, one that aims to subsume all possible kinds of identities under itself. Such a theory of identity will always be an expression of the craving for generality. In its effort to achieve an understanding of identity that excludes no one, such theories often reach fantastic levels of abstraction. For example, in *Mappings*, her celebrated exploration of the interaction of gender and other identity forms, Susan Stanford Friedman outlines six "discourses of identity within this new geography of positionality ...: multiple oppression; multiple subject positions; contradictory subject positions; relationality; situationality; and hybridity."[25] These discourses complicate our understanding of what gender is. According to Friedman, we must consider them if we wish to move "beyond gender," which to her means moving beyond the belief that gender is one, unitary essence.

Friedman concludes that a "locational feminist criticism" must constantly "negoti[ate] between attention to sexual and gender difference ... and scrutiny of the multifaceted matrices in which gender is only one among many axes of identity."[26] Thus the theorist lays down the requirements for what "woman" (or "gender") must—and must not—mean, in ever-spiraling circles of abstraction. (I hope it is clear that I am not arguing that Friedman is wrong to want to escape the idea that gender is a simple, unitary essence. I am arguing that she goes about it in the wrong way, by taking the question to require a general, theoretical answer.)

An anonymous reader of a draft of this chapter declared that "all identities [are] both situational and intersectional." She took me, rather generously from her point of view, to agree with this. From my point of view, however, such a claim is another example of the craving for generality. (I shall return to this.) But it doesn't follow that I am trying to *deny* that identity is situational, or intersectional, or anything else.[27] (To deny it would be to acknowledge the terms of the question.) Rather, I am questioning the underlying picture of theory that generates such questions in the first place, namely the idea that feminist theory needs a high-level, all-inclusive theory of identity before it can get going. As if the main task of feminist theory must be to settle the question of (female) identity once and for all, in general and in the abstract. As if the right theory could guarantee the right politics, the right feminist understanding of the specific case. (In an earlier book I call that attitude *theoreticism*.[28]) As if our understanding of identity doesn't require careful attention to the particular case. As if identity is always a problem, always *the* problem to be settled before feminists can say or do anything. Why do we think that feminist politics requires a theory of identity in the first place? What notion of politics makes us think that identity, rather than action (what we *are*, rather than what we *do*) is always the key feminist problem?[29] In short: What are the questions to which identity is the answer?

These are not rhetorical questions. Identity—a particular, concrete identity—*is* the answer to *some* questions. A Jewish student is accused of being unable to be impartial. A Black man is harassed by the police. A gay man is tortured and killed. In these cases the answer to why *this* person was singled out is identity: Because she was Jewish. Because he was Black. Because he was gay. But if we give in to the craving for generality, the drive to produce a general theory of identity and power that will cover all such cases, we will fail to pay sufficient attention to the particular case.

This is not just an ethical but an intellectual problem, for now we will be unable to learn anything from specific examples, unable to learn from the particular case.

The most important example of the feminist quest for perfectly inclusionary concepts is identity theory itself. The *negation* of identity theory is no better. Claims that identity has no essence, is always unstable, always constructed, always an effect of power or discursive matrices do not escape the constricting framework of identity theory. On the contrary: they are just different identity theories. We should not try to theorize identity in general. Rather we should investigate identity when it becomes a problem for us, when we experience a confusion, when our categories appear to fail in the encounter with concrete and specific identities in concrete and specific situations. This is in fact the starting point for some of the most powerful feminist work on identity. The impact of Judith Butler's *Gender Trouble* stems precisely from the author's investment in getting clear on a category that has kept tripping her up in her life. That Butler goes on to produce a general theory of meaning, which in turn becomes a general theory of identity (it's always performative), in precisely the way I find unhelpful, is a different matter.[30]

The Concept of Intersectionality

Today, many feminists would use the term "intersectionality theory" about a book like Friedman's *Mappings* (1998). Yet, in that book, Friedman herself never uses the word. This is not surprising, for although the term was coined in 1989 it didn't take off in feminist studies until the early 2000s. This shows that the kind of investigations we nowadays sort under the heading "intersectionality studies" don't require the term "intersectionality" to get off the ground.

Before I say anything else, I should explain what "intersectionality" is, for this rather unusual nominalization of a concrete noun is hardly a household word. The term is still not well known in academia outside women's studies. (I have often been asked whether I said "intersexuality.") In an influential article from 2005, Leslie McCall asserts that "intersectionality is the most important theoretical contribution that women's studies . . . has made so far." In 2013 Gail Lewis noted that "almost no disciplinary field within the social sciences and humanities has been untouched by it."[31] "Intersectionality" names the experiences of persons simultaneously exposed to multiple forms of discrimination. But intersectionality is also the name of a method, a field, a general attempt to understand race and gender, to theorize identity as well as intersecting forms of marginalization and oppression.

To get clearer on the concept, I'll go back to the beginning and look at the legal scholar Kimberlé Crenshaw's landmark 1989 essay called "Demarginalizing the Intersection of Race and Sex." Crenshaw begins by showing that in a number of legal cases, US antidiscrimination law was interpreted in ways highly detrimental to Black women. If the issue was racism, the court declared that they couldn't represent the class of Black people because of their gender. If the issue was sexism, they couldn't represent the class of women because of their race. Some courts wanted Black women to show that any discrimination they suffered was caused only by their race, or only by their gender, thus effectively barring any consideration of how one person may suffer from more than one type of discrimination at the same time. Crenshaw doesn't suggest that *all* antidiscrimination cases deny Black women justice by excluding them in this way. The fact that it *sometimes* happens is surely enough to make her point.

Crenshaw compares Black women's situation to that of a group of pedestrians finding themselves caught out in the intersection of two streets, as the traffic flows in all directions: "If a Black woman is harmed because she is in the intersection, her injury could result from sex discrimination or race discrimination." Even after a thorough investigation, we may not know which driver should be held responsible. Moreover, Black women's experiences don't divide neatly in a set of experiences of "pure" racism, and another set of "pure" sexism. Often the confluence of the two creates a new kind of experience that simply won't fit neatly into any of the old categories. Because feminist and antiracist theory, as well as legal theory, are "unidirectional," Crenshaw argues, they exclude Black women from their descriptions, analyses, and theories. The failure to understand the "cross-currents of racism and sexism" will produce unjust legal decisions and exclusionary theory.[32]

The solution to the problem, Crenshaw claims, must take the form of paying full attention to Black women's situation in all its complexity. Sojourner Truth used her own life, Crenshaw writes, to reveal the contradictions of white feminism at the time. In the same way, Crenshaw shares her own story of being denied the right to enter through the front door of an all-male Harvard club, not because she was Black, but because she was female. But the solution will also require a new understanding of simultaneous oppressions. As Crenshaw uses the term, "intersectionality" functions as a *description of a situation and an experience*; a *diagnosis* and *critique* of an intellectual problem; and as a *solution*, namely as an exhortation to pay attention to the lived experience of Black women. What it is not is a general theory of identity. (To my mind, this is a strength, not a weakness, of Crenshaw's paper.)

For Crenshaw's term to become ubiquitous, theory had to be added. In 2008 Kathy Davis described the meteoric rise of "intersectionality" in feminist theory and asked herself why this particular term had become such a buzzword so fast. Crenshaw's article alone didn't do it, for Crenshaw was hardly the first to call for the inclusion of Black women in feminist theory. In Davis's view, the concept owes its success to its power to capture something fundamental in feminist theory, namely its longstanding concern for diversity and differences among women, while at the same time giving these concerns a "new twist" by uniting them with the latest postmodern theory: "Intersectionality not only promises to address the 'fundamental and pervasive concern' of difference and diversity, but it does so in such a way that the old feminist ideal of generating theories which can speak to the concerns of all women can be sustained."[33]

By 2008, then, "intersectionality" had become a buzzword. Yet, Davis writes, the term remained vague and open-ended, and regularly generated "uncertainties and confusions." This situation sparked intense theoretical debate about the nature of the concept of intersectionality itself. In 2008 Jennifer Nash wrote that intersectionality theorists had yet to settle the question of what they were trying to theorize. Is intersectionality a theory of marginalized subjectivity? A theory of identity? Are all subjects intersectional, or only multiply marginalized subjects? In 2012 Patricia Hill Collins considered that the questions of what "intersectionality" is had yet to be resolved: "Is intersectionality a concept? Is it a paradigm, a heuristic device? Or is it a theory? Intersectionality may be one, some, all or none of the above." The following year, Barbara Tomlinson reminded her colleagues that many intersectionality scholars work on "structural power" and "structural injustice and subordination," not just on identity and subjectivity. In 2013 Crenshaw and others referred to intersectionality as a "theory," a "framework," a "work-in-progress," stressing that it is anything but a "contained entity."[34]

The sociologist Julia Orupabo writes that by now the effort to find the right metaphor to convey the "complex social reality" at stake in intersectionality theory has become a theoretical project in itself. Here are some of Orupabo's examples from the literature of the field: "dynamic processes," "a messy space of becoming," "layered cream-cakes," "curtain folds," and even "sugar."[35] One might be forgiven for feeling confused. Yet the variety shouldn't surprise us, for intersectionality theorists are trying to understand a set of phenomena as varied and multiple as the stars. Because they want all possible instances of "intersectionality" to fall under the term, it risks becoming empty: so inclusive that it no longer means anything in particular.

The refusal even to entertain the thought that intersectionality can be a "contained entity" mirrors the field's own relationship to concepts.[36] According to McCall, all forms of intersectionality research in the social sciences are deeply critical toward categories (she means social categories such as "woman," "man," "Black, "working-class," and so on).[37] The fear of "bounded" concepts is everywhere. The idea is that concepts, just by being concepts, will always be "exclusionary." Often this is combined with some vague idea that it is possible to produce perfectly "unbounded" concepts by simple declaration.

I'll give just one example of the yearning for unbounded concepts. In a 2014 essay Olena Hankivsky accuses care theorists of using "bounded categories," namely words and phrases such as "women," "poor women," "marginalized women," "women of color," "black and working class women," "migrants," or "migrant domestic workers." But what would Hankivsky prefer them to say? Are there "unbounded" words we should use instead? The answer is no. The trouble, Hankivsky declares, is not the terms, but the *attitude* of the care theorists who use them without "proper attention and investigation of within-group diversity."[38] The implication is that care theorists should begin by declaring that they have thought about "within-group diversity" before they go on to use the offending terms. This, in fact, is Hankivsky's own practice.

Hankivsky's worry about "bounded" categories doesn't appear to be grounded in a specific question or problem. It arises from the craving for generality, the wish to find words that somehow would never exclude anything. What is required, it appears, is a general reassurance about the meaning of any contentious words in advance of their use. This reminds me of Gayatri Spivak's famous call for "strategic essentialism," in which we begin our feminist analyses by admitting that the concept "woman" is essentialist, and also agree that essentialism is fundamentally incompatible with feminism. But given that we clearly need to use the word for political purposes, Spivak suggests that we continue to use the offending category, but stress that we only do so strategically.[39]

But what is the difference between use and strategic use? Do I use "woman" strategically if I make a mental reservation? (I say "woman," but my heart is not in it.) Nevertheless, I still use the word. Just as I usually can't avoid promising when I say, "I promise," I can't avoid the implications of saying "woman" or "Black woman" or some other identity term by *thinking*, as I utter them, that I really don't mean them in the usual, essentialist way. In what way does "woman" not mean "woman" when I speak "strategically"? Austin would diagnose this as the misguided idea that words are "(merely) the outward and visible sign ... of an inward and spiritual act." The alternative, he points out, is to stick to our promises: "our word is our bond."[40] In fact, the very idea of speaking "strategically" is bizarre: as if our intentions alone could determine the meaning of our words. It also introduces a split between what I know and what I do: I *know* women aren't a coherent category, but I will *act* strategically as if they were.[41]

Intersectionality theorists don't set out to be uninterested or neglectful of the particular case. On the contrary: the whole intersectionality project is grounded on the wish to avoid "exclusionary" generalizations. Yet, behind the scenes, the craving for generality does its work. Hankivsky declares that she wants to pay attention to the "specific care activity of migrant domestic workers," yet her essay never actually discusses the concrete experience of any such worker.[42] All we get are some general reminders that "migrant workers" isn't a homogeneous category.

In the same way, theorists worry about setting limits to the concept of "intersectionality" because they want it to capture everything from individual experience to general power structures, in all kinds of societies, in regard to every identity position. Davis thinks that intersectionality theory expresses the "old feminist ideal of generating theories which can speak to the concerns of all women."[43] As we have seen, some intersectionality theorists think that "intersectionality" speaks to the concerns—or identities—of everyone, including white, upper-class men. In its very concern for diversity and difference, whether among all women, or among all human beings, intersectionality theory becomes an extreme case of the craving for generality.

I'll spell out the logic. In its recoil against "exclusionary" concepts, intersectionality theory sets out to include all identity categories: Black, white, woman, man, working class, young, old, disabled, gay, lesbian, Chicana, African—the list potentially stretches to infinity. Identity, moreover, is not "additive," that is, it is *not* the sum of a number of discrete, fully bounded categories. There is no such thing as a purely "female" or "woman" identity, existing as it were on its own, without interference from all the other identity features the specific woman may have.[44] Intersectionality theory assumes that the relations among a person's different and differently interwoven identities are infinitely complex. In this way, "intersectional identity" becomes an ultra-abstract general term (a theory) under which all cases of identity are supposed to fall. (I am not suggesting that all intersectionality theorists are concerned with identity.) But if all identities are intersectional, the term does no work. I mean: the term fails to carve out any differences at all. At most, intersectionality can stand as a kind of metaphysical name-tag indicating that this theorist refuses to believe in "exclusionary" concepts and identities. But as soon as she must use words, the words remain the same. (We are back to the problem of "strategic essentialism.")

What is the alternative? For Wittgenstein it is to pay attention to particulars. If we begin with a genuine question, with an acknowledgment that we feel lost and confused in relation to a specific problem or situation, then we will only find the solution through an attentive examination of the particular case. Wittgenstein often refers to this as a "description" (as opposed to an explanation). Through such investigations, we may finally uncover the picture of how things must be that that caused our confusion. When we manage to describe how that picture works, the very description shows that it is not compulsory, that alternatives exist.[45]

To sum up: the problem for intersectionality theory isn't its wish to attend to differences, to complex identities, to understand how women (and men) react to different and complex forms of oppression. These are laudable goals. The fundamental problem is the underlying picture of how concepts work. This picture founds the craving for generality and shackles the investigation.

Criss-Crossing: Thinking after Wittgenstein

I began this chapter by saying that women's oppression is systematic and widespread. Yet now I appear to have argued that we can't provide a general theory of anything, including women's oppression. How does that square with my sense of its systematicity? And is it even possible to produce something like theory or philosophy without falling prey to the craving for generality? If we are willing to say that Wittgenstein, Austin, and Cavell are serious thinkers who reach new and original insights, some of which have vast implications, then the answer has to be yes. If they can do it, so can we. Then the question becomes: how do they go about getting clear on questions that matter to them? This question is large and can't be fully discussed here. Let me simply offer a few closing thoughts.

The search for what or what all the instances that fall under "intersectionality" or "women's oppression" have in common (their "essence") will always fail. But the denial that they have anything in common will also not lead anywhere, for that denial still binds us securely to the old picture, in which meaning turns on common features. Instead of trying to lay down rules for what intersectionality must mean—or in other words: instead of elaborating a conventional theory of intersectionality—it might help to think of it as the name of language we need to learn to speak. Here I am using language in Wittgenstein's sense, as an infinite number of utterances, an infinite number of cases of specific use (This is quite different from language as Saussure understands it, namely as a closed system consisting of a limited number of differential elements.[46])

For ordinary language philosophers, language can't be brought under a general theory. "What Wittgenstein ultimately wishes to show," Cavell writes, "is that it makes no sense at all to give a general explanation of the generality of language" (CR, 188.) At the same time, language is astonishingly systematic, both in obvious and startlingly unobvious ways. Anyone who tries to learn a foreign language soon discovers that it is fairly easy to lay out the grammar—the systematic rules—for *certain* areas of use. Thus it is not difficult to discover the rules for forming the future in Latin, or the third person singular present tense in English.

Yet other regions of the language don't appear to be rule-bound at all. Anyone who tries to learn English soon realizes that there is no magic shortcut to learning how to apply prepositions and adverbs. Each case appears to be different, and each case must be learned, one by one. I can back the car up or out, but unless I am parked on a hill, I can't back it down. Yet in a conversation with me *you* can back down quite without a car. I may try not to let on, yet you won't let up. The basketball game was a let-down. I refuse to give you a let-out. How is anyone supposed to *know* this? Yet if we are speakers of the language, we do know. What governs the application of words and expressions?

"Our uses of language are pervasively, almost unimaginably, systematic," Cavell writes (CR, 29). What governs this use, he suggests, is the application of shared criteria. When we try to get clear on something, we conduct what Wittgenstein calls a "grammatical" investigation. "Grammar tells what kind of object anything is" (§373). This means that if something puzzles us, something creates confusion and misunderstanding, we go over our criteria, lay them out, compare them and analyze them. We find our criteria for saying something by asking about the particular case, about what we just have said, for example. "Under what circumstances do we say ..." is one typical formulation (CR, 30).[47] If learning to understand women's oppression is like learning a language, then it is not incoherent to claim that women's oppression (or intersectionality, for example) is at once vastly complex, unimaginably varied, yet stunningly systematic. Just like a language.

A feminist inspired by ordinary language philosophy would be unlikely to set out to theorize "intersectionality" or "identity" as such. Instead, she would focus on a specific problem that troubles and confuses her, maybe by looking at some examples. The work of theory would be an effort to reach clarity—to find a clear view—of that problem. We can think of this as laying bare the criteria governing a certain *region* of women's oppression, or of intersectionality. We may call this a Wittgensteinian description, an attempt to lay out the articulations of one region of the crisscrossing strands that make up the concept. This is often extremely hard theoretical or philosophical work. But it never alienates us from concrete cases and actual experience. On the contrary: it *requires* the particular case.

Wittgenstein's most fundamental commitment in philosophy, Cora Diamond writes, was to make us give up thinking in terms of Big Questions. All we can ever do is to get clear on specific problems, one by one (cf. §133).[48] She suggests that Wittgenstein's effort to avoid setting up Big Problems accounts for the very form of *Philosophical Investigations*.[49] In his preface to *Philosophical Investigations*, Wittgenstein notes that the "very nature of [his] investigation" compelled him to "travel criss-cross in every direction over a wide field of thought" (3). Wittgenstein's criss-cross philosophy helps us to see why theory as it is practiced now prevents us from fully engaging in the feminist project of paying attention to—of acknowledging—women's experience. It frees us from unproductive discussion of "bounded" or "exclusionary" concepts, and enables us instead to figure out new ways of thinking seriously and systematically about the infinite variety of concrete experience.

I said that one can't "use" Wittgenstein like one "uses" more conventional theorists. The reason should now be clear: if my analysis of concepts and theory is right, it solves a problem in feminist theory. If the problem has been solved, it goes away. (There is no point in solving the same problem over again.) The Wittgensteinian analysis frees us from a theoretical yoke, a picture of how things must be. It puts us in a position to look at our field of interest with fresh eyes, to brush away the cobwebs of received opinion and to ask new questions.

What questions should we ask? Ordinary language philosophy doesn't say. It doesn't tell us what we must be interested in. It certainly doesn't tell us what to think about feminism. To find out about feminism, we still need to read *A Room of One's Own* and *The Second Sex*, and all the other feminist works that continue to inspire us. To me, *The Second Sex* stands as an excellent example of a kind of philosophical and feminist writing that is compatible with the spirit of ordinary language philosophy without being based on that philosophy in any way.

Beauvoir's existentialist interest in particular experience, in the meaning of individual actions and choices, her assumption that to speak is to act, to make an appeal to the other, helped her to produce a magnificent work of feminist analysis, packed with specific cases, specific examples of individual experience. The range and interdisciplinarity of *The Second Sex* is an effect of Beauvoir's interest in women's particular experiences, and in their myriad differences. At times it is as if she is piling up the examples, as if to force us to see that they have no single thing in common. Yet there still is a systematicity—a pattern—to it all, one which Beauvoir names by saying that "Woman is the Other."[50]

Words like "woman" and "Black" aren't more complex or more exclusionary than other words, but they are far more politically contentious. We can't solve political disagreements by focusing exclusively on definitions. To solve political problems we need to produce concrete analyses of specific cases, cases that genuinely trouble us. We also need to learn to express political judgments and try to persuade others to share them.[51] This requires attention to particulars.

PART II
Differences

5

Saussure

LANGUAGE, SIGN, WORLD

Introduction: Saussure's Project

The contemporary of Emile Durkheim and Sigmund Freud, Ferdinand de Saussure (1857–1913) belonged to the same generation as the French Symbolists. Among his close contemporaries we find many of the icons of "early" modernism, the artists who first broke with dominant artistic traditions, and laid the foundations for modernism. Oscar Wilde, Arthur Rimbaud, Anton Chekhov, Claude Debussy, Gustav Klimt, and Edvard Munch are all Saussure's contemporaries. By contrast, Wittgenstein (1889–1951) belongs to the generation of "high" modernists, the thinkers and artists who revolutionized twentieth-century art and culture. Figures such as James Joyce, Virginia Woolf, Charlie Chaplin, and Le Corbusier spring to mind.

After a meteoric early career as a historical philologist, Saussure stopped publishing. In a famous 1894 letter, he declares that he is "sick of it all and of the general difficulty of writing any ten lines of a common sense nature in connection with linguistic facts.... There is not a single term used in linguistics today which has any meaning for me whatsoever."[1] More than twenty years later, *Course in General Linguistics* conveyed the results of Saussure's attempts to develop a more scientific way to talk about language. Like Wittgenstein's *Philosophical Investigations*, *Course in General Linguistics* was published posthumously. Put together by Charles Bally and Albert Sechehaye, the 1916 Geneva edition constituted "Saussure" for twentieth-century intellectuals. Although further notes and drafts were discovered in 1996, the 1916 text remains the only one in print in English.[2]

In this chapter, I examine four key features of Saussure's linguistics. First I turn to his famous concepts "language" (*la langue*), "speech" (*le langage*), and "speaking" (*la parole*), and show how they map on to—or rather, fail to map on to—the concepts of ordinary language philosophy. I go on to examine the ambiguity of Saussure's theory of the split sign: is the signifier (or the sign) a meaningful form or a purely material "mark"? How useful is the concept of the signified? Saussure famously declared that the sign is arbitrary. What exactly is at stake in this claim? Finally, does Saussure have anything to say about "reference" or "representation," as his recent "materialist" readers—Vicki Kirby, and Perry Meisel and Haun Saussy—claim?

In order to show how *Course in General Linguistics* allows for the postwar "philosophizing" of Saussure, I focus on the fault lines in Saussure's own account. By "philosophizing" I mean the attempt to turn Saussure's linguistics into a general philosophy of language. I am not concerned to establish the "true" or "real" Saussure, but simply to bring out some significant differences between Saussure and his post-Saussurean interpreters, and between ordinary language philosophy and the post-Saussurean tradition. To grasp these differences is to grasp the depth and extent of the revolution proposed by ordinary language philosophy.

Saussure's Concepts

In his disenchanted 1894 letter, Saussure writes that linguistics would never begin to make sense unless it could "show what kind of an object language is in general."[3] In *Course in General Linguistics* he grasps the nettle. To establish a "true science of linguistics," he writes, one must begin by defining the "nature of its object of study" (CG, 3). In response to his own challenge, he proposes the tripartite distinction between "language" (*la langue*), "speech" (*le langage*), and "speaking" (*la parole*).[4]

Saussure's major contribution to linguistics is his concept of "language" (*la langue*), a completely new theoretical construct defined as a "self-contained whole and a principle of classification" (CG, 9). This definition makes "language" a theorizable entity, something one can grasp as a whole, something that can be the proper subject for a science. Turning language into a closed system, Saussure's definition also gives rise to the idea that it makes sense to talk about being "inside" or "outside" of language.

Saussure's "language" (*la langue*), then, is an artificially produced object, a "self-contained whole" carved out of the unwieldy chaos of "speech" (*le langage*). As even Saussure's warmest defenders acknowledge, *la langue* is a highly formal concept: "*La langue* is the system of a language, the language as a system of forms," Culler writes.[5] The Belgian linguist Emile Benveniste calls Saussure's linguistics "exclusively a science of forms."[6] This concept of language has no counterpart in ordinary language philosophy. Anyone who reads Wittgenstein or Austin or Cavell with Saussure's concept of "language" in mind is bound to misunderstand them.

"Speech" (*le langage*) is something like language in its raw, untheorized state, language understood as the countless number of utterances occurring every day. An infinite, untotalizable flood of linguistic data, "speech" defeats any attempt at systematic study: "Taken as a whole, speech is many-sided and heterogeneous; ... it belongs both to the individual and to society; we cannot put it into any category of human facts, for we cannot discover its unity" (CG, 9).

In some ways, Saussure's definition of speech (*le langage*) has affinities with "ordinary language," as Wittgenstein, Austin, and Cavell understand the term. At least they agree with Saussure that this phenomenon can't be brought under a theory. But Saussure has no concept of the "ordinary." On the contrary, as a linguist Saussure concludes that he simply cannot work with this unwieldy mass of words.[7] In other words: Saussure takes for granted that he could only say something useful about "speech" if he could grasp it from outside (bring it under a unifying concept). Since this is impossible, he leaves the concept aside. Ordinary language philosophy agrees that there can be no approach to the ordinary, for the very word "approach" implies that one takes up an external position in relation to one's "object." We are always *in* the ordinary. We live our lives in language and can't get outside it. To think the ordinary, we must give up the craving for generality and learn to think from within.[8]

Saussure's third term is "speaking" (*la parole*). This is the individual practice ("execution") of language (CG, 13). If speech (*le langage*) is the whole mass of utterances, speaking (*la parole*) is language as uttered by an individual speaker. This concept has strong affinities to Austin's "speech acts." This may explain why so many post-Saussureans have found it easier to engage with Austin than with Wittgenstein or Cavell.

Finally, Wittgenstein's "use" has no counterpart in Saussure's linguistics.[9] As we have seen in the first two chapters of this book, "use" intertwines language and the world, and asks about speakers and their intentions and motivations for saying what they say in highly specific circumstances. Such questions are of no interest to Saussure. Saussure sets out to found a science; Wittgenstein wants to understand our lives in language. These two projects don't necessarily conflict. An ordinary language philosopher has no reason to oppose the science of linguistics, or any other science for that matter. But she will challenge attempts to turn ordinary language (as Wittgenstein and Cavell understand the term) into an object for theory, as if we could ever stand outside the ordinary, outside our own words and actions. This is why ordinary language philosophy finds itself at greater odds with the post-Saussurean "philosophizing" or "theorizing" of Saussure than with Saussure's own text. This is also why the simple word "language" is at the root of so many post-Saussurean misunderstandings of Wittgenstein, Austin, and Cavell.

The Sign: Meaningful Form or Material Mark?

Saussure's definition of the sign, with its famous distinction between signifier and signified, is the most taken for granted part of his theory. Saussure begins by defining the sign as a "concept" united with a "sound-image [*image acoustique*]." Within a page, he replaces the terms "sound-image"/"concept" with "signifier"/"signified."

However celebrated it may be, this distinction is far from unproblematic.[10] Saussure's account of the sign is ambiguous. The text oscillates between the idea that the linguistic sign is a meaningful form, an indissociable bond between form (sound, graphic representation) and meaning (concept), and the rather different idea that the sign really is a form divorced from its concept or, if one prefers, an empty signifier, a mere material "mark." While Saussure explicitly defends the "meaningful form" thesis, the move from concept/sound-image to signified/signifier has the effect of making the "material mark" thesis look quite plausible. In modern intellectual history, the transition from "meaningful form" to "material mark" is crucial, for nothing is more characteristic of the post-Saussurean intellectual universe than the almost mystical belief in the "materiality of the signifier," and its sister concepts "the empty signifier" and the "mark."

How material is the "sound-image"? Every sound is not a "sound-image." Some sounds are just sounds. To hear "sound-images" we must know the relevant language, otherwise we wouldn't recognize the sounds as meaningful, as *language* (see CG, 13). The "sound-image" is material, but not in the way we usually expect: it is "*not* the material sound, a purely physical thing, but the *psychological imprint of the sound,* the impression that it makes on our senses" (66; my italics). The sound-image, then, is a *psychological event*, the experience of hearing something meaningful.[11]

This initial description of the "sound-image" strikes me as quite different from Saussure's illustration of the relationship between the Latin signifier "arbor" and the signified "tree," which is part of every literary scholar's DNA:[12]

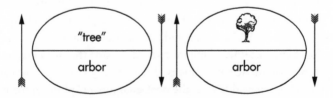

For generations, teachers (I am no exception) have explained that the sign is the whole (the circle); the signified ("tree") is the concept, or the meaning; and the signifier ("arbor") the material aspect of the sign, the sound-waves, the black marks on the page. In such formulations we reduce the signifier to something purely material, which Saussure explicitly warns against. But given this specific representation of the sign, with its clear dividing line between signifier and signified, it is hard to avoid precisely this "mistake."

When Saussure declares that the "bond between signifier and the sig-nified is arbitrary," he also legitimizes the idea that the bond might break (CG, 67). Once we assume that the signified can float free of the signifier, the signifier is no longer a meaningful but a meaningless form—a mate-rial mark, an empty shell. This turns the signifier/signified distinction into another version of the Augustinian picture of meaning.[13]

Technically, then, Saussure does define the signifier as a meaningful form, just like the sound-image. But somehow it is much harder to turn the "signifier" into a psychological event with only a faint trace of mate-riality attaching to it, than it was to do the same with the more ungainly term "sound-image." Maybe that's why Saussure keeps reminding his read-ers that the signifier can never come apart from the signified. In a posthu-mously discovered note he writes: "It is not true, indeed it is extremely false to imagine there to be a distinction between the sound and the idea. These are in fact inseparably one in our minds."[14] *Course* has similar dec-larations, for example this one: "Language can also be compared with a sheet of paper: thought is the front and the sound the back; on can-not cut the front without cutting the back at the same time; likewise in language, one can neither divide sound from thought nor thought from sound" (CG, 113).

Saussure himself, then, thinks of signifiers as meaningful forms. He considers meaning fundamental to the most formal linguist operations. Every time we split a sequence of sounds or letters into linguistic units, we do so *on the basis of their meaning*. We say that English distinguishes between the phonemes /k/ and /m/ because we already know that the meaning of "cat" is different from the meaning of "mat." If we didn't know this, we wouldn't know where to begin. To cast the play of such differences as the *ground* (site of production) of meaning, as generations of theo-rists have done, is to put the cart before the horse. The meanings of "cat" and "mat" don't emerge out of the free play of phonemes. It's the other way around: phonemes are established because these words *already* carry meaning for us. Saussure takes absolutely for granted that we can't deter-mine the simplest linguistic units without knowing the meaning: "mean-ing justifies the delimitation" (CG, 105).

In my view, then, the truly problematic aspect of Saussure's understanding of the sign is the introduction of the "signified." What work does this term do? If the signifier, like the sound-image, is supposed to be a meaningful form, why not just say so? I suspect that Saussure inherited his devotion to the signified (the concept) from the French symbolists, who tended to think of language as too brutish and too grossly material to convey the ineffable, the ideal, the inexpressible mysteries of the soul. There are striking parallels between Saussure's concepts and Arthur Symons's presentation of symbolism in his hugely influential 1899 anthology *The Symbolist Movement in Literature*, which inspired pioneering Anglophone modernists such as Yeats and Pound: "Without symbolism there can be no literature; indeed, not even language. What are words themselves but symbols, almost as arbitrary as the letters which compose them, mere sounds of the voice to which we have agreed to give certain significations, as we have agreed to translate these sounds by those combinations of letters?"[15] Such declarations makes the signified look like a moment of pure consciousness embodied in the sign, which again has the effect of turning the signifier into mere materiality. In such a theory, meaning does indeed appear as an "aura the word brings along with it," as Wittgenstein scornfully puts it (§116).

Saussure insists on the double nature of the sign because he wants to separate himself from the "nomenclature" understanding of language — the idea that language is a set of names, which implies that the meaning of a word is the thing the name refers to. But while Saussure gives up the "nomenclature" theory, he is incapable of divorcing himself from other versions of the "Augustinian" picture of meaning. There are three main versions of the "Augustinian" view. All of them posit a gap between a word and its meaning: meaning can be an essence; it can be the thing or idea the word stands for ("nomenclature" theory); or it can be a psychological (mental) entity. Saussure opts for psychology: meaning is psychological, it is in the mind, it is a concept.

Saussure, then, never explicitly endorses the "material mark" theory. It is hard to see how he could since it would condemn him to a strangely circular reasoning. For if I think of words as mere "material marks," I have to explain how I even recognize them as words. How do I know that a particular sound is a signifier and not simply a random sound? Only because I already know what it means. In this sense, an "empty signifier" or the "material mark" is a radically incoherent concept, simultaneously meaningless and meaningful.

If anything characterizes post-Saussurean thought, however, it is the belief that it is perfectly meaningful to speak of "marks" or "empty signifiers." The purely material signifier is the foundation for a huge amount of modern theory. It grounds every speculation about the "materiality of language." Elaborate theories of "materialism" have been based on the idea that the signifier is purely material. At one point in feminist theory it was quite common to hear the (outlandish) argument that language and the body can be "theorized" in the same way, since both are material. This is like saying that there is no theoretically significant difference between mice and mountains, asteroids and aspidistras, for after all, they're all material.[16]

When language is reduced to mere materiality, theorists have to explain how the gap between mark and meaning gets closed. This leads to theories claiming that the mark becomes meaningful through some mental operation ("interpretation," "authorial intention"); some external situation ("context," "*force de rupture*"), or some feature of the signifier itself ("iterability").

The Sign Is Arbitrary

Saussure famously claims that the sign is arbitrary: "The bond between the signifier and the signified is arbitrary. Since I mean by sign the whole that results from the associating of the signifier with the signified, I can simply say: the linguistic sign is arbitrary" (CG, 67). He takes this to be a perfectly uncontroversial observation, a principle "no one disputes" (68). At first glance, he simply means that there is *no reason* why "cow" means "cow" in English. There is, as it were, nothing cow-like about the word itself. This is proved by the fact that the French manage fine with *vache*. If the language had developed differently, we might have had a completely different word for the animal.

But Saussure also claims that the arbitrariness of the sign is of "primordial importance" (CG, 68), a principle from which momentous consequences spring. First, it entails that language is not a "nomenclature"—not a set of names of pre-existing concepts, essences, or things (see 65). Different languages "cut" the continuum of experience and thought differently. This wouldn't be the case, if they were all naming the same prelinguistic objects or essences. Second, the principle of arbitrariness ensures that words get meaning from their relations to other words (not from their relations to things or ideas)—language is not a set of labels, but a "system of differences *without positive terms*" (120). Third, for these reasons, language is expressive of a culture. Language is fundamentally social. Because "everyone participates at all times," it "blends with the life of society" (74).

Many theorists think that the arbitrariness of the sign implies that meaning is always unstable, always open to change. But this is not obvious.

"Arbitrary" simply means "not necessary." Language could have evolved differently—but it didn't. Now that we have *this* language, with *these* specific forms, we are pretty much stuck with it. For Saussure (as for Wittgenstein), there is no reason for words to mean what they mean. But this, he astutely points out, makes words *more*, not less, resistant to change, precisely because the sheer weight of traditional practice is not amenable to reason: "Because the sign is arbitrary, it follows no law other than that of tradition, and because it is based on tradition it is arbitrary" (CG, 74).

The sign, Saussure writes, is both "mutable" and "immutable." Its mutability is *diachronic*: temporal, historical, and mostly slow. But from a present-state (*synchronic*) point of view, language is extraordinary resistant to change: "The signifier, though to all appearances freely chosen with respect to the idea that it represents, is fixed, not free, with respect to the linguistic community that uses it. The masses have no choice in the matter, and the signifier chosen by language could be replaced by no other" (CG, 71). Saussure here sounds a Wittgensteinian theme: it is precisely because language is public and social that individual speakers can't simply endow words with their own private meanings. Or rather: if they do, they can't expect anyone to understand them.

Language may well be "conventional," but that doesn't make it particularly malleable (cf. CG, 78). Implicitly referring to his compatriot Rousseau, Saussure rejects the idea that language can "be identified with a contract pure and simple" (71). Language can't be a contract, Saussure explains, because it simply isn't a "convention that can be modified at the whim of interested parties" (78).

Saussure leaves us with a picture of language as a social institution transmitted from generation to generation, an institution with no origins, a system grounded on no reasons, and which cannot rightly be said to be "merely conventional" or the result of "agreement," if by that we imply that we are free to change it. Wittgenstein or Cavell would largely agree, although they would want to carry out a more serious investigation of what we mean by terms such as "convention" and "agreement."[17]

Arbitrary as opposed to what, then? The relevant answers seem to be "as opposed to Plato" (words express essences, or ideas) or "as opposed to eighteenth-century conceptualism" (words are names). This is indeed a position that "no one disputes."

Arbitrariness and Reference

Saussure's claim that the sign is arbitrary has spurred a vigorous debate about the relationship between the sign and the world. In some ways, this debate is truly arcane. It turns on the difference between saying that the "linguistic sign is arbitrary" and saying that the "bond between the signifier and the signified" is arbitrary. As we have seen, Saussure himself says both, in the same sentence, and appears to consider the two claims to be strictly equivalent (CG, 67). From the point of view of intellectual history, the debate is nevertheless important. Recently it has been invoked to ground some rather grand claims about matter (or "materiality"), and about the relationship between words and things (or "reference"). I will therefore give a brief account of the issues at stake, by first turning to Emile Benveniste's critique of Saussure's account of the sign, and then to Vicki Kirby's rereading of Saussure, which in part builds on Benveniste. In the next section, I'll examine some quite similar arguments made by Saussure's latest editors, Perry Meisel and Haun Saussy. I shall show that Kirby and Meisel and Saussy invoke Saussure's original understanding of language and the sign to ground a radically skeptical vision of a world without humans.

But first a few words about reference. Both Kirby and Benveniste assume that Saussure offers important insights about reference. This runs counter to classical readings of Saussure. For generations, scholars have wondered what to make of Saussure's apparent lack of interest in reference. As a first-year student at the University of Bergen, I had to take an introductory course in linguistics. I still remember my teacher's constant insistence that Saussure never once mentions the word "reference" or "referent."[18] He was hardly alone in making the point: already in 1923, C. K. Ogden and I. A. Richards upbraided Saussure for "neglecting entirely the things for which signs stand."[19]

The perennial discussions of "reference" in post-Saussurean theory take for granted that language as such either "refers" or fails to "refer." It is as if "language" just sits there as a huge, lumbering structure that constantly refers, or fails to. In this picture there are no speakers, nor any specific situations that might call for someone to refer to something. In such discussions, the word "language" is already tripping us up. For what is this "language" that either refers or fails to? Are we talking about *la langue*—Saussure's self-contained system of formal differences—or about *le langage*—language as we all use it every day? If it is *la langue*, then the "problem of reference" in Saussure simply isn't the same thing that most philosophers discuss under that heading. In fact, it is difficult to understand how *la langue* can have a relationship to anything at all. As a finite system of formal differences *la langue* rests in itself. *La langue* is an entity for which it makes no sense either to assert or deny that it has a relationship to the world. Saussure's refusal to discuss reference was well founded and perfectly coherent.

Among literary scholars, the most common view has been that Saussure's understanding of language posits an unbridgeable gap between reality and language.[20] This is certainly Fredric Jameson's view. His famous declaration that the "Real in Lacan ... is simply History itself" is based on the conviction that Lacan offers Marxism a "materialistic philosophy of language," whose "fundamental tenet is a rigorous distinction between the signified—the realm of semantics proper, of interpretation, of the study of the text's ostensible meaning—and the referent." As a result, Jameson writes, our language—our narratives—"can only approximate [the Real itself] in asymptotic fashion."[21] Here "the Real" is reality, history; language a set of symbols that approaches, but never quite coincides with the reality it seeks to represent.

Jameson's view is characteristic of the first generation of post-Saussureans. The self-confident second generation, exemplified by Kirby, and Meisel and Saussy, would dispute every one of Jameson's claims. In their view, Saussure has made the very term "referent" irrelevant by abolishing the gap between the signified and the referent. To put it more precisely: for them, the signified (the concept) simply *is* the referent. This is not an immediately plausible claim, to say the least. To understand their argument, it is necessary to return to Benveniste's 1939 article "The Nature of the Linguistic Sign."

Benveniste reminds us of Saussure's example of the arbitrariness of the sign, namely the word "ox" in French and German, which shows that two different signifiers—*böf* and *oks*—have the same signified. For Saussure, this shows that there is no essence, no necessary link between signifier and signified. Benveniste disagrees. If a German speaker hears the sound *oks*, she simply can't separate the sound from the idea. Benveniste writes: "Between the signifier and the signified, the connection is not arbitrary; on the contrary it is necessary. The concept (the "signified") *boeuf* is perforce identical in my consciousness with the sound sequence (the "signifier") *böf*. How could it be otherwise?"[22]

Benveniste is simply saying that words or signs are meaningful forms. If we know the language, they strike our ears as instantly meaningful. As we have seen, this is precisely Saussure's own original definition of the "sound-image." But Saussure's argument was historical; Benveniste's is phenomenological. Saussure wanted to know how language has become what it is (there is no reason; the sign is arbitrary). Benveniste raises the rather different question of whether, *here and now*, I, as a speaker of the language, am phenomenologically capable of hearing *böf* as anything but meaningful (no, I am not).

Benveniste is "asking for the meaning of a word in isolation."[23] Wittgenstein would remind him that meaning does not depend on the *word*, but on the *use*, on the word's place in the grammar of our lives. Both Benveniste and Saussure write as if *böf* had only one use. (However much they wish to escape from it, they remain locked up in the problematic of naming.) But, as Conant also shows, if one begins one's analysis by focusing on the individual word, rather than by looking at the work it carries out in its language-game, then we will end up positing a classically "Augustinian" gap between the word and its meaning.[24] This is precisely what Benveniste goes on to do.

Given that the connection between sound and meaning is necessary, Benveniste argues, what is arbitrary is the connection between the word (the sign) and the thing. Turning the sign into a name, Benveniste reintroduces the very "nomenclature" theory Saussure is at pains to avoid."[25] Moreover, Benveniste's philosophy of language is conventional in the extreme: "What is arbitrary is that one certain sign and no other is applied to a certain element of reality, and not to any other.... It is indeed the metaphysical problem between the mind and the world transposed into linguistic terms."[26]

In my view, Benveniste makes a complete hash of Saussure's original passage. Such a naive realism is nowhere to be found in Saussure's text. As John M. Ellis has shown, Saussure's point is not that the same animals ("referents") exist in two countries, but that a "similar *conception* of them exists in both places."[27] Saussure's claim about the arbitrariness of the sign has nothing to do with reference: his point is simply that the sign is unmotivated, that there is no *natural* connection between sound and meaning (see CG, 69).

Vicki Kirby builds on Benveniste's argument about the arbitrariness of the sign, but turns it upside-down. Given that Benveniste comprehensively misreads Saussure, Kirby's picture of Saussure's linguistics is hardly convincing. Yet her reading of Saussure is the first to sound a theme that Meisel and Saussy later repeat and amplify (without giving Kirby her due credit), namely the idea that Saussure's linguistics undermines the split between matter and consciousness, nature and culture, body and mind, by making matter signifying in its own right. Kirby's "materialist" rereading of Saussure grounds the grand (and to me quite bizarre) conclusion, namely that "nature is literate."[28]

Like Saussure and Benveniste, Kirby is boxed into the belief that we can discuss meaning by discussing individual words in isolation. Kirby also assumes that to understand "reference" is to understand language as such. Both assumptions are typical of the "Augustinian" picture of language. Kirby's self-declared radical vision of language is in fact highly traditional.

Kirby acknowledges that her interpretation of Saussure runs counter to

Saussure's own ideas. She also rightly points to the ambiguities and fault lines within his text as the starting point for her own theory.[29] Her argument goes roughly like this: the signified is defined as a "concept." But in fact Saussure conflates the "concept" (signified) and the "thing" (referent) throughout his text. For Kirby, this justifies the argument that the signified simply *is* the referent: the sign incorporates the thing in the world. While Benveniste insists on the gap between sign and thing, Kirby moves the thing into the sign. Saussure, she writes, "includ[ed] within the sign the reality to which the sign refers." The sign and the referent are no longer discrete entities, and since the sign is arbitrary, the whole world is now arbitrary: "The domain of 'the arbitrary' becomes the material world of reality."[30] I think this means that for Kirby everything is *literally* language. Not language as representation, for that would just be a flimsy overlay over "material reality," but actual "thing-language" or "language-things."

I have some difficulty understanding this. (In fact, I have some difficulty understanding Kirby's almost willfully opaque writing in general.) How are we to picture a sign containing reality, a sign incorporating the actual thing we usually think it refers to? If I say "pileated woodpecker," do I conjure up the actual woodpecker? And what about exclamations like "Help!" or "Bingo!"?[31] In what way is the "material world of reality" the "domain of the arbitrary"? Arbitrary as opposed to what? Kirby doesn't say. But no matter. However unfounded and implausible it may be, Kirby's reading of Saussure leaves us with a vision of language in which matter and "language/thought," as she calls it, are fully imbricated in one another; a vision of a fully signifying world, a world in which matter speaks. This vision has turned out to be attractive to many. As some recent commentators approvingly put it: "In the work of Kirby, matter appears as something that is not only spoken about or spoken with, but rather as itself simply *speaking*."[32] In Kirby's world, language and matter signify by themselves, without speakers, without any kind of human agency. Given that objects and language are imbricated in one another, "reference" itself now becomes a superfluous term.

As I read her, Kirby simply abolishes human consciousness by fiat, and for no particular reason. But this seems to be the point. As Karen Barad puts it, with reference to Kirby: "Intelligibility is not a human-based affair. It is a matter of differential articulations and differential responsiveness/engagement."[33] Kirby and Barad conjure up a world without human judgment and agency. In Kirby's work, Saussure's abstract conception of language as *la langue* becomes the unquestioned matrix for an utterly implausible vision of the world as a self-signifying soup. What specific problem is such a theory supposed to solve?

"The Problem of Reference"

Meisel and Saussy demonstrate with particular acuity how the "material mark" theory of the sign inevitably produces a skeptical vision of language and the world. They have no hesitations in "philosophizing" Saussure. On the contrary, in their eyes, Saussure *was* a philosopher, and not just any philosopher, but one who solved the "problem of reference" (CG, xv). One might want to ask what the problem of reference actually is. What specific difficulties does the idea of reference produce?

Meisel and Saussy don't get into specifics. For them, the "problem of reference" is the "problem of mimesis—of language as imitating or representing what it refers to" (CG, xv). Aligning "reference" with "mimesis" and "representation," they assume that to "solve" one is to solve all. I find this painfully vague and superficial. (Imitation! Representation! Reference! Language! So many concepts with 2,000 years of debate behind them!) Meisel and Saussy don't explain what's wrong with reference, or mimesis, or representation. But how can we assess the solution if we don't know what ills it is supposed to remedy?

For Meisel and Saussy, Saussure is a philosopher for whom "solving the problem of reference always comes first" (CG, xlii). Frequently veering over into grandiosity on Saussure's behalf, they declare that Saussure forces us to reimagine the "separation of word and thing, subject and object, self and world" (xvi). Thus he solves the "problem of both the subject and of history," develops a "wholly different conception of time and how it works," and undoes the "conventional chronological notion of cause and effect" (xlii).

Even the most ardent admirer of Saussure might balk at such extravagant claims. Certainly, they aren't all backed up by the 1916 text of *Course in General Linguistics*. Meisel and Saussy admit as much, for they blame the students who labored to put together the 1916 edition for having produced a "fallacious, self-contradictory Saussure" (CG, xxxiii). Their own Saussure is not in fact based on the 1916 text (the English translation of which they nevertheless reprint unchanged); rather, they declare, their Saussure is "the Saussure some readers have long desired to meet, the conjectural 'real Saussure,' the *Saussure who understands Saussure* emerg[ing] hesitantly from the variant notes and the manuscript materials" (xxxiii). I love this sentence, for it spells out exactly what they are trying to do, namely invent a post-Saussurean Saussure to replace the one we actually had.

How do Meisel and Saussy think Saussure "solves the problem of reference"? By "reconceiv[ing] reference as signification rather than as mimesis." Once reference has been "reconceived," we can no longer "take for granted the assumptions that mimesis as a notion traditionally puts in place: the separation of word and thing, subject and object, self and world. Saussure requires a reimagination of these categories and a makeover of the way we think." Meisel and Saussy go very fast here. For how does "reconceiving" reference as signification solve anything? Do Saussure's new editors believe that we can simply *will* away the difference between meaning and reference? How am I to take the idea that, thanks to Saussure, there is no longer any "separation between word and thing" (CG, xvi)?[34]

As far as I can see, Meisel and Saussy think that Saussure solved the "problem of reference" by eradicating the concept, that is, he solved it by not mentioning "reference" at all. Instead of talking about reference he talks about signifiers and signifieds. But if there is a genuine problem here, it won't disappear simply because Saussure doesn't mention it. Nor will it disappear just because we change the words we use to talk about it. (If the use is the same, the new words will do the same work as the old.) Even genuinely new concepts can't by themselves do the work of analysis, or what Wittgenstein calls a "grammatical investigation." In any case, if Wittgenstein teaches us anything, it is that the relationship between words and world simply can't be reduced to the single case of reference. The intertwinement of words and world is more complex, varied and subtle than Meisel and Saussy realize. As we have seen, the question of "reference" (or "representation") does not exhaust the question of how our words become aligned with the world, or fail to.

If Saussure has "solved" the problem of reference, what follows? As I read Meisel and Saussy, it appears that Saussure's *signified* now *replaces* concepts such as "thing in the world," and "referent." Terms like "reference" or "mimesis" or "representation" are therefore no longer required. (Meisel and Saussy casually deride anyone who still believes that people sometimes use language to name things.) After Saussure, apparently, both the sign and the world are at once material and signifying. They provide no argument as to why this would be the case. If, as I suspect, Saussure's "signified" represents the moment of pure consciousness in language, then Meisel and Saussy's vision is pure idealism.

The result, in any case, is a conflation of the sign and the world, in which the signified merges with the world. The result is a grand vision of a fully conceptualized world, which I confess to finding completely unintelligible:

In their reciprocity, signifier and signified produce a world that is both wholly concrete and wholly conceptual at one and the same time. Indeed, the world itself—the real, external world—is a matrix of signification, real because it is symbolic and symbolic because it is real. Language and the world are continuous. The object-world, including nature and our own bodies, is a web of signs continuous with the languages and images with which we describe them.... Saussure's signification is a process, not a product. Language is part of the reality to which it refers. It does not resemble social or organic life, nor is it simply a part of social or organic life. It is identical with them both.... Language is both subject and object in relation to itself, something to which it responds as much as something it uses. (CG, xvii–xviii)

There is much to ponder in this passage. The absence of human beings, for example. In this vision of meaning, nobody uses language; on the contrary, language uses and responds to itself. "Our" bodies appear, but only as part of the general "web of signs." This appears to be a version of Derrida's "general text."[35] Having turned signification into a radical idealism, Meisel and Saussy here radically objectify their own idealism, presenting signification as inscribed in and on a world in which there is nobody left to discover it, let alone be responsible for it.

How are we to imagine Meisel and Saussy's "wholly concrete and wholly conceptual" world? Are we to imagine a state in which words become things, or things become words? Or maybe a world in which things come with their labels as it were *engraved* on themselves? If so, we have arrived at the same fantasy that animates Kirby's vision of Saussure. In both cases the theorist ends up reproducing one of the classic fantasies of skepticism, namely a world in which language, meaning, and knowledge would no longer depend on fallible human subjectivity.[36] This is a version of what Cavell in *The Claim of Reason* calls the "fantasy of necessary inexpressiveness": "The wish underlying this fantasy covers a wish that underlies skepticism, a wish for the connection between my claims of knowledge and the objects upon which the claims are to fall to occur without my intervention, apart from my agreements. As the wish stands, it is unappeasable" (CR, 351–52).

Meisel and Saussy's dream of an "object-world" which is also a "web of signs," conjures up a world that spontaneously yields its meanings, a world in which the gap between the name and the thing have disappeared. But such a vision can't tell us anything about the nature of language, for it is a vision of a world in which there no longer is anything we would recognize as language.

Faced with what she perceives as a troublesome gap between language and the world, the skeptic has two options: she can celebrate (or deplore) language's incapacity to grasp reality, or she can, like Meisel and Saussy, dream of a world in which the gap has been overcome by the expulsion of the last traces of human subjectivity, human judgment. Thus the skeptic participates in what Cavell calls the grand philosophical project of the "Rejection of the Human" (see CR, 207). But let's not forget that nothing is more human than the denial of the human.[37]

6

Signs, Marks, and Archie Bunker

POST–SAUSSUREAN
VISIONS OF LANGUAGE

In this chapter I show how the post-Saussurean vision of language, particularly the concept of the mark, or the empty signifier, and the question of language and reference turn up in two classics of literary theory: Steven Knapp and Walter Benn Michaels's "Against Theory," and Paul de Man's "Semiology and Rhetoric."[1] Knapp and Michaels's neopragmatist understanding of intention and interpretation is similar to that of Stanley Fish. De Man's text is a cornerstone of the deconstructionist vision of literature and reading. De Man in particular enables us to see how the post-Saussurean vision of language constructs a specific notion of "literature" or "literariness." The point of these investigations is to enable readers to see the post-Saussurean heritage in a new light by bringing out, as clearly as I can, its underlying assumptions as they appear to a reader inspired by ordinary language philosophy. The result, I hope, will be a deeper understanding of the commitments of post-Saussurean tradition and of the difference between this tradition and that of ordinary language philosophy.[2]

From Signs to Marks, and Back Again

Walter Benn Michaels has long been a trenchant critic of the very idea of the "mark." "Mark" is the term used by Jacques Derrida in "Signature Event Context," and by Michaels himself, to name the "materiality of the signifier" or the "empty signifier," understood as purely material marks or soundwaves which in themselves have no meaning at all. (In chapter 5, I call it the "material mark.")[3]

In his 2004 book, *The Shape of the Signifier*, Michaels claims that the distinction between *marks* and *signs* brings out a crucial dividing line in contemporary literary theory. I largely agree with Michaels's critique of the mark, and of identity politics, too. He is exactly right about US postmodern culture being permeated by a mixture of a positivistic fascination with pure materiality and an investment in questions of identity and subjectivity. Michaels demonstrates that the commitment to "marks" actually produces the recent critical obsession with the physical object, the thing, pure materiality. This trend has, if anything, grown stronger in the decade since *The Shape of the Signifier* appeared. The same commitment to meaningless materiality, materiality without subjectivity, also surfaces in affect theory and "new materialism."

Michaels's incisive critique nevertheless relies on the concept it wishes to undo. For all his hatred of the idea of the mark, the very idea that signs can be "marks" remains the starting point for his own alternative vision of meaning. This becomes particularly clear in the 1982 essay "Against Theory," which he cowrote with Stephen Knapp.[4] The essay became famous for arguing that regardless what your theory of interpretation is, it won't affect what you actually do when you interpret a text. This distinctively neopragmatist aspect of Knapp and Michaels's essay is not my concern here. My concern is their understanding of meaning, signs, and mark, which underpins their claim that meaning is an effect of the author's intention.

From the point of view of ordinary language philosophy, this is a version of the "Augustinian" picture of meaning. For Knapp and Michaels, signifiers are empty. What fills them with meaning? The author's intentions. Like other post-Saussureans, Knapp and Michaels are awed at the thought that words (material marks, mere sounds) in principle can mean just *anything*. Their theoretical labor consists in showing that only the author's intention binds the mark to its meaning.

In "Against Theory," Knapp and Michaels invite us to imagine that one day, as we are walking along the beach, we come across the first stanza of Wordsworth's "A slumber did my spirit seal" written in the sand. We recognize the writing as writing, we understand the words, we may even recognize the lines as a rhymed poetic stanza, "all this without knowing anything about the author."[5] This, they write, "would seem to be a good case of intentionless meaning" (15/727). But imagine that as we stand there, a wave washes up, and when it recedes, we see that it has left the second stanza of the same poem in the sand. What then? According to Knapp and Michaels, we will either posit an author (God, the animated sea, the ghost of Wordsworth), or we will take the words in the sand to be an accidental material formation. In the second case, they ask, will the marks in the sand still be words? Knapp and Michaels think the answer is obvious: "Clearly not. They will merely seem to *resemble* words.... To deprive them of an author is to convert them into accidental likenesses of language. They are not, after all, an example of intentionless meaning; as soon as they become intentionless they become meaningless as well" (16/728).

But if Knapp and Michaels want to answer, "Clearly not," I want to answer, "Clearly yes."[6] In the situation outlined in the parable, we immediately recognize the words in the sand as words, even as a poem. Yet the moment I become convinced that the words are the result of accidental wave movements or, as P. D. Juhl suggests, "accidentally typed out by a monkey randomly depressing keys on a typewriter," I am supposed to turn them into marks.[7] How am I expected to achieve this? Through a willed forgetting, an instant self-blinding to the meaning of the words in the sand?

If I am convinced that the words on the beach are the random product of the waves, I will feel far *more* astonished at their existence than I otherwise would. That astonishment would be based precisely on the fact that we are speaking about *words*—whole sentences—("signs") not marks: how astounding that the random acts of the waves produced the words of a poem rather than mere squiggles! (It is of course true that if I no longer think of them as the expression of a human mind I may choose to *treat* the words quite differently, make a different use of them; my point is that regardless of what I go on to do with them, I can't just will myself into finding them meaningless.)

In this scenario, Knapp and Michaels introduce a distinction between two sets of perfectly identical signs: namely signs that are language (i.e., words), and signs that are merely an "accidental likeness of language" (i.e., marks). This is only possible because Knapp and Michaels do exactly what Derrida does in "Signature Event Context," namely strip all conceivable context, including the existence of language itself, away from the words they want to consider, all the while relying on the fact that we somewhere, somehow recognize them as words.

Only after carrying out that operation do they declare that since we are now dealing with "marks," (i.e., with mere material squiggles), we find ourselves in a situation in which we must produce a theory to explain how the marks will go from being marks to becoming words again. In Derrida's case, that theory is "iterability"; in Knapp and Michaels's case it is "authorial intention." Thus "Against Theory" exemplifies what its authors denounce, namely the "tendency to generate theoretical problems by splitting apart terms that are in fact inseparable" (12/724).

Like Derrida, Knapp and Michaels make the mistake of considering that the "particularity of words [consists] in their material or spatial integrity," as Cavell puts it.[8] For how would we ever recognize absolutely meaningless marks as words? As we have seen, Saussure initially avoided this problem by insisting that the "sound image" is a psychological event—the grasping of meaning—and not a mere physical phenomenon. If we turn the signifier into a meaningless mark, they aren't potentially signifying marks which for the moment fail to signify, but genuinely incomprehensible scratchings, a set of random sounds. Such phenomena have no existence in language.

Merleau-Ponty tells the story of a little boy who "put on his grandmother's spectacles and took up her book," hoping to find there the enchanting stories she used to read to him. He was horribly disappointed: all he could see was black and white marks.[9] Because he couldn't read, this boy was truly looking at empty signifiers. The point is the same: a mark, an empty signifier, isn't *language*, but a philosophical construct, produced *after* the fact or event of meaning.

Knapp and Michaels disagree. Faced with the wave poem, they can only imagine two possible reactions: amazement at the surprising identity of the author, or amazement at the discovery that "what you thought was poetry turns out not to be poetry at all. It isn't poetry because it isn't language; that's what it means to call it an accident" (16/728). As I have just said, I certainly agree that pure marks aren't language, but that's not the point here. The point is that once I have understood a word, or an utterance, I am in no position to rid myself of that understanding just because I no longer can explain where the utterance came from. To think of *words* as marks (mere material scratches, mere soundwaves) is radically counterintuitive, for it requires us to subtract the meaning from the "marks" we know perfectly well spell "slumber" or "dead."

Knapp and Michaels thus produce an utterly peculiar argument, namely that two sets of identical marks are in fact different: one set consists of words, while the other, identical set, merely *resemble* words. The first are linguistic marks (meaningful forms), the second are mere scratchings. Animated by the intention of an author, the first have meaning; the second are empty simulacra, mere marks. This is the mantra Knapp and Michaels can't stop repeating: "marks produced by chance are not words at all but only resemble them" (20/732); "marks without intention are not speech acts" (21/733); "marks without intention are not language" (21/733).

This distinction is meaningless. The concept of "author's intention" doesn't actually do any work in this argument. Certainly knowledge of the author and her intentions can make a huge difference to our understanding of an utterance, but not on this level, where we are trying to decide whether we are dealing with language or pure marks. "I'll teach you differences!" uttered by King Lear doesn't have the same meaning as if we imagine it uttered by Wittgenstein, or by Derrida. But Knapp and Michaels argue on the level of "meaning as such": no specific meanings are ever at stake. The formalism of the argument is breathtaking.

Although it begins by acknowledging that anyone who comes across the words in the sand will spontaneously take them to be language, the parable of the wave poem actually urges us to be ready to turn words into marks on a moment's notice. Knapp and Michaels's extravagant fiction is designed to make us stop doing what we ordinarily do, namely spontaneously understand the meaning of words. The underlying skepticism is palpable: theirs is a world in which words oscillate between meaning and pure materiality, a world in which we will lose all our bearings if we can't attach the words securely to an animated and human origin, the author. (I sympathize with the impulse to claim that without human beings there is no such thing as human language, but that argument can't be grounded in a vision of words as marks.)

If we decide that the words on the beach are marks, a new empirical fact can easily make us change our minds. Knapp and Michaels ask us to imagine, for example, that we suddenly see a small submarine, "out of which clamber a half dozen figures in white lab coats. One of them trains his binoculars on the beach and shouts triumphantly, 'It worked! It worked! Let's go down and try it again.'" At this point, the marks again turn into words: "Presumably," Knapp and Michaels write, "you will now once again change your mind, not because you have a new account of language, meaning or intention, but because you now have new evidence of an author. The question of authorship is and always was an empirical question, it has now received an empirical answer" (17/729).[10]

But such an oscillation between words and marks is only possible for someone who fundamentally thinks that words *are* marks. Anyone who can't stop thinking that words have meaning will find it impossible to transform them into marks and back again on command, let alone according to the presence or absence of a submarine. Knapp and Michaels's distinction between words and marks turns out to be at once weirdly idealistic (a matter of intention, as if of a spirit filling dead signs with life), and weirdly positivistic (a matter of being able to produce an empirical author for every speech act), just like the deconstructive theory of the mark that Michaels opposes so intensely in *The Shape of the Signifier*.

In a brilliant essay on "Against Theory," the philosopher George Wilson shows that Knapp and Michaels reject the "commonsense idea that words, phrases, and sentences mean something (and, often, mean several things) as expressions in a language." While Wilson is not concerned with "marks" or with literary theory, his conclusion is exactly the same as mine, namely that "Knapp and Michaels are committed to denying that words and sentences have meanings in a language in anything like the way we usually conceive this to be the case."[11]

In general, Knapp and Michaels's idea about meaning and intention is so simple as to be empty, consisting in the repetition of one mantra, namely that we take language to mean something only when we assume that someone intended to speak or write the words we see or hear. But this simply amounts to saying something like: "human language is the language of human beings." While this is preferable to the world without subjects conjured up by Meisel and Saussy, it is not a contribution to the understanding of meaning or intention.[12]

Given their staunch critique of thinkers like Derrida and de Man, it may seem excessive to claim, as I do, that Knapp and Michaels fully accept the post-Saussurean understanding of the "empty signifier" or the "mark." But their own text bears me out. In a famous moment in *Confessions*, Rousseau explains that when he was accused of stealing a ribbon, he uttered the sound "Marion," but without really meaning to accuse his fellow servant Marion of his own crime. While Knapp and Michaels go on to take issue with Paul de Man's analysis of Rousseau's "Marion," they agree with de Man's underlying idea, which is that the sound "Marion" can become an empty signifier: "The fact that the sound 'Marion' can mean nothing reminds us that language consists of inherently meaningless sounds to which one adds meanings—in other words, that the relation between signifier and signified is arbitrary." For Knapp and Michaels this is an "apparently uncontroversial description of language," namely the "recognition that the material condition of language is inherently meaningless" (22/734). Thus they reiterate the same claim as before, namely that the "meaningless noise "Marion" only *resembles* the signifier "Marion" (23/734).[13] I have tried to show that any such "recognition" is itself meaningless. Knapp and Michaels's vision of a gap between the mark and its meaning is a particularly pure iteration of the "Augustinian" picture of meaning Wittgenstein sets out to undo.

My own view of the episode is quite different. To understand Rousseau's "Marion," we need to understand the use. Which means understanding not just what he said, but to whom he said it, at what time, under what circumstances, and so on. Any use of language is an exercise of judgment. To speak is to act. Therefore we are responsible for what we say. If I say, "I promise," I actually promise regardless of whether I "mean it in my heart."[14] Whether he meant to or not, Rousseau successfully played the language-game of "accusation." He actually did accuse the poor Marion of theft. While he uttered her name in a moment of shame and panic, he did nothing to retract his accusation later, although he had plenty of opportunity to do so. In this situation, neither Rousseau nor de Man is free to unilaterally declare that the sound "Marion" is meaningless, particularly not when Rousseau was working alongside a woman bearing precisely that name.

Aware that there is a problem in declaring signifiers to be completely meaningless, Knapp and Michaels try to solve it by distinguishing between sounds and signifiers: "It is of course true," they write, "that sounds in themselves are meaningless. It is also true that sounds become signifiers when they function in language. But it is not true that sounds in themselves are signifiers; they become signifiers only when they acquire meanings, and when they lose their meanings they stop being signifiers" (23/734–35). But this is just to restate the same problem. Knapp and Michaels simply won't recognize that signifiers are only signifiers *because* they already have meaning in the language.[15] Instead they suggest that we at once recognize signifiers as signifiers, and take them to be utterly meaningless until we give them an author. If this theory is unconvincing, it is because it faithfully reproduces the incoherence installed at the very heart of the theory of the "empty signifier" or the "material mark."

In an op-ed piece in the *New York Times* in 2005 Stanley Fish argues an almost identical case:

> Suppose you're looking at a rock formation and see in it what seems to be the word "help." You look more closely and decide that, no, what you are seeing is an effect of erosion, random marks that just happen to resemble an English word. The moment you decide that nature caused the effect, you will have lost all interest in interpreting the formation, because you no longer believe that it has been produced intentionally, and therefore you no longer believe that it's a word, a bearer of meaning.[16]

Fish assumes that as soon as I realize that the word "help" is the result of erosion, I will no longer wish to "interpret" it. Again, I am supposed suddenly to forget what I clearly understood a split second earlier, namely that the marks scratched into the rock spell "help." And what does Fish imagine will happen once I lose "all interest in interpreting the formation"? Maybe he thinks I'll just keep on walking, oblivious to the random marks on the rock. But surely I can't just walk on. Again, the question isn't one of epistemological uncertainty, but of action and responsibility.

Against Fish, I think that the question I have to decide is not whether to "interpret" the word "help," but whether to call out the mountain rescue squad. As in the case of the wave poem, the problem of the author actually does matter. But it doesn't matter for the meaning of the words. Rather it matters for *how I take* that meaning, that is, for *what I do* once I grasp that these scratchings spell "Help!" Before I walk on, I must come to some conclusion about how and when the marks got scratched onto the rock face. If I am now responsible for my decision—walk on? call the rescue squad?—it is precisely because I know perfectly well that "help" means "help" and not, say, "coffee." Interpretation is simply not required here.[17] That's what it means to say that words have meaning: that the meaning of a word is alive in its use, that use relies on shared criteria and shared forms of life, which every child learns as it learns to speak.

"Against Theory" shocked many literary critics, not because of its theory of the mark, but because of its explicit espousal of authorial intentions, a topic that had become more or less taboo in the wake of W. K. Wimsatt and Monroe Beardsley's 1946 essay "The Intentional Fallacy."[18] I won't discuss literary texts and authorial intention here (I return to the subject in chapter 9). It is nevertheless worth saying, as Wilson also does, that intentions don't play the same role in relation to literary texts as they do in relation to individual words. Words don't usually have authors; literary texts always do. A word has meaning in the language (that's what dictionaries try to account for), but until someone actually uses it, it's impossible to talk about intentions. A literary text, on the other hand, is intentional through and through simply because it is made to be read.

In his brief comments on "Against Theory," Cavell finds himself marveling at the "will to emptiness" in modern thought.[19] To show what he means, he asks whether Knapp and Michaels "meant, or intended the extremity of [this claim]: "In all speech what is intended and what is meant are identical" (17/729). Then he produces the following devastating demonstration of the difference between intention and meaning:

> For consider: if I glance at you meaningfully, that is between us, but if I glance at you intentionally, I am including a third.... I know how to give the meaning of a word but not how to give the intention of a word, though I might tell you what someone intended in using a certain word in a certain place. If Hamlet had asked, "Do you think I intended country matters?" Ophelia might well have been even more alarmed than she was.[20]

Knapp and Michaels repeatedly speak of "intentionless meaning," which is a highly unusual turn of phrase, a theoreticist construct that seems intended to replace (or block from view) the ordinary expression "unintended meaning," which makes perfect sense, but a sense that contradicts the very foundation of "Against Theory."[21] We can only speak of unintended meanings because we take for granted that words have meaning in the language, which here means that their use is governed by shared criteria, which we can't just neglect in our utterances. But that's precisely what Knapp and Michaels deny.[22]

But if Knapp and Michaels deny that words have meaning in the language, so does everyone else who thinks that they are speaking about language when they speak about marks, empty signifiers, or about the materiality of the signifier. This is a fundamental difference between post-Saussurean thought and ordinary language philosophy.

What's the Difference? Disagreeing about Archie Bunker

I'll now turn to Paul de Man's "Semiology and Rhetoric." There are several reasons for this. First, de Man returns us to the question of language and reference. Second, he raises the question of literary language, which he defines as fundamentally figural or "rhetorical." To de Man, "rhetoric" always undoes or destabilizes meaning. Third, his mode of reasoning exemplifies a certain idea of what it means to "do theory," which clashes with the very different notion to be found in ordinary language philosophy. Finally, "Semiology and Rhetoric" provoked a response from Stanley Cavell, a response that helps to brings out the difference between the two men's philosophical and literary sensibilities.

In the 1970s *All in the Family* was the most popular sit-com on American television, "famous," as Marco Roth puts it, "for the casual racism, misogyny, anti-Semitism, maudlin traditionalism and proud ignorance of its lead character."[23] That lead character was Archie Bunker, a reactionary and cantankerous working-class guy constantly trying the patience of his wife, Edith. The series ran on CBS from January 1971 until 1979, when it morphed into *Archie Bunker's Place*, which lasted for another four years.

In "Archie and the Bowling Team," an episode first aired on December 16, 1972, Archie comes home brandishing a pair of new laces for his bowling shoes.[24] A place has opened up on the best bowling team in the league, and Archie will get a tryout! All excited, he tells Edith to hurry up and lace his shoes for him. A few minutes later, she returns with the shoes still unlaced, and an urgent question for Archie:

EDITH: Archie, how do you want me to lace these?
ARCHIE: Through the holes, Edith, through the holes!
EDITH: No, I mean, do you want me to lace them over or under?
ARCHIE: What's the difference?

EDITH: Well, you see, if you lace them over, they show more, and these—

ARCHIE (*interrupts*): Edith, I didn't say what's the difference explain it to me, I said what's the difference who the hell cares.

EDITH: Oh, I am sorry Archie, I misunderstood you, you see when you say—

ARCHIE (*interrupts*): Will you stop with your stuff and lace these shoes? I ain't got much time![25]

Four months later, Paul de Man referred to the scene in "Semiology and Rhetoric," a lecture given at Cornell University as part of a symposium organized by *Diacritics*, then an up-and-coming journal with a mission to promote poststructuralist theory. In 1979 de Man made it the lead essay in his influential collection *Allegories of Reading*.[26]

Pouncing on Archie's exasperated exclamation "What's the difference?" as a brilliant example of the "tension between grammar and rhetoric," de Man draws some startling conclusions: "Rhetoric," he writes, "radically suspends logic and opens up vertiginous possibilities of referential aberration" (SR, 9). This is not all: the "rhetorical, figural potentiality of language" mobilized by Archie is the equivalent of "literature itself" (10). After reading Yeats's poem "Among School Children," and some passages from Proust's *In Search of Time Past*, de Man concludes that a rigorous reading will always uncover the "impossibility of knowing what [language] might be up to," always land the serious reader in a state of "suspended ignorance" (19).

Widely taught for more than a generation, "Semiology and Rhetoric" has had enormous impact on theorists inside and outside literary studies. "De Man's influence on academic literary and cultural criticism," Marc Redfield writes, "far exceeds the limits of an identifiable school or clique."[27] Teachers and commentators have usually taken de Man's message to be that "[since] you cannot reconcile rhetoric and grammar," the meaning of language, and literature, is "radically undecidable." They also stress de Man's "demonstrations of the confusions entailed by assuming that language performs an unproblematic designation of the world," of the text's "inability to designate."[28] At stake, then, is the relationship between language and the world, which here (again) is reduced to the single question of reference.

Stanley Cavell provided the first serious philosophical response to de Man's essay. In "The Politics of Interpretation (Politics as Opposed to What?)," a lecture delivered in Chicago in 1981, he presented a politely worded but philosophically scathing critique of de Man's essay.[29] Incensed at the Yale deconstructionist's procedures, Cavell objected to everything from de Man's reading of the scene from *All in the Family*, to his claims about grammar and rhetoric and his generalizations about language. De Man's essay, Cavell writes, "ignores the paradigms of comprehensibility" of philosophy as Cavell understands them. To Cavell, de Man's claims about the relationship between grammar and rhetoric are meaningless. There simply is no "inevitable relation between grammar and rhetoric." It is difficult to imagine a clearer rejection of de Man's analysis. Moreover, Cavell makes it clear that his disagreement goes deep: at stake is nothing less than the "moral of ordinary language philosophy...and of the practice of art." That moral is that "grammar cannot, or ought not, of itself dictate what you mean, what it is up to you to say.[30] In drawing a contrast between the rules of grammar and the responsibility of speakers, Cavell builds on a vision of language and meaning, and of the responsibility of speakers and listeners, writers and readers, fundamentally at odds with de Man's.

Grammar, Rhetoric, and Austin

"Semiology and Rhetoric" is an ambitious attempt to arrive at a new, radical definition of literature. De Man's explicit goal is to defeat the idea, often voiced by literary critics interested in history and society, that literary criticism should move "beyond formalism" (SR, 3).[31] His strategy will be to investigate the relationship between grammar and rhetoric. Here "rhetoric" is defined not as "eloquence" or "persuasion," but as the "study of tropes and of figures" (6). A trope is a poetic image (metaphor, metonymy); a figure a specific sequential arrangement of words. De Man uses "grammar" in the usual sense of rules for how to combine different linguistic elements.

In this project, de Man's opponents are, first, structuralists like Barthes, Gérard Genette, Tzvétan Todorov, and Algirdas Greimas and, second, Austin, all of whom commit the unpardonable sin of "letting grammar and rhetoric function in perfect continuity" (SR, 6). But as Cavell points out, it is hard to understand why de Man thinks that Austin posits anything of the kind.

Before I turn to de Man's misreading of Austin, I should say that I find most of de Man's specific claims about the relationship between grammar, logic, and reference opaque. I simply don't understand why any belief I might have about the relationship between grammar and rhetoric (even the rather strange belief that they always go hand in hand, in perfect continuity) would make me either assert or deny anything about logic or reference. I note that de Man uses the word "proposition" once, and wonder whether this is a gesture toward logical positivism. But if that is the case, de Man certainly doesn't say so, and never explains why people like Todorov or Genette, let alone Austin, would be aligned with that philosophy (SR, 7). In fact I don't even understand why de Man assumes that grammar and rhetoric constitute a binary opposition. Above all, however, I don't see why grammar and logic are always aligned (as if one can't be illogical in perfectly grammatical sentences), or why de Man believes that there is a logical connection between grammatical sentences and a belief in the referential powers of language.

According to de Man, Austin and his followers believe that an order always takes the form of an imperative, a question always the form of an interrogative, and so on (see SR, 8). As Cavell points out, this is a serious misrepresentation of Austin, who begins *How to Do Things with Words* precisely by criticizing the view that one can comfortably distinguish between propositions ("statements") and other linguistic structures:

> It was for too long the assumption of philosophers that the business of a "statement" can only be to "describe" some state of affairs, or to "state some fact," which it must do either truly or falsely.... Doubtless ... both grammarians and philosophers have been aware that it is by no means easy to distinguish even questions, commands, and so on from statements by means of the few and jejune grammatical marks available, such as word order, mood and the like: though perhaps it has not been usual to dwell on the difficulties which this fact obviously raises. For how do we decide which is which?[32]

Austin also explicitly declares that he could find no "grammatical criterion for performatives."[33] For Austin, grammar simply doesn't stand in any one, specific relationship to logic or truth. In fact, the philosophical *work* of *How to Do Things with Words* is precisely to show us that the same grammatical sentence can be used to do any number of different things. As Cavell reminds us, Austin introduced the famous distinction between constative and performative utterances precisely to show that "certain utterances that are grammatically statements are rhetorically something else" ("Politics," 43).

Reading Archie Bunker

By choosing a scene from *All in the Family*, de Man comes close to a subject that happens to be the focus of Cavell's deepest philosophical commitment, namely the ordinary and the everyday. Here's de Man's reading:

I take the first example from the sub-literature of the mass media: asked by his wife whether he wants to have his bowling shoes laced over or laced under, Archie Bunker answers with a question: "What's the difference?" Being a reader of sublime simplicity, his wife replies by patiently explaining the difference between lacing over and lacing under, whatever this may be, but provokes only ire. "What's the difference" did not ask for difference but means instead "I don't give a damn what the difference is." The same grammatical pattern engenders two meanings that are mutually exclusive: the literal meaning asks for the concept (difference) whose existence is denied by the figurative meaning. (SR, 9)

Introducing his "example from the sub-literature of the mass media," de Man sounds as if he is holding his nose. Given his obvious distaste for the material, why bother? What does de Man see in Archie and Edith? To be honest: de Man sees nothing in Edith, whom he dismisses as a "reader of sublime simplicity." In de Man's estimation, Archie is not much brighter: he "muddles along in a world where literal and figurative meanings get in each other's way, though not without discomforts" (SR, 9). De Man's interest is exclusively focused on one line, namely Archie's rhetorical question "What's the difference?"

According to de Man, the literal meaning of Archie's line asks for the difference. The figurative meaning, however, is "I don't give a damn what the difference is." Therefore, he concludes, the figurative meaning *denies the existence* of the concept ("difference") asked for in the literal meaning. The two meanings are mutually exclusive.

De Man is very quick to write off Edith's question about how to lace the shoes—in fact his casual "whatever this may be" reveals that he himself has no idea what the difference is. Because he is hazy on the question of shoe-lacing techniques, he is primed to slip into the erroneous assumption that there is no difference at all. Maybe that's why he is so confident that "I don't give a damn what the difference is" actually denies the existence of a difference. But there is more here: de Man's quick rejection of the difference between "lacing over" and "lacing under" reveals that he simply cannot imagine that ordinary language spoken by ordinary men and women has the power to make distinctions that, in this case at least, are *more* precise than de Man's own efforts to distinguish between "grammar," "logic," and "rhetoric."

Cavell is not so impatient with the minutia of everyday life. He takes Edith quite seriously:

> Let us to begin with be sure we remember that there are definite, practical differences between ways of lacing shoes, say between lacing them so that they crisscross and lacing them so that they are parallel. The former might be called lacing over, the latter lacing under. Apart from neatness of appearance, lacing under butts the edges better but takes a longer lace. ("Politics," 44)

Edith's question shows that she knows both her husband, and the difference between lacing over and lacing under, a difference that may well have an effect on the footwork of a competitive bowler. There really is no reason for de Man to accuse her of being a "reader of sublime simplicity" just because she decides to give a straight answer to a rhetorical question. Given Archie's temper, Edith would surely be unwise not to draw his attention to the difference.

As for de Man's key assertion, that Archie's "I don't give a damn what the difference is," actually *denies the existence* of a difference, Cavell begs to differ: "This form of words is likely to be used either to mean 'I'm not interested in the difference' (which in this case may be quite false) or else to mean 'The difference won't change my plans' (which would make good sense if, say, Mrs. Bunker were trying to *prevail* on Archie to wear the shoes)" ("Politics," 44). Against de Man, Cavell shows that Archie's line, if anything, *affirms* the difference: the point is that Archie doesn't want to hear about it, and certainly not from Edith.

Here I think de Man's formalism—his lack of interest in the actual speakers in their concrete situation—makes him deaf to the nuances of Archie's response. To my ears, the exchange between Archie and Edith is not a clash between two "mutually exclusive" meanings, but between a wife who wishes to explain something, and a husband who refuses to listen. This has more to do with the sexual politics of marriage than with some inherent tension between grammar and rhetoric.

De Man's gloss on Archie's exclamation is not his final word on the matter. A few lines later, he uses quite different terms to spell out the point: "A perfectly clear syntactical paradigm (the question) engenders a sentence that has at least two meanings, of which the one asserts and the other denies its own illocutionary mode" (SR, 10). But this adds nothing new. Here too something is being denied: not the "concept" provided by the literal meaning, but the sentence's own "illocutionary mode." The term "illocutionary" comes from Austin, who defines it as "the performance of an act *in* saying something."[34]

De Man appears to reasons as follows: Grammatically, "What's the difference?" is a question. But at the same time it's a *rhetorical* question, which means that it doesn't *really* ask about anything. Therefore it's a question denying that it's a question. Thus the sentence has two meanings, one asserting what the other denies. But this is unpersuasive. Of course, de Man is right to say that there is a difference between a rhetorical question and an actual question. But the *value* of that difference must be established anew in every case. Furthermore, de Man (again) assumes that *not to ask* a question is the same thing as to *deny* that the relevant sentence has the form of a question. But surely that's not the case. (Archie himself glosses his question as "who the hell cares," thus replacing one rhetorical question with another.)

But even if de Man were right, a natural question arises. Doesn't de Man's claims just amount to saying that "I can produce two different (or even contradictory) readings of the same sequence of signs"? (Here my rhetorical reading, there my grammatical reading.) After all, any sequence of signs can be interpreted in *any* way (cf. §28). But if so, de Man isn't telling us anything about rhetoric and grammar in general, let alone about their intrinsic tension; he is simply showing us two different perspectives on the same utterance. De Man is aware of the problem:

> It is not so that there are simply two meanings, one literal and the other figural, and that we have to decide which one of these meanings is the right one in this particular situation. The confusion can only be cleared up by the intervention of an extra-textual intention, such as Archie Bunker putting his wife straight; but the very anger he displays is indicative of more than impatience; it reveals his despair when confronted with a structure of linguistic meaning that he cannot control and that holds the discouraging prospect of an infinity of similar future confusions, all of them potentially catastrophic in their consequences. (SR, 10)

The objection calls forth de Man's staunchest enemy, the "extra-textual intention," the very thing that "Semiology and Rhetoric" sets out to exclude from literary studies. (Note the picture of intentions as clearly extra-textual, clearly outside the text. I return to this picture in chapter 9.) However, there is no argument here. De Man simply decides to up the stakes and interpret Archie's "extra-textual" anger as a desperate reaction to the truth of de Man's rhetorical analysis. This will simply not do. Either Archie's anger is "extra-textual" and thus irrelevant, or it is not. Right here, de Man's struggle to keep *context*—the human gestures, feelings, intentions, and convictions that accompany or find expression in our words and give them their precise value—out of his analysis and his theory fails.

What motivates de Man's rhetoric of despair and catastrophe? After

all, Archie doesn't seem to be anywhere close to despair, and his alterca-
tion with Edith does not have remarkable consequences. (Archie fails to
make the team, but not because Edith laced his shoes the wrong way.) It
is difficult to imagine that Archie's exasperation is caused, not by Edith,
but by a vision of an "infinity of similar future confusions" between literal
and figurative meanings.

But let us grant de Man his point, which seems to be that when we ask a
rhetorical question, we aren't usually asking a question. This is fair enough,
but hardly news. As I read on, I realize that de Man is inviting me to feel a
kind of dizzying intellectual exhilaration at the implications of this insight:
"The grammatical model of the question becomes rhetorical ... when it is
impossible to decide by grammatical or other linguistic devices which of
the two meanings (that can be entirely incompatible) prevails. Rhetoric
radically suspends logic and opens up vertiginous possibilities of referential aberration" (SR 10).

Now grammar and rhetoric have become something like two independent entities at war with one another. The conflict between them leaves
us unable to "decide" what the true meaning of the sentence is. We have
landed in the state of "suspended ignorance" which de Man sees as the inevitable result of a truly rigorous rhetorical reading (SR, 19). But if Archie's
rhetorical question doesn't in fact deny any difference, the very foundation
of the "undecidability" conclusion falls.

Cavell is not denying that one can say what de Man says. There is nothing to stop de Man from interpreting the same utterance in two contradictory ways, to label those interpretations "grammatical" and "rhetorical" and claim that they stand in melodramatic tension with one another.
The real question is *why* do so? The problem for Cavell is that de Man has
provided *no reason* to believe his claims about grammar, rhetoric, logic,
and literature.

Cavell is not entering into de Man's logic: he is not saying the opposite of de Man; he is saying that de Man's argument is not intelligible as
philosophy to him:

> In [*Allegories of Reading*] the claim to philosophical rigor is repeatedly
> made, but the work's discourse is one that pretty well, to my ear, ignores
> the paradigms of comprehensibility established in Anglo-American
> philosophy. Perhaps they should be ignored; it has occurred to me more
> than once over the years that they should. But I have said that I remain,
> instead, in quarrel with them; to that extent I cannot accept de Man's
> carelessness of them. ("Politics," 41)

Where de Man sees a dramatic deconstruction of the relationship between grammar and rhetoric, Cavell sees a willful imposition of melodrama on an ordinary phenomenon, namely the fact that we constantly use the "same grammatical pattern ... for different rhetorical effects" ("Politics," 43). To an ordinary language philosopher, this is hardly news:

> Austin's constative-performative distinction is about [the fact that] certain utterances that are grammatically statements are rhetorically something else. Shall we say that their rhetoric deconstructs their grammar, or is in tension with it, or that their grammatical pattern or their rhetorical function is somehow aberrant? ... But why say so?—as if the grammatical or rhetorical facts should be other than they are. You might as well say that it is perverse or aberrant of the normally functioning human hand that it can grasp, and make a fist, and play arpeggios, and shade the eyes, and be held up to bless or to swear. Does one of these possibilities repress or otherwise oppress the others? ("Politics," 43–44)[35]

For de Man, meaning arises from the sign. For ordinary language philosophy meaning arises only in use. Use is always a matter of what we *do*: When we speak, we are not just uttering signs, but engaging in all kinds of practices and relationships. An utterance, a speech act, is not just an example of a certain *form*, and it does not just describe (or otherwise relate to) the world, it also reveals the speaker's commitments. For Cavell, the "moral of the example" of Archie and Edith, is that there is "no inevitable relation" between grammar and rhetoric. He continues: "This seems to me the moral of ordinary language philosophy as well, and of the practice of art. Put it this way: Grammar cannot, or ought not, of itself dictate what you mean, what it is up to you to say" ("Politics," 45). For Cavell, the question of what we say and mean is always also ethical and political, a question of the responsibility we take for our words.

Unlike de Man, Cavell can draw no dizzying conclusions, not just because there is nothing "vertiginous" at stake, but because he takes an interest in the specific speakers and their situation. To him, the scene between Archie and Edith doesn't tell us anything about grammar or rhetoric, but rather something about a particular man and a particular woman, and maybe also something about comic marriages on television. If there is an ambivalence in Archie's response to Edith, Cavell writes, "that is a fact about some Archie, not about the inevitable relation between grammar and rhetoric" ("Politics," 45).

The Archie Debunker? Condescension, Jokes, and Puns

De Man is aware that the Archie Bunker example alone doesn't warrant his extreme conclusions: "As long as we are talking about bowling shoes, the consequences are relatively trivial" (SR, 9). To make his point, therefore, he asks us to imagine that a different speaker now utters the same sentence:

> But suppose that it is a *de*-bunker rather than a "Bunker," and a de-bunker of the arche (or origin), an archie Debunker such as Nietzsche or Jacques Derrida for instance, who asks the question "What is the Difference"—and we cannot even tell from his grammar whether he "really" wants to know "what" difference is or is just telling us that we shouldn't even try to find out.... For what is the use of asking, I ask, when we cannot even authoritatively decide whether a question asks or doesn't ask? (SR 9–10).[36]

The new speaking situation has two key features: it is entirely abstract: we know nothing about the situation, or what the conversation is about. All we know is that Archie and Edith have been replaced by two philosophical authority figures. Now we are no longer talking about shoelaces, but about difference as such. We also realize, as Cavell did, that the only reason de Man even bothered to mention Archie and Edith was to set up this "exceptionally elaborate gag" ("Politics," 43).

Cavell does not find it funny, and neither do I. The gag is condescending in a way I find slightly distasteful: While the working-class Archie "muddles along" without fully realizing what he is saying; the "archie Debunkers" of this world utter their rhetorical questions with consummate self-ironic expertise. In any case, I don't see why de Man should care about origins. And doesn't he place rather too much faith in his Archie Debunkers? As if Derrida or Nietzsche could never exclaim "What's the difference!" in a fit of misogynist exasperation? I find this joke too condescending toward ordinary speakers of the language to be able to enjoy it.

This may sound nitpicking. Can't we just let de Man enjoy his pun without making such a meal of it? But few things signal a difference in sensibility, in outlook on the world, in fundamental assumptions, better than a joke that succeeds with some listeners and fails with others. Cavell notes that de Man's supporters upbraided him for failing to appreciate the joke about the "archie Debunker" ("Politics," 47 n. 10). This reminds me of the accusation that feminists who fail to laugh at sexist jokes have no sense of humor. In both cases the failure to appreciate the joke is taken to prove that there is something wrong with the hearer. Moreover, there is always more than a touch of aggression or disappointment in such accusations, for they arise from a sense of pain or rejection, likely to arise in a situation when we realize that we are facing someone who doesn't get our jokes, someone who is not quite sharing our world, someone whose reactions reveal that we are not, or not quite, in community with one another.

When a joke succeeds, teller and hearer "are joined in feeling," Ted Cohen writes. When it fails, "what has failed is the effort to achieve an intimacy between teller and hearer. It is a failure to join one another in a community of appreciation."[37] When we cannot share each other's jokes, we become a peculiar sort of stranger to one another. It's not that we can't understand each other at all (you could explain your joke to me, and I could surely come to see the point, but that isn't the same thing as finding it funny), it is rather that the failed joke reveals that we don't share enough of a world, of a form of life, to be spontaneously at ease together. Whether this is a problem depends on one's hopes and wishes in relation to the other person.

But what does it mean to share or not share a world? When we learn to speak, we also learn to respond to other people's words, their concepts. We grow up to share with others "routes of interest and feeling, modes of response, senses of humor and of significance and of fulfillment," Cavell writes.[38] But this means that we grow up to become exquisitely aware of the moments when we don't quite share such things. Maybe the first inkling is a fleeting feeling of annoyance at a far too elaborate pun.

Cavell doesn't share de Man's sense of what counts as a convincing conclusion. To Cavell, the discovery of such a profound separation is not just a matter of personal taste, but of the standards of intelligibility in philosophy. Drawing on the passage about forms of life that I just quoted, Cora Diamond writes: "You take yourself not to be sharing the same moral world if your response to something he says is, for example, 'How can he have adduced that here? How can he so much as think that relevant?'"[39] This is exactly what I think when I consider some of de Man's claims.

In the case of Archie Bunker and the archie Debunker, the joke that fails to join us in feeling is a pun of modest wit. While the unexpected juxtaposition of Archie Bunker, Jacques Derrida, and Friedrich Nietzsche produces a slight shock, even hardcore poststructuralists surely can't have found it more than mildly funny. Why would de Man think it worthwhile to go to such elaborate lengths to set it up? One reason, surely, is that he considers puns exemplary of the case he wants to make. "Puns," Jonathan Culler writes, "are not a marginal form of wit but an exemplary product of language or mind."[40]

For poststructuralists, puns are the "foundation of letters," the very "model of language" because they demonstrate that the same sounds or letters can have different meanings, and thus reveals a deep truth about language itself: "Puns both evoke prior formulations, with the meanings they have deployed, and demonstrate their instability, the mutability of meaning, the production of meaning by linguistic motivation. Puns ... produce effects of meaning—with a looseness, unpredictability, excessiveness, shall we say, that cannot but disrupt the model of language as nomenclature."[41] For post-Saussureans like de Man and Culler, puns provide an attractive model of language because they show that words aren't names intrinsically connected to things, a point which is then taken to prove that reference itself is always unstable.

Gordon Bearn makes the case even more explicitly. He is fascinated by inadvertent puns, which he takes to show that we "have to give up the idea that a word or concept has one central meaning, perhaps its literal meaning." And since no meaning qualifies as the "real" or "literal" one any longer, Bearn writes, then "there is no one thing which is the meaning of a text, ... no one thing which is our meaning, no one thing which is what we meant to say, no one thing which we are understood as saying."[42] Thus de Man's elaborate pun both illustrates and enacts the point he wants to make: that Archie's "What's the difference" can have more than one meaning, and that meaning therefore is far more unstable than Archie could ever have imagined. I don't object to any of this. I am rather thinking that de Man is breaking down open doors. For who believes that words are names in this way, or that a text or an utterance can have only one meaning? Surely we don't need elaborate puns to realize this?

Like Culler and Bearn, de Man is committed to the project of elaborating a *theory* of language as such. Here the word "theory" means something like a conceptual description capable of subsuming under itself all the possible features and phenomena of language. For de Man, language is a system or a structure that lends itself to a general theory; for Cavell, it is an infinite number of past, present, and future speech acts, which can't be theorized once and for all. "Wittgenstein," Cavell notes, "has no philosophy of language at all. He can better be read as attacking philosophy's wish to provide theories of language" (CR, 15).

We have returned, then, to the difference between seeing a pun (or Archie's rhetorical question) as representative of "language as such," and seeing it as a specific speech act uttered by a specific person in a specific context. Both de Man and Cavell believe that the same utterance can have many meanings. But they frame that observation very differently, and the conclusions they draw, or refuse to draw, from it are also very different.

As we have seen, while de Man deconstructs the relationship between rhetoric and grammar, Cavell asks why anyone would want to do so in the first place. When de Man claims that Archie's "What's the difference?" contains the key to a whole theory of language, Cavell thinks it only shows something about "some Archie." If Cavell has little sympathy for de Man's case it is not because he believes in the "naïve" view of grammar, or thinks that language is a set of stable names with secure reference, it is because he doesn't think that it is either possible or desirable to have a general theory of language, and, ultimately, it is because his notion of what counts as philosophy or "theory" is fundamentally different from de Man's.

Critique, Clarity, and Common Sense

ORDINARY LANGUAGE PHILOSOPHY AND POLITICS

Marcuse's Mandarin Sensibilities

Is ordinary language philosophy reactionary? Ernest Gellner (*Words and Things*, 1959) and Herbert Marcuse (*One-Dimensional Man*, 1964) certainly thought so. Today, political critiques of Austin and Wittgenstein still give voice to their views: Ordinary language philosophy is doomed to repeat and reinforce the reactionary ideology embedded in common sense; Austin's philosophy expresses nothing but the complacent conservatism of the Oxford common room in the 1950s; Wittgenstein endorses a passive, contemplative stance towards social and political problems.[1]

Although Gellner's arguments have largely been discredited, they shouldn't be overlooked. For he influenced many other philosophers, not least Marcuse.[2] But if anyone ever convinced intellectuals that Wittgenstein and Austin are the enemies of "critique," it was Marcuse. In *One-Dimensional Man*, Marcuse's ostensive target is "linguistic analysis," which is his term for the rather varied landscape of the so-called "Oxford philosophy" in the 1940s and 1950s. Nevertheless, Wittgenstein and Austin are his main targets and provide almost all his examples.[3] In Marcuse's account, his own "negative thinking" contrasts starkly with Wittgenstein and Austin's "positive thinking." Negative thinkers are "radically non-conformist," free spirits capable of challenging the most stifling ideologies. In contrast, "linguistic analysis" is a sour and schoolmaster-like positivism eager to make us submit to the tyranny of the "common usage of words." As such it is "intrinsically ideological," incapable of thinking outside the "societal framework," enforcing slavish conformity in words and behavior: "It leaves the established reality untouched; it abhors transgression," Marcuse declares (OM, 171–73).

Marcuse's antipathy toward Wittgenstein and Austin is so pervasive that even a casual reader feels that more is at stake than just the usual philosophical disagreements. This is a clash of radically different philosophical sensibilities. Marcuse and Wittgenstein have different views on what philosophy is and what it should do. Their assessment of what is interesting and significant is also dramatically different. Marcuse champions the hidden and the deep. Wittgenstein yearns for clarity. Marcuse has no devotion to the "common, the familiar, the everyday, the low, the near."[4] He scoffs at Wittgenstein's "almost masochistic reduction of speech to the humble and common," and even objects to Wittgenstein's use of the "intimate or condescending '*du*' [*you*]" (as opposed to the more formal *Sie*) (OM, 174, 177). In his mandarin disdain for the ordinary, Marcuse even takes Austin to task for using the "colloquial abridgments of ordinary speech: 'Don't …' 'isn't …'" (175). He is also outraged by the stunning banality, the utter insignificance of Wittgenstein's and Austin's examples. Imagine, Wittgenstein talks about broomsticks! And Austin spends pages analyzing nuances of taste and smell! (See 175–77.)[5]

I am not sure that such an abyss can be bridged. It certainly can't be bridged by simple persuasion. Maybe it will take something more like a conversion experience.[6] When I first read Austin discussing goldfinches and dead donkeys, I was elated. I enjoyed his quirky and witty examples. What a change from the usual turgid theoretical prose![7] But where I find philosophical relevance, wit, and understanding, Marcuse only finds unwarranted familiarity and petty-minded banality. Marcuse's contempt for the particular case—his lack of respect for the intellectual power of examples—makes him unable to see that Austin's discussion of ordinary experiences of taste and smell illuminate long-standing philosophical questions concerning human knowledge, or that the case of the dead donkeys has a bearing on how we think about freedom and responsibility.

This attitude isn't unique to Marcuse or to Marxist thinkers. The hermeneuticist Paul Ricoeur shared the same disdain for the ordinary. Criticizing Wittgenstein for "situat[ing] himself immediately in this world of everyday experience, in which language is a form of activity like eating, drinking, and sleeping," Ricoeur praised Saussure's understanding of language precisely because it manages to remove us from the everyday. For Ricoeur, language "does not belong to life," and neither does philosophy.[8]

Marcuse's philosophical imagination is dramatic, even melodramatic. He wants to discuss the atomic bomb, capitalist consumer society, the meaning of life. This is (of course) fine. Marcuse even agrees that we can *begin* interesting work by paying close attention to "the most banal examples of speech" (OM, 176). But the agreement with ordinary language philosophy goes no further. At this point a chasm opens: "Critical philosophical thought" may well be concerned with ordinary language, Marcuse writes, but only in so far as it sets out to "reveal that 'hidden' something which is of no interest to Wittgenstein" (181). Marcuse thinks of critique as a form of suspicion, as the hard work of delving beneath misleading surfaces. Wittgenstein, who declares that "nothing is hidden," is taken to be incapable of even discovering a misleading surface (§435).[9]

For Marcuse, philosophy is incompatible with the ordinary. There is, he writes, an "irreducible difference ... between the universe of everyday thinking and language on the one side, and that of philosophic thinking and language on the other" (OM, 178). The ordinary is hopelessly vague and muddled: "exactness and clarity in philosophy cannot be attained within the universe of the ordinary" (179). To do his work, the critical philosopher must keep his distance, not submerge himself in the messiness of the ordinary: "Critical analysis must dissociate itself from that which it strives to comprehend; the philosophic terms must be other than the ordinary ones in order to elucidate the full meaning of the latter" (193). The critical philosopher needs concepts uncontaminated by ordinary language.

Wittgenstein strongly disagrees. He points out that even the most scientific or philosophical language, including language about language, is ordinary language: "When I talk about language (word, sentence, etc.), I must speak the language of every day. So is this language too coarse, too material, for what we want to say? *Well then, how is another one to be constructed?*" (§120). Marcuse makes no attempt to answer. He has no recipe for how to construct a language that could escape the concepts and distinctions of ordinary language—that is, human language as we use it now. It is as if Marcuse thinks that his critique of Wittgenstein is constructed in something other than ordinary language.

Marcuse believes that the "ordinary universe" is synonymous with the flattened, one-dimensional world of consumer society, a world in which the ruling powers unilaterally "shape the restricted experience" available to ordinary human beings. In such a universe, ordinary language can only express banal thoughts (OM, 180). In Marcuse's mind, the "chap in the street" simply can't say anything that goes against the grain of the ideological universe shaped for him by the powers that be (174). Genuine critique can only come from intellectuals, philosophers capable of deploying a specialist philosophical language beyond the grasp of the common "chap in the street." More self-conscious, more politically alert, such intellectuals alone can cut through the "prevailing variety of meanings and usages" (175).

Because they trust the ordinary, and believe that perfectly ordinary people are at least as capable as philosophers of making relevant and useful distinctions, Marcuse assumes that Wittgenstein and Austin must be marching in lockstep with dominant ideology. For Marcuse, their philosophy "militates against intelligent non-conformity" (OM, 174) and can do nothing but kowtow to power.

For a long time, I thought Marcuse's and Gellner's arguments against Wittgenstein and Austin were so obviously polemical, and so intellectually feeble, that there was no need to discuss them. Surely, anyone who bothered to read Wittgenstein and Austin would see right through them, I thought. This was both too simplistic and too optimistic. Marcuse remains part of our intellectual heritage. We—critics on the left—still can't "just read" Wittgenstein and Austin as if we had never heard of Marcuse.

This chapter, then, will deal with political critiques of ordinary language philosophy. I shall show that there is no reason why politically engaged intellectuals should turn their backs on Wittgenstein, Austin, and Cavell.[10] Both Gellner and Marcuse misread the philosophy they were so quick to attack. The misreadings surface most strikingly in relation to two concepts, namely "ordinary" or "everyday" language, and "forms of life."

Marcuse's disdain for the ordinary, the everyday, and common sense, as well as his conviction that critical thought requires a special "philosophical" language, also fuel the recurrent debates about the writing style of radical theorists, which usually always return to the questions of common sense (is it always reactionary?) and clarity, and thus to the question of how to write theory. Must radical theory always be excruciatingly difficult to read? Is there something intrinsically radical about impenetrable prose? These are the questions I'll examine in this chapter. But I'll begin with Gellner, since he came first.

Gellner: Forms of Life

The philosopher and sociologist Ernst Gellner published *Words and Things*, his hugely influential attack on "linguistic philosophy," in 1959. By "linguistic philosophers" Gellner originally meant anyone working on the philosophy of language in Britain.[11] However, there is no doubt that Wittgenstein was Gellner's *bête noire*.[12] Gellner's breezily dismissive style of anti-Wittgensteinian polemics, T. P. Uschanov writes, was quickly taken up by "thinkers as diverse as Marcuse, Popper, Habermas and Deleuze."[13] Gellner's visceral distaste for Wittgenstein is certainly echoed by Gilles Deleuze, who (in)famously calls Wittgenstein a "philosophical disaster" (*un catastrophe philosophique*), and declares that all Wittgensteinians are "terrorists."[14]

Gellner's critique of Wittgenstein's "forms of life" has been particularly influential. In §43, Wittgenstein writes: "The meaning of a word is its use in the language." I don't mean to imply that it is easy to grasp Wittgenstein's vision of "use."[15] But Gellner doesn't even try. First, he turns the phrase into a handy mantra: "meaning is use." Inexplicably, he takes this to mean that Wittgenstein "endorses anything that 'has a use.'"[16] This is like arguing that anyone who understands English must agree with every utterance made in the English language. By saying that meaning is use, Wittgenstein obviously isn't *endorsing* any particular utterance.

Wittgenstein never says that we can't challenge what people say. (He certainly never hesitated to do so himself.) On the contrary: "What is true or false is what human being *say*; and it is in their *language* that human beings agree. This is agreement not in opinions, but rather in forms of life" (§241). Even the most violent disagreements arise within a shared language. What is common sense to me may be pure madness to you. But if I don't share your language, I will never even realize that your utterances are fundamentally unacceptable to me. The more adept I am at ferreting out your hidden ideological agenda, the better I demonstrate my grasp of the finest nuances of your specific way of speaking. The more astute my critique, the better it demonstrates that we share both the words and the world we are fighting over.

Because Gellner believes that Wittgenstein simply endorses whatever is said in a language, he also believes that the discovery that we live in a world with more than one culture strikes a fatal blow against Wittgenstein's philosophy. For when cultures clash, when different communities have different uses, how do we decide which use to go with? To Gellner, the answer is obvious: we need to examine our forms of life dispassionately and rationally, and then choose the best. Because Wittgenstein's philosophy considers language to be grounded in "forms of life" which we can't escape, Gellner claims, it obliges us to accept existing norms, practices, and ideologies as the only truth, for it offers no vantage point for us rationally to evaluate competing institutions and worldviews.[17]

This argument hasn't aged well, mostly because it assumes that in order to assess our forms of life, we need to stand outside them.[18] On this point, Gellner finds himself at odds with a long Marxist tradition that insists that critique is immanent, that it consists in showing up the contradictions and assumptions of our own system, ideology, discursive regime, or mode of production.

But here we must tread carefully. My argument—that Gellner is wrong to assume that critique requires an external vantage point—can itself be profoundly misleading, for it may give rise to the idea that while Gellner is wrong about the external vantage point, he is right about what Wittgenstein means by "forms of life," namely worldviews, ideologies, social conventions—the sort of things we can actually be critical about, the sort of things we can change by personal or collective decision. But he is not. Gellner, and Marcuse too, have a far too "conventionalist" understanding of "forms of life." Wittgenstein's "forms of life" aren't synonymous with "social norms" or "social conventions." They go deeper than that. To assume that we can simply choose between forms of life, as if they were so many different options on the shop shelves, is not to understand the concept at all.[19]

Gellner also thinks that Wittgenstein's philosophy is insulated from reality, and thus from politics and society, because "linguistic philosophy" only deals with language, not with the world. This argument is based on Gellner's "mirror theory of meaning," which holds that the meaning of a word is the thing it refers to.[20] According to Gellner, anyone who denies this self-evident claim will find himself locked up in a self-enclosed linguistic capsule drifting free of reality.

Most intellectuals today would utterly disagree with Gellner's "mirror theory or meaning," which also happens to be a version of the "Augustinian" picture of language Wittgenstein sets out to dismantle. As we have seen in *Philosophical Investigations*, he shows that use is a form of action, that word and world are enmeshed, that anyone who thinks that language only does one thing—namely represent or refer—will soon discover that they can't even explain how we understand the simplest sentence, such as a request for "five red apples" (§1).

How to Read §124

Both Marcuse and Gellner accuse Wittgenstein of quietism. The claim is that he thought that philosophers should let things be, refrain from intervening in social and political affairs. Such arguments usually draw on §124:

> Philosophy must not interfere in any way with the actual use of language, so it can in the end only describe it.
> For it cannot justify it either.
> It leaves everything as it is.

To politically committed critics, Wittgenstein's warning against "interfering" with language appears to be the negation of everything critical philosophy represents. Marcuse's outraged response to §124 exemplifies the attitude. For Marcuse, §124 is a "general proposition on philosophical thought." As such it exemplifies "academic sado-masochism, self-humiliation, and self-denunciation of the intellectual whose labor does not issue in scientific, technical or like achievements" (OM, 173).

Of course, Marcuse misreads. But his reaction is representative. This particular paragraph has caused widespread consternation among left-wing intellectuals. Ben Ware shows that the British Marxist Raymond Williams also shared Marcuse's views.[21] Why do so many intellectuals feel horrified by the idea that philosophy shouldn't "interfere with" the ordinary use of language? What cherished project do they take Wittgenstein to forbid? I imagine that many think of racist, sexist, and homophobic uses of language. Perhaps they take Wittgenstein to be saying that philosophers should simply describe ugly racist slurs, and otherwise leave them be. If so, no wonder they get upset.

To such readers, Cavell's comment, "What the statement means is that, though of course there are any number of ways of changing ordinary language, philosophizing does not change it," may look as if it begs the question.[22] Surely, they will say, we need to change language! And surely the task of philosophy is to help us change it! But does §124 prevent us from trying to change language, or anything else? In other words: what exactly is Wittgenstein saying here?

Marcuse may be misled by the simplicity of Wittgenstein's prose. The paragraph is more difficult than he assumes. Taken together, these three sentences raise three interwoven questions: What is ordinary language (the "actual use of language")? What is philosophy? And what counts as "interfering" with ordinary language? In German, Wittgenstein's "to interfere with" (antasten) has two major fields of meaning: (1) to touch or to finger; and (2) to break into, to violate, to infringe, or to encroach. Wittgenstein is saying that philosophy mustn't violate ordinary language. But what does this mean? What exactly is it philosophy mustn't do? Wittgenstein distinguishes between what philosophy *must not in any way* (*darf...in keiner Weise*) do and what it *can* and *cannot* (*kann; kann ... nicht*) do. One way of reading the first sentence is to say that he is exhorting philosophers *not* to do something that in any case can't be done. If that is to make sense, he must mean *both* that philosophers are constantly tempted to build programs — develop ways of thinking — that do set out to "interfere with" the actual use of language, *and* that such programs are doomed to fail. This is in fact Wittgenstein's view.

Section 124 appears just as Wittgenstein has completed a long critique of positivist attempts to build a language consisting of "crystalline" concepts, a language positivists hoped would grasp the world as it is, without the vagueness, imprecision, and "noise" of ordinary language. Cavell explains, rightly, that the idea of "interfering" with language refers to Wittgenstein's critique of philosophy's tendency to distort perfectly ordinary words, such as "see," "believe," "doubt" and so on, to use them in ways that conflict with their ordinary use, yet all the while trading on that use for philosophical effect.[23] This is how philosophy removes words from their "everyday use" and turns them into metaphysics (see §116). The result is a peculiar kind of incoherence, which prevents us from seeing our own situation clearly, and which can be extremely hard to diagnose.

For Wittgenstein, the task of philosophy is to dissolve the confusions produced when we lose touch with the everyday in this way. (Note that he is talking about getting clear on *our own* confusions, not about correcting other people from a position of superiority.) But this is harder than we think, for we tend to get lost in our own words, to fall victim to the illusion that our way of framing the problem makes sense. And as long as we are convinced we have no problems, we won't seek therapy. But if we won't acknowledge that we are lost, we can't even begin the philosophical work: "A philosophical problem has the form: 'I don't know my way about'" (§123). Such a therapy consists in getting to a point where we can see clearly the picture that "[holds] us captive" (§115). Then we will realize that there was, after all, no necessity in seeing things in that way. What we took to be our philosophical problems were nothing but illusions, "houses of cards" (*Luftgebäude*; §118). Ideally, this therapy should reach "*complete* clarity," Wittgenstein writes, "but this simply means that the philosophical problems should *completely* disappear" (§133).[24] The therapeutic understanding of philosophy is the opposite of philosophy as a master-discourse, or philosophy as the "queen of the disciplines," as the French used to call it. Wittgenstein doesn't tell us what to do. Rather, he waits, patiently, for us to realize that we have a problem. Ordinary language philosophy doesn't speak first: it *responds*.

What Wittgenstein actually says in §124, then, is that philosophy can neither ground nor justify the actual use of language. *Nothing* grounds use. This doesn't mean that use is grounded on nothing. (Whether one asserts or denies that use has a ground, one is stuck in the same old picture.) It means, rather, that the very picture of a ground is misleading. Section 124 does not deny that language changes, it just denies that *philosophers* have any special power over the evolution of language. It also denies that philosophical attempts to construct ideal languages—more exact, more logical, more critical than ordinary language—will ever work. Wittgenstein is keenly aware of linguistic change. He insists that use is infinitely open, that language is ever-changing and endlessly diverse: "And this diversity is not something fixed, given once for all; but new types of language, new language-games, as we may say, come into existence, and others become obsolete and get forgotten" (§23).

In §124, then, Wittgenstein is not saying that we shouldn't try to change the world. Rather, he is saying that some philosophers have the wrong picture of how language works and fail to realize that they too use ordinary language. To Wittgenstein, the way we speak reveals the way we live: "And to imagine a language means to imagine a form of life" (§19). To change our language means to change our attitude, our way of dealing with others, our way of being in the world. Coining new, super-rigorous ("crystalline") philosophical terms won't help. If the best philosophy, the best theories of racism, or sexism, or homophobia, contribute powerfully to social and political change, it is not because they "interfere ... with the actual use of language," but because they help us to see the world, and other people, more clearly.

Wittgenstein's §124 doesn't tell us that we just have to accept sexist or racist slurs. Nor does it deny that language changes in many ways, including in response to intellectual or scientific developments. The real question is whether Wittgenstein's kind of therapeutic philosophy can be useful to radical thinkers. I obviously think the answer is yes. Every time a critical or political project runs aground because of the confusion of its own concepts, it needs Wittgensteinian therapy.[25]

The purpose of his kind of philosophy is to dispel illusions, undo the false ideas, free us from the prison-houses created by our own uses of language, to help us make our way back to the ordinary and the everyday, help us to see clearly what Wittgenstein calls our "real need" (§108). We don't enter into philosophical therapy in order to offer a new *theory* of anything, but rather to get clear on beliefs and assumptions that hold us captive, that prevent us from moving on. There is no contradiction between such a philosophical project and the wish to change the world.

Power, Unmasking, Critique

Critics of ordinary language philosophy believe that this philosophy can't carry out vigorous critique of anything. In literary studies the underlying assumption is usually that since ordinary language philosophy refuses to accept the picture of language as intrinsically hiding anything, it can't ferret out the ideological crimes lurking beneath the surface of language. It is certainly true that Wittgenstein and Cavell challenge the very idea of a "surface of language." But we don't need to accept the idea that language has surface and depths in order to think critically.[26]

In fact, ordinary language philosophy excels at critique, unmasking, undoing of illusion. For Cavell "ordinary language philosophy is a mode of interpretation and inherently involved in the politics of interpretation."[27] Austin, Cavell writes, is also a philosopher of "unmasking" in the lineage of Marx, Nietzsche, and Freud.[28] As for Wittgenstein, one of his major themes is the undoing of illusions. The very aspiration to clarity, to get to a clear view (*übersichtliche Darstellung*; §122), the wish to get out of the prison-house of the picture that holds us captive (§115), the wish to turn the inquiry around "on the pivot of our real need" (§108) ought to be cherished by anyone who wants to engage in critique.

But one objection to ordinary language philosophy is justified. Wittgenstein, Austin, and Cavell offer no theory of the relationship between language and power. Ordinary language philosophy offers no theory of anything, and certainly not of "language as such," or of "power" in its broad generality.[29] From an ordinary language philosophy point of view, the very request for a theory of "the relationship" between language and power is troublesome. For it sets up a picture in which "language" appears to be a totalizable entity that could have a "theorizable" relationship to another totalizable entity called "power." That picture needs to be challenged. Not by claiming that language has no relationship to power—to deny a meaningless picture is as meaningless as to assert it—but by giving up the idea that we can ever make "language as such" fall under a theory. Wittgenstein, Austin, and Cavell aren't denying anything at all about power and language. There is nothing to stop us from analyzing the imbrication of power and language. We just have to do it by paying attention to particulars.

We have returned to the most fundamental difference between ordinary language philosophy and more conventional philosophies, namely Wittgenstein's refusal to give in to the craving for generality.[30] Claims such as "there is power in everything" cancel all the way through. There may well be "power in everything," but this still leaves us with the task of investigating how power works in the particular case. Such claims don't tell us what we need to know about power.

Nancy Bauer provides a good example of how one can pay attention to particulars as a feminist. When feminists first began to talk about "sexual objectification," she writes, it was part of a "feminist shift in how to understand the world and one's experience in it."[31] Once feminists began to see the world as one in which women were systematically oppressed and disadvantaged, the term "sexual objectification" began to "light up" experiences in new ways. It became part of a new understanding of what it is to be a woman. Bauer shows how an oppressed group began to use language to challenge ingrained patterns of power, while emphasizing both the difficulty and the possibility of creating new insights in a situation of oppression. Such work is far more illuminating and helpful than blanket statements about power and language.

In the 1980s and 1990s many feminists embraced the post-Saussurean configuration of politics (power) and language. We took the new insistence on the "signifying process" (as opposed to "reference") to mean that language shapes reality, that cultural and social values enter into our most fundamental discourses and practices.[32] There is nothing here that a Wittgensteinian needs to disagree with. And, as I hope I have shown, ordinary language philosophy does a much better job of connecting world and words than post-Saussurean visions of language. There simply is no reason for feminists to prefer Saussure over Wittgenstein.

Wittgenstein certainly doesn't offer a theory of class, gender, or race. But ordinary language philosophy doesn't try to be a *substitute* for specific knowledge about the world. If you want to understand the role of the working class in history, you need to read Marx. If you want to understand the oppression of women, you need to read Beauvoir, and so on. If we want to fight sexism and racism, or challenge capitalism, we need to understand sexism, racism, or capitalism. (If we want to launch a revolution, we need to learn the language of revolution.) Ordinary language philosophy doesn't prevent us from reading Freud or Foucault. It leaves us free to work on power in all its manifestations, without falling victim to the philosophical confusions that will arise from conventional theory's craving for generality.

Ordinary language philosophy refuses to lay down requirements for what we *must* do, what we must or must not be interested in. It leaves the responsibility for our political and intellectual investments to us. It certainly makes us wish for radical change in intellectual life. Yet Wittgenstein himself thought intellectual change was secondary to a change in *Lebensweise*—"a change in the way we live."[33]

What Is Ordinary Language?

Marcuse is convinced that ordinary language philosophy is a kind of positivism. This belief underpins his political critique of "positive" as opposed to "negative" thinking. But what is a positivist understanding of language? Stanley Fish, who also believes that "ordinary language" is a positivist notion, provides an excellent definition. For him, ordinary language is a "kind of language that 'merely' presents or mirrors facts independently of any consideration of value, interest, perspective, purpose, and so on."[34] Marcuse and Fish agree, in short, that proponents of "ordinary language" believe that language always conveys the objective truth, always presents facts neutrally.

For Marcuse, the accusation of positivism has far-reaching political implications. Such a scientistic view of language, he claims, leaves no space for ideology, false consciousness, or for utopias and visions of change. This is why he declares that Wittgenstein and Austin uncritically endorse the "prevailing variety of meanings and usages, [and] the power and common sense of ordinary speech" and imprison us in the "universe of ordinary discourse" (OM, 175, 177). For Fish, "ordinary language" leaves no space for affective, emotional, and figurative language, which to him means no space for literature. Values belong to literature; ordinary language is the tool of science.

But such oppositions cannot hold. Wittgenstein and Austin aren't logical positivists. Their vision of language has nothing to do with scientism. On the contrary, they developed their philosophies in stark *opposition* to the positivist program, which wanted philosophy to develop a language consisting of nothing but "propositions," statements that are either true or false, and therefore represent the world (or fail to) without interference. For the positivists, only "propositions" convey knowledge. They are "cognitive" utterances. Other kinds of utterances are "emotive," for they simply express the speaker's feelings and subjective judgments. But as Cavell reminds us, the "single most telling blow against the tyranny of this distinction between cognitive and emotive meaning came with Austin's counter-distinction between constative and performative utterances."[35] For Austin, there can be no such thing as a purely descriptive, literal, or objective language. For Wittgenstein, *use* always requires judgment, and reveals both how I see the world and what my own investments and values are.

For Wittgenstein, Austin, and Cavell "ordinary language" is not a particular kind of language, whether scientistic or artistic. Ordinary language is not restricted to "the common usage of words" understood as the talk of "the chap on the street," as Marcuse believes (OM, 171, 174). Ordinary language is not limited to one specific socioeconomic group, nor is it a simplified or "basic" version of some kind of "standard" language. Ordinary language is not a normative notion. It is simply "what we say." And "we" here means every speaker of the language, not just a select high-status group. It is, simply, language that *works*, language that helps us to draw useful distinctions, carry out tasks, engage fruitfully with others—in short, language as the medium in which we live our lives, language as it is used every day in myriad different speech acts. Ordinary language, in short, comprises the full resources of human language, all its powers to draw distinctions.

Wittgenstein even places "the symbolism of chemistry and the notation of the infinitesimal calculus" in the "new suburbs" of the "ancient city of language" (§18). As the ancient city grows, we expand and rebuild some old houses, and tear others down to make way for modern buildings. Language does not change by philosophical decree, but with the needs and practices of human life. Of course, philosophy is one of those practices, but it has no privileged status as a kind of master-practice of language, any more than it has a special status as a kind of master-practice of mathematics.

For Wittgenstein, there is only ordinary language. The "opposite" of ordinary language, if we can call it that, does not escape the ordinary. On the contrary, it trades on ordinary use precisely by trying to "interfere" with it. Wittgenstein calls such attempts to lead us away from the ordinary "metaphysics." To think well we must find our way back to the ordinary: "What *we* do is to bring words back from their metaphysical to their everyday use" (§116). Metaphysical language is language "on holiday" (§38), language that misleads us by looking as if it is doing important work, but in fact isn't doing anything: it is just like an engine "idling" (§132). Cavell sees both skepticism and "whatever metaphysics is designed to overcome skepticism" as departures from the ordinary.[36] But metaphysics and skepticism aren't matters of individual words (as if some words were intrinsically more philosophical than others): they emerge in *use*, in the way we deploy our words. Such language may *look* ordinary, but it does no work.

Ordinary language is language that teaches us differences. This is why ordinary language does not stand in opposition to specialist vocabularies, technical expressions, or to the language of chemistry and mathematics. Ordinary language is certainly not the opposite of "literary" language. (In my view, there is no such thing as "literary language.") Nor is ordinary language the opposite of "extraordinary language."[37] The extraordinary is at home in the ordinary. (We share perfectly ordinary criteria for when to apply the concept.) There is nothing extraordinary about the extraordinary.

Specialized languages are ordinary. Think of the language of, say, *haute couture, haute cuisine,* or car mechanics. Just because many of us don't know what "molecular cuisine" or "*sous vide*" cooking is, have no clue how to tell a padstitch from a slipstitch, and are utterly ignorant of what a float chamber has to do with a carburetor, it doesn't follow that such terms aren't ordinary. They work just like other words, and hold no mystery for the practitioners of these arts. (The same is true for philosophical terms, unless they are used in ways that unmoor them from the ordinary.) If you are interested in learning the language-games in which such words are normally at home (this usually means: if you are interested in learning to *do* these things), the practitioners will be able to train you, to teach you their criteria, initiate you into their world. Eventually you will be able to go on, to project these terms in new contexts.

Clarity: The "Bad Writing Contest"

Nothing is more ironic than Marcuse's idea that ordinary language philosophy must be the enemy of difficult or stylistically challenging writing. If this were true, we would have to begin by denouncing the writing of Wittgenstein (gnomic and startlingly counterintuitive), Austin (those off-putting lists with headings and subheadings, packed with neologisms that usually come to nothing), and Cavell (the self-consciousness! the endless doubling back! the constant effort to say it and qualify it at the same time!). Ordinary language philosophy neither recommends nor forbids any particular writing style. How you write will depend on who you are, who you are writing for, and what you want to do with your writing. The style of theory or philosophy can't be discussed in general and in the abstract.[38]

Unfortunately, discussions of academic writing on the left are still conducted almost exclusively on Marcuse's terms. That was certainly the case for the battle over the so-called Bad Writing Contest, which left me feeling quite despondent. I can't subscribe to Marcuse's understanding of the difference between "ordinary" and "philosophical" language. I certainly can't join him in his disdain for the critical capacities of ordinary people. Nor do I believe that common sense is always conservative. At the same time, I despise the smug anti-intellectualism of the conservative critics who organized the "contest." How could they ever think that one sentence taken out of context proves anything about serious intellectual work? The debate placed me in a position I have come to know well: the discovery that premises that make sense to my colleagues appear alienating and unproductive to me. (This is how one begins to wish for a revolution.)

What was the "Bad Writing Contest"? From 1995 to 1998 the journal *Philosophy and Literature* ran a flagrantly biased "competition" designed to "[celebrate] the most stylistically lamentable passages found in scholarly books and articles published in the last few years."[39] Among the winners were Roy Bhaskar, Fredric Jameson, and Judith Butler. In 1998 Homi Bhaba was named runner-up after Judith Butler. These "winners" are all left-wing critics: Bhaskar and Jameson are Marxists, Butler a founder of queer theory, Bhaba a leading postcolonial scholar. In each case, the journal's editors selected a single convoluted sentence to be held up as exemplary of radical gobbledygook. The "award" clearly targeted a certain kind of politics, a certain kind of theory, and a certain kind of guru-status. As such it was a belated entry into the "theory-wars" of the 1980s, without much interest in its own right.

The 1998 "award" to Judith Butler nevertheless sparked intense debate.

The editor of *Philosophy and Literature*, Denis Dutton, published an op-ed in the *Wall Street Journal*.[40] Judith Butler responded with an op-ed in the *New York Times*.[41] The fallout reached magazines like *Lingua Franca* and the *London Review of Books*.[42] Eventually, a group of well-known academics, including Butler, defended their ways of writing in the 2003 anthology *Just Being Difficult*.[43] While the sixteen literary scholars and theorists contributing to *Just Being Difficult* have significant theoretical and political differences, they generally agree that common sense is always conservative, and that difficult writing is necessary to shake up uncritical consumers of dominant ideology. Some, rightly, also defend the humanities' right to produce just as much specialist language as the sciences.

Nobody in *Just Being Difficult* speaks up for the ordinary, the everyday, or the low. Nobody is willing to admit that some academics, whether radical or not, actually do write excruciatingly awful prose.[44] As I read through the book, I feel Ibsen's "compact majority" closing in on me. The wish to challenge common sense is ubiquitous. It's hard to avoid the conclusion that the knee-jerk rejection of common sense has become the new common sense. In the same way, any demand for readable or stylish writing is rejected as a misplaced demand for clarity, which is taken to be inherently conservative. This is Marcuse all over again.

It is not a coincidence, then, that in her 1999 *New York Times* op-ed, Butler enlisted *One-Dimensional Man* in her defense. Contrasting "philosophers who champion common sense" with "those who propagate a more radical perspective," Butler quotes a passage in which Marcuse accuses ordinary language philosophers of behaving like a Stalinist politburo in their attempts to enforce their conformist demand for clarity: "The intellectual is called on the carpet. What do you mean when you say ... ? Don't you conceal something?" (OM, 192, quoted by Butler). Butler continues: "The accused then responds that 'if what he says could be said in terms of ordinary language he would probably have done so in the first place.'"

To make the argument stick, both Marcuse and Butler rely on a verbal sleight of hand. In *One-Dimensional Man*, Marcuse begins by saying that the intellectual is called on the carpet. But halfway through the paragraph, the "intellectual" inexplicably morphs into a "poet." It's the *poet* (neither the "intellectual" nor the "accused") who replies: "if what he says could be said in terms of ordinary language he would probably have done so in the first place." This is the usual defense of modernist poetry against philistinism. (Marcuse was writing in the early 1960s, at a time when debates about modernist art were raging.) But intellectuals can't just help themselves to the status of poets. If intellectuals want to claim the privileges of poets, they should write like poets. Do we really choose our words and our syntax with the same rigorous exactitude as a world-class poet? Why is it even controversial to acknowledge that the winners of the "Bad Writing Contest" don't write with the elegance and precision of a Wallace Stevens or a Wislawa Szymborska?

I rarely read an academic text that wouldn't have benefited from another round of editing (or just editing), another effort to clarify sentences, improve the organization of paragraphs, set up chapters in the best possible way. (My own work is certainly no exception.) Surely we sometimes write as if we were deaf to the nuances of language, and surely we sometimes forget to think about the poor readers who have to slog through our leaden prose. Wouldn't it be more gracious simply to acknowledge that even the greatest intellectuals are not always the greatest masters of style? And, conversely, to cherish radical intellectuals who do write with clarity and grace? Orwell, Sartre, Beauvoir, Barthes, for example?

In 2003, at least, no such acknowledgment was made. Most of the contributors to *Just Being Difficult* treat clarity as a synonym for unthinking naivety, a sign of servitude to dominant ideology. Many object to the very idea that subjects express themselves, which they see as kowtowing to liberal humanism. For them, any wish to "communicate"—a wish to produce readable prose—is enmeshed with retrograde forms of humanism. I don't see why the simple recognition that human beings exist, that they express themselves (or fail to), and that we often need to understand one another, must entail any of this. My wish for readable—even graceful—academic prose commits me neither to a simple model of communication nor to an unsophisticated picture of language and meaning.

As I was reading through *Just Being Difficult* I felt as if I was being invited to be either for or against clarity, for or against difficulty, once and for all. But the effect of clarity or difficulty will depend on the circumstances. In any case, clarity is not incompatible with difficulty. Some ideas just *are* difficult, even in the most lucid presentation. As Einstein is supposed to have said: "Everything should be made as simple as possible, not simpler." Wittgenstein's own writing is at once clear, experimental, and fiendishly difficult. It is no coincidence that so many scholars have concluded that Wittgenstein's writing style itself is a form of modernism.[45]

A form or a style considered in isolation has no inherent meaning, no ideological essence that it always trails with it. The meaning of an utterance depends on who says what to whom under what circumstances. Clarity and grace are not always ideological, and certainly not always ideological in the same way.[46] The idea that anyone truly subversive of the status quo *must* express herself in ways that will come across to ordinary people as difficult, obscure, or opaque is belittling to ordinary speakers of the language, and naive about the relationship between ordinary and "special-ist" language.

We should stop casting clarity as the opposite of difficulty. The oppo-site of clarity is obscurity. The opposite of difficulty is easiness. Easy think-ing was certainly never Wittgenstein's goal. As he puts it in the preface to *Philosophical Investigations*: "I should not like my writing to spare other people the trouble of thinking. But if possible, to stimulate someone to thoughts of his own."[47]

If we—left-wing intellectuals—were willing to admit that our own writing isn't always perfect, we would be all the more convincing when we tackle the real issues, which I here take to be the "Bad Writing Contest'"s anti-intellectualism and reactionary understanding of the role of the intel-lectual in society. Why fight the battle through an implacable defense of impenetrable prose? Why dig ourselves into a position in which we have to defend every ambiguous "that" and "it," every infelicitous word, every clunky sentence, every incoherent paragraph and badly constructed chap-ter?[48] Why disdain the writing skills of the best nonfiction writers?[49] The answer has to do with Marcuse's idea that clarity is somehow connected to common sense, which he takes to be self-evidently reactionary.

Common Sense and the Writing of Theory

What exactly is common sense? Why must we—theorists who wish to change society—oppose it so ferociously? Butler writes that the task of the radical intellectual is to "question common sense, interrogate its tacit presumptions and provoke new ways of looking at a familiar world."[50] As examples of the "nefarious ideologies [that] pass for common sense," she mentions slavery and the idea that women should not have the right to vote. In such examples, common sense means something like "conven-tional wisdom," or "received opinion" (a term Butler herself uses else-where).[51]

But even received opinion is rarely shared by all. During the French Revolution, male revolutionaries took women's exclusion from politics to be a matter of common sense, yet some brave women—Olympe de Gouges, Mme Roland, and others—nevertheless agitated for their right to political participation. Butler recognizes this. Noting that "common sense ... is not always common," she acknowledges that the right of les-bians and gays to be "protected against discrimination and violence" is commonsensical to some and deeply threatening to others.

Surely Butler is right to say that what is received opinion to me may be anathema to you. But once we accept this view, a contradiction arises, for

Butler also explicitly endorses Adorno's view that "nothing radical could come of common sense."[52] However, if we admit, as she appears to do, that today it is commonsensical to endorse women's right to vote, and equally commonsensical to abhor slavery, and also that many of us find gay rights to be a matter of common sense, she presumably won't conclude that these positions are examples of the "nefarious ideologies" that radical intellectuals have a duty to challenge.

My point is simple: even Butler doesn't really believe that common sense (in the sense of received opinion) is *always* conservative. Rather, she rightly thinks that we should question the tacit presuppositions of *certain kinds* of common sense, namely the uncritical acceptance of oppression, exploitation, and injustice. It follows that common sense is not always conservative. What is always conservative is *what passes for common sense among conservatives*. But then the injunction always to challenge common sense is tautologous, for now it simply means that left-wing intellectuals should behave as left-wing intellectuals, and challenge conservative opinions. (I am sure writers as different as Zola, Orwell, Beauvoir, and Sartre would agree.) This is no longer a case against common sense as such.

But, you may object, maybe the political critique of common sense as such is built on a different argument? Maybe the real difference between critique and common sense is that critique challenges and contests, while common sense thoughtlessly acquiesces? In such arguments the meaning of "common sense" changes from "received opinion" to a certain kind of mental attitude or capacity—the willingness to oppose and contest. This argument lands us in a kind of formalism, for it implies that it makes no difference *what* common-sense ideas one challenges, as long as one vigorously challenges them. Unfortunately, it is perfectly possible to thoughtlessly acquiesce in radical as well as in conservative opinions.

By casting common sense as the *opposite* of critical sense, the champions of critique turn the traditional meaning of the concept upside down. For now "critique" (or "critical sense") appears to refer to the virtue Descartes and the Enlightenment philosophers called "good sense" or "common sense," namely reason understood as intelligence and the capacity for independent judgment. For Descartes, nothing was more ordinary: "Good sense is the most evenly distributed thing in the world" is the first sentence in *A Discourse on the Method*.[53]

None of this seems to have much to do with writing style. What is the connection between arguments about common sense and arguments about how to write theory? The usual argument is well put by Butler, who claims that difficult language produces defamiliarization, and thus opens our eyes to that which we have taken for granted: "One of the most important ways to call into question the status quo is by engaging language in nonconventional ways," she writes: "[Adorno] worried ... that language gives us a world, a sense of its meaning and its intelligibility, and that many assumptions about how the world should be are built into language use."[54] I agree that language gives us a world. I also agree that defamiliarization, unconventional use of language, may shake us out of our ingrained habits of thought and wake us up to the ideological implications of everyday activities.

But "defamiliarization" is also a strategy of modernism. Make it new! Again, left-wing intellectuals help themselves to the status of poets. It's not that easy to produce powerful, defamiliarizing prose. The underlying assumption remains the same: that a specific form or style (vaguely described as "unconventional") is inherently radical. (The picture is of a deadening norm, a conventional academic language, that the intrepid radical writer must shake up.) But it is perfectly possible to be conceptually and linguistically adventurous and yet deeply conservative, fascist, or racist (Pound, Heidegger, and Céline come to mind.) It is impossible to assess the effects of a theoretical style without considering who the text is addressed to, and what it actually is about.

Nevertheless, I am all for defamilarization through brilliantly refreshing and unusual writing. In fact, I would like radical theorists to behave *more* like avant-garde writers. Imagine a world in which radical theorists took a real interest in their own writing style, passionately discussed strategies for how best to develop the craft of theory writing, took for granted that theorists too need to work hard to master their chosen medium! Imagine if we all began to make serious efforts to write in strikingly fresh, powerful, invigorating ways, so as truly to make us see the world anew! Unfortunately, this is not what happens. Instead such arguments are used to defend "difficulty" in general, without making any attempt to take style seriously, and without even a token effort to distinguish between syntactical helplessness, conceptual opacity, and genuinely challenging writing.

The argument for defamiliarizing language is based on yet a third definition of common sense. Slavoj Žižek puts it succinctly when he complains that some people fail to realize that the ordinary itself is thoroughly ideological: they fail to realize that their "non-ideological common-sense form of life, [really is] the spontaneously accepted background which is ideology par excellence."[55] In this case, common sense appears to mean something like unformulated and implicit attitudes and assumptions arising from the very fabric of everyday life: not so much what we explicitly think, as what we take for granted, or what we obscurely feel to be the case, without expressing it in words.

I note that Žižek uses Wittgenstein's term "form of life" to describe the fake neutrality of the ideologically saturated universe. Žižek's ideologically saturated universe is a postmodern replica of Marcuse's "one-dimensional society."[56] Both of them saddle Wittgenstein and Austin with the chore of representing ideology-soaked banality. Both Marcuse and Žižek believe that we need a special philosophical language to see through the implicit assumptions of ordinary life. Butler's call for "unconventional" language use is a different version of the same idea. As we have seen, the trouble with this idea is its explicit or implicit condescension to ordinary people, and its almost magical faith in the power of philosophy (or "high theory") to see through the ideology that misleads everyone else. But even left-wing intellectuals are immersed in everyday practices, and participate in our ordinary forms of life. Why are we so sure that we will manage to tear the first rift in the ideological veil constituted by everyday practices? And if ideology goes as deep as Žižek implies, how can we have faith that mere unfamiliar writing, formal experiments alone, will shake us out of our ingrained assumptions?

Much of the "Bad Writing" battle was fought over the question of "specialized" language. At stake was intellectuals' right to use difficult concepts, such as "hegemony," for example. From an ordinary language philosophy point of view, this is not an issue. As we have already seen, Wittgenstein's question is not whether you are using esoteric or common terms, but whether the terms you use do any work. The organizers of the "Bad Writing Contest" never claimed that scientific terms (whether the symbolism of chemistry or the terms of infinitesimal calculus) are unclear. But the same goes for the humanities: carefully defined terms used stringently are per definition not unclear, however difficult and specialized they may be.

Clarity or obscurity are never features of individual words. Nor is clear (or obscure) writing just a matter of syntax and the organization of paragraphs. It is a matter of the whole conception of a work: its organization and address. In a powerfully conceived work, the odd knotty sentence will not prevent the reader from grasping what is going on. Whether something is accessible certainly can't be decided on the basis of a single sentence taken out of context, as the organizers of the "Bad Writing Contest" blithely assumed. The question is never an individual word, but who you are writing for, and what intervention you want to make.

Butler and her defenders are right to resist the idea that all their writing has to be immediately accessible to anyone who picks it up. Clarity, accessibility, readability, difficulty are relative entities: what is crystal clear to a Kant scholar is not going to be equally clear to readers with no background in philosophy. In *Just Being Difficult,* Michael Warner sensibly suggests that we ask whether a given text has been made as accessible as possible, given its specific target audience.[57] But sometimes academics forget that even close colleagues haven't necessarily read exactly the same books as they have. Steven Pinker calls the inability to imagine "what it is like for someone else not to know something that you know," the "curse of knowledge," and considers it the single best explanation of "why good people write bad prose."[58] Can it really hurt to provide just a little more information for interested, yet uninitiated colleagues?

Looking back, it would seem that the "bad writing" debate changed little one way or the other. Both sides persist in their bad habits. Anti-intellectuals and anti-theorists continue to find any challenging theoretical writing "bad," and the theorists themselves continue to believe that the more convoluted their writing, the more challenging it is to common sense and the status quo. We still haven't had the creative debates we need to have about how to write theory, who to write it for, and what we hope to do with our writing.

"My Spade Is Turned": On §217

In a discussion of Wittgenstein and politics, someone brought up Wittgenstein's §217: "Once I have exhausted the justifications, I have reached bedrock, and my spade is turned. Then I am inclined to say: 'This is simply what I do.'" To me, this is one of Wittgenstein's most arresting, and inspiring, images. To my interlocutor, it was a sellout. Is this really what Wittgenstein recommends we do when faced with a racist, a sexist, a homophobe? And how about the racist who rests on his spade?

While the passage isn't really about politics, it can certainly be taken that way. Wittgenstein is trying to convey the situation that arises when we have tried every conceivable argument, come to an end of all our attempts to explain to someone else why we do what we do, or why we think what we think. It is fundamentally connected to Wittgenstein's abiding sense that we place far too much faith in explanations, as if they could provide a firm ground beneath our feet. It is no coincidence that he begins *Philosophical Investigations* by reminding us that "explanations come to an end somewhere" (§1). Sooner or later, we run out of explanations. Then what do we do?

Imagine that I have failed to convince a racist to change her views. Although I have tried every argument, every consideration I can think of (I have "exhausted the justifications"), she simply won't be swayed. What do I do? What *can* I do? Wittgenstein's image of digging down until one hits bedrock conveys the frustration one might rightly feel in such a case.

Imagine that you have been digging really hard for a long time, that you are sweaty and thirsty, and then your spade hits rock and bends. Now you are not only exhausted, but you also have a damaged spade. Further work seems impossible. In such a situation, what are your options? Wittgenstein says that he is *inclined* to say "this is simply what I do." (It's not clear that he actually says anything.)

What else *could* he say? Are there other options? What *do* we do when further explanations are futile? (We may, of course, be unsure whether we have reached that point. But in this example I am assuming we have.) Sometimes we simply can't convince others, however hard we try. Wittgenstein chooses the peaceful option: rather than hitting his interlocutor with his bent spade, he rests on it. But he doesn't give in, he doesn't abandon his own practice, his own convictions, just because he can't convince the other. Imagine an antiracist deciding that since she can't convince the racist, she will simply give up her own convictions. (But imagine the opposite, too: the racist who won't give up her convictions.)

Wittgenstein's example points to the gulf that may suddenly open up between two human beings: the passage is telling us that *explanations* will never solve all the issues that arise when we are forced to face our finitude and separation, face the fact that we are *other* to each other. He draws our attention to a situation that requires a different vocabulary, a situation that not only raises questions of power, but of acknowledgment and response. (I am not saying that acknowledgment and response are always unrelated to power. On the contrary. Think of *King Lear*.) He reminds us of the obvious: that sometimes, however hard we try, we fail to make others see what we see, see the world as we see it. Then what are our options?

Wittgenstein's philosophy does not prevent us from wanting to change the world. It does not prevent us from being feminists or Marxists, or anything else. Rather it makes us respect the awesome powers of ordinary language. It makes us respect the ordinary and the everyday. And it gives us no reason to think that professional intellectuals, whether we call ourselves philosophers or theorists, are always better at seeing through the ruses of power than ordinary men and women. These are monumental achievements.

PART III

Reading

"Nothing Is Hidden"

BEYOND THE HERMENEUTICS
OF SUSPICION

Critique, Reading, Method

It used to go without saying that the purpose of literary studies was to produce critique, and that to do so one had to practice some form of the "hermeneutics of suspicion." These assumptions long ruled unchallenged. In the late 1990s Eve Sedgwick observed that the hermeneutics of suspicion had become "nearly synonymous with criticism itself."[1] Recently, Rita Felski has shown how the mindset—the mood or attitude—characteristic of the hermeneutics of suspicion came to dominate literary studies. Whether they are deconstructionists, Marxists, feminists, Foucauldian historicists, or something else, Felski writes, most literary critics share the same suspicious "knowing, self-conscious, hardheaded, tirelessly vigilant"—attitude.[2] To suspicious critics, the text is never what it seems, or never *only* what it seems.

On this vision, to engage in critique is to expose hidden ideology, uncover the workings of power, encourage resistance, and generally contribute to social and political change. Practitioners of critique must therefore be fundamentally suspicious of anything that appears to be ordinary and commonsensical, and anything that presents itself as an "established fact," including the so-called facts of the text (its words, its language). The conclusion imposes itself: radical, committed, political, left-wing critics must read "against the grain."

To read the text suspiciously is to see it as a symptom of something else. That "something else" usually turns out to be a theoretical or political insight possessed by the critic in advance of the reading. Instead of responding to the text's concerns, the critic forces it to submit to his or her own theoretical or political schemes. The result is often entirely predictable readings. Even critics totally committed to critique admit that the results can become stultifying.[3]

By now, however, critique has begun to lose its status as the self-evident goal and method of literary studies. We no longer believe that power always seeks to cover its tracks. Well before terrorists began to release videos of their atrocities—well before they began to commit their atrocities in order to release their videos—Eve Sedgwick asked: "What does a hermeneutics of suspicion and exposure have to say to social formations in which visibility itself constitutes much of the violence?" Moreover, she argued, the hermeneutics of suspicion's obsession with the opposition between *the hidden* and *the shown* encourages paranoid readings.[4] Bruno Latour notes that the techniques of critique are no longer the exclusive province of radicals. In particular, its trademark skepticism about "established facts" has long since been hijacked by everyone from defenders of the Iraq War to climate-change deniers.[5] For him, critique removes us from the things we actually care about: instead of writing about the things we cherish, we focus on their conditions of possibility. When we have exposed them as socially constructed, and thus as contingent, we feel that our work is done. But, Latour asks, what good does it do to know that something we love is contingent, or socially constructed? Is that really all we can say about the objects of our affection and admiration?

In spite of their misgivings, neither Sedgwick nor Latour opposes critique. Sedgwick simply wants to make room for "reparative" readings alongside the usual paranoid readings. Latour wants us to get closer to the facts, to "cultivate a stubbornly realist attitude" by turning to the "matters of concern we cherish."[6] For critique to renew itself, they both imply, we must learn to recognize situations in which suspicion is *not* called for, situations requiring us to speak up for the things we care about. Sometimes skepticism and suspicion will simply be less politically useful than admiration, care, love. Even Stephen Best and Sharon Marcus, who in their 2009 essay "Surface Reading" controversially argued that critique—"political activism by another name"—can't conceivably be the *only* purpose of literary studies, consider that "surface reading broadens the scope of critique."[7]

As a feminist, I am convinced that we still need to produce compelling critiques of injustice and oppression. But let's remember that it is perfectly possible to produce critical readings without invoking terms like "the hermeneutics of suspicion" or "symptomatic reading." Before intellectuals began to speak of critique as a mode of reading, Simone de Beauvoir took apart the sexism in the writing of Henry de Montherlant, Paul Claudel, D. H. Lawrence, and André Breton. Kate Millett's blistering political critique of writers from Lawrence to Henry Miller and Norman Mailer, proceeded quite without reference to hidden depths.[8] Such examples remind us of the obvious: critical readings existed well before professional literary critics began to believe that critique requires a particular vision of language, meaning, and texts, or a particular method of reading.

In "Surface Reading," Best and Marcus don't use the term "hermeneutics of suspicion." They prefer "symptomatic reading," a term first elaborated by Marxist thinkers, notably Louis Althusser and Fredric Jameson. In Jameson's words, symptomatic readings set out to "seek a latent meaning behind a manifest one [and] rewrite the surface categories of a text in the stronger language of a more fundamental interpretive code."[9] Over time, Best and Marcus note, the term has come to name any reading that "[takes] meaning to be hidden, repressed, deep, and in need of detection and disclosure by an interpreter."[10] In their view, we should oppose the idea that the task of literary criticism is to disclose the hidden and the deep. We should reject symptomatic reading, or "depth" reading, and embrace "surface reading" instead.

The essay provoked innumerable, more or less irate reactions.[11] In a particularly well-argued essay, the Marxist critic Carolyn Lesjak accuses Best and Marcus of positing a "benign" and "culturally conservative" reader who is "neutral, objective, self-effacing, humbled before the text." The surface reader, Lesjak argues, "accommodates herself to the given, to common sense, against the now discredited excesses of the theory years."[12] Lesjak, who is certainly not alone, is convinced that critique or symptomatic reading requires critics to probe beneath the surface of the text. Any other way of proceeding condemns us to supine acceptance of common sense, and thus the political status quo.[13] In this way, a specific picture of texts (as things with surfaces and depths) and reading (as critique, which brings the hidden to light) gets entangled in a political project: to undo an oppressive status quo, to raise our political consciousness. This logic produces the idea that critics who refuse to accept this specific picture of texts and reading must be conservative. There is an underlying formalism at work here: as if a particular picture of texts or reading by itself always imposes a reactionary politics, regardless of the critic's explicit thematic and political interest.

If we look more closely at the disagreement between Best and Marcus and Lesjak, it's easy to see that they share the same picture of the text, namely as a thing or object with surface and depths. While Lesjak prefers depths, and Best and Marcus surfaces, all agree that there *are* two different methods of reading, namely one that delves beneath the surface, and one that more or less contentedly accepts the same surface. In this chapter I challenge this picture. To get beyond the by-now exhausted terms of the debate about surface reading and critique, we need to learn how to think differently about texts, reading, and language.

This is where Wittgenstein comes in. I shall show that in Wittgenstein's vision of language there simply is no need to think of texts and language as hiding something. This goes against the grain of the post-Saussurean assumption that language itself, just by being language, is always hiding something; that words, sentences, utterances themselves always wear masks; that there is always something else beneath or behind our words, a shadow of meanings covered up by the words themselves. This picture of language and meaning, which is far from compulsory, helps to shore up the idea that texts have surfaces and depths, and thus that it makes sense to oppose surface reading to depth reading.

I shall also show that critics who think they are uncovering hidden truths don't read any differently from critics who simply think they are discovering the text's concerns and insights. In fact, even the most suspicious critics, the very poster-figures for the hermeneutics of suspicion—Sherlock Holmes and Sigmund Freud—don't do anything special. They simply look and think. I also oppose the idea that only "suspicious" or "symptomatic" readings are capable of acknowledging and exploring difficulty and obscurity. I do this by turning to Søren Kierkegaard's practice of reading in *Fear and Trembling*.

In my view, literary criticism—by which I mean what we now call "reading"—doesn't have anything we can plausibly call competing methods, at least not in the sense widely used in the sciences and social sciences: a set of explicit—and repeatable—strategies for how to generate new knowledge. This is why literary critics often have trouble explaining their "method" to colleagues in other disciplines. When Rita Felski discusses critique, she rightly refrains from calling it a method, and rather defines it by using terms such as "mood" and "mindset," and by focusing on characteristic rhetorical patterns. Critics do have specific thematic interests and political investments. But whether I do a postcolonial or a feminist or a psychoanalytic reading, methodologically I do the same sort of thing: I read. And to read is to pay attention to the particular text, to look and think in response to particular questions. Is reading a "method"? In literary studies the methodological alternatives to reading are things like conducting interviews, setting up focus groups, doing chemical analyses of paper quality and watermarks, or using computers to crunch big data.[14]

Understood as the work of reading, literary criticism has no method. There simply is no special "suspicious" as opposed to a "gullible" method of reading. While readers and readings may be more or less sophisticated, more or less knowing, even more or less suspicious, it doesn't follow that a suspicious reader deploys a particular method for reading, unused by others. A suspicious reader reads in a spirit or mood of suspicion, as opposed to, say, a spirit of curiosity or admiration. Clearly, our mood colors the expression of our insights and interests. But a mood is still not a method.

In my view, literary criticism doesn't have anything we can plausibly call competing methods. Most handbooks and courses in "method" either provide useful instructions in how to do research (how to use archives and bibliographies, how to read seventeenth-century handwriting), or they turn out to be overviews of various kinds of theory. But a theory is not a method. It is, rather, the name of a particular (often political or ethical) field of interests. As Felski has shown in *The Limits of Critique*, different interests generate different moods. If we think of "deconstruction" or "feminist theory" as methods, we are simply encouraging students to take a given theory and apply it to a text. This is truly the last thing we should teach our students to do.[15]

The way we (literary critics) talk about what we do (often under headings such as "method" or "approach" and the like) is at odds with what we actually do. We mistake political and existential investments for methods, specific practices of reading. Whether they speak of depths or surfaces, readers do pretty much the same sort of thing regardless of their understanding of what they are doing. What we — literary critics — call different "methods of reading" are really different interests, and different views of what is important in literature (and life).

The implications are radical: the fetishization of the hidden and the deep does *no work* for literary critics. This is why Best and Marcus are right to challenge the ubiquitous invocations of depth and hiddenness. But it is also why Best and Marcus are wrong to believe that a call for "surface reading" will liberate us from the metaphor of depth. After all, the two are inextricably linked: talk of surfaces calls forth thoughts of depths. In my view, claims about hiddenness and depth in literary criticism are empty. They don't underpin anything, not even critique.

This is a liberating insight, for it follows that radical critics no longer have to feel bound to the hermeneutics of suspicion. We can reject its characteristic oppositions—latent/manifest, hidden/shown, depth/surface—without losing anything at all. By "reject" I don't mean "exclude from our vocabulary." There can be no point in forbidding literary critics from using the word "deep," for example (in this chapter, I use the word about Kierkegaard's reading of the sacrifice of Abraham). I mean rejecting the belief that these oppositions tell us something interesting about how to read or not to read a literary text. Abandoning this view leaves the field of reading wide open. In the encounter with the literary text, the only "method" that imposes itself is the willingness to look and see, to pay maximal attention to the words on the page, to the point that we feel compelled to ask "Why this?" How we go about answering that question will depend on what we want to know.[16] But whatever we do, we are responsible for our reading. This is liberating, but it is daunting too.

"Nothing Is Hidden," or from Confusion to Clarity

The suspicious reader assumes that language itself hides its meanings from us. This belief is rooted in the post-Saussurean idea that the sign is split in a purely formal or material part (the signifier, the visible surface), and a buried or hidden part (the signified, the meaning). On the theory of the "split sign" any attempt to establish meaning will per definition become a hunt for the hidden. The sign here, the meaning there. Or as Wittgenstein dismissively puts it: "Here the word, there the meaning. The money, and the cow one can buy with it" (§120). Anyone who accepts the idea of the split sign builds the idea of the hidden into their very idea of language. And once they do that, they will find it impossible to break with the hermeneutics of suspicion.

Wittgenstein flatly denies that language hides anything: "How does a sentence manage to represent? . . . How does a sentence do it?—Don't you know? After all, nothing is hidden" (§435). The main reason why he insists that sentences don't hide anything is that for him, the meaning of a word isn't divorced from its use.[17] When Wittgenstein insists that nothing is hidden, he does not mean that everything is self-evident. He means that we shouldn't go around thinking that language itself—our sentences, our utterances—hides something just because it is language. Sometimes we lie, deceive, cheat; sometimes we are honest and truthful. This isn't something "language" does. It is something *we* do. We, as speakers, are responsible for our words. Language as such can't be blamed for our prevarications.

As we have seen, Wittgenstein thinks of utterances as actions, as something we *do*. If we think of a poem, a play, a novel as a particularly complex action, or intervention, we immediately escape the hold of some of the hermeneutics of suspicion's most entrenched beliefs. Actions aren't objects, and they don't have surfaces or depths. To understand an action isn't the same thing as to open the lid of a box. Partisans of the "death of the author" thesis forget that actions aren't divorced from their doers in the same way as objects from their makers. Think of the simplest of actions, such as reaching for a pen, or jumping over a puddle in the road. To understand the action is to understand why I or you do this particular thing, and to grasp the implications of doing it in the particular situation.

On this view, to understand an utterance may require us to ask about the speaker's motivations, reasons, and intentions; about its repercussions, ramifications, consequences, and effects; and to consider issues of responsibility, ethics, and politics arising in and through the utterance. (I write "may require" since all these questions are not going to be equally relevant in all situations.) From now on I'll refer to the whole range of such investigations as the *"Why This?"* question. Cavell notes that "a certain sense of the question 'Why This?' is essential to criticism."[18] We can't ask it unless we have noticed something, seen something that surprises or strikes us. Anything we notice—a specific word, a way of applying paint strokes, a surprising camera angle—can become the starting point for an investigation. Whether the investigation will be important depends on what we noticed in the first place. Training, experience, skill, knowledge are required if we are to be able to notice something of genuine interest.

"Why this?" is unrelated to the metaphysics of the hidden: it neither presupposes anything in particular about surfaces and depths nor prescribes any particular critical mood or attitude. We can ask "Why this?" in a spirit of confusion, in a spirit of really wanting to know. But we can also ask it in a spirit of suspicion. (To ban suspicion is no better than to require it.) The point is to be able to show *why* suspicion is called for in the particular case.

The suspicious reader is convinced that the text leads us astray. Wittgenstein thinks that we get lost in our own words, in our own unacknowledged or imperfectly understood assumptions. Philosophical problems arise when we let our words drift away from their ordinary use, yet still trade on that use. The result is not meaning, but the illusion of meaning. If I tell you that "I hid the car keys," you will usually understand. But what if you replied: "And I hid the meaning of my words"? It would take me aback, puzzle me, make me wonder what you mean. There is something odd about your saying this *here*, in *this* particular sentence, uttered in *this* particular context. In philosophy, Wittgenstein writes, we easily end up doing something similar, namely using ordinary words ("see," for example), but twisting their ordinary meanings ever so slightly. Problems arise when we fail to realize that we have done this: "A *picture* held us captive. And we couldn't get outside it, for it lay in our language, and language seemed only to repeat it to us inexorably" (§115). Then we are lost in the fog of our own language.

For Wittgenstein, philosophy begins in the acknowledgment of this lostness: "A philosophical problem has the form: 'I don't know my way about'" (§123). Note the difference between assuming that a text is hiding something from us, and assuming that the problem is *in me, in us*. If Wittgensteinian philosophy is a kind of therapy, it is not a therapy of others but of ourselves. If we assume that the work of reading is akin to the work of philosophy, then reading isn't an excavation but a self-examination. The work of philosophy is to dispel the fog and get to a clear view of the particular problem that troubled us. In literary criticism we can begin by asking "Why this?" We begin, then, not with a method, but with our own sense of confusion. If the critic doesn't have a problem, if nothing really puzzles her about the text, she really has no reason to investigate it. A reading is an attempt to get clear on something. (But this means that we have to see something, notice something in the text. To notice something interesting requires learning, knowledge, insight.)

To give an example: I began writing a paper on *Hedda Gabler* because I was struck by three different moments in the play when Hedda remains puzzlingly or shockingly silent.[19] The paper is an attempt to answer the question: "Why these silences?" The answer wasn't obvious, at least not to me. Nor was it self-evident where or how the reading would end. To bring out the meaning—value, mode—of Hedda's silences, I chose to contrast Ibsen's modern and Kierkegaard's romantic notion of despair. I can certainly imagine moving in some other direction. I can also imagine asking different questions. Why does Hedda say such awful things about Aunt Julie's hat? What does this tell us about her relationship to language? Different questions lead to different kinds of investigations. I don't think there is any way of deciding in advance of the reading what the *best* option would be, as if the path was already there, waiting for us. We just have to risk it. There are no guarantees.

A Clear View, or Description According to Wittgenstein

"Why this?" questions arise every time we are confused by a word, a sentence, an utterance. To find the answer, we try to get clear on how the word or sentence is used in this particular case. This can be so hard that we begin to feel we are banging our head against a brick wall. We may get stuck, feel we go around in circles. Then we get bumps on our understanding, as Wittgenstein puts it.[20] When we reach this point, a "grammatical investigation" is called for. The aim of the investigation is to reach a clear overview—a "surveyable representation" (*übersichtliche Darstellung*; §122)—of the way we use our words. Wittgenstein often refers to such an overview as a description. Think of something like an engineer's drawings of a machine, which lays out the different parts and their connections as clearly as possible. But note also that such drawings won't do anything for us unless they are offered in response to a confusion.

Here surface/depth metaphors no longer work. Of course, we can say that the drawings reveal how the machine is put together. Maybe you want to say that it unveils the inner workings of the machine (although that would be a bit odd, for it just "unveils" the machine). Yet it makes no sense to think of the machine as somehow hiding its own construction or structure. The drawings remind us of what was already there. We began by being confused, by failing to realize why the engine stopped working, but now we see what went wrong. The clear view allows us to relax, to stop worrying about this particular problem. It "gives philosophy peace," Wittgenstein writes (§133). At least for a while, until we begin to feel confused about something else.

In Wittgenstein's understanding of philosophy, then, a description is the therapy we need to see clearly. To describe, for him, is to point out connections, do comparisons, pay attention to distinctions, and so on. In literary studies, however, description has long been a contentious term. Proponents of "description" have been accused of being empiricists, of taking language to be "transparent," or of believing that texts only have one "literal" meaning. In *The Political Unconscious*, Jameson imagines an "ordinary reader" who "when confronted with elaborate and ingenious interpretations [objects] that the text means just what it says." According to Jameson such a reader can only be a mystified victim of ideology.[21] When Best and Marcus bravely declared that "surface reading... strives to describe texts accurately," they knew that they were asking for trouble.[22]

In "Live Free or Describe," her wittily entitled response to Best and Marcus, Ellen Rooney goes for the jugular: "Description ... celebrates obviousness, that which (allegedly) lies in plain view; it consequently embraces (the form of) paraphrase. Paraphrase is precisely a reading practice that disavows reading's own formal activities, which are thus rendered transparent in the sense of 'neutral' ..., allowing a paradoxical mediation without (the complicating factor of) mediators."[23] According to Rooney, description simply reiterates the obvious, that which is in plain view; it is no more than paraphrase. For her, paraphrase is a reading practice that wrongly takes itself to be neutral, even objective, as if it weren't an interested, ideologically suspect exercise in its own right. Whether we talk about "description" or about "what the text says," we are, according to Jameson and Rooney, dealing with quintessential cases of the kind of self-understanding, and the kind of language, that truly cries out for critique, unveiling, demystification.

Such critiques have no purchase on Wittgenstein's notion of description as *übersichtliche Darstellung*. A Wittgensteinian description is a response to a confusion, not an unmotivated call for an empirical survey. Wittgenstein, moreover, doesn't believe that human beings can ever escape their own embodied point of view. To him, we always speak as the fallible creatures we are. All utterances are situated: to understand an utterance is to understand how it is used in a specific situation, for a particular purpose. Yet it doesn't follow that all utterances are equally biased or equally unreliable. We can still get some things right, still get clear on a specific problem. Moreover, some utterances *are* more neutral, or more objective, than others. Even enthusiastic proponents of critique will denounce their opponents for providing a "flagrantly biased" account of reality, for example. But in so doing, they implicitly invoke the idea of a better—more accurate, more objective, more illuminating—account. Or at least I hope they do, for otherwise critique would be pointless.

Nevertheless, in literary studies "description" still invites misunderstandings. My use of the term may be easier to follow if I stress that until relatively recently the English-language editions of *Philosophical Investigations* translated *übersichtliche Darstellung* as a "clear view." The description *is* the clear view. This is why I often use expressions such as "provide a clear view," "get clear on something," or simply talk about reaching some kind of clarity.

When Wittgenstein declares that nothing is hidden, or that everything is in plain view, he doesn't mean that everything is obvious, in the sense of easily grasped, self-evident, or banal. First of all, we often don't notice the obvious. And if something really is obvious to us, we will not feel confused. Then we don't have a philosophical problem. Maybe we *should* have a philosophical problem. For what we take to be obvious may precisely be the picture that holds us captive. But as long as we haven't discovered that we *are* held captive, we are not in a position to realize that. So we still don't realize that we have a philosophical problem. To do philosophy—to engage in critical thinking—we must begin with our own personal experience of intellectual trouble. Unless *something* grates, gives us a headache, wakes us up from the conviction that our current view works just fine, we'll never even realize that we are confused.

Adherents of the hermeneutics of suspicion try to avoid the inevitable appeal to the critic's own experience of the text, the critic's own act of reading, by recommending constant suspicion. The result is a radical narrowing of the literary critic's register of attitudes and, in the worst cases, a permanent pose of knowing cynicism. And it won't help. For even the most suspicious critic will never be able to see her own blind spots. Wittgenstein helps us to understand that this is an inevitable part of the very process of thinking. For him, philosophy isn't a steady state of eternal vigilance, but rather a series of new forays, new efforts to clear up new confusions.

When the fog in our head lifts, we often feel that we should have seen

what the problem was all along. For then the solution often seems excruciatingly obvious. How *could* we have missed it? It was never hidden.
We just failed to see it. This is like Poe's purloined letter: what we seek is
hiding in plain view. But to see it is nevertheless not that easy. It requires
self-therapy, a change in outlook, an escape from the picture that held us
captive. This has nothing to do with empiricism, or with supine acceptance of the status quo.

Nor does Wittgenstein's notion of description—a clear view—stand in
a specific relationship to paraphrase. Yet paraphrase has been unjustly ma-
ligned. There is no point in being either for or against paraphrase as such.
A paraphrase can be an indispensable aid to understanding. As Cavell
has shown, metaphors *demand* paraphrase, while other kinds of poetic
language absolutely resist it.[24] Like all the other tools in the critic's toolbox, paraphrase can be illuminating when it is offered as a response to a
genuine problem. The question, as always, turns on use. Nobody is in favor of bad uses of paraphrase. The challenge is to distinguish good uses
from bad ones.

Looking and Thinking: Sherlock and Freud

I now want to show that reading practices that are routinely described as
quintessential cases of the hermeneutics of suspicion don't in fact require
us to think in terms of the traditional oppositions. The implications are
revolutionary, for it follows that metaphors of depth and surfaces, hidden
and shown, don't actually describe what readers are doing, or how reading
works. Whether a critic takes herself to be digging beneath the surface or
not makes no difference to her actual reading practice.

To clarify what I mean, I'll give two examples. The first concerns a detective, one of the favorite figures of the hermeneutics of suspicion. My
example comes from the TV series *Sherlock*. How does it represent Sherlock's detection process? In the first episode of season 1, Sherlock examines the body of a woman dressed in a pink suit, sprawled on the floor of
an empty warehouse.[25] He notices that there is humidity on the inside of
her collar. He looks at her umbrella, which is dry. He examines her jew-
elry, takes off her wedding ring and looks carefully at the inside. He notices small splatterings of mud on her calves.

During this process, Sherlock doesn't say anything. He is just looking,
touching, smelling, and thinking. To convey a sense of action—his hec-
tic process of thinking—words in Courier font, styled to look like rough
data output, flash across the screen. "Umbrella: dry," for example. At the
end of the scene, Sherlock declares that the woman has just arrived from

Cardiff where it rained that morning, she is a serial adulterer, there has to be a missing pink suitcase, and so on.

Is Sherlock uncovering the hidden? Well, if you like you can say so, but then it becomes your responsibility to explain why you think that metaphor captures what Sherlock is doing better than the alternatives. I prefer to say that Sherlock is *looking and thinking* in response to a specific question: Why this? What brought this woman to her death in this dismal place? What Sherlock notices is already there, in plain view. The other characters—the police detective, Watson—simply fail to take an interest in the features that grab Sherlock's attention. It's not that the others look at the surface, whereas Sherlock looks beneath it. It is that he *pays attention* to details they didn't think to look at. Wittgenstein's "Nothing is hidden" explains Sherlock's activities better than metaphors of hiding/showing. Sherlock is a master in his field because he pays meticulous attention to what is before him. Master readers do the same thing.

My second example comes from one of the founding fathers of the hermeneutics of suspicion, namely Freud. Freud regularly used metaphors of the hidden and the buried to describe the unconscious, and drew on the language of archaeology and detection to explain his method of interpretation. In the famous "Dora" case, Freud writes that his strategy was to "follow the example" of great archaeologists who "bring to the light of day after their long burial the priceless though mutilated relics of antiquity." Like such archaeologists, he too has "restored what is missing."[26]

Freud's metaphors stress the hidden/shown opposition. But his account of what he actually does, is at odds with the imagery of burial and excavation. He has set himself the "task of bringing to light what human beings keep hidden within them ... by observing what they say and what they show." To discover human secrets turns out to be easier than one might think: "He that has eyes to see and ears to hear may convince himself that no mortal can keep a secret. If his lips are silent, he chatters with his finger tips; betrayal oozes out of him at every pore."[27] Our secrets are all too evident: all it takes to reveal them are "eyes to see and ears to hear." Freud isn't digging under the surface. The psychoanalyst observes and listens. He looks at and listens to his analysand's expressions, and thinks.

Wittgenstein too thought that human beings are, as Cavell puts it, "condemned to expression, to meaning" (CR, 357). The famous aphorism "The human body is the best picture of the human soul" is an attempt to make us stop thinking of the body as something that *hides* the soul, and to make us realize that the body is *expressive* of soul, which means that it is expressive also of our attempts to hide, disguise, or mask our feelings and reactions (PPF, §25). For Wittgenstein, gestures and activities inflect our words: language cannot be isolated from our tone, our facial expressions, or from what we do with our bodies as we speak or remain silent. Silence can be as easy—or as hard—to read as words.

In Freud's celebrated model analysis of one of his own dreams, the "Dream of Irma's Injection," or more formally "An Analysis of a Specimen Dream," he shares his method of interpretation with his readers. He begins by writing down the dream as soon as he wakes up. This writing is the "dream-text," the text to be analyzed. The "specimen dream" concerns a patient Freud calls "Irma," a woman who in spite of Freud's psychoanalytic therapy still complained of pains. To analyze the dream, Freud breaks the dream-text up into small fragments. Some are full sentences, others single words, or, in one case, a chemical formula. Then he produces, as fully as he can, his thoughts and associations to each fragment. The aim of the process is to figure out what the dream means. The effort is crowned with success. Freud concludes that the dream shows that: "I was not responsible for the persistence of Irma's pains, but [my colleague] Otto was." The famous conclusion follows: a "dream is the fulfillment of a wish."[28]

This strategy can easily be redescribed as a version of the "Why this?" question. Here, as in his other interpretations of dreams, or jokes, or literary texts, Freud is looking for motivations and intentions, showing *why* the individual elements of the dreams are as they are, why each word, each sentence, appears where it does, what work it does, and so on. Sherlock does the same thing: he explains *why* the umbrella is dry, but the inside of the coat collar is humid, and so on.

How do the surface/depth metaphors fit Freud's method? What is hidden here? The dream-text is not hidden. On the contrary, it is the text to be interpreted. The new associations and thoughts produced by Freud are not hidden either. Although he must prod himself to produce them, he doesn't appear to consider them either "deeper" or more "superficial" than the dream-text itself. What *is* hidden, according to Freud, is the meaning of it all—let's call it his *conclusion*—namely that the dream expresses his wish to blame Otto for Irma's pain. He himself was not aware of this wish. What is hidden, then, is the unconscious *motivation* for the dream. Freud's point is that we don't always know our own feelings, attitudes, and investments. This is certainly true. But this is a claim about the human mind, not about language, texts, or interpretation.

The Italian historian Carlo Ginzburg would say that Sherlock and Freud behave like master hunters who know how to piece together a detailed picture of the animal from its traces. The master hunter does not move from surface to depth, but rather from scattered details, traces, and clues to an idea of the whole. When Freud discovers the meaning of his dream, when

Sherlock uncovers the murderer, they are like the brothers in the oriental fable who "demonstrate[d] in a flash how, by means of myriad small clues, they could reconstruct the appearance of an animal on which they have never laid eyes."[29]

For Ginzburg, both Sherlock and Freud practice *conjectural knowledge*. They are among the early practitioners of a new "evidential paradigm" that began to enter European intellectual life in the 1870s and 1880s. Rooted in medicine, jurisprudence, historiography, and philology, the conjectural paradigm soon became the very foundation of the emerging human sciences. Any "highly qualitative" discipline, any form of knowledge concerned with "individual cases, situations and documents," Ginzburg writes, will build its cases in this conjectural way.[30] Where Ginzburg writes "conjecture," others might want to say "interpretation." But whatever we call it, Ginzburg manages to show that interpretation can discover the unknown without having recourse to the oppositions hidden/shown or depth/surface.

The Difficult, the Dark, and the Deep: Kierkegaard

We have seen that partisans of critique believe that the only alternative to "deep" reading is banal paraphrase, simplistic and superficial descriptions. I have already shown that Wittgenstein's search for clarity doesn't entail a rejection of difficulty. Now I want to show that the language of the hidden and the shown, of mystery and revelation, isn't the private property of the hermeneutics of suspicion, but can be used in other, different ways. To show what I mean, I'll turn to Søren Kierkegaard, a magnificent reader of difficult texts, but in no way a hermeneuticist of suspicion.

I choose Kierkegaard because he appears to be a hard case for my argument. Kierkegaard is almost obsessed with revelation and recognition. And, as he himself stresses: "Whenever and wherever it is possible to speak of recognition, there is *eo ipso* a prior hiddenness."[31] In *Fear and Trembling* he reminds us that ancient Greek drama is constructed on the model of the hidden and the shown. In Aristotle's *Poetics*, recognition (*anagnorisis*) is an unveiling, a discovery, a disclosure, as when Oedipus suddenly realizes that *he* is the one who brought the plague to Thebes. For Aristotle *anagnorisis* is something a tragic hero experiences when he realizes who he is, what he has done. In the moment of recognition, the hero moves from ignorance to knowledge. This can also be experienced as a conversion: "I was blind, but now I see." Wittgenstein's search for the path from confusion to clarity has some kinship with such scenes.

For Kierkegaard, the hiddenness of the Greek drama connects to the

Greeks' sense of the "dark, mysterious source" of dramatic action (84). But it lingers on in modern drama, which depends on recognition and hiddenness for its very existence. (He is thinking of nineteenth-century melodramas, in which the plot almost always turns on sudden revelations of identity: "Ah, so *you* are my long-lost son!") However, neither Greek recognitions nor modern revelations are hidden from the audience; on the contrary, they take the form of explicit dramatic action, there for all to see.

The Bible's story of Abraham's willingness to sacrifice Isaac is remarkably simple. God tells Abraham to sacrifice his only son. Abraham takes his son, a knife, and some firewood to Mount Moriah, and begins to prepare the sacrifice. At the last minute, an angel stays Abraham's hand. Nearby Abraham suddenly notices a ram caught in a bush and sacrifices the ram instead. In this story nothing is hidden and nothing is revealed. God's intervention isn't the revelation of a secret, it's just what God does. Yet for Kierkegaard, this story is so difficult to understand that it disturbs his sense of reason. He simply can't fathom how Abraham can *do* such a thing.

Kierkegaard's method for getting clear on what this story means is fascinating. He begins *Fear and Trembling* by rewriting it four times. In each retelling he makes an enormous effort to imagine what the situation must have felt like to the different protagonists, how they might have experienced it, what it might have been like. To him, such a literary rewriting—a retelling or recounting—of the story is an act of intense interpretation. (Why don't we ask our students to do this sort of thing more frequently?) By supplying new contexts, adding details about the characters' feelings and experiences, he tries to get closer to understanding Abraham's action, understanding his intentions, motivations, state of mind as he prepares to kill his son. Then, in the much longer rest of the book, he meditates on the philosophical—religious, ethical, existential—confusion this story throws him into.

Kierkegaard's various retellings are attempts to understand a text that challenges him totally as a thinker and as a human being. As he struggles to get clear on Abraham's relationship to God, he keeps returning to the idea that faith is "distress, anxiety and paradox" (63, 65, and so on). At the end of the book, the story of Abraham still defeats him, not because it is obscurely written, or particularly puzzling in style or form, but because it presents us with a fundamentally incomprehensible act, one that will only ever make sense to a great religious soul, a "knight of faith." The effort to bring Abraham's act back to human (social, ethical) categories of understanding will always fail.

Few texts equal *Fear and Trembling* in its strenuous, iconoclastic, imaginative, deeply philosophical effort to read a difficult text as thoughtfully and intensely as possible. *Fear and Trembling* exemplifies a form of reading that fully acknowledges difficulty, obscurity, and mystery without falling under the categories of the hermeneutics of suspicion. At the beginning of his reading of *Walden*, Cavell writes: "My opening hypothesis is that this book is perfectly complete, that it means in every word it says, and that it is fully sensible of its mysteries and fully open about them."[32] Cavell reads in the same spirit as Kierkegaard: there is no assumption that the critic is superior, more knowledgeable, more sophisticated than the text. Nor is there an assumption that the text hides anything. There is just the idea that the text is an enormous challenge to the reader, that the reader's task is to understand why every word is exactly the way it is. This attitude turns reading into an arduous expedition of discovery, a genuine adventure.

I want to say that Kierkegaard's reading of the story of Abraham is deep. What does the word mean here? In his reading of *Walden*, Cavell writes: "A deep reading is not one in which you sink away from the surface of the words. Words already engulf us. It is one in which you depart from a given word as from a point of origin; you go deep as into the woods."[33] Kierkegaard's reading sends us deeper into the woods, to a place we have never been before. In such a place new discoveries can be made, at least by those who know how to read the signs. We are back to Ginzburg's hunter, back to what he calls "the oldest act in the intellectual history of the human race: the hunter squatting on the ground, studying the tracks of his quarry."[34]

"Why This?" Critique, Admiration, Responsibility

As we have seen, Cavell notes that "a certain sense of the question 'Why this?' is essential to criticism." But to ask "Why this?" in relevant and interesting ways is difficult. It takes extensive training and experience to become a good critic. If you know nothing about metaphors in Romantic poetry, you will fail to notice anything puzzling or unusual about a specific metaphor in a particular poem. And if you notice nothing special, you won't be in a position to begin an investigation: "The best critic will know the best points," Cavell writes. "Because if you do not see *something*, without explanation, then there is nothing further to discuss."[35] A critic always stakes herself—her experience, her judgment—in her observations. That's why the very work of criticism can conjure up anxiety, fear of exposure, dread of being misunderstood.

We can ask "Why this?" about anything. This doesn't mean that the words of the text can be made to *mean* just anything. It just means that we can do more than one thing with texts. A Marxist may be interested in the class struggle, or in modes of production or ideology; a feminist in women, their social status, their relationships, their actions and expressions; and so on. Different interests will inspire different questions.

If we want to know whether the Marxist or the feminist reading is better, the answer will depend on the particular case. They are not necessarily mutually exclusive. In any case, we shouldn't lay down requirements about what thematic interests, what worldview, what politics the critic should deploy in advance of the reading. The reading—the critic's expression of her reading—either justifies itself or it doesn't. The best critic will not just know the best points, and ask the best questions, she will also choose to work on the best texts, by which I don't mean the established canon, but the texts that best respond to her own interests and purposes, the texts to which she herself responds most fully.

Wittgenstein, Austin, and Cavell can be formidable allies for anyone interested in unmasking pretense, deceit, and illusions.[36] But *we* are the ones who decide to unmask or not to unmask. Whether we write literary criticism to critique or to admire, to investigate or to explore, is up to us. The politics of literary criticism does not lie in the method, or in the way we picture texts. It lies in the critic. *We* are responsible for our words, for our own practice. Our readers will always be justified in asking what we want to do with our writing, what intervention we take ourselves to be making. They will also always be justified in asking how far our reading genuinely illuminates the text, how far it helps us to understand something we didn't understand before. In literary criticism, both politics and aesthetics are matters of response, judgment, and responsibility.

The *doxa* of critique makes us fear that if we were to write in admiration, were to reveal what we cherish, we may come across as blindly submissive and unthinkingly accepting, as if picking fault with a text is always more difficult, more challenging, more serious than giving an account of why it deserves our full attention. This is to confuse critique with critical thinking. Once we learn to read beyond the traditional parameters of critique and suspicion, we will find it easier to show other people why literature matters, why they might want to care about it, and why it is important to create a society that takes it for granted that such things are to be cherished and preserved.

No Approach: Reading without a Method

Literary studies comprise a number of research programs that do have methods: the history of the book; bibliographical research; philology, including the edition of ancient manuscripts; neuro-criticism (insofar as it involves the type of experiments usually done in the sciences); the use of "big data" to reconstruct literary history. But I am not convinced that literary *criticism*—professional readings of literature—has a method in the usual sense of the word. Franco Moretti, who has pioneered the use of big data and experimental research in literary studies, thinks the traditional method in literary studies is close reading, which he denounces as an essentially canonizing "theological exercise," consisting in a "very solemn treatment of very few texts taken very seriously."[37] Instead, Moretti proposes, we should practice "distance reading": don't read the books, read what critics have to say about the books instead. While this is innovative advice, and an intriguing starting point for research in literary history, it is obviously not a method for actually reading literary texts.

Is "close reading" the method for literary criticism, as Moretti claims? As far as I can see, "close reading" simply means "attentive reading." A "close reading" can mean any kind of detailed textual analysis. (It's not incoherent to speak of postcolonial or feminist or Marxist close readings.) This is hardly a method. The word "method" means something like "along the way," for it comes from the Greek *meta* (with, after) and *hodos* (way, road). In the social and natural sciences, a method *is* a road-map: a systematic protocol, a clearly defined series of steps to be taken in a specific order in order to reach a replicable result. Without a method, science simply wouldn't be science. But literary critics are humanists, not scientists. We don't try to produce replicable results. On the contrary: When we evaluate literary criticism, we look for the unique, the individual, the original. If we feel that a job candidate is simply "saying the same thing" as everyone else, we remain unimpressed. The closer a literary theory comes to generating a characteristic repertoire of moves (New Criticism, deconstruction, New Historicism, psychoanalytic criticism), the quicker we start complaining that the approach has become entirely predictable, and therefore boring.[38]

I understand the temptation to call such theories "methods." I just find it confusing. A theory is not a method.[39] Talk about "approaches" doesn't help either. David Rudrum reports that some British universities changed the name of the "Introduction to Literary Theory" course to "Approaches to Literature." The idea was this would be "less intimidating" to first-year students. Rudrum points out that this is mere play with words: "Why should it be … more exciting to have an 'approach' to literature than to have a 'theory' of it?"[40]

Literary critics regularly use the words "method," "theory," and "approach" without much stringency.[41] But if we routinely call theories methods, the distinction does no work for us. The solution is not to call for more rigorous training in "methods" (for we still have no clear notion of what "method" might mean), but to recognize that literary criticism isn't the kind of practice that responds to the distinction between "theory" and "method," as this has been laid down by the natural and social sciences. Let us acknowledge that we are humanists. In our practice, "theory," "method," and "approach" are simply names for the knowledge and the thematic, formal, political, and ethical interests that critics bring to texts and explore in their readings.

We owe our talk about "method" to the New Critics. In the 1950s the insistence on method may have expressed a certain longing for literary criticism to become a more scientific and less humanistic enterprise than it actually is. Today, humanists are exposed to intense pressure to make our research and writing conform to the standards of the sciences. We are surrounded by interdisciplinary initiatives that take the norms and paradigms of the sciences or the social sciences for granted, which inevitably make humanists feel excluded and undervalued. In such contexts, literary critics are increasingly asked to give an account of their "method," whether it makes intellectual sense or not. And in such contexts, the honest answer — "just reading" — simply won't be taken seriously.[42] In such situations, we fall back on describing our "approach" or our "theory," which usually just confuses our colleagues in disciplines that actually have methods.

But what about "Why this?" I have, after all, recommended this question as a starting point for critical investigations. Isn't that a kind of method? As Cavell notes: "What you need to learn will depend on what specifically it is you want to know; and how you can find out will depend specifically on what you already command."[43] There is no road map given in advance, nothing that guarantees that others can repeat my specific journey. I ask "Why this?" because *I* feel lost and confused, because *I* feel the need to get clear on something, the need to understand something. There is no guarantee that everyone else will feel confused at the same spot, in the same situation as I do. But by making my own responses exemplary (not representative) — by trying to convey them to you — I invite you to respond. You may react with surprised delight, or with cold disdain. You may not respond at all. To ask "Why this?" is to take a risk, to stick to one's judgment that *this* particular feature of the text is worth our full attention.

We may ask "Why this?" suspiciously or admiringly, in anger or in elation, or in any other spirit, mood, or state of mind. (Felski is certainly right to emphasize mood and attitude in criticism.) Reading in a state of increasing suspicion certainly *feels* different from reading in a state of mounting enthusiasm. The suspicious and the enthusiastic reader will surely produce different kinds of literary criticism, different responses to the text, for they have had quite different reading experiences. But this is not to say that they used different *methods*.

At the beginning of *The Claim of Reason*, Cavell writes that he has no "approach" to *Philosophical Investigations*: "There is no approach to it, anyway I have none. Approach suggests moving nearer, getting closer; hence it suggests that we are not already near or close enough; hence suggests we know some orderly direction to it not already taken within it; that we sense some distance between us and it which useful criticism could close" (6). The metaphor of "approach" conjures up an object, a phenomenon, which we could understand better if we only could move closer to it. But this is to picture reading a text as something akin to studying Mars or Saturn.

Like "surface" and "depth," the metaphor of "approach" casts the text as an object, and ourselves as the inquiring subject. But works made of words don't work like that. If we can read the words, we are close enough. And we already know the words. (If we don't, we need to look them up, or learn the language.) To read a text isn't to discover new facts about it. (But that's exactly what talk about the "materiality of the signifier" leads us to believe.) It is to figure out what it has to say to us. There is no "orderly direction," no method for how to do this.

In such a case, what do we do? Cavell simply tells us what he did: "Leaving myself, I trust, without an approach, I find a blur or block from which to start, a turn in Wittgenstein's thought that I can report as having for a long time seemed to me both strange and familiar, far and near" (CR, 6). Deliberately choosing the words "far" and "near," Cavell shows that here, in relation to this text, they are not indicators of distance. Wittgenstein's text is *at once* "far" and "near," "strange" and "familiar": these words don't describe a scientific object, but rather name Cavell's *experience* of *Philosophical Investigations*.

The "blur or block from which to start" combines the philosopher's own experience of confusion, difficulty, obscurity, with an intuition or a hunch that *this* is where he will find his beginning. At the beginning, the reader must stake everything on that hunch. There is no guarantee that beginning from this rather than that blur will lead to illuminating insights. But we don't have anything else to go on. Even if I decide to take your word for where to start—decide to accept your judgment for where to go—I can't substitute your judgment for mine throughout the reading. At *some* point, I have to risk my own judgment as to what may be a significant or insignificant question. What bothers and confuses me, may bother nobody else: "I have nothing more to go on than my conviction, my sense that I make sense" (CR, 20). This is why reading can feel so risky.

To read—and to find the words in which to express one's reading—is to stake one's claims on one's own perceptions, on one's own experience of the text. There is no recipe—no method—for how to do this. The most perceptive, the most attentive, the most learned, and the most knowledge-able critic will do the best job. We fear that when we voice our view, we will discover that we are alone, maybe mad, certainly cast out. But unless we take the risk, and engage ourselves in the "adventure of reading" as Cora Diamond calls it, we will never discover who our intellectual companions are.[44]

Reading as a Practice of Acknowledgment

THE TEXT AS ACTION
AND EXPRESSION

To say that texts are actions and expressions is to remind us of the obvious: that sentences, utterances, texts don't generate themselves; that they are spoken or written by someone at a particular time, in a particular place; that words reveal the speaker; that once words are uttered they can't be undone; that utterances, like other actions, have consequences, ripple effects spreading far beyond the original moment of utterance. In this chapter, I'll show that this picture of texts frees us from the old taboo on the author's intentions and enables us to think of reading as a practice of acknowledgment. On this view, to give an account of a reading is to give an account of an experience, the experience of an adventure.

I originally wanted to say that texts are actions, expressions, and interventions. Then I started to wonder how much "intervention" adds to "action and expression." According to the OED, an intervention is "the action of intervening, 'stepping in,' or interfering in any affair, so as to affect its course or issue." To say that a text is an intervention is to say that its appearance creates effects in the world. But since most actions interfere in some existing state of affairs, however minimally, I concluded that "intervention" is implied in "action and expression."

Texts are actions, for they are made of language. But they are physical objects, too. Scholars of bibliography and the history of the book work on the material aspects of texts. By studying watermarks and binding, annotations and marginalia, they produce new knowledge about book production, readership, circulation, collectors, and collections. Hieroglyphs, runes, print, computer code are as material as mountains. But to study the "materiality" of the inscription is not to study its meaning. We shouldn't be carried away by the fantasy that we can understand a text by studying its "materiality" alone, as in the old fetishization of the "materiality of the signifier."[1]

I am interested in reading and understanding, in how the reader responds to the text. For these purposes, it usually doesn't matter whether we read *Madame Bovary* on a Kindle, in paperback, or in the Pléiade edition. There are exceptions: Apollinaire's "Calligrammes"—poems laid out to look like pictures—have to be read in the original layout and no other. The same is true for the kind of acrostic poetry in which a code is embedded in the first letter of every new line.

To think of texts as either action or expression is hardly new. What *is* new in recent literary theory is ordinary language philosophy's distinctive combination of action *and* expression. The Romantics took for granted that literature was expressive of mind or soul. The expressivity of literature remained relevant to literary criticism until the New Critics denounced the intentional fallacy and the poststructuralists announced the death of the author. The idea that texts are actions has had better press, for it has long been bound up with the concept of "discourse," which I'll now go on to discuss.

Discourse and Intention

In her much admired 1977 book *Towards a Speech Act Theory of Literary Discourse*, Mary Louise Pratt defines "discourse theory" as the study of language in use, and argues that texts are acts or utterances, and that there is no such thing as "literariness" or "literary language."[2] I couldn't agree more. But Pratt, who reads Austin in the spirit of Searle and Grice, sets out to produce a systematic theory of "literary discourse." I don't share that ambition. Moreover, the literary field has moved on. After the French *autofiction* of the 1960s and 1970s, the explosion of the memoir genre, and Karl Ove Knausgård's *My Struggle*, it seems futile to try to draw some fundamental boundary line between fiction and nonfiction, or between "literary" and "nonliterary" prose.

Pratt hoped that "discourse theory" would become a thriving new field bridging the gap between linguistics and literary studies. This both has and hasn't happened. Today "discourse theory," or "discourse studies," or "discourse analysis" flourishes, but mostly outside literary studies. Linguists take "discourse analysis" to mean the "study of language in use" and debate whether or not it is the same thing as "pragmatics."[3] In the social sciences, "discourse theory" means the study of any kind of social communication, anything to do with "people communicating and using language to do things," as one handbook puts it.[4] Social scientists interested in discourse studies often acknowledge Wittgenstein and Austin as precursors, but they don't draw on them for their own empirical studies.[5]

When they hear the concept of "discourse," literary critics often think of the linguistics of Émile Benveniste and the literary theory of Mikhail Bakhtin. In vastly different ways, both men stress the connection between the word and the speaking subject, and both use "discourse" to mean language in use. Benveniste distinguished between "statement" (*énoncé*) and "utterance" (*énonciation*). *Énonciation* is the act of producing a "statement." This act reveals the "I" and implies a "you." To be interested in this act is to be interested in "discourse."[6]

Benveniste's concept of discourse may well have inspired Foucault's. But in Foucault, discourse is no longer a purely linguistic or textual concept. For Foucault, architecture, as well as all kinds of practices and habits, is part of the "discourse" of an institution or a social phenomenon. The panopticon—a particular prison design and the habits and practices that go with it—tells us a lot about a certain way of thinking about prisons, prisoners, crime, and punishment. This concept of "discourse" is fascinating, and not inimical to ordinary language philosophy, but it is not my topic here.[7] Both Benveniste's and Bakhtin's understanding of language as utterance, action, and expression inspired Julia Kristeva's early work. By combining their notions of discourse with linguistics and psychoanalysis, she developed her own theory of the speaking subject and desire in language.[8]

The classical theorist most congenial to ordinary language philosophy's interest in particular cases, and in language as action and expression, is surely Bakhtin, who sets out to study "concrete language." According to Ken Hirschkop, we study "concrete language" when we include not just the words, but the "feelings, motivations, and values of speakers"; acknowledge "[language's] own historical mutability and social variability"; and consider language "as an *act* ... as a moment of commitment or position-taking."[9]

In his celebrated essay "Discourse in the Novel," Bakhtin defines discourse as language *use*, a fundamentally dialogic "social phenomenon," taking place among specific interlocutors and interacting with other socially and culturally specific discourses. As soon as it is uttered the word "enters a dialogically agitated and tension-filled environment," a space in which the word's original object is already "overlain with qualifications, open to dispute ... shot through with shared thoughts, points of view, alien value judgments and accents."[10] Bakhtin, in short, thinks of language use as an intervention in a complex social space. To me, this is entirely compatible with ordinary language philosophy.

As Benveniste and Bakhtin understand it, the concept of discourse requires a speaker, a subject. The concept does not require us to hold a homogeneous, unitary picture of the subject; we just have to acknowledge that *somebody* speaks. But once we think of speakers and action, the question of authors and authors' intentions naturally arises. If we are puzzled by an action, no question is more natural than "Why?"—"Why did she do *that*?" Yet, surprisingly, admirers of the concept of discourse have not challenged the taboo on talking about intentions in literary criticism.

How did champions of the concept of discourse avoid having to consider authors and intentions? A 1973 paper by Paul Ricoeur, "The Model of the Text," provides a perspicuous example. Interpretation, Ricoeur writes, requires both a linguistics of *language* (Saussure) and one of *discourse* (Benveniste). Stressing the parallels between Benveniste's "discourse" and Austin's "speech acts," Ricoeur defines discourse as temporal utterances, always addressed to someone, always both referential and self-referential. Discourse stands in stark contrast to Saussure's *langue*, defined as a closed system, "virtual and outside time."[11] On Ricoeur's model, language is system; discourse event. (This distinction echoes Saussure's distinction between *langue* and *parole*.)

Ricoeur acknowledges that both texts and speech are discourse, language uttered by a speaking subject. But once we write the utterance down everything changes. Writing (inscription) is not action, only the frozen trace of an action. Written down, discourse escapes its original temporal situation, addresses a universal audience, and no longer refers, but rather, in Heidegger's term, "discloses" a world. Texts, then, are discourse only in name: in reality, they are the opposite of speech.

There is much truth in this. I agree that writing cuts a text loose from its original situation. The less we know about its origins, its specific situation of utterance and reception, the more open to interpretation a text becomes. (Consider Nietzsche's "I have forgotten my umbrella," discussed in chapter 3.) Yet Ricoeur's theory about the absolute difference between speech and writing seems forced. To make it stick, he reduces speech to cartoonish simplicity. On Ricoeur's view, speech is never an interpretive challenge. Speech is fixed in a particular moment in time, always addresses a specific other, always has a concrete reference, always conveys the speaker's intentions. In speech, the speaker's intentions and her meaning always coincide, and the question of reference is never problematic. Ricoeur even claims that reference in speech is always ostensive, that is, of the kind in which one points to an object while defining it (96). In short: Ricoeur's account of speech implies that face-to-face conversation is devoid of misunderstandings, opacity, ambiguity, uncertainty, and always concerns objects one can point to. Such a patently unsatisfactory notion of speech serves only as a foil to writing. If speech is governed by intention, writing is not. If speech is action, writing is object-like (frozen traces), and so on.

Ricoeur's underestimation of the complexity of speech and overestimation of writing has deep roots. It is characteristic of postwar modernist aesthetics, and particularly of the French strand, which goes back to the *nouveau roman* and continues with Derrida, and the *Tel Quel* group. In Ricoeur's case, the purpose of setting up such a dubious opposition is precisely to divorce the text from the author. "With written discourse," Ricoeur writes, "the author's intention and the meaning of the text cease to coincide.... What the text says now matters more than what the author meant to say, and every exegesis unfolds its procedures within the circumference of a meaning that has broken its moorings to the psychology of its author" (95). Ricoeur's concept of intention—as something "mental," as a matter of the author's psychology, of some inner state of mind—is no different from that of the New Critics, and just as unsatisfying.

Intentions

What is unsatisfying about the New Critics' concept of intention? In "The Intentional Fallacy" Wimsatt and Beardsley define intention as "design or plan in the author's mind."[12] On this picture, an intention is a mental phenomenon—a thought, a vision, an idea—that precedes the text, often pictured as an urn or an icon.[13] As we have just seen, Ricoeur shares this picture. The "author's intentions," then, are imagined to reside outside the text, and to precede it as cause to effect. An intention becomes an ethereal object in the mind, a matter of the author's psychology. This mental phenomenon is imagined to cause the work, pictured as an atemporal object with clear spatial boundaries.

The New Critics postulate this picture of intentions in order to denounce it. They don't deny that authors *have* intentions, but claim that there is no way to establish what they might have been and that, in any case, readers have no business asking after them. The meaning of the text resides in the text itself, not in whatever intentions the author might once have had.

Convinced that the author is dead, poststructuralists haven't been kinder to questions of intentions than the New Critics. Yet Roland Barthes' classic "The Death of the Author" is not so much an essay on intentions as an essay trying to replace the old liberal subject with language itself: "For Mallarmé, as for us, it is language which speaks, not the author; to write is to reach ... that point where not 'I' but only language functions."[14]

Nevertheless, to eradicate the writing subject is to place a taboo on asking about intentions.

In her influential 1980s handbook in poststructuralist literary criticism, *Critical Practice*, Catherine Belsey asserts that questions like "What is he trying to tell us?" or "What does she mean in this passage?" are questions about something "anterior to [the text]," attempts to "explain it ... in terms of the author's ideas, psychological state or social background."[15] But there is no reason to outlaw such questions. Usually they are answered by pointing to specific passages in the text. Why rule out the relevance of an interview with the author, in advance and on principle? The interest of the interview will depend on how it sheds light on the elements that puzzle us in the text.[16]

The picture of intentions conjured up by the New Critics and shared by Belsey, is a theoretical fiction. If I intend to write a novel, it doesn't follow that the text resides in my brain as a kind of homunculus, a fully formed work in miniature. Writers know that intentions don't work in this way. Writing is thinking. Texts grow and change as the writer works on her sentences. As Flaubert struggled with every word and every comma of *Madame Bovary*, he wasn't taking dictation from a pre-existing mental image of the finished work. He was paying close attention to the words on the page. Then he crossed them out and rewrote them, over and over again, until each sentence seemed right. The "rightness" of those specific words emerged from the work of writing, not from a pre-existing mini-work in his head. For why would it take Flaubert so long to figure out what sentences he would accept as the ones he meant to say if he already had a perfectly formed intention to say exactly those sentences? In the work of writing, intentions work in the opposite direction: only by looking at what he had done could Flaubert decide whether it was what he wanted to do. It is true that, at some point, Flaubert decided to—intended to—write a novel about provincial life in Normandy. But that is not much help to a literary critic wanting to understand that novel. As a guide to reading, the picture of intentions as a mental plan preceding the work is mostly useless. (The New Critics got that right.)

The New Critics and their fellow-travelers were right to oppose such a bad picture of intentions. Unfortunately, they opposed it not by showing that it is a bad picture, but by preserving it under a taboo. Instead of providing a better explanation of what we do when we talk about intentions, the New Critics enthroned the bad picture of intentions as the only term in which to discuss the matter. In this way, they succeeded in making questions about what the author wants to say or do signs of unbearable critical naivety. The result was to create an all or nothing choice: either we embrace the bad picture of intentions, or we can't mention intentions at all. We should resist this move.

Strangely enough, the traditional view of intentions still lingers on in literary theory, even though many critics no longer have strong allegiances to New Criticism or poststructuralism. Recently, both David Rudrum and Ingeborg Löfgren have wondered why Cavell's trenchant critique of the New Critics' positions, first published in the late 1960s, has gone unnoticed.[17] In my view, the answer has to do with the critics' underlying picture of texts. Anyone who thinks of a text as an object will have trouble escaping the New Critics' view of intentions as "outside" the text. At the same time, anyone who, like Saussure, thinks of language as a closed system of signs will reject any discussion of speakers. Or they will insist, like Barthes, that the speaker is an effect of the language, rather than the other way around. The "posthumanist" turn has made it even more difficult for critics to acknowledge the obvious, namely that texts are made by someone. As a result, critics who are otherwise quite different come together in banning the word "intention" from their critical vocabulary.

Luckily, it is possible to talk about intentions in relation to a literary work in a more philosophically interesting way. In 1967, when the New Critics still dominated literary criticism, Cavell published two articles on intentions: "Music Discomposed," and "A Matter of Meaning It." The latter was written as a response to Monroe Beardsley's criticism of Cavell's view of intentions in the former. Here I'll focus on "A Matter of Meaning It," an essay in which he acknowledges the importance of Elizabeth Anscombe's book *Intention* for any discussion of this topic (see MM, 235 n. 7).

For anyone interested in the literary discussion of intentions, Anscombe's key move is to show that we read intentions off actions. Like Wittgenstein's and Austin's, Anscombe's perspective on actions is *retrospective*. If we want to understand what the intention was, we must analyze the act after it has happened. The question "why?" always comes after the fact. An intentional action, Anscombe writes, is an action "to which a certain sense of the question 'Why' is given application; the sense is of course that in which the answer if positive, gives a reason for acting."[18]

To ask about the author's intentions is to ask about her reasons for doing a certain thing, once that thing has been done. Readers naturally begin by looking to the text itself for such reasons. Say that a literary critic reads *King Lear* and notices a striking number of references to eyes, sight, blindness. If she then asks "Why this?" the answer will take the form of providing reasons for their appearance, reasons that help us understand the play better. In *King Lear* we will discover that the play is practically inexhaustible in the depth and range of reasons it provides. (Like other great works, *King Lear* can take any amount of interpretive pressure.)

Cavell's understanding of intention is also retrospective, in Anscombe's sense. (In contrast, the New Critics think of intention as causal and predictive.) Tackling the question head-on, Cavell declares that "the first fact of works of art is that they are meant, meant to be understood. A poem, whatever else it is is an *utterance* (outer-ance)" (MM, 227–28). By coining the term "outer-ance" Cavell conveys both a sense of action, and a sense of expression, in contrast to the New Critic's understanding of the poem as "more or less like a physical object." Beardsley and the other New Critics' "bad picture of intention," he shows, goes hand in hand with their "bad picture of what a poem is" (227). If you picture the poem as an object, you will also picture intentions as something mental that precedes and causes it.

What happens to intentions if we consider a text a kind of action? Or, as Cavell puts it, as something someone has *done*, something that is *meant to be exactly as it is*? This idea often gets expressed by calling texts (and paintings, and pottery, and other artworks) "intentional objects." The word "object" works better for the visual arts than for literature. A literary text does not become an object—a sculpture, a painting—just because it is written down. Language remains action and expression.[19] Yet the idea behind the term "intentional object" is sound: the text is made to be exactly the way it is.

If we think of a text as something someone has wanted to be precisely the way it is, Cavell argues, there is no difference between "what is intended" and "what is there." What is there is what is intended. To ask "Why this?"—for example why the author wants *this* word *here*, in this specific position in the line, is not to ask about "something anterior" to the poem. It is to ask about what's *there*, on full display, in the poem, or painting, or film. Nothing is hidden.

To ask "Why this?" or, if you prefer, "What did the author want from this?" about a textual feature is to ask what *work* this feature does in the text. It is simply not to ask about the contents of the author's brain at a specific point in the past: "Intention," Cavell writes (in Anscombe's spirit), "is no more an efficient cause of an object of art than it is of a human action: in both cases it is a way of understanding the thing done, of describing what happens" (MM, 230). It follows that "Why did Shakespeare make Hamlet delay so long?" and "Why does Hamlet delay so long?" are versions of the same question.[20]

Intentions are by no means always hidden. Cavell writes: "In … the case of ordinary conduct, nothing is more visible than actions which are not meant, visible in the slip, the mistake, the accident, the inadvertence ..., and [in] what follows (the embarrassment, confusion, remorse, apology, attempt to correct....)" (MM, 226–27). Consider actions such as stumbling, dropping the ball, missing the basket. In such cases we don't speculate on the person's intentions. The intentions are stunningly obvious, built into the action itself. Our language reveals that we know this. We call what she did "stumbling," because we can tell *from her behavior* that her intention was to "walk." The *grammar* of "stumbling" implies "walking." It also implies lack of intention to stumble. Yet *some* stumbles may strike us as artificial or theatrical or odd in some way. There is something about them—maybe a hint of exaggeration, maybe a too obvious buckling of the knee—that makes us suspect that the action was intentional, that it was "done on purpose." In such cases, we immediately begin to wonder why the person would stumble in that specific way, at that specific time. (We ask for her reasons.)

The moment we talk about actions, questions of repercussions and responsibility arise. On this point, Sartre's "What Is Literature?" complements Cavell's understanding of language and writing. Sartre, who thinks of texts as intentional objects, doesn't hesitate to ask the writer: "What aspect of the world do you want to disclose? What change do you want to bring into the world by this disclosure?"[21] Such questions are not extrinsic to the text. They acknowledge that the writer has *done* something, that she has intervened in an existing state of affairs, that she therefore is *responsible* for something.[22]

Intentions matter for the question of responsibility, including political responsibility. In a court of law the difference between murder and manslaughter is a matter of intentions. The difference between a crime and liability in tort can also turn on intentions. If I deliberately set fire to your house, I am a criminal. But if I inadvertently set fire to your kitchen while trying to deep-fry potato chips, I probably am not. We can't assess responsibility without taking intentions into account.

But there are degrees of responsibility. Sartre stresses that the writer has absolute responsibility for her text. This is not exactly false. But Sartre makes the question of responsibility too general, too metaphysical. He is right to say that an author must always and at all times be ready to explain himself. But he occasionally forgets that the question of political responsibility is just as situated, just as specific as the question of who one is writing for. One doesn't demand an explanation—a defense, a justification, an excuse, an apology—unless a problem has arisen. If nobody responds to the writer's text by asking "How could you write *this*?" she is not in a position either to apologize or to justify herself. In literary criticism the question of intentions, like the question of responsibility, cannot arise unless someone (the critic, the reader) *notices something* and asks, "Why this?" Usually, this question doesn't take us "outside the text," as the New Critics feared it would. (And if it does, that is no disaster.) Rather it makes us examine the "outerance" of the text with renewed attention.

Acknowledgment

Expressions and actions place claims on us. If texts are expressions and actions, then they call for our *acknowledgment*. But what is acknowledgment? Cavell developed the term in an attempt to free us from the skeptical picture of what it is to understand others. By "free us from" I don't mean "refute" or "disprove" but, rather, "propose a different picture" of what it is to know—to understand—another mind. I want now to suggest that "acknowledgment" can also provide a different picture of what it is to read a text. The concept can serve as an antidote to the idea that to read a text is to impose our own pre-existing theories on it. It can also free us from the idea that all readings must begin in suspicion. (A particular reading may well *end* in suspicion, or develop suspicion as it goes, but that is another matter.) I'll begin by explaining what acknowledgment is, in Cavell's sense of the term.[23]

Cavell introduces the concept of "acknowledgment" in a discussion of skepticism of other minds. The question is how I can know what another human being is thinking, feeling, sensing. The skeptic holds that we can't ever know this with certainty. Cavell agrees that the skeptic has a strong position. On what criteria could I be 100 percent certain that I know what is going on inside another human being? *Of course* I can't feel his pain the way he does. *Of course* he could be faking his symptoms. Yet Cavell balks at the seemingly inevitable skeptical conclusion: that it follows that I can *never* know another human being. To understand what it is to know another, Cavell argues, we need to shift our frame and break with the skeptic's picture of human beings.

The skeptic pictures the human being as split between an outside and an inside (this is a version of the body/mind split). The outside consists of expressions and behavior (including gestures, mimicry, and so on). The skeptic rightly argues that expressions and behavior may be deceitful. How, he asks, can we get beyond such outer displays to what we actually want to know, namely the feeling, thought, sensation? He takes the question of how to know others to be a question of how to bring behavior and mind together with certainty. Given this picture, the skeptical conclusion—we can *never* know, or know only for "practical purposes"—seems inevitable. Against this, Cavell argues that we often do know. The skeptic sets up an all-or-nothing choice: either I know other minds fully and transparently, or I don't know them at all. This is not how knowledge of other minds work, in ordinary life, when we often (but certainly not always) know perfectly well what other people are thinking and feeling. I may not understand all others perfectly all the time. But sometimes, I do understand some particular other. Think of the situations in which parents understand their teenager better than she understands herself.

I am struck by the parallel between linguistic skepticism and skepticism with respect to other minds. In both cases, the skeptic pictures the question of knowledge as the need to bring the outer together with the inner: the signifier with the signified, the body with the soul.[24] Since nothing provides an absolute guarantee for the connection between outer and inner, the skeptic concludes that certainty can't be reached: meaning will always be indeterminate and undecidable, the inner life of another human being always inaccessible.

The picture of an outer form (signifier, behavior) cut off from its inner meaning (signified, mind or soul) is not compulsory. Cavell and the skeptic agree that we only have the other's behavior and expressions to go on. But, Cavell argues, in casting behavior as an outer shell, to be filled with inner meaning, the skeptic forgets that behavior is "expressive of mind, that only in rare cases is behavior utterly random or arbitrary" (KA, 262). "The human body is the best picture of the human mind," Wittgenstein writes (PPF, §25). This is not a behaviorist idea, for Wittgenstein isn't saying there is nothing but the body. He is saying that the body and its expressions—the expressive body—are what we have to go on when we try to understand the soul—the inner life—of a human being. This is why ordinary language philosophy is so relevant for theater, for theater presents this aspect of the human condition in pure form: to understand the characters on stage, all we have to go on are their actions and expressions, in this particular setting, at this particular time. Theater teaches us how much we can tell about the mind from paying attention to the expressive body.[25]

The skeptic is on to something. He reminds us of something most people have experienced, namely situations in which we feel powerless to know the thoughts and feelings of another human being. Such experiences arise because human beings are *separate*. There is no solution to the problem of human separation. The umbilical cord is cut at birth; no mother-matrix connects us all. Nor are we connected by invisible sensory channels, like the two brothers in Dion Boucicault's 1852 play *The Corsican Brothers*.[26] Earthlings are finite, mortal, and separate. This is a fundamental metaphysical (or, if one prefers, ontological) condition, a feature of all human forms of life.

The skeptic, Cavell writes, takes this metaphysical condition to be an epistemological limitation. Without explanation, the skeptic represents "metaphysical finitude as intellectual lack," as if this move goes without saying (KA, 263). But it doesn't. The skeptic doesn't treat other ontological or metaphysical facts in this way. Human beings are earth dwellers. Our perspective on life, the universe, and everything is that of earthlings. Nevertheless, skeptics don't invoke earth-boundness as a ground for skepticism with respect to biology or astronomy. Earth-boundness isn't considered an epistemological *perspective*, it's just our form of life, what we are. In other words: We live with our earthling-ness. Why can't we live with our separation? Why do we insist on turning human separation into an epistemological perspective? (There are so many answers, so many reasons—but they have nothing to do with epistemology.) Cavell wants us to realize that our finitude—our bodily existence, which entails our separation from each other and our mortality—is the condition of possibility for, not an obstacle to, human knowledge.

Acknowledgment is not a state of mind, or a particular mental content, but a *response*, something we *do*. Acknowledgment is not the opposite of knowledge, rather it *acts on* knowledge: "From my acknowledging that I am late it follows that I know I am late …; but from my knowing I am late, it does not follow that I acknowledge I am late …. One could say: Acknowledgment goes beyond knowledge … in its requirement that I *do* something or reveal something" (KA, 257). Attempts at acknowledgment reveal us: who we take ourselves to be, how we picture our relationship to the other. It goes without saying that my attempt at response may fail and thus reveal me as cruel, selfish, inattentive, and so on.

By intellectualizing and epistemologizing human finitude, the skeptic forgets the most fundamental thing about knowledge of other minds, namely that expressions and behavior *place a claim on others*. If you suddenly begin moaning and clutching your stomach, I will respond by calling the ambulance, trying to make the pain more bearable until it arrives. Or maybe I'll kick you in the groin to make it worse. Either action acknowledges your pain, and reveals my relationship to you. But unless you have a long history of putting on your "pain-act" with me, I will not first step back and consider whether I can be absolutely certain that you really are in pain. Acknowledgment thus always has a moral dimension (but it isn't reducible to matters of morality): our response to the expressions and actions of another inevitably reveals our judgment of the situation, the other, and our own responsibilities.

Acknowledgment is not an operation a subject performs on an object, and its goal is not scientific certainty. If the other's expressions, actions, behavior amount to a claim on us, to respond to that claim is to establish between us a kind of community based on the recognition of our separateness. To acknowledge your expressions and behavior is to show that I understand how it is with you. In all these ways acknowledgment "goes beyond" knowledge.

Acknowledgment also requires self-revelation: my actions and expressions reveal my position in relation to the other. King Lear can't acknowledge Cordelia's love unless he manages to acknowledge—reveal—his own failure of love. His tragedy, Cavell argues, is that Lear never can face this fact about himself. Cordelia dies because of Lear's "avoidance of love."[27] Failure of acknowledgment is the absence of an action, the absence of response, or a noncomprehending, inept, callous response. A failure to acknowledge something isn't a nothing, it is "the presence of something, a confusion, an indifference, a callousness, an exhaustion, a coldness" (KA, 264).

Acknowledgment isn't a second-class replacement for certainty, as if certainty were the gold standard, and acknowledgment what we settle for in the absence of knowledge. Nor is it a supplement to knowledge, as if we always have knowledge first, and then, in a second move, decide what to do with that knowledge. On the contrary: our response to another may surprise us, reveal a knowledge we didn't even know we possessed.[28] Acknowledgment *changes the dimension* in which we assess our understanding of others.

Acknowledgment does not begin in suspicion, although it may well conclude that suspicion is called for. It resists the positivistic model of knowledge from which skepticism is a recoil. If we picture our relationship to a work of literature as one of acknowledgment, then the category of "certainty" is no longer the relevant dimension in which to assess the kind of knowledge a literary critic has of a literary work. Acknowledgment includes knowledge, but in its insistence on response, on action and self-revelation, it moves beyond epistemology to raise questions of ethics and morality.

Acknowledgment is individual and particular. It isn't a "description of a given response," Cavell notes, "but a category in terms of which a given response is evaluated" (KA, 263–64). There is no such thing as universal acknowledgment, acknowledgment given once and for all. Each case, each human situation, requires a specific response. There is no end to the claims of others on us, and ours on them.

Acknowledgment, then, is always specific. A mother's expressions of pain place different claims on her daughter than on her nurses. If the daughter behaves as a competent, professional nurse in relation to her mother, this may (or may not) represent a radical failure to acknowledge her mother's pain. The concept of acknowledgment helps us to understand why even the most stunning reading of a text doesn't block the way for new ones. Different brilliant readings aren't competing to reveal the same (absolutely certain) knowledge of the text, as if the text only offered us one truth. That is like saying that there is only one truth to be had about a human being. Rather, different readings reveal different readers' different ways of acknowledging the text. To acknowledge the text in the right way, each reader needs to work out his or her own position in relation to it. This requires humility, self-knowledge, and good judgment.

In short, the mere existence of different interpretations is not a reason to start worrying about the old question of "validity in interpretation." That would be like saying that there is only one right way to acknowledge the actions and expressions of another human being. One reason why the great classics demand new readings in new times is that the reader's relationship to the text changes with the reader's position in time, and in geographical location, too. To read Shakespeare in England in the nineteenth century is vastly different from reading him in Sri Lanka in the twenty-first century. If reading is a practice of acknowledgment, then reading requires us to discover our own position in relation to the work.

In his essay on *King Lear*, Cavell writes that the "epistemology of other minds is the same as the metaphysics of other times and places."[29] Everything I have said about acknowledgment, then, is also relevant in cases where we are trying to understand works from different times and places. Whether we are trying to understand Euripides, Shakespeare, or Ibsen, we can't acknowledge the characters, their situation, their plight of soul—we can't understand them—unless we attempt to make their present ours, attempt to see what they see.

We can't abandon the effort of acknowledgment on the grounds that we are separated from the characters and the works by deserts and oceans, or by centuries, as if we were persuaded that there exists only one right place and time for the reading, a place and time that we fail to occupy. "There is no *place* from which we can see the past. Our position is to be discovered, and this is done in the painful way it is always done, in piecing it out totally," Cavell writes.[30] There is no place—no right place and no wrong place—from which to see a work. (This amounts to saying there is *no approach* to the work; that when we read, we aren't *outside* the work.) If there were one right place—the perfect, external vantage point—from which to look at the work, then we could simply search for it, find it, and then invite all future readers to go to that spot. (I suppose this would be a form of dogmatism.) Luckily, this is not how reading works. Our task is far more difficult: we have to acknowledge the work and its concerns here and now, as they appear to this particular reader in this particular moment in history.

But how can I acknowledge a text? What will I have to do? The first step is to remember that there is no approach. As with ordinary language itself, we can't grasp the text as a totality from the outside. Reading implicates us in the text's language from the start. Rather than seeing the totality from afar, we find a "blur or block from which to start" (CR, 6). That "blur or block" may be a passage or a theme that haunts us, to which we always return, something that grabs our attention and refuses to let it go. Something we need to understand. Something that makes us ask "Why this?" There is no method to be had here. For how we go about answering the question will depend on what we want to know.[31]

In any case, if acknowledgment is response, I have to try to understand the work's claim on me.[32] But since acknowledgment is personal, particular, and specific, I—the reader—now have a double task: to understand the work—to acknowledge its concepts and concerns—I also have to figure out where I stand in relation to it.

What Is Literature? On Literariness and Literary Language

Is all this talk of acknowledgment specific to literature? Or maybe to fiction? The short answer is: I don't think so. All kinds of storytelling—not just novels, plays, and films, but fairytales, myths, parables, legends—invite response and acknowledgment. So does philosophy, literary criticism, nonfiction, and journalism. Whether we read philosophy or literature, we can try to discover the work's own concepts and concerns, and figure out our response to them.

The long answer would return to the age-old debates about whether there is something that holds all examples of literature together. What is literature? Is there a literary language? Maybe there is something called "literariness"? That term goes back to the Russian and Czech formalists, particularly to Jan Mukařovský and Roman Jakobson. The fundamental idea is that literary texts share certain formal strategies ("devices") that signal that they are literature. Today, variations on this (highly modernist) view are everywhere: ordinary language is simplistic, familiar, and referential; literary language is complex, unfamiliar, and self-referential or not referential at all.

Mukařovský declares that poetic language is the "systematic violation" of the "norm of the standard [language]." But the argument relies on an extreme definition of the "norm": the "standard language in its purest form [is] the language of science."[33] There is no place here for ordinary language in Wittgenstein's or Austin's understanding of the term. Jakobson and Mukařovský agree that poetic language focuses "on the utterance" (Mukařovský), or on the "poetic function" (Jakobson).[34] For Jakobson, poetry foregrounds its own "palpability"—today many would call this its own materiality.[35] Viktor Shklovsky's view—that literature uses various "defamiliarizing" techniques to make us wake up, fall out of the routine—is also an attempt to define poetic or literary language.[36] This view, fortunately, doesn't have to be understood in strictly formalist terms. Shklovsky is right to say that the best writing—whether fiction or non-fiction—makes us pay attention to things we took for granted, makes us see some aspect of the world more clearly.

Since it is all too easy to find literary works that don't exhibit the features we have decided to count as "literary," other critics throw up their hands and declare that literature can't be defined at all. John M. Ellis rightly argues that both groups are looking for something that all cases of literature have in common. Rejecting both camps, Ellis proposes instead that we consider the concept of literature to be similar to "weeds." No one feature holds the concept of "weeds" together. Weeds are whatever the gardener doesn't want in his garden. Definitions aren't a matter of essences, but of use. To discover what literature is, Ellis writes, we should examine use, find out when (under what circumstances) "speakers of the language" are willing or unwilling to use the word.[37]

I agree with Ellis's Wittgenstein-inspired critique of the quest for the perfect definition of literature. I am less enamored of the example of "weeds," which depends too much on us knowing pretty clearly what we will *not* consider weeds. Fiction, for example: Ellis goes on to claim that we should only use the word "literature" about texts in relation to which we don't ask about truth and falsity. This questionable move makes "literature" synonymous with "fiction." This is a traditional view, which no longer works. When we read memoirs, or Knausgård's *My Struggle*, the truth of the account is crucial to the text's literary value. Moreover, like so many other critics and philosophers who set out to define literature, Ellis forgets that excruciatingly *bad* literature is literature, too.

As a concept, "literature" works much like "game": attempts to find the essence that unites all members of the group will always fail. But it doesn't follow that the term is meaningless. In case of doubt, we point to examples, and spend time discussing borderline cases.[38] "Here giving examples is not an indirect way of explaining—in default of a better one," Wittgenstein notes (§71). Many literary genres work in the same way. To define the genre of the "novel" is as difficult as to define "literature." Just as we can talk about games, or weeds, and make perfect sense, we can talk about literature, or call some styles "literary" (as opposed to, say, "academic" or "bureaucratic" or "journalistic") without implying that all cases that fall under the concept must have something in common.[39]

If we need to draw more rigid boundaries "for a special purpose," we can of course do so (§69). Then we should begin by reminding ourselves of the purpose. Why do we need this particular boundary in this particular case? If a student asks me what "literature" is, I can't even begin to provide a useful answer until I understand why she wants to know. Is she trying to learn the meaning of the word, from scratch as it were? Then I must assume that until now she has lived in a different world.[40] My answer had better acknowledge that her task is not just to learn the word, but to learn something about a world in which "literature" is (still) part of shared practices, sensibilities, ways of talking, responding, and judging, so that with respect to "literature" she will have to learn "all the whirl of organism Wittgenstein calls 'forms of life.'"[41] Until she has learned all that, she won't be able to project the word appropriately in new contexts—to use it in the way we do.[42] Here "we" means whatever the use is in the world she is trying to become part of. That world may be mired in conflicts over the concept. If so, learning to use the concept means learning how those conflicts work, too. Once she knows how to use the word as we do, she will know what literature is in our world. But that just means that she will now be in the same pickle as everyone else, namely unable to come up with one clear definition of this phenomenon she now can discuss with ease.

But maybe she asks what literature is because she is a graduate student of English who wants to know whether Gibbon's *The History of the Decline and Fall of the Roman Empire* is literature. She will soon discover that one set of criteria for literature (literature is fiction as opposed to truth) clashes rather awkwardly with another (literature is writing that exhibit a mysterious feature we call "literariness"). To get a clear answer, she will have to explain why she asks. Does she need to know whether she can put Gibbon on her prelims reading list? Or does she want to compare Gibbon's prose style with Defoe's? In the first case, she needs a bureaucratic answer; in the second, she may be looking for the beginning of a dissertation. Perhaps she is really asking whether certain generic differences that we think of as important mattered to eighteenth-century readers and writers. One day, her work may help us to understand the origins of certain contemporary notions of literature, but it will not define literature once and for all.

We can certainly establish the grammar of "literature" in a particular tradition, or for a particular institution and so on, but attempts to define "literariness" or "literary language" once and for all will be futile. No theory I know of has managed to show what specific features unite the language of Shakespeare, Proust, Brecht, and Knausgård. A great writer is someone capable of mobilizing the full resources of ordinary language, someone who helps us to "sharpen our perceptions," not someone who leaves ordinary language behind.[43] There are as many different uses of language in literature as in life. The best literary language is ordinary language used exceptionally well.

All kinds of texts can place a claim on us, call out for response and acknowledgment. There is no point in restricting discussion of literature to discussions of fiction. Or rather, there is no point in confusing "literature" with "fiction." If readers begin to respond to new, previously "nonliterary" genres in "literary" ways, then those genres too will become literary. Like the rest of language, the concept of literature changes over time. Literary critics contribute crucially to such changes, not by laying down new definitions, but by responding to new kinds of writing, by making us see something new. Over the past generation, for example, critics have helped to change "comic books" into "graphic novels" by showing that such works too can carry the weight of a good reader's full attention and response.

Uses of Literature

Because I don't think it is useful to try to define literature, and because I resist equating literature with fiction, I find myself at odds with many critics who offer theories of why literature is valuable, for example by arguing that reading literature (or just fiction) makes us better people, or more active citizens, or that such reading makes us more responsive, more thoughtful, more caring, or more critical.[44]

I am certainly not denying that literature can be supremely valuable, existentially and ethically. Reading can change lives. It can help us to expand our sense of possibilities in life. The French critic Marielle Macé rightly argues that reading literature gives us a personal archive, a set of narratives that "give our existence form, flavor, and even style."[45] Reading gives us access to the cultural imaginary and supplies us with figures and situations that help us to understand our own experience. But so do stories and characters from film and television, or the continuous soap opera offered by celebrities featured in *People* magazine. And we have all heard the stories of the concentration camp commander who read Goethe and Schiller in his spare time.

Most academic defenses of literature rest on one particular aesthetic norm, one particular definition of literature, namely that of late modernism. Wolfgang Huemer, for example, thinks that we can "define what is particular about literary texts" by saying that they "put an emphasis not on *what* is said, but on *how* it is said."[46] Such definitions are variations on the usual formalist definitions of "literariness," as if attention to form were the key feature of all literature, or at least of all valuable literature (but here the defense of literature becomes tautological: valuable literature is valuable).

In the same way, Richard Eldridge considers "the literary as a site of formal disruption." Literature, he writes, always works with a specifically "literary" set of devices, such as "emplotment, metaphor, allegory, irony, hyperbole, understatement, and assonance." By using such devices, the writer achieves "fullness of attention (ideational, emotional, and sensuous)." I don't deny that some literature works in this way. But the insistence on formal disruption and specific "literary" devices reinforces the late modernist dispensation. So does the constant preference for the tragic over the comic, the idea that (valuable) literature always emerges from "occasions of crisis and loss."[47] What happened to the muse of comedy? To visions of creativity and joy? Is the comic vision not enlarging of mind and soul?

Late modernist aesthetics turns reading into an immensely self-conscious affair. Thus Charles Altieri, a distinguished scholar of modern poetry, wants us to value aesthetic valuation, the very activity of valuing and appreciating literature. For him, "appreciation" stands in contrast to critique, which he reduces to resentment. I certainly agree that cultivation of good judgment is a valuable activity. It is also true that literary critics need to learn the art of admiration as well as that of critique. But Altieri's "appreciation" is so self-conscious it seems to lose sight of the work we are supposedly admiring: "In the process of valuing we adjust to invitations to ... define the persons we become as readers because we become capable of seeing our imaginative activities as valuable in their own right."[48] Such readers are likely to admire themselves for being capable of self-conscious admiring.

In general, contemporary academics privilege self-conscious, late modernist reading over the kind of spellbound reading Beauvoir valued so highly. All her life she praised the experience of immersed, absorbed, spellbound reading. A good novel, she wrote, "imitates the opacity, ambiguity, impartiality of life; spellbound by the story he is told, the reader responds as he would to events in real life."[49] To read is to have experiences one would otherwise not have. Readers of fiction, Beauvoir tells us, enlarge their world.

In contrast, the late modernist reader is a self-aware, knowing formalist. She wouldn't dream of identifying with a character, let alone the author, and would dismiss spellbound reading as naively uncritical. Late modernist reading works brilliantly on texts written to be read that way. Professional literary critics certainly need to know how to practice it. But late modernist reading isn't the only kind. Like Beauvoir, I believe that the experience of being completely absorbed by a book is valuable, and thrilling, too.[50] For most people, that experience is usually a major reason for reading literature in the first place.[51] The thrill of complete absorption gets many young people hooked on reading for life. When I read *Harry Potter* or *Game of Thrones*, I was so immersed that I certainly didn't pay attention to the shape of every sentence. In fact, to begin worrying about the sentences would be to destroy the immersive experience entirely. But spellbound reading isn't a response limited to popular, world-creating fiction. Reading novels by Dickens, George Eliot, Balzac, and Tolstoy is equally immersive. Karl Ove Knausgård's *My Struggle* and Elena Ferrante's Naples-quartet also have that spellbinding or "unputdownable" quality.

Readers are as variable as the texts we call literature. Why do we persist in looking for *one* general defense of literature? One single reason to value reading? Historically, as Joshua Landy shows, theorists have come up with all kinds of reasons to value fiction: for its moral exemplarity, for its affective power, and for its development of a whole range of cognitive insights or capacities.[52] In Landy's view (and in mine), a number of these theories are quite convincing, and there is always *some* work that will brilliantly illustrate the theory.

Landy doesn't leave it at that. On the contrary, resolutely set against moralizing and didactic reasons to value fiction, he proposes that *some* fictions—the ones he calls "formative"—are valuable because they train us to "fine-tune our mental capacities." As he sees it, such fictions don't preach, they don't tell us what to think, they *train* us to acquire new mental habits, habits which, in the end, may well help us to develop "virtue of character."[53] Different "formative fictions" teach us different skills or habits. Landy isn't trying to say something about how all literature works. Rather he aims to say something true about a specific kind of fiction.

Landy's argument avoids large generalizations about literature as such. Although he would not use this language, I would say that Landy investigates the (Wittgensteinian) grammar of a specific region of literature, that of "formative fictions." To decide whether his concept picks out certain

works in an illuminating way, we would, among other things, need to figure out whether we are capable of going on with it. Can we use it ourselves,
project it in new contexts? If not, is it because of some issue with its original formulation? To decide, we would need to re-examine the works he
cites as exemplary for his case. Whether we agree or disagree with him,
Landy's mode of argument makes us pay attention to particulars.

Reading as a Practice of Acknowledgment

I have said that acknowledgment is a response to the expressions of another. It is an effort to understand those expressions. I now want to suggest that reading is a practice of acknowledgment. The concept helps us
to reconceive what we do when we try to understand a work of literature.
(Here I am simply using "literature" in its ordinary sense, which has no
rigid boundaries. There will always be hard cases, texts we don't know
how to define.) To understand other minds we need to understand other
people's reasons and motivations for saying and doing what they do: "In
all cases," Cavell notes, "[the] problem is to discover the specific plight
of mind and circumstance within which a human being gives voice to his
condition" (KA, 240).

How does this affect our work with texts? We aren't acknowledging
the work's concern if we simply project our own preoccupations on to
it. So we will have to try to discover the works own concepts. But how
do I avoid forcing the work to conform to my own pre-existing theories?
How do I read in a spirit of "just response," as Sarah Beckwith calls it?[54] If
I turn to Cavell for guidance, I find nothing. As usual, ordinary language
philosophy doesn't propose a method; it is utterly uninterested in laying
down requirements for how to read. All I can find is a passage in *Pursuits of
Happiness*—a book about film, not literature—telling the reader to try "to
let the object or the work of your interest teach you how to consider it."[55]

The first time I tried to figure out what this might mean in practice,
with a novel, a play, a film, I was completely baffled. The only hint Cavell
provides is to say that we usually have no trouble letting a work of theory
or philosophy teach us how to read it. It finally dawned upon me that the
right sort of reading will emerge if we simply let ourselves read literature
or watch films in much the same way as we read theory and philosophy.

But how do we read theory? Well, we often begin by trying to get at
least a general idea of what the work is about, maybe get a vague sense of
what its major concerns and concepts are. We find the "blur or block from
which to start" (CR, 6): a moment in the text that in some way grabs us,
calls out for investigation. At first, we may only form a hazy idea of what is

going on in the text. To get a clearer view, we zoom in on some concepts, study the examples, circle back to passages that appear to illuminate them, look for the arguments, the contradictions, the exceptions. If we persist, we usually emerge with a workable understanding of the book's concerns. We have learned something new. If the book really fascinates us, we may engage with it again, maybe revise some of our initial impressions, try to get clear on why it strikes us as important, reflect on what we can use it for in our own work.

Why do we imagine that it is always much harder to do this with a novel or a play than with a work of theory or philosophy? Maybe because we lack practice. Maybe we fear that the reading emerging from such a process might not look all that impressive. We are not used to looking for the work's own concepts when that work is a novel or a play. Instead we rush in with concepts taken from theorists and philosophers. Or with the unbearable knowingness of skepticism. But if we dare to trust our experience, dare to develop our response, dare to figure out where we stand in relation to the text—dare to acknowledge it—then reading will become a discovery of the unexpected and the new. It will become an adventure.

But acknowledgment isn't just a matter of accounting for the work's concepts. It also requires us to understand our own position in relation to the work's concerns. To articulate a just response, we must do justice both to the work and ourselves. Just as I try not to impose my own theories on the work, I need to acknowledge my own investments, interests, and reactions. After all, if they drive me toward this particular work, I need to account for them, too. Understood as a practice of acknowledgment, reading becomes a conversation between the work and the reader.

This can be daunting, for who am I to assume that my concerns should be voiced in conversation with Goethe or Shakespeare? But it is impossible to write literary criticism without revealing one's own judgment. Literary criticism depends on judgment. Judgment that something is interesting, worth teaching, worth writing about; judgment that our own insights are worth expressing, judgment in finding the right words to express them. And however great it may be, literature requires readers. Without the generosity of the reader, Sartre writes, the work cannot come into existence.[56]

To make an aesthetic judgment is to stake one's authority on nothing but one's own experience: when we declare that something is beautiful we have nothing but our own judgment to go on. While we may spontaneously feel that others simply *must* see what we see, we can't ground this conviction on anything more tangible than our own judgment that this is beautiful (or fascinating, or significant, or unexpectedly moving, and so on).[57] This feels risky. To say what we see is to expose our judgment to the potential ridicule of the world.

To account for one's experience of a work of art requires willingness to pay close attention to that experience. It requires us to trust it, and to find it worth expressing: "Without this trust in one's experience, expressed as a willingness to find words for it, without thus taking an interest in it, one is without authority in one's experience," Cavell writes.[58] There are four tasks here: to be willing to have the experience (in the sense of paying attention to it), to judge it important enough to be expressed, to find words for it, and to claim authority for it. These tasks require judgment, and courage.

But this is true for accounts of every kind of experience. Aesthetic experience—I mean simply the experience of reading, watching, seeing a work of art—is a specific region of ordinary experience. Cavell's understanding of what it is to trust one's experience of a film reminds me of the work going on in feminist consciousness-raising groups in the 1960s and 1970s. The purpose of these groups was precisely to encourage women to take an interest in their own experience, to be willing to voice it, and to claim authority for it. The result was revolutionary. The women's understanding of themselves, their experiences, their place in the world was transformed.

The difficulties involved in "taking an interest in one's experience" are the same in life and in art, as Cavell points out: "The difficulty of assessing [one's experience of a film] is the same as the difficulty of assessing everyday experience, the difficulty of expressing oneself satisfactorily, of making oneself find words for what one is specifically interested to say, which comes to the difficulty, as I put it, of finding the right to be thus interested."[59]

Aesthetic experience is ordinary: to find out what our aesthetic experience means entails the same difficulties and joys as the investigation of other experiences. In the 1970s many feminists made the mistake of taking experience to be infallible. To them the "authority of experience" meant that once a woman had found the words to express it, she could never be wrong about the nature of her own experience—as if our capacity to understand our own experience did not stand in need of education, training, development. This is not Cavell's view. Nor is it the psychoanalytic view. All critics, whether literary or not, take for granted that new practitioners need long and serious training. It "needs constant admission," Cavell writes, "that one's experience may be wrong, or misformed or inattentive and inconstant" (MM, 218).

Cavell's sense of the fallibility of experience coalesces around the idea of "checking one's experience" against the work of art. He uses the term "checking" to "capture the sense at the same time of consulting one's experience and of subjecting it to examination, and beyond these, of momentarily stopping, turning yourself away from whatever your preoccupations and turning your experience away from its expected, habitual track, to find itself, its own track: coming to attention. The moral of this practice is to educate your experience sufficiently so that it is worthy of trust."[60]

The education of one's experience by paying careful attention to it: what a hopeful idea! Experience is not fixed; previous experience does not doom me forever to repeat the same mistakes. (This too is like psychoanalysis: There is a way to break the old patterns! Experience can be trained!) I must be prepared to discover that my sense of the work was profoundly mistaken, but that discovery will itself be part of my further education as a critic. Here too there is no difference between aesthetic experience (our experience of the work of art), and ordinary experience (what we experience in life).

Aesthetic experience is ordinary experience. I don't mean to say that it doesn't require special insights, knowledge, skills, and judgment. But so do other experiences as well: truly to appreciate great cooking, a particularly excellent fishing spot, or great growing soil also requires specific knowledge, judgment, and skills. That's why it's so helpful to know that we can train our experience. Like other experiences, the experience of film, theater, literature has the power to change us, to help us overcome or undo our existing beliefs. Of course, most of the time nothing much will happen. We aren't regularly transformed by reading, just as we aren't regularly transformed by ordinary experiences either. But sometimes reading becomes a genuine adventure. When it does, it can transform our understanding of ourselves, and the world.

Reading as an Adventure: Discovering the New

If reading is a practice of acknowledgment, it can teach us something new. It can become an adventure. I take the word "adventure" from Simone de Beauvoir and from Cora Diamond. In her 1946 essay "Literature and Metaphysics," Beauvoir declares that a good novel is an invitation to the reader to share the author's sense of exploration (*recherche*) and discovery, to join her on an "authentic adventure of the mind" (272).[61] Beauvoir's reader is open to new discoveries, willing to follow the writer, ready to set off on their joint adventure. If the experience disappoints, the responsibility does not always rest with the writer. The reader can fail a book, Beauvoir writes, by refusing to "participate sincerely in the experience the author is trying to involve him in; he does not read as he demands that one writes, he is afraid of risks, of adventure" (276).[62]

Although it lacks the concept of acknowledgment, Beauvoir's account of "spellbound" or "absorbed" reading overlaps with my understanding of reading in significant ways. To her, the miracle of literature is its power to convey the "taste of another life" (*le goût d'une autre vie*).[63] Literature allows us to see the world as it appears to another, not by becoming them, but by being able to let ourselves be imaginatively absorbed by the vision offered by the literary work. Thus literature helps to bridge the separation between human beings: immersed in your text, I can see what you see, but without losing myself, without becoming you. (This is the point where the work of acknowledgment can take place.) I don't take Beauvoir to say that reading *necessarily* makes us willing to open ourselves up to the point of view of the other. It is perfectly possible to fail in our efforts to acknowledge the other. Or never make the effort at all.

In Beauvoir's account, a capacity for identification—for putting ourselves in the other's place—is not a sign of naivety, but of a willingness to be open to the other's point of view. Identification can help us to see the other's world more clearly, and thus give us better grounds for judging it. Beauvoir reads as ordinary readers do. She has the intellectual self-confidence to know that she won't lose her powers of discernment and critique by allowing herself to be immersed in the world of a novel. A suspicious reader can't read in this way. She has to be constantly self-conscious, constantly on her guard, constantly anxious about being tricked by the text, and thus come across as naive. In this way, she runs the risk of missing the adventure, as Diamond would say.

Beauvoir speaks of the "taste of another life." Other thinkers use different terms to get at very similar ideas. Martha Nussbaum calls the "ability to see the world from another creature's viewpoint" *empathy*.[64] Hannah Arendt thinks that critical thinking—political thinking—requires us to learn to "think with an enlarged mentality," which means "train[ing] one's imagination to go visiting."[65] Iris Murdoch speaks of a "compassion" and a "just and loving gaze." (I discuss Murdoch's ideas further in chapter 10.) All these thinkers stress the moral or political importance of being able to share the point of view of another person, to see what she sees. This is also required for the work of acknowledgment.

For Diamond, to read well is to bring to the text a certain quality of attention, a willingness to participate in the adventure offered by the text. Diamond introduces the idea by quoting the legendary British mountaineer George Mallory, who disappeared on Mount Everest in 1924. Asked why mountaineers climb mountains, he answered: "Our case ... is not unlike that of one who has, for instance, a gift for music. There may be inconvenience, and even damage, to be sustained in devoting time to music; but the greatest danger is in not devoting enough, for music is this man's adventure.... To refuse the adventure is to run the risk of drying up like a pea in its shell."[66]

For Diamond, adventure and attention are intrinsically linked. The bad reader is the inattentive reader who "misses the characters' adventures, "misses his own possible adventure in reading"; misses the chance to emerge from his shell, to open himself to the new, the different, the challenging: "The greater danger is inattention, the refusal of adventure," Diamond writes. "The risk there, as Mallory puts it, is of drying up like a pea in its shell."[67]

To be open to adventure is to be attentive, ready to be illuminated by the text, to assume that it can work the "miracle of literature" and show us something new. Reading as a practice of acknowledgment requires full attention to particulars. It requires us to emerge from our shell and open ourselves up to the experience offered by the text. It requires us to take our own experience seriously, and to trust it. It requires us to mobilize our powers of identification and empathy when called for: not as final resting places, but as one dimension of the work of understanding the text's claim on us. Moreover, if we want to be literary critics, we need to be writers, too, for our task is to find the right words to express *our* adventure. Acknowledgment requires attention to particulars, and to language, our own as well as that of others.

10

Language, Judgment, and Attention

WRITING IN THE WORLD

On July 22, 2011, Anders Behring Breivik detonated a bomb in Oslo that killed eight people and injured over 200 others. Then he headed to Utøya, a small island in the lake of Tyrifjorden where the Norwegian Labor Party's annual youth camp was taking place. At Utøya, he killed 69 men and women, one by one, at extremely close range: inches, not yards. Almost all the victims at Utøya were under twenty. Some were only fourteen.

Hours before he killed the children on Utøya, the terrorist sent off his manifesto to the world. For him, the manifesto was the point, his intellectual legacy, the expression of his "mission." The bombing and the callous killing of children were, in his own words, the "marketing operation" for his manifesto.[1] Strikingly, the manifesto contained hardly a word of his own. For years, the Norwegian terrorist had been "writing," which to him meant plagiarizing—cutting and pasting, copying and repeating, citing and recirculating—snippets of text from reactionary and racist websites. His relationship to language was as alienated as his relationship to reality. He had lost—or maybe he never really had—any sense of the weight of words.

His horrific acts challenged our sense of language. We—Norwegians—could not find the words. Yet we needed words, more than ever. In an article with the telling title "Reality Shock," Anders Johansen, a professor of nonfiction at the University of Bergen, wrote that the terror on Utøya changed Norwegian culture's relationship to language: "We no longer immediately dismiss as naïve serious attempts to make words conform to reality. For many of us, it has been crucial to find ways to say something true about what happened, in a language that is accurate both to facts and emotions."[2]

One doesn't have to be a Norwegian in the aftermath of Utøya to yearn for language in touch with reality. Every day, we face reports of new atrocities, new acts of terror. At the same time, the language of politicians increasingly drifts free of reality. Back in 2004 President George W. Bush's advisor, Karl Rove, scolded the journalist Ronald Suskind for still living in a quaintly old-fashioned "reality-based community."[3] In 2005 Stephen Colbert coined the word "truthiness" to convey his sense of the peculiar unreality of the political language surrounding him.[4] When politicians, advertisers, bureaucrats, academics produce a quagmire of words that don't mean anything, their words serve one purpose: to make us acquiesce in ideas, actions, and projects we don't actually understand. This is as dangerous for intellectual life as it is for democracy.[5]

In such a situation we need a philosophically serious alternative to theories promoting the idea that language is in some fundamental way disconnected from reality, just as we need an alternative to linguistic positivism and/or scientism. As I have shown in this book, ordinary language philosophy provides such an alternative. In this final chapter, I'll bring out the ethical dimension of ordinary language philosophy by turning to the philosophy of attention developed by three women philosophers: Simone Weil, Iris Murdoch, and Cora Diamond. Their work enables us to understand how literature—good writing—can teach us to see the world with greater clarity. To bring out the point, I'll place the philosophers' views on language, judgment, and attention in conversation with texts by Ibsen, Rilke, Woolf, and Hjorth.

Language, Judgment, Criteria

In chapter 9 I said that aesthetic experience is a specific region of ordinary experience. In the same way, aesthetic judgment is a specific region of ordinary judgment. To make an aesthetic judgment is to stake one's authority on nothing but one's own experience. While we hope others will see what we see, we can't count on it, for we can't compel anyone to judge a view or a painting in the same way we do. This is hardly news: Kant stressed the essentially subjective nature of aesthetic judgment in 1790.[6] If we are in a position of power in relation to them, we can compel others to *say* they agree with our judgment, but they can't be compelled truly to see what we see. At the heart of judgment, there is always an element of freedom. (But this is where ideology and marketing operations come in: they consist in efforts to shape, and change, our most fundamental ways of seeing. Sometimes they succeed. But not every time.) If, even after our most strenuous efforts to explain our judgment, our interlocutors truly don't see what we are talking about, then our spade is turned.[7]

For Wittgenstein and Cavell, every speech act—even scientific claims—takes place against a background of shared judgment: "It is not only agreement [*Übereinsstimmung*] in definitions, but also (odd as it may sound) agreement in judgements that is required for communication by means of language," Wittgenstein writes (§242). Agreement in judgment, moreover, is "agreement not in opinions, but rather in form of life" (§241).

In the stunning first part of *The Claim of Reason*, Cavell brings out the relationship between speaking and judging. To agree in judgment is to *share criteria* for how and when to apply concepts. Use is governed by criteria. But, as Steven Affeldt brilliantly demonstrates, "governed by" doesn't mean that criteria pre-exist language, or that criteria somehow form a set of rules that provide a "ground of intelligibility" for our words. The wonder of human language, Cavell notes, is precisely that it does *not* depend "upon such a structure and conception of rules."[8] Criteria don't underpin or ground language. Rather, criteria and language are on the same level. "Agreement in language" and "agreement in criteria" are two ways of describing the same thing.[9]

We don't ask about criteria unless we feel confused. ("What do you mean?" or "I don't get it?" are common ways of calling for criteria.) Cavell gives the example of arriving in an unfamiliar culture and coming upon a (to us) strange plank with three pegs (two for the armholes, one to "sit" on): "We might feel he's not so much sitting on the thing as hanging from it. But he looks comfortable enough" (CR, 71). Do we want to call what he does "sitting"? The question calls for us to examine our criteria for "sitting" afresh. Can one "sit" without bending the knees or without folding at the hips?

But criteria don't exist apart from the specific situation, apart from the "specific occasion of asking and the specific need which our asking is to address," Affeldt notes.[10] Back in my own culture, I go to a bar and see a woman half-perched, half-leaning on a barstool, with one leg on the floor, head bent over the counter. Would I call what she does "sitting"? As I observe her, I feel more tempted to call it "slouching." But why? Examining my criteria, I realize that "slouching" has more to do with the shoulders and upper spine than with the hips and knees. Apparently, in this case, I am more struck by the curve of her spine and shoulders than by her hips and legs.

In a most crucial paragraph, which I will quote at length, Cavell writes:

> Wittgenstein's insight, or implied claim, seems to be something like this, that all our knowledge, everything we assert of question (or doubt or wonder about ...) is governed not merely by what we understand as "evidence" or "truth conditions," but by criteria. ("Not merely" suggests a misleading emphasis. Criteria are not alternatives or additions

to evidence. Without the control of criteria in applying concepts, we would not know what counts as evidence for any claim, nor for what claims evidence is needed.) And that suggests, according to what has so far emerged, that every surmise and each tested conviction depend upon the same structure of background of necessities and agreements that judgments of value explicitly do. (CR, 14)

Facts remain facts. But we couldn't establish them unless we shared the "background of necessities and agreements" that make up our form of life. Criteria, moreover, do not precede judgment. (If they did, they would be some kind of ground of language. But that is not the picture proposed by either Wittgenstein or Cavell.) We discover—lay bare, uncover—our criteria by investigating what we say. The stunning systematicity of language reveals itself in the discovery—the fact—that we share criteria for what to say when.

But if to speak is to utter something against a background of shared judgments, we see why Cavell emphasizes the concept of *voice*, which I connect to the inescapable element of subjectivity in every human utterance. Here "subjectivity" does not stand in opposition to "objectivity." It signals, rather, that "objectivity" is something we achieve in language. Even the most objective or matter-of-fact statement takes place against a background of shared judgments. Cavell stresses the point: "I do not say that, according to Wittgenstein statements of fact are judgments of value. That would simply mean that there are no facts, that nothing can be established in the way statements of fact evidently can be. The case is rather that, as I wish to put it, both statements of fact and judgments of value rest upon the same capacities of human nature; that, so to speak, only a creature that can judge of value can state a fact" (CR, 14–15).

"Language itself" makes no judgments. *We* do. This emphasis on the subject's judgments, at work in every utterance, enables ordinary language philosophy to move us beyond both linguistic skepticism (the sense that language never grasps the world) and various kinds of scientism and positivism (the idea that only a certain kind of objective, "scientific" language provides true knowledge).

Once we grasp Wittgenstein's vision of language, Cavell writes, we may begin to worry that "maybe language (and understanding, and knowledge) rests upon very shaky foundations—a thin net over an abyss" (CR, 178). To speak is to appeal to others: "Can you see what I see?" If they can't, and we wish to go on talking to them, we may call for criteria. Inspecting our different criteria for saying what we say, we may discover why we fail to understand each other (this can be the beginning of philosophy). Or we may discover that no further conversation is possible, that we have become unintelligible, at least to these specific others. Then the abyss gapes open at our feet.

Writing and Attention

We make our lives in language. If we care about language, then we have good reason to care about literature, too, not because it necessarily uplifts us and makes us better, but because writers specialize in language. Using words is their specific craft. And, as Austin reminds us, a "sharpened awareness of words" is intertwined with sharpened attention to reality. Just think of the specialist distinctions that appear to come naturally to chefs, fashion designers, farmers, and fishermen. They instantly see features I don't even notice, both because I don't know how to do what they do, and because I don't know how to talk like they do. Craftsmen and practitioners develop ways of talking that register the finest gradations in their craft, their activity, whether it is sewing, cooking, fishing, hunting, tennis, soccer, bullfighting, motorcycle repair—every human practice gives rise to its own expressions, its own ways of speaking. The language of such practitioners "embodies the inherited experience and acumen of many generations," as Austin puts it, but it also constantly projects old words in new contexts and invents new expressions in response to new practices and technologies.[11]

To people who don't share their skills, highly experienced craftspeople appear to have uncannily heightened powers of perception. "Experts see the world differently. They notice things that nonexperts don't see," Joshua Foer writes. By "expert," Foer means exceptionally highly trained and experienced practitioners. Among his examples are master chess players, successful chicken sexers, and skillful police officers. Such practitioners can't always explain what they do. Expert chicken sexers, for example, appear to have no way of explaining how they decide whether a chicken is male or female. "Their art is inexplicable," Foer writes.[12] Yet someone teaches chicken sexers to see. Those teachers must say and do *something* to convey their art to their successors. Maybe learning chicken sexing is like learning our first language: we don't know how we learn it (there's no point in lecturing a two-year-old on language), yet we learn it, by example, by imitation and response, and always in constant interaction with others.

Writers spend their lives trying to find the right words. They can teach us differences. The best writers have an exceptional capacity to convey nuanced sense impressions, emotions, experiences, imaginative ruminations, reflections, thoughts. Their writing reveals and expresses the precision of their attention. When Henry James had to give advice to writers, he didn't tell them to work hard to develop a specifically literary language. He simply said that they should try to notice everything: "Try to be one of the people on whom nothing is lost."[13]

Attentive writing doesn't have to be fiction. Good writing requires a capacity to think concretely, to imagine specific situations, to consider how different situations endow words with different nuances. This is not a skill limited to literature, or to a particular genre of writing. Austin exhorted philosophers to use their imagination, to "imagine the situation in detail with a background of story," and to "imagin[e] cases with vividness and fullness."[14]

The highly imaginative essayist Guy Davenport reminds us that the imagination is more than the capacity to make things up. For him, the "skills of the imagination" require the capacity to dream, to recognize, to guess and suppose: "Language itself is continuously an imaginative act."[15] David Foster Wallace's essays are luminous in their explorations of the resources of the English language. Wallace makes us see both language and reality afresh. "A Supposedly Fun Thing I'll Never Do Again" changed my ideas about the meaning of "fun" forever. (It also made me think quite differently about cruises and cruise ships.)[16] When Karl Ove Knausgård describes a day in his teenage life in all its banal details, he isn't taking dictation from his memory. Rather, he remembers, he dreams, he thinks, to the point that he can conjure up—create—the scene in language. (No wonder he insists that *My Struggle* is a novel, not a memoir.)

An Attentive Gaze Is a Just and Loving Gaze

Writers, then, can teach us to pay attention to particulars, including the particulars of language. But what exactly is attention? As a concept, "attention" has a wide range of meanings. It comes from the Latin *ad* + *tendere*: to reach or stretch toward something. To attend to something is to direct the mind or the senses toward something, to apply oneself; to watch over, minister to, wait upon, follow, frequent; to wait for, await, expect. In this concept, the idea of caring for, or serving others converges on the idea of listening, waiting, and watching.

Iris Murdoch defines an attentive gaze as a "just and loving gaze."[17] For a long time I resisted this formulation. I suspected "just and loving" to be code for "moralizing and sentimental," or "judgmental and saccharine." These terms scared me. As Leslie Jamison puts it: "If sentimentality is the word people use to insult emotion—in its simplified, degraded, and indulgent forms—then "saccharine" is the word they use to insult sentimentality."[18] Nevertheless, I came round. I now find Murdoch's "just and loving gaze" to be an excellent description of the kind of attention required for anyone who wishes to cultivate a realistic spirit. I'll try to explain why.

Murdoch's philosophy of attention was inspired by Simone Weil. For Weil, to be *attentif* is to be waiting, watchful, open to what may arise: "Above all our thought should be empty, waiting, not seeking anything, but ready to receive in its naked truth the object that is to penetrate it," Weil writes. To be attentive is to be *disponible pour la vérité*: to be open, ready, available for the truth.[19]

For Weil the ultimate truth is God: "prayer consists of attention." But one doesn't have to be a mystic to follow Weil; an interest in earthly truth will suffice. Weil herself, in fact, analyzes the value of attention through a discussion of schoolwork. Even the most banal school studies, such as math problems or translation to or from a foreign language, provide valuable training in attention. The right sort of attention, however, only arises if we manage to find joy and pleasure in the work: "The joy of learning is as indispensable in study as breathing is in running," she writes.[20]

For Weil, attention is neutral, waiting, and open. It rests on joy, a pleasurable wish to contemplate the truth. Attention is neither striving nor self-promoting. It tries to understand, not destroy. Attention is the very essence of the love of God: "Not only does the love of God have attention for its substance; the love of our neighbor, which we know to be the same love, is made of this same substance." Love is not the same thing as warmth and compassion. Too much sympathy can blind us to reality. To manage to see another human being with the openness of genuine attention is truly difficult: "it is almost a miracle; it is a miracle," Weil writes.[21]

Unlike Weil, Murdoch is not religious. She writes about attention because she wants to turn us into "active moral agent[s]," persons capable of having a genuinely moral relationship to reality and to act accordingly. Yet, like Weil, she considers attention to be at once impartial and loving. Attention, Murdoch writes, "express[es] the idea of a just and loving gaze directed upon an individual reality."[22] A just and loving gaze is open and waiting in relation to reality, but it is not passive. To be attentive is to let reality reverberate in us. Attention answers, responds and takes responsibility.

But why is "just and loving" the right expression? Like Weil, Murdoch stresses repeatedly that she wants nothing to do with sentimentality and misplaced compassion. A just and loving gaze enables us to see the world as it is. It is the best strategy we have when we want to discover the truth about a person or a situation. We will never understand whatever it is we are looking at if we don't do our utmost to see the situation from the other person's point of view, yet without relinquishing our own perspective. (This is clearly relevant for the idea that reading is a practice of acknowledgment, as I present it in chapter 9.) The attentive gaze combines justice and love. For Weil and Murdoch, love is not less objective than justice. Just like justice, love requires a realistic gaze. Cavell's understanding that we establish facts against a background of shared judgment seems exactly relevant here.

Murdoch does not write about politics. But a just and loving gaze is needed in politics, too, perhaps more than anywhere else. The boundary between morality and politics is not absolute. It is both politically and morally urgent, for example, to find the right relationship to the Other. (We all have our [different] others.) Weil herself directed her attention toward the poor and the oppressed, and supported the radical causes of her time. In spite of her bad health, she worked in a factory before leaving to fight in the Spanish Civil War. Her attention was as political as it was religious.

Attention and Moral Philosophy: Cora Diamond

Perhaps it is because of the depth of her understanding of Wittgenstein that Cora Diamond writes so well about attention in relation to moral philosophy. For her, as for Weil and Murdoch, moral reflection is a specific kind of attention, a particular response to the world, a way of seeing things (the world, other people, oneself). For Diamond, moral philosophy—moral thought—must focus on the particular case, on the individual, the specific and the unique.[23] Murdoch writes that there are "moral attitudes which emphasise the inexhaustible detail of the world, the endlessness of the task of understanding."[24] Diamond agrees. We never finish the work of understanding. As the best literature demonstrates, there is always more to see. As an example, Diamond quotes the last stanza of "Ducks," a children's poem by Walter de la Mare. Having described many different kinds of ducks, the poet concludes:

> All these are *kinds*. But every Duck
> Himself is, and himself alone:
> Fleet wing, arched neck, webbed foot, round eye,
> And marvellous cage of bone.
> Clad in this beauty a creature dwells,
> Of sovran instinct, sense and skill;
> Yet secret as the hidden wells
> Whence Life itself doth rill.[25]

The poem shows, in a very simple way, that a duck is a creature of beauty and dignity, deserving of respect and admiration. Diamond wants us to see that there is something morally important about the quality of the poet's attention to a common duck. The stanza is an example of a just and loving gaze.

Diamond disagrees with the widespread idea that moral reflection always takes the form of deliberation on clear-cut choices, or explicit evaluations: right, wrong, evil, good. Traditional moral philosophy, she writes, takes a far too narrow view of what counts as morally relevant insights. The famous trolley problem — on which there are innumerable variations — is the quintessential example. Here's one version: A runaway railway trolley comes down the railway line. If nothing is done, it will kill five workers further down the track. I am standing on a bridge over the track, next to a very fat man. Should I push this stranger down on the line in order to save the five workers?

When it comes to explaining the kind of moral reasoning we actually engage in in everyday life, Diamond thinks the trolley problem is truly useless (my interpretation, not her words). First, it is overly focused on dramatic choices. Second, it divorces the question of moral action from the question of how we see the world. In this way, it turns morality into something added to already existing knowledge, a kind of moral icing on an already existing cake. Diamond objects to the idea that epistemology and metaphysics provide the framework for what we can say about reality, and then, once that framework is in place, moral philosophy can step in and tell us what is to count as good or evil, right or wrong. This view reduces morality to the question of how to label people and their actions, and divorces it from questions concerning truth and insight (for those questions are taken to be settled before the moral reflection can begin).

Diamond reminds us that moral action only rarely takes the form of a clear choice, in which we sit down and make lists of arguments for and against. In real life, we often feel that we "have no choice." Or we discover that we already have done something with huge moral implications, without really thinking about it. Sometimes we make long lists of arguments, consider them carefully, and decide what to do. Then we go out and do exactly the opposite. Or we don't actually do anything. In such situations, the trolley problem is no help.

At the beginning of Iris Murdoch's novel *The Bell* (1958), Dora Greenfield takes the train on a hot summer's day. The train, of the kind with a long corridor running along the side of the compartments, is hot and overcrowded. As Dora squeezes into her middle seat, she feels sweaty and fat, for her skirt is tight and she is only too aware that she has put on weight.

An old lady struggles through the crowded corridor and reaches Dora's compartment, delighted finally to have found Dora's neighbor, a rather large old lady: "Dora stopped listening because a dreadful thought has struck her. She ought to give up her seat. She rejected the thought, but it came back."[26]

Dora now has a moral dilemma. Should she give up her seat? Couldn't the elderly lady stand in the corridor herself? But she looks rather frail, and the corridor is terribly crowded. Nobody else in the compartment look as if they are even thinking of getting up. But Dora took the trouble to get to the train early. She deserves her seat. In any case, Dora is tired. She certainly deserves to rest:

> She regarded her state of distress as completely neurotic. She decided not to give up her seat.
> She got up and said to the standing lady "Do sit down here, please. I'm not going very far, and I'd much rather stand anyway."[27]

It turns out that the elderly lady already has a corner seat by the window in a different carriage, and that she is delighted to change seats with Dora. "Everyone in this carriage was thinner," Dora thinks as she settles into her comfortable corner.[28]

The contrast between Dora's smug deliberations and her spontaneous leap out of her seat is comic. But there is an edge to the comedy: the relationship between moral reflection and action turns out to be more complicated than we think. Dora is by no means a saint. Her reflections aren't particularly subtle. She has a tendency to be selfish, and she loves feeling physically comfortable. She is also a little too pleased to be rewarded with a better seat.[29]

Dora clearly has a fairly shaky understanding of why she does whatever she does. This turns out to be the case for her train journey, too. Without really understanding why, she is on her way to be reunited with her husband, a man she fears. Nevertheless, she still has the right attitude. While the other passengers bury themselves in their newspapers or determinedly stare out of the window, Dora is attentive. She takes in the situation. She gets up. Murdoch's attitude toward Dora is humorous, but just and loving, too.

The Difficulty of Reality

To devote one's full attention to a phenomenon or a person, and to find a language in which to express what we see, is difficult. Even when we do our best, others may never understand us. Sometimes we are overcome by our own inadequacy: we simply can't find the words. We turn away. We don't want to pay attention. Diamond writes about the "difficulty of reality," which she defines as something we aren't capable of thinking about, something we can't express in words, maybe because it is too painful, maybe because it is inexplicably good:

> The difficulty of reality.... That is a phrase [for] experiences in which we take something in reality to be resistant to our thinking it, or possibly to be painful in its inexplicability, difficult in that way, or perhaps awesome and astonishing in its inexplicability. *We take things so.* And the things we take so may simply not, to others, present the kind of difficulty, of being hard or impossible or agonizing to get one's mind round.[30]

Diamond is not just talking about traumas. And even when she does discuss traumatic experiences, she does not share the widespread conviction that trauma always falls "outside language." To her, the difficulty of reality is something that has to do with the way we "take it." When we can't find words, the problem is not language, it is us.

The problem of the difficulty of reality—the problem of the unsayable—won't be the same for everyone. In her magnificent essay "Slouching Towards Bethlehem," the psychoanalyst Nina Coltart reaches a similar insight: "There is always in our work a dimension that is beyond words. Some people *suffer* more from the unthinkable than others."[31] What is unthinkable for one person needs not be for another. There is no such thing as *the* unthinkable, if by that we mean some essential something that nobody can think, but which we nevertheless can name.[32] Yet it doesn't follow that we will be able to express everything. Coltart writes that "in all of us there are some things which will never be within our reach; there is always a mystery at the heart of every person, and therefore in our jobs as analysts."[33] She makes me think of Wittgenstein's "explanations come to an end some time" (§1). Coltart's understanding of psychic life clashes with positivistic forms of psychiatry, which operate on the assumption that scientific explanations go—or one day will go—all the way down. (The recoil from that belief is skepticism.)

Diamond uses Ted Hughes's poem "Six Young Men," as one of her examples. The poet looks at a photograph of six young men, taken in 1914. Six months later they were all dead, some in gruesome ways. Staring at their "celluloid smiles," the poet feels the "contradictory permanent horrors" of the scene, feels it invading and threatening his own sense of aliveness. Yet not everyone takes the scene so. Diamond writes: "What is capable of astonishing one in its incomprehensibility, its not being fittable in with the world as one understands it, may be seen by others as unsurprising."[34] Writers can open our eyes to the difficulty of reality. But we may not be able to respond. Instead of feeling our own mortality to be as fragile as celluloid, instead of feeling the horror of the young men's death, we'll talk about the sacrifice of heroes willing to give their lives for king and country. Then we take something the writer wants us to see as horrible, unthinkable, and reduce it to a cliché.

Trauma isn't the only experience that we may find difficult to express in words. Finding the words to convey the inexplicable reality of goodness is not always easier than finding the words to express evil. Diamond writes about Ruth Klüger, who was sent to Auschwitz when she was thirteen.[35] During the selection, the SS officer's female assistant, herself a prisoner, walked up to Ruth and asked how old she was. Thirteen, she replied. Tell him you are fifteen, the woman said. When the SS officer asked about her age, Ruth said fifteen. The officer thought she was small. The assistant pointed out that she seemed strong. That's how she became registered as a prisoner in the camp, and thus got a small chance to survive. Klüger writes:

> I have always told this story in wonder, and people wonder at my wonder. They say, okay, some persons are altruistic. We understand that; it doesn't surprise us. The girl who helped you was one of those who likes to help.... But don't just look at the scene. Focus on it, zero in on it, and consider what happened.... Her decision broke the chain of knowable causes.... She saw me stand in line, a kid sentenced to death, she approached me, she defended me, and she got me through. What more do you need for an example of perfect goodness? ... Listen to me, don't take it apart, absorb it as I am telling it and remember it.[36]

Klüger experiences this moment as an incomprehensible miracle, something she simply can't understand with ordinary logical criteria. After the war, she encounters people who don't think there is anything special at all in her experience. They completely fail to acknowledge her own deep and lasting sense of wonder. Diamond makes us see that there is something morally defective about this. If we are to acknowledge Ruth Klüger, we need to meet her with a "just and loving gaze," and try to take in the permanent state of amazement and wonder in which she lives.

The Realism of Compassion: *Little Eyolf*

Ruth Klüger's case shows that the right kind of attention isn't simply a cool, clinical noting down of features of reality. Truly to "get inside" the experiences of the other is difficult. It requires us to mobilize our powers of imagination, compassion, identification, alongside our powers of reflection and reason. I think this is what Simone de Beauvoir has in mind when she speaks of being absorbed by a novel, to the point of feeling the "taste of another life."[37] But here I must stress that the "just and loving gaze" works in the service of realism. According to Murdoch we engage in fantasy— not realism—when we project our own "proliferation of blinding self-centred aims and images" on to reality. The just and loving gaze requires detachment, a kind of impersonality: "The freedom which is a proper human goal is the freedom from fantasy, that is the realism of compassion."[38] Compassion is realism, not misplaced sentimentality.

Both Murdoch and Diamond use the word "realism" about the capacity for attentive moral response: "in the elaboration and application of moral concepts, we come to an understanding of what the world is, what life is," Diamond writes.[39] For Murdoch, realism is a moral achievement, a liberation of the self, the result of an unusual capacity for unselfish attention. Moral philosophy therefore has to be a kind of realism. But this kind of realism is almost impossible to achieve: "How is one to connect the realism which must involve a clear-eyed contemplation of the misery and evil of the world with a sense of the uncorrupted good without the latter idea becoming the merest consolatory dream?"[40] I am not quite sure what Murdoch means by "uncorrupted good." If she means something like a perfect, Platonic ideal, I can't follow her. But I if I consider goodness as an ordinary, everyday phenomenon, I see what she means, for the implication is that to learn to love is to learn to see.

In his late play *Little Eyolf* (1894), Ibsen investigates the connection between compassion and the capacity to face reality.[41] Ibsen's critics have often complained that *Little Eyolf* is difficult to understand. They have been particularly concerned with what they take to be the play's inferior structure, in which Rita and Alfred Allmers's ten-year-old son, Eyolf, drowns already at the end of the first act. Critics who think that the death of the child ought to be the focus and high point of the dramatic action can't figure out why Ibsen even thought he needed the remaining two acts.

Little Eyolf ends with a scene in which the Allmers decide to help the poor boys who live down by the fjordside, the same boys who often bullied Eyolf, who was lame in one leg.[42] Then they hoist the flag (as one did after funerals in Norway at the time). Many critics have found this ending unbearably sentimental and melodramatic. I am struck by the parallel between misreadings of *Little Eyolf* and misreadings of Murdoch: In both cases, critics fail to see the clear-eyed realism, the unblinking attention at the heart of the "just and loving gaze."

If we take Weil, Murdoch, and Diamond seriously, it's not that difficult to understand what Ibsen sets out to investigate in *Little Eyolf.* The play is about two ordinary, well-intentioned human beings who refuse to look attentively at themselves, other people, or the world. When their son dies, suffering finally enters the Allmers's lives. In the first act, Ibsen shows us the full extent of Rita's and Alfred Allmers's egoism and blindness. Then little Eyolf drowns. Ibsen places the death of the child in the first act because he is interested in exploring the *aftermath* of trauma: the numbness, the grief, the horror. *Little Eyolf* is concerned with what we do when the worst has happened.

In the second act, we witness the emergence of the protagonists' increasing self-insight, which in the third act culminates in the wish to care for others. The last two acts show how suffering—the awareness of death, of human finitude—changes the protagonists, how it slowly makes them realize that they can't continue to live in their egocentric cocoon. At the end of the play, Rita wants to develop "something that could resemble a kind of love" for other people.[43] This leads Rita and Alfred to decide to do something for the poor children down by the fjordside, the children whose screams we hear, but whom we never get to see on stage.

It is quite possible that they will fail, for this project requires them to give up their fantasies and learn to look at themselves, and others, with a realistic—a just and loving—gaze. This may well be too much for them. But as they stand there hoisting the flag in the last scene, they want to try. Ibsen's own gaze at these characters is neither sentimental nor judgmental. At the end of the play, they are neither heroes nor villains, but two ordinary people who have to live in a world they now know to be as fallen and imperfect as they are.

Even the structure of Ibsen's play brings out the connection between realism and love. For *Little Eyolf* is structured as a double movement away from selfishness and toward love, away from fantasy and toward reality. The controversial end emphasizes the protagonists' attempt to go on living without closing their eyes to suffering. Metatheatrically, the play struggles to develop a "just and loving gaze" on its own imperfect characters. But the play is not just a narrative of their attempts. The very form of the play, the form that annoyed so many critics, represents an enormous effort to escape from traditional forms of theater (*Little Eyolf* is neither tragedy nor comedy, and not melodrama either) and reach a new form of realism, a realism capable of showing the right kind of compassion.

"I Am Learning to See": *The Notebooks of Malte Laurids Brigge*

The Notebooks of Malte Laurids Brigge (1910) is as different from *Little Eyolf* as it is possible to be. Yet Rilke too is interested in the way egoism blocks the possibility of an attentive gaze. *The Notebooks of Malte Laurids Brigge* is a fiery defense of the modernist understanding of writing. In order to grasp what is real, important, and necessary in an alienated and alienating world, one must write. Through his writing, Malte questions absolutely everything he has been told by others, everything he has learned and heard. Writing is a counterstrategy to deception and inauthenticity. To write is to convey something genuine, something true. A true writer needs to be able to see, to experience the world for himself:

> I am learning to see. Why, I cannot say, but all things enter more deeply into me; nor do impressions remain at the level where they used to cease. There is a place within me of which I knew nothing. Now all things tend that way. I do not know what happens there.[44]

This fascinating passage sets up the *Notebooks*' investigations of the relationship between the inner and the outer. By "inner" I mean the inner life, what Wittgenstein sometimes calls the "soul." By "outer," I mean either the person's actions and behavior, or simply whatever surrounds the writer. Rilke brings out the paradoxical nature of writing. Writing is expression, in the most literal sense of the word, for it turns the inner into something outer. At the same time, however, the writer doesn't have a soul, an inner life, until he learns to see. The implication is that if we don't notice anything, if we don't pay attention to the outer world, we will have no inner life. It is as if judgment—the act of taking notice of something—creates subjectivity.

The more Malte learns to see, the more he ends up feeling unknown and unknowable. The more his inner world expands, the less he feels known by others. There is an incipient skepticism at work here, a skepticism that necessarily leads to thoughts of loneliness, madness, and death. But the alternative, which is *not* to open one's eyes, is worse, for that leads to inner emptiness, to the death of the soul. If we don't turn our attention to the world around us, we will not develop that unknown inner space that both enriches and separates Malte from others. Then we will become utterly predictable, fully knowable, quite without interiority.

This is exactly what has happened to the local parson, Dr. Jespersen:

> When he visited us, Dr. Jespersen had to content himself with being some sort of private person; but that was precisely what he had never been. As long as he could remember, he had been in the souls department. The soul was a public institution, which he represented, and he contrived never to be off duty, not in even in his relations with his wife, "his modest, faithful Rebekka, beatified by the bearing of children," as Lavater put it when writing of another case.[45]

The passage reveals that Jespersen's problem is that something that should be inner— the soul—somehow has become something outer. This externalized interiority is clearly neither a mask nor a costume, nor is it a deliberate performance. Rilke describes it as a department, an institution, a clunky and impractical administrative unit. As a result, Jespersen has become impossible to relate to for anyone who doesn't piously submit to his ecclesiastical authority. He simply no longer knows how to behave like an ordinary human being ("a private person"). No wonder, then, that young Malte's parents find Jespersen the most boring guest imaginable: "To be candid, there was nothing whatsoever to talk about; remnants were dragged out and disposed of at unbelievable prices—everything had to go."[46] Without an inner life, language and expression becomes impossible. But to get an inner life, we need to learn to see.

If authenticity requires the outer to correspond to the inner, then Jespersen can neither be authentic or inauthentic. Since Jespersen *is* the outer shell he shows the world, the distinction becomes meaningless. For this reason, we can't call him a hypocrite. In a way, Jespersen is a postmodern subject a hundred years ahead of time: he *is* his priestly performance. No concept of falsity or inauthenticity can apply to him, yet paradoxically, this is precisely what makes him seem so hopelessly inauthentic. The difference between the young Malte and Jespersen is that Malte tries to see, to take in the world, whereas Jespersen has become a bureaucrat of the soul.

Rilke isn't explicitly concerned with moral issues. To convey what a shallow and self-obsessed person is like, he simply shows us how he talks, without sticking moral labels on any specific point, but also without shrinking from judgment. Yet his insistence that we must learn to see has obvious moral (or political) implications. Rilke's style, his way of presenting his material, his utterly original engagement with the relationship or nonrelationship between the inner and the outer challenges his readers: can we see what he sees?

A Room of One's Own and Reality

In *A Room of One's Own*, Virginia Woolf presents a stunning defense of the value of women's attention and women's writing. Women must write, not just for their own sake, but for the sake of the world: "When I ask you to write more books I am urging you to do what will be for your good and for the good of the world at large."[47]

Why is writing good for the world? Woolf's answer focuses on attention, on our capacity to see. In ordinary life, we only catch fleeting glimpses of reality. Usually we are far too filled with superficial and selfish thoughts to notice reality. Unless she learns to see, a human being risks living her whole life in a kind of unreality. The writer, Woolf notes, is privileged to "live more than other people in the presence of this reality. It is his business to find it and collect it and communicate it to the rest of us" (108). (I find Woolf a touch too Romantic here, just a shade too convinced that writers always have god-given powers of insight, but I can't let that deter me. At least I agree that writers specialize in language and attention.)

Reading also teaches us to see. (Few writers have read as much as Woolf did.) By focusing her attention on the text, the reader learns to see what the author sees. The reader learns to see reality. To read texts like *King Lear*, *Emma*, or *In Search of Lost Time* opens one's senses: "one sees more intensely afterwards; the world seems bared of its covering and given an intenser life" (109).

For Woolf, attention is disinterested and impersonal. A writer, she insists, must "communicat[e] his experience with perfect fullness. There must be freedom and there must be peace" (103). Self-consciousness is destructive for any writer, but particularly for women: "It is fatal for any one who writes to think of their sex," she declares (102–3). "Don't dream of influencing other people.... Think of things in themselves" (109).

If it is crucial for women to enter literature, it isn't because they have to write about their gender, but rather because each individual woman writer can give voice to her experience, her particular vision of the world.[48] Her singular perspective adds to our understanding of reality and is therefore valuable in itself. This is why Woolf encourages an imaginary young woman writer, who will never become a Dante or a Shakespeare, but still can teach us to see something we hadn't noticed before. In an age unused to women scientists, an age in which women in fiction were almost exclusively placed in plots turning on heterosexual love, "Mary Carmichael" widens her culture's understanding of literature, and reality, by writing two simple sentences: "Chloe liked Olivia. They shared a laboratory together" (82).

For Woolf, each woman has to find her own voice, focus her attention on the world, and find a language in which to express her vision. Although Woolf doesn't say that this is a political task, it can easily become one. In the 1970s, we learned from the women's movement that under the right circumstances, such a seemingly simple project can be political dynamite. Woolf's fundamental insight is simple: it is valuable to try to see reality as it is, and to find a language for what one sees. The result doesn't have to be *War and Peace*. A society needs to see itself through the eyes of writers, not least writers who occupy marginal and excluded positions. This is not an invitation to identity politics, but to a democratic vision of writing.

Literature after July 22: *Long Live the Post Horn!*

The Norwegian critic Ane Farsethås has shown that in the decade leading up to the massacre of 2011 Norwegian literature was haunted by a sense of unreality. After 2000, she notes, the postmodern fascination with performance and performativity began to lose its hold, and writers as well as characters often worried about authenticity, veering between a fear of being seen and the wish to remain hidden. In this decade, Norway, with its combination of oil-fueled affluence and social-democratic traditions, bred a desire for reality in many of its most talented artists.[49]

What is the point of writing in a world in which language appears to float free of the world? This question drives *Leve posthornet!* (Long live the post horn!), the 2012 novel by one of Norway's best-known writers, Vigdis Hjorth.[50] Written in the aftermath of July 22, the novel sets out to break down the gap between language and reality. In this book, language does real work. As the novel opens, Ellinor, a communications advisor, has lost all sense of the meaning of her words. When she looks out of the window, she literally can't see clearly, and she has become unable to feel anything for others, whether it is her lover, her family, or her colleagues.

The title "Long live the post horn!" is taken from Kierkegaard's *Repetition*.[51] In *Repetition*, Kierkegaard praises the post horn because it never sounds the same tone twice. But the title may also contain a sly reference to that pioneering postmodern novel, Thomas Pynchon's *The Crying of Lot 49*, in which a post horn is the symbol of a conspiracy that may or may not exist. Furthermore, Derrida's claim that the letter never arrives is also under attack here, for in Hjorth's novel the mail carrier is a hero who will go to extreme lengths to deliver the mail.

As the novel develops, Ellinor learns to mean what she says, and to work with something she has faith in, namely the heroic struggle to stop Norway from adopting the European Union's Third Postal Directive. She even manages to shed her habitual disdain for clichés, for she realizes that sometimes a cliché expresses exactly what she feels. Over time, her emotional numbness disappears, and she begins to admire and learn from the experiences of others. Hjorth turns Ellinor's story into a fine comic novel, a satire of political and commercial bureaucratic complacency, a profound and witty allegory of postmodern society's alienated relationship to language.

Although Hjorth's novel was written after the massacre on Utøya, the plot ends a few months before the horrors of 2011. The novel expresses the longing for reality, for a more genuine faith in language that intensified in the aftermath of those atrocious events, but the massacre itself can find no place in Ellinor's rather hopeful story. For a Norwegian novelist writing in 2012, the horrors of Utøya remain the unspeakable difficulty of reality. To read about Utøya we must turn to nonfiction, to Åge Borchgrevink and Åsne Seierstad.[52]

Language and Judgment after July 22

For Norwegians the terror of July 22 was a profoundly traumatic example of the difficulty of reality. Only saints can look at *everything* that happened that day with a just and loving gaze. Yet Oslo District Court made efforts to organize the trial in a way that gave room for love as well as justice. After the presentation of the gruesome details of each post-mortem report, a photograph of the victim was projected in court, while a one-minute long biography, usually written by the victim's family, was read out. The court record thus enshrines the memory of the victims not just in their death, but in life. Many badly wounded survivors from Utøya spoke in court about their suffering. The accused was also given hours to express himself, both at the beginning and at the very end of the trial.

One particular moment in the trial of the Norwegian terrorist turned on language, namely the judge's cross-examination of the first psychiatric team. (The court had asked for two psychiatric reports. The first found the terrorist criminally insane, the second not.) The authors of the first report, Synne Sørheim and Torgeir Husby, based their conclusions strictly on the checklists provided by the diagnostic manual ICD-10.[53]

To me, the two psychiatrists' testimony embodied one of the attitudes deplored by Diamond, namely the idea that objective description of reality somehow precedes and is independent from moral judgment. I got the impression that they thought that the categories on their checklists somehow were cut loose from ordinary judgment. But their own explanation showed the limits of that attitude. They claimed, for example, that the mass murderer's language exhibited neologisms characteristic of psychosis. Under cross-examination, however, it turned out that their criterion for a neologism was their own ordinary sense of language: a neologism, they said, is a "word that we take to be used in an incomprehensible way."[54]

At another moment, the presiding judge, Wenche Arntzen, explicitly raised the question of morality. The context is that the terrorist had said that he considered himself a "knight" who had to decide who should live and who should die in the new and ethnically pure Norway that his actions were intended to produce. The two psychiatrists claimed that this was a typically psychotic delusion:

JUDGE ARNTZEN: As to this question about who shall live and who shall die. Is it a delusion because it so immoral?

PSYCHIATRIST SØRHEIM: Now you confuse me.

ARNTZEN: You are saying that nobody can decide who shall die, that morally speaking nobody can have this responsibility?

SØRHEIM: The way we see it, no single individual has the responsibility for who lives and dies.

ARNTZEN: Well, many people have that responsibility in the sense of the death penalty, and in war. Such phenomena exist.

SØRHEIM: Yes, you are of course right.

ARNTZEN: But to call it a delusion. Is it because it is so immoral?

SØRHEIM: No, I am thinking of the examples you mentioned about war, and to sentence someone to death, it's impossible that he, sitting in his old bedroom, would belong to one of those categories and really believe that he was in a position to discover who should live and who should die.[55]

If Sørheim was "confused" by Arntzen's clear questions about morality and ideology, it is because her vision of psychiatry considers moral reflection irrelevant. At best moral reflection is secondary to the establishment of (scientific) facts, but that just proves that it has no place inside the science of psychiatry. (On this point, Sørheim exemplifies the position criticized by Cora Diamond.) Judge Arntzen's questions, in contrast, are the questions of a person who carries the burden of judgment, who has to decide on the sanity or insanity of the mass murderer. In the end, the court sided with the second, more humanistically oriented psychiatric team, and refused to find the terrorist psychotic. At least in this case, we learned something about the shortcomings of a scientistic understanding of the soul.

In the way it organized the July 22 trial, Oslo District Court acknowledged that a traumatized society needs more than just facts. Or rather: it acknowledged that facts cannot be divorced from judgment. The trial itself showed that we do need a different gaze, and a language that doesn't reduce the difficulty of reality to the flat and flattening categories on a general questionnaire. Not long after the trial ended, a scathing report on the events of July 22 revealed stunning failures in coordination and preparedness in police and government. In the ensuing debate, it became clear that bureaucrats too use language to avoid responsibility.

A society that loses faith in language will also lose its sense of reality. A society that rejects the very idea of a just and loving gaze as so much unscientific sentimentalism will try to replace judgment with measurements. In such a society, leaders won't ask themselves if they have truly looked at the situations for which they are responsible. Instead, they will proceed as if rules, benchmarks, and checklists abolish the need for human judgment. When disaster strikes, they will hide behind their rules and regulations, and their vague, lifeless, and peculiarly impersonal language. They will forget that "man's faculty of judgment ... rules out blind obedience," as Arendt puts it.[56] When we ask what such leaders take responsibility for, their answers will certainly make us feel that reality is slipping through our fingers.

In a world in which so many powerful persons and institutions have a vested interest in making us lose faith in language's power to respond to and reveal reality, precise and attentive use of words is an act of resistance. In "Politics and the English Language," George Orwell declares that "one ought to recognize that the present political chaos is connected with the decay of language, and that one can probably bring about some improvement by starting at the verbal end."[57] Every imaginatively crafted sentence, every perceptive reflection, every clear formulation, every accurate description is a small victory.

Notes

Introduction

1. For readers looking for a way into the ordinary reading of Wittgenstein, I recommend Cavell's "Availability of Wittgenstein's Later Philosophy" and "Excursus on Wittgenstein's Vision of Language," and Conant, "Wittgenstein on Meaning and Use." For Austin, I recommend Cavell's writings, beginning with the title essay in *Must We*, and continuing with two other essays in that volume, namely "Aesthetic Problems" and "Austin at Criticism." This initial course of reading could then continue with the whole first part of *The Claim of Reason*, move on to "What Did Derrida Want of Austin?" and "Counter-Philosophy and the Pawn of Voice," and culminate in Cavell's fascinating late essay on "Performative and Passionate Utterances." After this, it may be time to return to *The Claim of Reason* and read the rest of it, particularly part 4 on skepticism and tragedy. Fleming's *The State of Philosophy* is an excellent companion to *The Claim of Reason*.

2. See Felski, *Limits of Critique*, 2, 1; Diamond, *The Realistic Spirit*; Fleming, *The State of Philosophy*, 151–63.

3. For introductions to and discussions of Cavell, see, e.g., Fischer, *Stanley Cavell and Literary Skepticism*; Fleming and Payne, eds., *The Senses of Stanley Cavell*; Fleming, *The State of Philosophy*; Fleming, *First Word Philosophy*; Mulhall, *Stanley Cavell*; Gould, *Hearing Things*; Hammer, *Stanley Cavell*; Eldridge, ed., *Stanley Cavell*; Crary and Shieh, eds., *Reading Cavell*.

4. Hacker, "Preface," in *Wittgenstein: Comparisons and Contexts*, xviii.

5. Ibid., xx, xvii

6. For the first use of "reality-based community," see Suskind, "Faith, Certainty"; "truthiness" was the inspired invention of Stephen Colbert.

7. Diamond, "The Difficulty of Reality and the Difficulty of Philosophy," 44–45.

8. Fleming, "A Lecture on the History of Ordinary Language Philosophy," in *First Word Philosophy*, 115 (see also 39–40). For an example of a more recent analytic approach, which is alien to ordinary language philosophy as I use the term, see Hansen, "Contemporary Ordinary Language Philosophy."

9. The last two sentences are based on the introduction to a cluster of essays on ordinary language philosophy and feminism, which I cowrote. See Bauer *et al.*, "Introduction," v.

10. See Cavell, "Existentialism and Analytical Philosophy," 950–51.

11. For "post-positivism," see "Aesthetic Problems," 90, and Cavell, *Little Did I Know*, 414; for "appealing to ordinary language," see "Aesthetic Problems," 95.

12. Fleming, *First Word Philosophy*, 117.

13. Cavell, *In Quest of the Ordinary*, 6.

14. Austin, "A Plea for Excuses," 181.

15. See Kripke, *Wittgenstein on Rules and Private Language*.

16. Derrida first presented "Signature Event Context" as a lecture in Montreal in 1971. See Graff, "Editor's Foreword," vii.

17. One of the first and most ambitious attempts to harness Austin for a poststructuralist project is Felman, *The Scandal of the Speaking Body*, first published in English in 1983.

18. It would be instructive, for example, to examine what goes wrong in J. Hillis Miller's reading of Austin in *Speech Acts in Literature*, and in Judith Butler's *Excitable Speech*, but this isn't the place for that project. For a somewhat exasperated, yet still useful account of some common misreadings of Austin, see Gorman, "The Use and Abuse of Speech-Act Theory."

19. Altieri, "Wittgenstein on Consciousness and Language."

20. For the early debate about Wittgenstein and Derrida, see Staten, *Wittgenstein and Derrida*, and, on the antideconstructionist side, Quigley, "Wittgenstein's Philosophizing," and Ellis, *Against Deconstruction*. For later debates see the essays collected in Nagl and Mouffe, *The Legacy of Wittgenstein*, which includes Staten's "Wittgenstein's Deconstructive Legacy," as well as Schalkwyk's analysis of reference in Saussure, Derrida, and Wittgenstein, in *Literature and the Touch of the Real*. Glendinning's sensitive and thoughtful work on Derrida and Wittgenstein in *On Being with Others* stands out.

21. See Cavell, "Counter-Philosophy and the Pawn of Voice." An excerpt from an earlier version of this essay was published in 1995 as "What Did Derrida Want of Austin?" in Cavell, *Philosophical Passages*, 42–65. While the two versions overlap, they are not identical. The 1995 version is followed by an illuminating discussion (see Cavell, "Seminar," in *Philosophical Passages*, 66–90).

22. According to Perloff, Wittgenstein, like the avant-garde modernists, succeeded in bringing out the "strangeness, the enigmatic nature of everyday language." Perloff, *Wittgenstein's Ladder, 20*. Wittgenstein brought out the awesome power of ordinary language. He showed us why it is worthy of wonder, but he doesn't imply that this makes ordinary, everyday language consistently "strange" or "enigmatic."

23. "Much as I admire Cavell, I am resolutely opposed to his emphasis on therapy," Altieri writes in *Reckoning with the Imagination*, 218 n. 7.

24. Altieri, "Wittgenstein on Consciousness and Language," 1400.

25. Ware, *Dialectic of the Ladder*.

26. Fischer, *Stanley Cavell and Literary Skepticism*.

27. I can't begin to list all the relevant works. But see, e.g., Rhu, *Stanley Cavell's American Dream*; Beckwith, *Shakespeare and the Grammar of Forgiveness*; Moi, *Henrik Ibsen and the Birth of Modernism*; and, in a different mode, the discussion of Beckett in Critchley, *Very Little … Almost Nothing*.

28. I do try to use "philosophy" and "philosopher" about people who use those words about themselves: Cavell does philosophy, while Julia Kristeva does theory.

29. Cavell, "Existentialism," 954.

30. Austin, *How to Do Things with Words*, 6.

31. For "revolution," see "Politics," 28 and 30; for "revolutionary tasks," see *Must We*, xxxix.

32. Cavell, "Counter-Philosophy," 58.

33. The following discussion of Derrida and deconstruction, and Kuhn, is an edited version of a few pages in Moi, "They Practice Their Trades."

34. Cavell, "Aesthetic Problems of Modern Philosophy," 90.

35. Kuhn, *Structure of Scientific Revolutions*, 150.

36. Cavell, *Must We*, xxiii.

37. Kuhn, *Structure of Scientific Revolutions*, xiii.

38. Cavell, "Counter-Philosophy," 63.

39. For the claim that the two traditions are binary opposites, see Jost and Dauber, eds., *Ordinary Language Criticism*, xvi–xx.

40. To gain a sense of the complexity involved in getting clear on the relationship between the two traditions, see Cavell on Derrida in "Counter-Philosophy"; on de Man in "Politics"; and on Levinas in "What Is the Scandal of Skepticism?" See also two indispensable essays: Gould, "The Unhappy Performative," and Stone, "Wittgenstein on Deconstruction." For a general overview of Cavell's engagement with poststructuralism, see chapter 6 in Hammer, *Stanley Cavell*.

41. Cavell, "Existentialism," 948.

42. See Cavell, "Politics," 41.

43. For an excellent discussion of the problem of beginnings in Wittgenstein and Cavell, see Fleming, *The State of Philosophy*.

44. Cavell, *Little Did I Know*, 414.

45. Diamond, *The Realistic Spirit*, 24.

46. Ziarek, *Rhetoric of Failure*, 31.

47. See Hekman, *Material of Knowledge*, 31–46.

48. Moi, *What Is a Woman?* 59 n. 86.

49. I discuss theoreticism further in Moi, "Meaning What We Say."

50. Drury, "*Conversations with Wittgenstein*," 171.

51. See Kirby, *Telling Flesh*; and Meisel and Saussy, "Saussure and His Contexts."

52. Belsey, *Critical Practice*, 35.

53. I realize that Perry Meisel and Haun Saussy, the editors of the most recent English-language edition of *Course of General Linguistics*, disagree. I return to their view in chapter 5.

54. Barad, "Posthumanist Performativity," 802.

55. Ibid., 829 n. 38; see Kirby, *Telling Flesh*.

56. Wittgenstein, *Culture and Value*, 77.

57. Drury, *The Danger of Words*, xii.

58. See Cavell, "Aesthetic Problems of Modern Philosophy," 96.

59. Sartre, *Being and Nothingness*, 349.

60. See Fleming's magisterial analyses of silence in *Evil and Silence*, and "Listening to Cage"; and also my own "Hedda's Silences."

Chapter 1

1. A version of this section appeared in Norwegian as Moi, "Fem røde epler."

2. Cavell, "Division of Talent," 532. Cavell has also published his own reading of this beginning; see "Notes and Afterthoughts."

3. Wittgenstein quotes the Latin text, and the editors place this English text in a footnote.

4. Unless I indicate otherwise, all quotations from *Philosophical Investigations* in this section come from §1.

5. I am thinking of Paul Cézanne, *Five Apples*, 1877–78, Collection of Mr. and Mrs. Eugene V. Thaw.

6. Plato writes: "This feeling—a sense of wonder—is perfectly proper to a philoso-

pher: philosophy has no other foundation" (*Theaetetus*, 37). See also Descartes' discussion of wonder [*admiration*] in *Les Passions de l'ame*, 116–21.

7. "It is of no importance here whether Wittgenstein is right or wrong about Augustine's understanding of language, as long as we can recognize his account as a description of the 'background presuppositions' for a range of different views held by philosophers throughout history." Baker and Hacker, *Wittgenstein, Understanding and Meaning: Part I*, 3.

8. "As the text of the *Investigations* now stands," Wetzel writes in his learned and thoughtful meditation on the confessional voice in Wittgenstein and Augustine, "Augustine holds a place of honor and authority. Wittgenstein allows Augustine to supply him with his most perspicuous picture of a subtle, but profound, temptation" ("Wittgenstein's Augustine," 233).

9. The jars and the teddy bears appear in "Excursus on Wittgenstein's Vision of Language."

10. For an excellent article laying out the parallels and differences between Platonism and Derridean deconstruction, see Stone, "Wittgenstein on Deconstruction."

11. The phrase "grounded in use" can be found, for example, in Yu, "Wittgenstein, Pedagogy, and Literary Criticism," 366. The idea is quite ubiquitous in literary critical writings on Wittgenstein.

12. The best readings—the best introductions and most illuminating analyses—of the beginning of PI are by Cavell. I recommend "The Availability of Wittgenstein's Later Philosophy," "Excursus on Wittgenstein's Vision of Language," and "Notes and Afterthoughts on the Opening of Wittgenstein's *Investigations*."

13. Cortázar, *A Certain Lucas*, 24–25, 26.

14. Joaquín Vidal, "Faena cumbre."

15. Cortázar, *A Certain Lucas*, 26.

16. "El galache, precioso, terciado, mas con trapío, muy bien armado y astifino, encastado, que era noble, seguía entregado a los vuelos de la muleta, que el maestro salmantino manejaba con soltura y mando. Relajada la figura, trenzaba los muletazos, y cada uno de ellos era el dominio absoluto por el que tenía que seguir el toro un semicírculo en torno del diestro, y el remate, limpio y preciso, para dejar a la fiera en la distancia adecuada. Hubo naturales inmejorables y de pecho grandiosos, y ayudados por alto y por bajo a dos manos, y pases de la firma, pero no se nos irá de la retina un natural ligado con el de pecho, y el dibujo de éste, con salida por el hombro contrario, quizá los más acabados muletazos que haya dado nunca El Viti."—A "galache" is not, as the translation has it, a "monster" (25), but a bull from the Galache bull breeding farm in Salamanca.

17. Cortázar, *A Certain Lucas*, 25.

18. Cavell, "Must We Mean What We Say," 19.

19. Ibid., 20.

20. Austin, "A Plea for Excuses," 182.

21. I realized the importance of this section by reading Drury, who quotes 6.371, on p. xii in *The Danger of Words*.

22. Drury's discussion of the difference between philosophical clarity as Wittgenstein understood it, and scientific clarity is most illuminating (see Drury, *The Danger of Words*, xi–xii.)

23. See Wittgenstein, *Blue and Brown Books*, 17. I return to the craving for generality in chapter 4.

24. Culler, *On Deconstruction*, 123.

25. Conant, "Wittgenstein on Meaning and Use," 239.

26. Ibid., 241.

27. To use a metaphor is to project a word in a new, unexpected context (see Cavell, "Excursus on Wittgenstein's Vision of Language," 189–90). To understand a metaphor is not to translate it back to its "literal" meaning, but to understand the work *this* image does *here*, in this specific utterance. (See Cavell's suggestive discussion of metaphors in Cavell, "Aesthetic Problems," 79–81.)

28. Conant, "Wittgenstein on Meaning and Use," 235.

29. For a full account, see ibid., 231–38.

30. "Attempts to describe limits always make possible a displacement of those limits, so that Wittgenstein's suggestion that one cannot say 'bububu' and mean 'if it does not rain I shall go out for a walk,' has, paradoxically, made it possible to do just that. Its denial establishes a connection that can be exploited" (Culler, *On Deconstruction*, 124).

31. For a detailed account, see my discussion of Meisel and Saussy, and of Kirby, in chapter 5.

32. This is exactly what happens in Miller's reading of Austin in *Speech Acts in Literature*.

Chapter 2

1. It will be obvious how much my discussion of grammar and forms of life in this chapter owes to Stanley Cavell's understanding of Wittgenstein, particularly to his discussions of judgment and criteria.

2. Cavell, "Must We Mean What We Say," 19.

3. Drury, "Conversations with Wittgenstein," 171.

4. Here I draw on Wittgenstein's crucial discussion of concepts in §65–71, to which I return in chapters 3 and 4.

5. Terada, "Philosophical Self-Denial," 465.

6. Cavell, "Must We Mean What We Say," 33–34.

7. Noggle, "The Wittgensteinian Sublime," 605.

8. Read makes the same point; see "Ordinary/Everyday Language," 65.

9. Witherspoon, "Conceptions of Nonsense," 345.

10. Conant, "Wittgenstein on Meaning and Use," 249.

11. In a 1948 letter to Norman Malcolm, Wittgenstein mentions how much he liked a novel by the American crime writer Norbert Davis (1909–49). Wittgenstein calls the novel *Rendez-vous with fear*. When I set out to read it, I couldn't find any novel with that title. It turns out that *Rendez-vous with Fear* was the British title. In the United States, the book was published as *The Mouse in the Mountain* (1943). Apparently, there is also an edition called *Dead Little Rich Girl*. For more information on Wittgenstein and Davis, see Hoffman, "Hard-boiled Wit." Set in a mountaintop village in Mexico, this comic thriller features an unlikely band of heroes and villains, plus an absolutely amazing dog called Carstairs.

12. Conant, "Wittgenstein on Meaning and Use," 249.

13. Rhees, *Discussions of Wittgenstein*, 45, quoted by Diamond in "Rules," 12.

14. Diamond, "Rules," 15.

15. Ibid., 24–25.

16. This controversial paragraph has been the object of much political critique, which I discuss in chapter 7.

17. Diamond, "Rules," 20.

18. Such readings often draw on Saul Kripke's skepticist and "constructionist" reading

of Wittgenstein in *Wittgenstein on Rules and Private Language*. Stanley Fish introduces the term "interpretive community" in *Is There a Text in This Class* ("Introduction," 14). Ziarek translates "forms of life" as "discursive community" (*Rhetoric of Failure*, 26). See also Cavell's critique of Kripke in "The Argument of the Ordinary," 64–100.

19. I discuss their critiques of Wittgenstein in chapter 7.

20. Belsey, *Critical Practice*, 39.

21. On this question, Hacking, *The Social Construction of What?* is invaluable.

22. See chapter 4 for more on concepts and essences.

23. There will be exceptions: the naming of products of various kinds is often done by committee; some scientific terms may be decided in the same way.

24. See also: "What we are supplying are really remarks on the natural history of human beings: not curiosities, however, but facts that no one has doubted, which have escaped notice only because they are always before our eyes" (§415).

25. Cavell, *This New Yet Unapproachable America*, 41.

26. Cavell, "Availability of Wittgenstein's Later Philosophy," 52.

27. "You cannot refrain from understanding simple sentences in your own language"; Kahneman, *Thinking, Fast and Slow*, 22.

28. Ziarek, *Rhetoric of Failure*, 50.

29. Merleau-Ponty, *Phenomenology of Perception*, 170, 189.

30. Drury, *The Danger of Words*, x. A slightly different version of the same story can be found in Drury, "Conversations with Wittgenstein," 134.

31. Everett, *Don't Sleep, There Are Snakes*, 117–18.

32. Cavell's discussion of the status of conventions in Wittgenstein's understanding of grammar and forms of life is breathtakingly brilliant. See the chapter called "Natural and Conventional," in *Claim of Reason*, 86–125.

33. To follow Cavell through these themes, I recommend reading part 4 of *Claim of Reason*, and then continue with *Pursuits of Happiness*, *Disowning Knowledge*, *Contesting Tears*, and *A Pitch of Philosophy*. This is the part of Cavell's work that has inspired the greatest number of literary critics so far.

34. For a brilliant discussion of the intertwinement of words and world, see Laugier, *Why We Need Ordinary Language Philosophy*, particularly chapter 8, "The Myth of Inexpressiveness," 85–96.

35. Austin, "Plea for Excuses," 182.

36. See, e.g., Hillis Miller's reading of Austin in *Speech Acts in Literature*.

37. For Austin, Laugier notes, "language is not only true or false, but … confused, inadequate, misplaced and so on" (Laugier, *Why We Need Ordinary Language Philosophy*, 72).

38. Wittgenstein, *Remarks on the Foundations of Mathematics*, 325; quoted by Diamond in *The Realistic Spirit*, 39, and by Laugier in *Why We Need Ordinary Language Philosophy*, 20 and 22.

39. Laugier, *Why We Need Ordinary Language Philosophy*, 109; Diamond, *Realistic Spirit*, particularly chapter 1.

40. Diamond, *Realistic Spirit*, 44.

41. Ibid., 40. "Attention" is such a crucial concept for ordinary language philosophy that I return to it in chapter 10.

42. Marcuse detests both Wittgenstein's and Austin's "banal" examples (*One-Dimensional Man*, 176–77), and Ziarek expresses her distaste for Cavell's "trivial examples" (*Rhetoric of Failure*, 57).

43. Diamond, *Realistic Spirit*, 47.

Chapter 3

1. For further discussion of ordinary language philosophy as revolutionary, see the introduction.

2. Fish, *Doing What Comes Naturally*, 319. See also Knapp and Michaels, "Against Theory."

3. See chapter 8 for my own intervention in the discussion of suspicious reading.

4. See my discussion of this in the introduction.

5. Staten, *Wittgenstein and Derrida*.

6. Stone, "Wittgenstein on Deconstruction."

7. Cavell, "Counter-Philosophy," 63. An earlier version of the middle part of this text was published as "What Did Derrida Want of Austin?" in Cavell, *Philosophical Passages*, 42–65.

8. Cavell, "Counter-Philosophy," 100, 112.

9. Austin, *Sense and Sensibilia*, 41n, 142.

10. Here Cavell too hears the "drone of the unserious" ("Counter-Philosophy," 100).

11. Another explanation is that the author's or the speaker's *intention* limits the field of meaning. I return to intentions in chapter 9.

12. Derrida must have been aware of Cavell's essay. In 2000 *Ratio* published a special issue called *Arguing with Derrida* collecting the papers from a conference held in Reading, England, in 1999 where both Derrida and the Cavell scholar Stephen Mulhall were present. Glendinning writes that "an important part of its background [was] Derrida's controversial engagements with the 'ordinary language philosophy' of J. L. Austin" ("Preface: Arguing with Derrida," 299n).

13. For Searle's reply to Derrida, see Searle, "Reiterating the Differences." Searle's review of Jonathan Culler's *On Deconstruction* ("The Word Turned Upside Down") provoked Derrida's "Afterword."

14. Searle, "Word Turned Upside Down," 78. The phrase is quoted in Derrida, "Afterword," 115, 123.

15. Wittgenstein wonders whether we can point to the color blue in §33; Cavell asks about our dress sense in "Must We Mean What We Say?" 9; and Austin discusses donkeys in "A Plea for Excuses," 185n.

16. Derrida, *Of Grammatology*, 56.

17. Commenting on this point, one Derridean unhesitatingly repeats the word "vulgar" four times on the same page. See Arthur Bradley, *Derrida's "Of Grammatology,"* 68.

18. These concepts are explicitly mentioned by Derrida in "Afterword," 117, 117n, 127, 155.

19. There is an obvious parallel to Deleuze and Guattari's well-known claim that the task of philosophy is to produce concepts. See *Qu'est-ce que la philosophie?* 26–27.

20. Cavell, "Counter-Philosophy," 85; Derrida, "Signature Event Context," 15.

21. Stone, "Wittgenstein on Deconstruction," 91; Glendinning, "Inheriting 'Philosophy,'" 329.

22. Austin, "A Plea for Excuses," 182.

23. Also quoted in "Counter-Philosophy," 70.

24. The young Derrida was deeply fascinated by Husserl's theory of the "ideality" of words and concepts, to the point that his first dissertation proposal was on the "ideality of the literary object." For an account of early Husserlian influences on Derrida, see Kates, "A Transcendental Sense of Death?" 1017.

25. I am grateful to Simon Glendinning for taking the time to write to me after the

publication of an earlier version of this chapter. I also learned a lot from reading Glendin-ning's two papers on Wittgenstein, "Wittgenstein's Apocalyptic Library" and "Wittgen-stein's Nomadism."

26. I take "Big Questions" from Diamond, "Criss-Cross Philosophy."

27. Frege, *Grundgesetze der Arithmetik*, vol. 2, §56; in *The Frege Reader*, 259.

28. That Wittgenstein's critique of logical positivism also can be used as a critique of deconstruction points to what Hammer has called the "latent positivism" of the decon-structive tradition (Hammer, *Stanley Cavell*, 152).

29. For a discussion of the relationship between ordinary and mathematical language, see Cavell, "The Argument of the Ordinary," 90–91.

30. It is symptomatic of the poststructuralist attitude toward the ordinary that a formi-dable deconstructionist like Geoffrey Bennington gets this exactly the wrong way round. According to Bennington, Wittgenstein thinks that *philosophy* should set itself up as a "hygienic intervention" into ordinary language, and that the "philosopher has a therapeu-tic or hygienic role in clearing up the misunderstandings fostered by ordinary language." Bennington, *Frontiers*, 381 and 392n. Available as pdf file (ISBN 0-9754996-0-2) at http://bennington.zsoft.co.uk (downloaded April 14, 2009).

31. Cavell, "What Did Derrida Want of Austin?" 61. These specific formulations don't appear in "Counter-Philosophy."

32. Derrida once said that "there is only ordinary language—philosophy too is 'ordi-nary language.' But, since there is no opposed term here, since 'there is only ordinary lan-guage,' this concept is empty." He also spoke of Austin's irony as "an 'ordinary language' which can always be supplanted by an extraordinary use." I have difficulty understanding this opposition, let alone how it applies to Austin. But this will have to be left for another discussion. Derrida, "Derrida's Response to Mulhall," 415, 416, 417.

33. Austin, *Sense and Sensibilia*, 127–28. Austin would not dream of asking for an ex-haustive description of the "total context" of every speech act, yet this is precisely what Derrida accuses him of doing. Austin uses the phrase "total context" in *How to Do Things with Words*, 148. Derrida takes this to mean "exhaustively definable context" ("Signature Event Context," 15). Cavell shows that Austin "seeks no systematic account, either of con-text or of its oblivion" ("Counter-Philosophy," 113).

34. To understand what that something is, it would be necessary to explain Cavell's account of Wittgensteinian criteria in *Claim of Reason*, 3–125. The best essay on the topic is Affeldt, "The Ground of Mutuality." See also Mulhall's response to Affeldt: "The Given-ness of Grammar.

35. Derrida, "Signature Event Context," 19; Cavell, "Counter-Philosophy," 63.

36. Bennington, *Frontiers*, 386–87.

37. Ibid., 387, 450, 428.

38. See Cavell, "Excursus on Wittgenstein's Vision of Language," 180–90.

39. Cavell, "Must We Mean What We Say?" 19.

40. Cavell, "Excursus on Wittgenstein's Vision of Language," 187–88.

41. This was also a major emphasis in Richard Fleming's seminars on *Philosophical Investigations* organized by the Ordinary Language Working Group at Duke University in 2008/9.

42. In addition to the marvelous account of a child learning language in "Excursus on Wittgenstein's Vision of Language," see also Cavell, "Notes and Afterthoughts," and Cavell, "The Argument of the Ordinary," 64–100.

43. The first quote is from Fleming, "Ordinary Language Philosophy," 518; the second is

from *Claim of Reason*, 177–78. See also the discussion of learning what an "umiak" means or what an "umiak" is in chapter 1, and in Cavell, "Must We Mean What We Say?" 19–20.

44. Cavell, "Must We Mean What We Say?" 19.

45. See also *Claim of Reason*, 449–50.

46. I return to this definition of theory in chapter 4.

47. I became aware of this quote in Stone, "Wittgenstein on Deconstruction," 83. Wittgenstein's quotation can be found in "Philosophy" (sections 86–93 of the so-called Big Typescript), included in *Philosophical Occasions*, 171.

48. Stone, "Wittgenstein on Deconstruction," 99.

49. See my discussion of grammar in chapter 2.

50. See my discussion of critique in chapter 7 and of the hermeneutics of suspicion in chapter 8.

51. Culler's quote comes from *On Certainty*, §559.

52. Cavell too stresses that Wittgenstein's vision of language is slanted toward the past: "Wittgenstein pictures [the iteration necessary for language] as a continuation, or discrete continuability, knowing or seeing how to go on, but as if something is always over. The step creates the path as it relinquishes the path" ("Counter-Philosophy," 72).

53. Wittgenstein, *On Certainty*, §555.

54. Ibid., §558–59.

Chapter 4

1. Here I was tempted to create a lovely binary opposition between a "logic of representation" and a "logic of exemplarity." But, in the end, it seemed too pat. I don't want to imply that all representations really are examples, or that we should always replace representations with examples: both have their uses.

2. See particularly the title essay in Moi, *What Is a Woman?*

3. See, e.g., Modleski, *Feminism without Women*, particularly chapter 1. Cavell's response can be found in *Contesting Tears*, 32–36. Singling out Cavell's discussion of *Now, Voyager*, Modleski claims that Cavell fails to quote and discuss feminist writings on the film. It is true that Cavell doesn't cite any women in his analysis. But, as he points out, he doesn't cite any men either. Cavell is right to say that his own work on melodrama, and particularly on *Now, Voyager*, is *sui generis*, and arises from his previous book on remarriage comedy (see *Contesting Tears*, 33). I share Modleski's frustration with male theorists' systematic neglect of feminist contributions. However, such complaints are most effective when we can show that the man's key arguments are flawed because of such omissions, which I don't think is true for Cavell's work on the melodrama of the unknown woman.

4. In chapter 8 I write more about Wittgenstein's notion of philosophy as a movement from confusion to clarity, and why this view is a powerful alternative to the hermeneutics of suspicion.

5. See Felski, *Limits of Critique*, for a critical analysis of "critique." There is excellent feminist work on the ordinary and the everyday. But most of that work is not considered part of "theory." Felski's essay on the lower-middle class is an excellent analysis of the neglect of the ordinary ("Nothing to Declare.") A completely different example of feminist analysis of ordinary experience is Steedman, *Landscape for a Good Woman*. I have always found the work of Simone de Beauvoir and Pierre Bourdieu congenial to my interest in the ordinary. See Beauvoir, *The Second Sex*, and Bourdieu, *Distinction*. See also Moi, "Appropriating Bourdieu."

6. For a discussion of such beliefs, see chapter 7.

7. There are of course nonphilosophical reasons, too, for example, the fact that contemporary feminist theory has become an academic discipline.

8. Frye, *Politics of Reality*, xi, xii.

9. Beauvoir, *L'Existentialisme et la sagesse des nations*, 12. My translation.

10. See Diamond and Edwards, eds., *The Authority of Experience*.

11. Scott, "Evidence of Experience," 777, 797.

12. Ibid., 797.

13. For a discussion of experience in literary criticism, with reference to feminist consciousness-raising groups, see chapter 9.

14. Cavell, "Aesthetic Problems," 95.

15. Ibid., 95–96.

16. Beauvoir discusses action as an appeal to the other's freedom in *Pyrrhus and Cineas*.

17. For "clear boundaries," see §71, which I discuss in chapter 3.

18. In §67, Wittgenstein calls this "family resemblances." I don't use this term, for I fear that it can easily be taken to constitute Wittgenstein's "theory" of concepts, which is precisely what I think it is not. I share Cavell's view that "all the idea of 'family resemblances' is meant to do, or need do, is to make us dissatisfied with the idea of universals as explanations of language, of how a word can refer to this and that and that other thing, to suggest that it fails to meet 'our real need'" (*Claim of Reason*, 187).

19. See chapters 1 and 2 for a discussion of use and grammar.

20. Austin, *Sense and Sensibilia*, 127–28.

21. I discuss the feminist unease with the word "woman" at length in "What Is a Woman?"

22. See, e.g., Grosz, "The Practice of Feminist Theory."

23. See Moi, "Språkets tvangstrøye."

24. Søndergaard, "Poststructuralist Approaches to Empirical Analysis," 190.

25. Friedman, *Mappings*, 20.

26. Ibid., 34–35.

27. Cf. Wittgenstein: "What gives the impression that we want to deny anything?" (§305).

28. See Moi, "What Is a Woman?," 59 n. 86.

29. For a recent essay on intersectionality that exemplifies the assumption that we need to conceptualize identity or identities *before* we can sort out our politics, see Carastathis, "Identity Categories as Potential Coalitions." Carastathis is also the author of a clear-headed, critical analysis of intersectionality theory, "The Invisibility of Privilege."

30. See Butler, *Gender Trouble*; my critique of Butler in "What Is a Woman?," particularly 30–59. See also Segerdal, "Gender, Language and Philosophical Reconciliation."

31. McCall, "The Complexity of Intersectionality," 1771; Lewis, "Unsafe Travel," 869.

32. Crenshaw, "Demarginalizing the Intersection of Race and Sex," 149, 155.

33. Davis, "Intersectionality as Buzzword," 71–72, 73. Davis places "fundamental and pervasive" in quotation marks, not because she is quoting a particular text right here, but because throughout her essay she uses the phrase as a shorthand reference to Murray S. Davis's explanation of why some social theories manage to "capture the imagination of a broad audience of academics" (69).

34. Ibid., 69; Nash, "Re-Thinking Intersectionality," particularly 9–10; Collins, "Looking Back, Moving Ahead," 22; Tomlinson, "To Tell the Truth and Not Get Trapped," 999–1000; Carbado, Crenshaw, Mays, and Tomlinson, "Intersectionality," 304.

35. Orupabo, "Interseksjonalitet i praksis," 334. My translation from the Norwegian.

36. Carbado, Crenshaw, Mays, and Tomlinson, "Intersectionality," 304.

37. In "The Complexity of Intersectionality," McCall distinguishes between "anticategorial," "intracategorial," and "intercategorial" (or simply "categorial") approaches. The first approach considers categories "simplifying social fictions" (1773), the second recommends "strategic use of categories" (1773), and the third urges the "provisional adoption of existing categories" (1785).

38. Hankivsky, "Rethinking Care Ethics," 256.

39. "I think it's absolutely on target to take a stand against the discourses of essentialism.... But strategically we cannot. Even as we talk about feminist practice, or privileging practice over theory, we are universalizing—not only generalizing but universalizing." Spivak, "Criticism, Feminism and the Institution," 166.

40. Austin, *How to Do Things with Words*, 9, 10.

41. Linda Zerilli helped me to see this.

42. Hankivsky, "Rethinking Care Ethics," 253.

43. Davis, "Intersectionality as Buzzword," 72.

44. I certainly agree with this claim. The idea that one can somehow separate someone's race from their gender, or sexuality (and so on) is absurd. In *What Is a Woman?* I discuss Beauvoir's very different account of identity and gender through the concept of the body as a situation (see particularly 59–84).

45. I discuss Wittgenstein's notion of description in chapter 8.

46. For more on Saussure, see chapter 5.

47. For more on grammar and grammatical investigations, see chapter 2.

48. The intersectionality theorist Jennifer Nash also concludes that we should avoid general theories of intersectionality. She quotes the Bourdieu-inspired sociologist Loïc Wacquant, who recommends abandoning the search for origins, or the "search for a single overarching concept to develop an analytic of racial domination" ("Re-Thinking Intersectionality," 13).

49. See Diamond, "Criss-Cross Philosophy," particularly 208–11, but the whole essay provides an illuminating analysis of Wittgenstein's "piecemeal" method.

50. This compatibility in spirit explains why it is so rewarding to reconceive Beauvoir's achievement in the light of ordinary language philosophy, as Nancy Bauer does in her brilliant book *Simone de Beauvoir, Philosophy, and Feminism*.

51. See chapter 1 in Zerilli, *A Democratic Theory of Judgment*.

Chapter 5

1. Saussure, "Lettres de Ferdinand de Saussure à Antoine Meillet," 95. I am quoting Jameson's elegant translation in *The Prison-House of Language*, 12–13.

2. The new texts were published as Saussure, *Writings in General Linguistics*. For in-depth information on Saussure's life and work, see Mauro, "Sur F. de Saussure," the magisterial afterword to his edition of *Cours de linguistique générale*.

3. Saussure, "Lettres de Ferdinand de Saussure à Antoine Meillet," 95. Jameson's translation in *The Prison-House of Language*, 13.

4. I can't judge how useful Saussure's concepts are for present-day linguists. For some discussion of this question, see Harris, *Saussure and His Interpreters*.

5. Culler, *Ferdinand de Saussure*, 39.

6. Benveniste, "Nature of the Linguistic Sign," 44.

7. This is surely why "speech" tends to disappear from post-Saussurean accounts of Saussure. Many textbooks discuss only *langue* and *parole*. Even the excellent Jonathan Culler fails to mention *le langage* in his discussion; see *Ferdinand de Saussure*, 39–45.

8. See chapter 4 for more on how to think through examples.

9. Ziarek considers Wittgenstein's "use" to be "closely related to structuralist linguistics" because "in both cases the meaning of the word is not determined on the basis of reference to the object or to an inner subjective process but through relations to other words" (Ziarek, *Rhetoric of Failure*, 34). It is true that we investigate specific cases of use by exploring alternative formulations. But Ziarek's formulation cuts the world out of Wittgenstein's understanding of language, leaving language exactly as what the post-Saussurean tradition says it is, namely as a chain of signifiers.

10. I am hardly the first to notice the trouble with the distinction! Benveniste, "Nature of the Linguistic Sign," and Kirby, *Telling Flesh*, both show up its ambiguities, in different ways.

11. By "psychology," Saussure means any mental activity, anything that goes on in our brain or consciousness. To him, language is "psychological" or it is nothing. Sounds without meaning, are "nonpsychological" (*Course in General Linguistics*, 13), "purely physical" (66), i.e., irrelevant to linguistics. By "non-psychological" Saussure means the "physiological productions of the vocal organs as well as the physical facts that are outside the individual" (12).

12. The illustration appears in *Course in General Linguistics*, 67.

13. See chapter 1 for a full discussion of Wittgenstein's analysis of the Augustinian picture of meaning.

14. Quoted by Meisel and Saussy, "Saussure and His Contexts," xlii. They quote Saussure, *Writings on General Linguistics*, 41.

15. Symons, *The Symbolist Movement in Literature*, 1.

16. I discuss Judith Butler's account of matter in "What Is a Woman?" 47–51.

17. See my discussion of "forms of life" in chapter 2.

18. In fact, expressions like "with reference to" or "refer to" occur five times in the English translation of *Course*, always in contexts where Saussure explains how a word is used, or what a thing is called in a specific language or a specific context.

19. Ogden and Richards, *The Meaning of Meaning*, 6.

20. In *Literature and the Touch of the Real*, Schalkwyk gives a detailed overview and analysis of the question of reference in Saussure (see chapter 1, 27–62).

21. Jameson, "Imaginary and Symbolic in Lacan," 384, 388–90.

22. Benveniste, "Nature of the Linguistic Sign," 45.

23. Conant, "Wittgenstein on Meaning and Use," 231.

24. I spell out the logic of this claim in chapter 1.

25. "Here, then, is the thing, expressly excluded at first from the definition of the sign, now creeping into it by a detour, and permanently installing a contradiction there" (Benveniste, "Nature," 44).

26. Ibid., 46.

27. Ellis, *Against Deconstruction*, 47 n. 36.

28. Kirby, *Telling Flesh*, 127.

29. Kirby also attributes to Saussure the idea that the "substance of reality, or what we take to be the referent, is produced through language" (ibid., 17). This sounds less like Saussure and more like a debased version of Judith Butler's "performativity" to me. I can't find anything in Saussure to substantiate this view, and Kirby gives no reference.

30. Ibid., 18, 19.

31. These are examples I use in chapter 1.

32. Dolphijn and van der Tuin, *New Materialism*, 108.

33. Barad, "Posthumanist Performativity," 824, n. 30.

34. I leave aside the editors' equally extravagant claims concerning subject/object and self/world.

35. I discuss the "general text" in chapter 3.

36. I discuss this fantasy more extensively in Moi, "A Woman's Desire to Be Known: Expressivity and Silence in *Corinne*," 166–69.

37. I am echoing Cavell's "Nothing is more human than to deny [the necessities common to us all]" (Cavell, "Aesthetic Problems," 96).

Chapter 6

1. I first discussed Archie Bunker in "'What's the Difference?': Om Stanley Cavells lesning av Paul de Man." While I don't reuse any of the actual text here, some of the ideas in this chapter were first expressed in that Norwegian essay.

2. I don't discuss the concept of the "outside" or "beyond" of language in this chapter. I do spend some pages discussing Lacan's idea of femininity as "beyond" language in Moi, "From Femininity to Finitude." But this particular topic would require a far more extensive discussion, for it touches on the idea of the "limits of language," and thus brings up questions concerning how to understand Wittgenstein's view of nonsense (meaninglessness) at the end of the *Tractatus*. For discussions of the latter, see, e.g., Conant, "Elucidation and Nonsense," and Diamond "Ethics, Imagination."

3. For Michaels's critique of Derrida, see particularly *The Shape of the Signifier*, 61–66.

4. *The Shape of the Signifier* builds on "Against Theory." As far as I can see, the understanding of signs and marks is the same in both texts.

5. Knapp and Michaels, "Against Theory," 15/727. The first reference is to Knapp and Michaels in Mitchell, ed., *Against Theory* (1985); the second to Knapp and Michaels, "Against Theory" (1982). Subsequent page numbers appear in the text.

6. I'm hardly the only one. For a similar reaction, see Hirsch, "Against Theory?"; Panagia, "The Shape of the Signifier"; Rorty, "Philosophy without Principles"; Staten, "Review"; and Wang, "Against Theory Beside Romanticism."

7. Juhl, *Interpretation*, 83. Juhl also suggests that the lines could be a result of "water erosion." See also Hirsch, *Validity in Interpretation*.

8. Cavell, "Counter-Philosophy," 70. See also Cavell's critique of the idea that to explain the meaning of a word we must begin by considering it in itself, i.e., as a "particular" in search of its universal, in "Excursus on Wittgenstein's Vision of Language."

9. Merleau-Ponty, *Phenomenology of Perception*, 401.

10. Kamuf challenges Knapp and Michaels's understanding of what an author is, by pointing out that if Wordsworth is the "author" of the lines, then the scientists are merely citing the original ("Floating Authorship").

11. Wilson, "Again, Theory," 171.

12. Wilson also concludes that "there is no contribution of substance to the topic of meaning in 'Against Theory'" (ibid., 173).

13. In *Theory at Yale*, Marc Redfield also picks up on Knapp and Michaels's distinction between "language and language's simulacrum" (81). But he faults them not for establishing it in the first place (as I do), but for thinking that the difference between language and

not-language is a matter of "human agents" (82). Faithful to the post-Saussurean belief in the empty signifier, Redfield thinks that Knapp and Michaels have unwittingly rediscovered the logic of undecidability championed by de Man, for the difference in question, he proclaims, is "absolute and yet absolutely invisible, impalpable, and unsecureable" (82). The result is skepticism, or as Redfield puts it, "that neither 'you' nor we nor anyone else can know for sure whether or not 'Marion' is a signifier" (82).

14. See Austin's discussion of promises in *How to Do Things with Words*, 9–10.

15. By "meaning in the language" I mean that they have acquired meaning through use. I don't mean that the meaning could never change, or that we'll always understand every utterance. See chapters 1 and 2 for more on use.

16. Fish, "Intentional Neglect."

17. For an excellent analysis of Fish's belief that interpretation is always necessary, see Stone, "On the Old Saw."

18. "The Intentional Fallacy" was first published in the *Sewanee Review* in 1946, before becoming the lead essay in Wimsatt, *The Verbal Icon*.

19. Cavell, "Division of Talent," 524.

20. Ibid.

21. Kamuf points out that the phrase "intentionless meaning" also occurs in John Searle's reply to Derrida's "Signature Event Context" ("Floating Authorship," 6–8).

22. See Wilson, "Again, Theory," 171–73, for a similar argument.

23. Roth, "I Don't Want Your Revolution," 25.

24. For full credits, and the date of first broadcast, see http://www.imdb.com/title/tt0509804/.

25. On YouTube, the scene runs from 3:24 to 3:58.

26. The Cornell conference was held on April 20–21, 1973. "Semiology and Rhetoric" was first published in *Diacritics* 3, no. 3 (Fall 1973). Unless otherwise noted, page references are to *Allegories of Reading*.

27. Redfield, "Introduction," 3.

28. The first quote is from Paul Fry's lively presentation of de Man's essay in his online lecture "Deconstruction II." The section on "Semiology and Rhetoric" begins around minute 43; my quote comes from around minute 48. Redfield writes of the "radical undecidability dramatized in 'Semiology and Rhetoric'" ("Introduction," 8). The third quote is from Brooks, "The Strange Case of Paul de Man," 47.

29. Cavell's paper was first delivered in Chicago in 1981, at a conference called "The Politics of Interpretation," organized by the journal *Critical Inquiry*, and was first published in September 1982. Page references to the reprint in Cavell, *Themes Out of School* will be given in the text, marked as "Politics."

30. All quotes in this paragraph come from Cavell, "Politics," 41, 45.

31. De Man names no names. But he is clearly thinking of Hartman and Jameson. In 1970 Hartman wrote about the need to "go beyond formalism and to define art's role in the life of the artist, his culture, and the human community" (*Beyond Formalism*, ix). De Man quotes part of this sentence ("Semiology and Rhetoric," 3). He also refers to the title of Jameson's *The Prison-House of Language*, first published in 1972 (see "Semiology and Rhetoric," 4).

32. Austin, *How to Do Things with Words*, 1–2.

33. Ibid., 91.

34. Ibid., 99.

35. Cavell also reminds us of §21: "We could imagine a language in which all assertions

had the form and tone of rhetorical questions; or every command had the form of the question 'Would you like to … ?'"

36. The 1979 version of the text has a line split on the last Debunker. So should it be spelled Debunker or De-bunker? The 1973 *Diacritics* version provides the answer: Debunker (*Diacritics*, 29).

37. Cohen, *Jokes*, 25–26.

38. Cavell, "Availability of Wittgenstein's Later Philosophy," 52. See also the discussion of grammar, and forms of life in chapter 2.

39. Diamond, "Losing Your Concepts," 273–74.

40. Culler, "The Call of the Phoneme," 4.

41. Ibid., 4, 14.

42. Bearn, "The Possibility of Puns," 331, 332–33.

Chapter 7

1. I leave Cavell out of this, for he had barely begun to publish when Gellner and Marcuse published their attacks on Wittgenstein and Austin. For Cavell's response to Gellner, see "Austin at Criticism," 112–13.

2. Read also notes that "Ernest Gellner's gross misreadings are not taken very seriously any more" ("Marx and Wittgenstein," 273). Marcuse mentions Gellner in *One-Dimensional Man*, 173 n. 2.

3. Marcuse's chapter on "linguistic analysis" is called "The Triumph of Positive Thinking: One-Dimensional Philosophy," *One-Dimensional Man*, 170–99.

4. Cavell, "Politics," 33.

5. Similarly, Ziarek recoils from "Cavell's trivial examples" precisely because they fail to deal with political issues (Ziarek, *The Rhetoric of Failure*, 57).

6. "The transfer of allegiance from paradigm to paradigm is a conversion experience that cannot be forced," Kuhn, *Structure of Scientific Revolutions*, 151.

7. For the donkey story, see Austin, "Plea for Excuses," 185n. For taste, smell, and goldfinches, see Austin, "Other Minds."

8. Ricoeur, "Husserl and Wittgenstein," 217.

9. I discuss the hermeneutics of suspicion in chapter 8.

10. For more on Wittgenstein and Marx, see Kitching and Pleasants, eds., *Marx and Wittgenstein*; Vinten, "Leave Everything as It Is"; Vinten, "Eagleton's Wittgenstein"; and chapter 3 in Ware, *Dialectic of the Ladder*.

11. In 1959 the targets of Gellner's critique were not just Wittgenstein and Austin, but also philosophers now recognized as among the founders of analytic philosophy, such as Gilbert Ryle, Stuart Hampshire, R. M. Hare, J. O. Urmson, and many others.

12. "Wittgensteiniansism" is Gellner's only target in "The Saltmines of Salzburg or Wittgensteinianism Reconsidered in a Historical Context"; the substantial introduction added to the 1979 edition of *Words and Things* (Gellner, *Words and Things*, 1–44).

13. See Uschanov, "Ernest Gellner's Criticisms of Wittgenstein," 24. Uschanov's article offers an excellent overview of the reception of Gellner's book and the development of Gellner's increasingly rabid anti-Wittgensteinianism.

14. See the section on "W" in Deleuze, *Gilles Deleuze from A to Z* (*L'Abécédaire de Gilles Deleuze*). This video excerpt is also widely available online.

15. See chapters 1 and 2 for more on "use."

16. Gellner, *Words and Things*, 31.

17. See ibid., 14–15. Gellner calls this the "problem of validation," the problem of deciding what kind or religious, philosophical, political, or social organizations and convictions we want to live by (3).

18. Crary provides a useful critique of the "idea of an external standpoint on language" from a Wittgensteinian point of view (Crary, "Introduction," in Crary and Read, *The New Wittgenstein*, 3).

19. For more on "forms of life," see chapter 2.

20. Gellner, *Words and Things*, 52.

21. See Ware, *Dialectic of the Ladder*, 85–92.

22. Cavell, "Availability of Wittgenstein's Later Philosophy," 57–58.

23. Ibid., 60.

24. I discuss the need to experience one's own lostness in chapter 8.

25. Ben Ware agrees. To him, Wittgenstein's §124 has a crucial place in materialist thought (see *Dialectic of the Ladder*, 90–91).

26. See chapter 8 for my discussion of the hermeneutics of suspicion.

27. Cavell, "Politics," 28.

28. See Cavell, "Austin at Criticism," 113.

29. See chapters 3 and 4.

30. See particularly chapter 4.

31. Bauer, "What Philosophy Can't Teach Us," 28.

32. In the introduction to *Signifying Woman*, Zerilli gives a good account of these assumptions (1–15).

33. Wittgenstein, *Culture and Value*, 61. This edition translates *eine Veränderung der Lebensweise* as "a change in the way people live"; the revised 1998 edition has "a change in the way we live."

34. Fish, "How Ordinary Is Ordinary Language?" 97. (Confusingly, Fish thinks that Austin is *not* an ordinary language philosopher.) See also Cavell's heartfelt dismay at Fish's misleading presentation of Austin's understanding of "ordinary language" ("Politics," 34–41).

35. Cavell, "Politics," 36.

36. Ibid., 52.

37. Fish goes for the clever paradox: "Ordinary language is extraordinary, because at its heart is precisely that realm of values, intentions, and purposes which is often assumed to be the exclusive property of literature" ("How Ordinary Is Ordinary Language?" 108). But this paradox only works if one sets up a distinction between cognitive and emotive statements in the first place.

38. I compare the theoretical styles of Beauvoir and Irigaray in *What Is a Woman?* 171–77.

39. Dutton, "The Bad Writing Contest."

40. Dutton, "Language Crimes."

41. Butler, "A 'Bad Writer' Bites Back."

42. Miller, "Is Bad Writing Necessary?"; Butler, "Exacting Solidarities: Letter to the Editor."

43. Culler and Lamb, eds., *Just Being Difficult*.

44. Graff willingly admitted the problem. See "Scholars and Sound Bites."

45. See Perloff, *Wittgenstein's Ladder*, and Ware, *Dialectic of the Ladder*.

46. The reference is to the title of Williams and Colomb's useful handbook, *Style: Toward Clarity and Grace*.

47. *Philosophical Investigations*, 4.

48. Recently Pinker, in *The Sense of Style*, and Sword, in *Stylish Academic Writing*, have voiced similar concerns.

49. No book has taught me more about sentences than Verlyn Klinkenborg, *Several Short Sentences about Writing*, a book imbued with the spirit of the ordinary.

50. Butler, "A 'Bad Writer' Bites Back."

51. See Butler's defense of Gayatri Spivak's writing style, in which she lauded Spivak for "staying ... the death of thought," in contrast to "those who recirculate received opinion" (Butler, "Exacting Solidarities").

52. Butler repeats the claim in the preface to the second edition of *Gender Trouble*, xviii.

53. Descartes, *A Discourse on the Method*, 5.

54. Culler and Lamb, eds., *Just Being Difficult*, 200.

55. Žižek, *In Defense of Lost Causes*, 21.

56. This is the title of part 1 of *One-Dimensional Man*.

57. Warner, "Styles of Intellectual Publics," 116.

58. Pinker, *The Sense of Style*, 59 and 61.

Chapter 8

1. Sedgwick, "Paranoid Reading and Reparative Reading," 124. (A version of this text appeared as early as 1997, in the introduction to Sedgwick, *Novel Gazing: Queer Readings in Fiction*. Durham, NC: Duke University Press, 1997.) Paul Ricoeur was the first to call Marx, Nietzsche, and Freud "masters of suspicion" (*Freud and Philosophy*, 33). Already in 1983 the philosopher Alexander Nehamas pointed out that literary critics had become over-reliant on "metaphors of depth and concealment" (Nehamas, "What an Author Is," 687).

2. Felski, *Limits of Critique*, 6. Felski also explores critique and the hermeneutics of suspicion in "After Suspicion"; "Context Stinks!"; "Critique and the Hermeneutics of Suspicion"; and "Suspicious Minds."

3. Bartolovich writes that "some versions of symptomatic reading" suffer from "stultification," and that "producing yet another article on, say, race in novel X, Y, or Z ... can now seem like a hollow exercise" ("Humanities of Scale," 116–17).

4. Sedgwick, "Paranoid Reading and Reparative Reading," 140, 125.

5. See Bruno Latour, "Why Has Critique Run Out of Steam?" particularly 228–32.

6. Sedgwick, "Paranoid Reading and Reparative Reading," 126; Latour, "Why Has Critique Run Out of Steam?," 231 and 248.

7. Stephen Best and Sharon Marcus, "Surface Reading: An Introduction," *Representations*, no. 108 (2009): 2, 1.

8. See Beauvoir, *The Second Sex*, and Millett, *Sexual Politics*

9. Jameson, *The Political Unconscious*, 60.

10. Best and Marcus, "Surface Reading," 1.

11. Marcus gave an excellent talk on responses to "Surface Reading" at the conference "Interpretation and Its Rivals," at the University of Virginia, September 19–20, 2013. Love's two articles "Close but Not Deep," and "Close Reading and Thin Description" build on Best and Marcus's arguments by taking them in the direction of the social sciences, particularly cultural anthropology.

12. Lesjak, "Reading Dialectically," 241, 248.

13. See my discussion of common sense in chapter 7.

14. In *The Limits of Critique*, Felski considers Latour's Actor Network Theory to be a new method for literary criticism. She may be right. Given my definition of "method," I would only call it a method if the theory provides ways for the critic to do something else or something more than reading, thinking, judging.

15. See Moi, "The Adventure of Reading."

16. I write more about this in chapter 9.

17. For more on "use," see chapters 1 and 2.

18. Cavell, "A Matter of Meaning It," 227.

19. See Moi, "Hedda's Silences."

20. "The results of philosophy are the discovery of some piece of plain nonsense and the bumps that the understanding has got by running up against the limits of language. They—these bumps—make us see the value of that discovery" (§119).

21. See Jameson, *Political Unconscious*, 60, 61.

22. Best and Marcus, "Surface Reading," 16.

23. Rooney, "Live Free or Describe," 116.

24. See Cavell, "Aesthetic Problems," particularly 78–79.

25. Sherlock, "A Study in Pink."

26. Freud, "Fragment of an Analysis of a Case of Hysteria ["Dora"]," 12.

27. Ibid., 77–78.

28. Freud, "The Method of Interpreting Dreams," 118, 121.

29. Ginzburg, "Clues," 102.

30. Ibid., 106.

31. Kierkegaard, *Fear and Trembling*, 83. Subsequent page numbers appear in the text.

32. Cavell, *The Senses of Walden*, 3–4.

33. Ibid., 65.

34. Ginzburg, "Clues," 105.

35. Cavell, "A Matter of Meaning It," 227; Cavell, "Aesthetic Problems," 93.

36. For a discussion of Austin as an unmasker, see Cavell, "Austin at Criticism," 113.

37. Moretti, "Conjectures on World Literature," 57.

38. The desire for surprise is a key theme in Straub's response to Best and Marcus (see Straub, "The Suspicious Reader Surprised").

39. See also Felski, "From Literary Theory to Critical Method."

40. Rudrum, *Stanley Cavell and the Claim of Literature*, 6. I find Rudrum's discussion of the trouble with "approaches" to literature congenial (see 6–11).

41. However, Anna Klara Bojö convinced me that while we regularly call theories methods, we rarely call methods theories.

42. I take the term "just reading" from Marcus, who coins it in *Between Women*, 75, and returns to it in Best and Marcus, "Surface Reading," 12.

43. Cavell, "Must We Mean What We Say?" 20.

44. Diamond, "Missing the Adventure," 313.

Chapter 9

1. See my discussion of the "material mark" in chapters 5 and 6.

2. See Pratt, *Toward a Speech Act Theory of Literary Discourse*, particularly chapter 3 (79–99).

3. Gee and Handford, "Introduction," *Routledge Handbook of Discourse Analysis*, 1.

4. Wetherell, Taylor, and Yates, "Introduction," *Discourse Theory and Practice*, 3.

5. See, e.g., Potter, "Wittgenstein and Austin."

6. Benveniste, "L'appareil formel de l'énonciation," is a good introduction to these concepts.

7. For a fascinating account of Foucault, which gives attention to his affinities to Wittgenstein, see Davidson, ed., *Foucault and His Interlocutors*, and also Davidson, *The Emergence of Sexuality*, particularly the essay called "Foucault and the Analysis of Concepts," 178–92.

8. See Kristeva, "The System and the Speaking Subject"; Kristeva, "Word, Dialogue and Novel"; and Kristeva, *Revolution in Poetic Language*.

9. Hirschkop, *Mikhail Bakhtin*, 35.

10. Bakhtin, "Discourse in the Novel," 275, 276.

11. See Ricoeur, "Model of the Text," 92. Subsequent page numbers appear in the text.

12. Wimsatt and Beardsley, "Intentional Fallacy," 4.

13. The references are to Brooks, *The Well Wrought Urn*, and Wimsatt and Beardsley, *The Verbal Icon*.

14. Barthes, "Death of the Author," 50. Foucault's "What Is an Author?" has different concerns: above all to investigate the "author-function" as a historical "discourse" in Western society, to map its rise and fall.

15. Belsey, *Critical Practice*, 13.

16. See Cavell's discussion of what he might (or might not) get out of asking Fellini whether he intended a certain scene in *La Strada* to be a version of the story of Philomela ("A Matter of Meaning It," 240–41).

17. See Rudrum, *Stanley Cavell and the Claim of Literature*, particularly 74–83, and Löfgren, *Interpretive Skepticism*, particularly chapter 5.

18. Anscombe, *Intention*, §5.

19. See also Cavell, "A Matter of Meaning It," 231. This is also why Sartre, in *What Is Literature?* claims that the writer is responsible for *everything* in her work.

20. This is the kernel of truth around which Stephen Knapp and Walter Benn Michaels build their extravagant claim that "not only in serious literal speech but in all speech what is intended and what is meant are identical" ("Against Theory," 17/729). See chapter 6 for a discussion of Knapp and Michaels's vision of language.

21. Sartre, *What Is Literature?*, 37.

22. I discuss the question of meaning and responsibility at greater length in "Meaning What We Say."

23. Cavell first elaborated the distinction in "Knowing and Acknowledging," developed it further in "The Avoidance of Love," his magisterial essay on *King Lear*, and then turned it into the foundation of part 4 of *The Claim of Reason*. Cavell's "acknowledgment" is not the same as "recognition," as this concept is often used in political debates. Rather, as Nikolas Kompridis has shown, "acknowledgment" adds a vital new dimension to debates concerning "recognition" (see "Recognition and Receptivity").

24. For a splendid discussion of this picture of the inner and the outer see Finkelstein, *Expression and the Inner*. Chapter 4, "Meaning, Expression and Expressivism," is particularly interesting. See also my discussion of the Saussurean picture of language in chapters 5 and 6.

25. See Cavell, *Disowning Knowledge*; Beckwith, *Shakespeare and the Grammar of Forgiveness*; Moi, *Henrik Ibsen and the Birth of Modernism*.

26. Cavell uses *The Corsican Brothers* as an example in "Knowing and Acknowledging." Boucicault based his play on an 1844 novella by Alexandre Dumas.

27. Cavell, "Avoidance of Love," particularly 296–301.

28. On this point, I disagree with Gibson, in *Fiction and the Weave of Life*, who thinks we always "move from knowledge to acknowledgment" (111), and therefore considers acknowledgment to be the "fulfilment of knowledge" (112). An example of this may be the scene in Murdoch's novel *The Bell*, which I discuss in chapter 10.

29. Cavell, "Avoidance of Love," 337.

30. Ibid.

31. I am echoing Cavell's: "What you need to learn will depend on what specifically it is you want to know; and how you can find out will depend specifically on what you already command," in "Must We Mean What We Say?" 20.

32. I use "acknowledgment" to say something about readers and reading. Gibson draws on his somewhat different understanding of the term to argue that "literary works represent ways of acknowledging the world rather than knowing it" (*Fiction and the Weave of Life*, 117). I disagree with the idea that acknowledgment is an *alternative* to knowledge: there surely can be no "rather than" here.

33. Mukařovský, "Standard Language and Poetic Language," 226.

34. Ibid.; Jakobson "Closing Statement," 356.

35. Jakobson, "Closing Statement," 356.

36. See Shklovsky, "Art as Device."

37. Ellis, *Theory of Literary Criticism*, 34.

38. Ellis too recommends focusing on the "edges," the "marginal members"; ibid., 35.

39. I discuss Wittgenstein's understanding of concepts and his critique of the craving for generality in chapters 3 and 4.

40. "And to imagine a language means to imagine a form of life" (§19).

41. Cavell, "Availability of Wittgenstein's Later Philosophy," 52.

42. For more on "projecting a word," see Cavell, "Excursus on Wittgenstein's Vision of Language."

43. For "sharpen our perceptions," see Austin, "Plea for Excuses," 182.

44. For an interesting overview of different views of the uses of literature, see Felski, *Uses of Literature*. For a Wittgenstein-inspired defense of literary humanism, see Harrison, *What Is Fiction For?* One of the best known defenses of the uplifting effects of reading is Nussbaum, *Not for Profit*.

45. Macé, "Ways of Reading, Modes of Being," 213.

46. Huemer, "Introduction," 5.

47. Eldridge, *Literature, Life and Modernity*, 7, 5, 22.

48. Altieri, *Reckoning with the Imagination*, 187, 210–13.

49. Beauvoir, "Literature and Metaphysics," 270. I amended the translation. The original can be found in "Littérature et métaphysique," 106.

50. Felski calls this "enchantment" in *Uses of Literature*, 51–76.

51. In his trilogy about the emergence of modern painting, *Absorption and Theatricality, Courbet's Realism,* and *Manet's Modernism*, Fried provides a brilliant framework for thinking about absorption as a value that modernism had to overcome. I want to stress that Fried writes about absorption as a feature of paintings; whereas I am thinking of the state of the reader, or beholder.

52. See Landy, *How to Do Things with Fictions*, 3–19.

53. Ibid., 10, 19.

54. Beckwith, "Are There Any Women in Shakespeare's Plays?" I take her "just response" to be one way of talking about reading as acknowledgment of the other.

55. *Pursuits of Happiness*, 10.

56. See Sartre, *What Is Literature?* particularly chapter 2, "Why Write?" 49–69.

57. See particularly the discussion of the two "peculiarities" of the judgment of taste in Kant, *Critique of the Power of Judgment*, 162–66.

58. *Pursuits of Happiness*, 12.

59. Ibid., 41–42.

60. Ibid., 12.

61. "Exploration" is my translation of *recherche*, from "Littérature et métaphysique," 109. The English translation has "search" ("Literature and Metaphysics," 271).

62. My translation from "Littérature et métaphysique," 122–23.

63. Beauvoir, "Que peut la littérature?" 83, my translation.

64. Nussbaum, *Not for Profit*, 36.

65. Arendt, *Lectures on Kant's Political Philosophy*, 43.

66. Quoted by Diamond, "Missing the Adventure," 313. The square brackets are my omissions, the dots are Diamond's. I have corrected a misprint in Diamond's quotation. The original can be found in Robertson, *George Mallory*, 217.

67. Diamond, "Missing the Adventure," 315.

Chapter 10

1. I discuss the case further in Moi, "Markedslogikk og kulturkritikk."

2. Johansen, "Virkelighetssjokk," 18. In this chapter, all translations from the Norwegian are mine.

3. Suskind, "Faith, Certainty," 2004. The article doesn't mention Rove's name, but the speaker has been widely identified as Rove, for example in Danner, "Words in a Time of War."

4. Colbert, "The Word: Truthiness."

5. Errol Morris's 2014 documentary on Donald Rumsfeld, *The Unknown Known*, contains some brilliant examples of Rumsfeld's deliberate deployment of misleading language.

6. See Kant, *Critique of the Power of Judgment*.

7. See my discussion of Wittgenstein's §217, in chapter 7.

8. Cavell, "Availability," 48.

9. See Affeldt, "The Ground of Mutuality," 2, 15.

10. Ibid., 14.

11. Austin, "A Plea for Excuses," 182, 185.

12. Foer, *Moonwalking with Einstein*, 51, 55.

13. James, "The Art of Fiction," 510.

14. Austin, "Plea for Excuses," 184, 198.

15. Davenport, "The Geography of the Imagination," 3.

16. See Wallace, *A Supposedly Fun Thing I'll Never Do Again*. See also Garner and Wallace, *Quack This Way*, for Wallace's views on language and writing.

17. Murdoch, *Sovereignty of Good*, 33.

18. Jamison, "In Defense of Saccharin(e)," in *The Empathy Exams*, Kindle loc. 1821–22.

19. Weil, "Reflections on the Right Use of School Studies with a View to the Love of God," 112.

20. Ibid., 105, 110.

21. Ibid., 114.

22. Murdoch, *Sovereignty of Good*, 33.

23. My account of Diamond's view in this section is based on Diamond, "Murdoch the Explorer."

24. Murdoch, "Symposium: Vision and Choice in Morality," 46.

25. de la Mare, "Ducks," 817.

26. Murdoch, *The Bell*, 9–10.

27. Ibid., 10.

28. Ibid., 11.

29. Murdoch herself considered thoughts of rewards to be alien to moral deliberations (see *Sovereignty of Good*, 65).

30. Diamond, "The Difficulty of Reality and the Difficulty of Philosophy," 44–45.

31. Coltart, "Slouching Towards Bethlehem … or Thinking the Unthinkable in Psychoanalysis," 14.

32. This makes me think of Diamond's and Conant's investigations of the idea of nonsense in Wittgenstein's *Tractatus*. See Diamond, "What Nonsense Might Be," and Conant, "Must We Show What We Cannot Say?"

33. Coltart, "Slouching Towards Bethlehem," 14.

34. Diamond, "The Difficulty of Reality and the Difficulty of Philosophy," 62.

35. I am expanding on Diamond's example in ibid., 61–62.

36. Klüger, *Still Alive*, 108–9.

37. See chapter 9.

38. Murdoch, *Sovereignty of Good*, 65.

39. Diamond, "Murdoch the Explorer," 57.

40. Murdoch, *Sovereignty of Good*, 59.

41. This section draws on my essay on *Little Eyolf*, "Something that Might Resemble a Kind of Love."

42. I follow Ibsen's habit of referring to male principal characters with their last names.

43. Ibsen, *Lille Eyolf*, 266.

44. Rilke, *Notebooks of Malte Laurids Brigge*, 4.

45. Ibid., 71.

46. Ibid., 70–71.

47. Woolf, *A Room of One's Own*, 108. Subsequent page numbers appear in the text.

48. I discuss some of the implications of this view in "I Am Not a Woman Writer" (2008).

49. See Farsethås, *Herfra til virkeligheten*.

50. Hjorth, *Leve posthornet!*

51. Howard Hong and Edna Hong translate Kierkegaard's *Posthorn* as "stagecoach horn." Kierkegaard, *Repetition*, in *Fear and Trembling and Repetition*, 175.

52. See Borchgrevink, *A Norwegian Tragedy*; Seierstad, *One of Us*.

53. ICD-10 is WHO's diagnostic manual, organized according to the same principles as the American Psychiatric Association's handbook *DSM-V*.

54. *VG-Nett*, "22/7-rettssaken: Ord-for-ord—dag 38" (torsdag 14. juni) http://www.vg.no/nyheter/innenriks/22-juli/rettssaken/artikkel.php?artid=10058131.

55. *VG-Nett*, "22/7-rettssaken: Ord-for-ord—dag 38."

56. Arendt, *Eichmann in Jerusalem*, 136.

57. Orwell, "Politics and the English Language," 170.

Works Cited

Affeldt, Steven G. "The Ground of Mutuality: Criteria, Judgment, and Intelligibility in Stephen Mulhall and Stanley Cavell." *European Journal of Philosophy* 6, no. 1 (1998): 1–31.

Altieri, Charles. *Reckoning with the Imagination: Wittgenstein and the Aesthetics of Literary Experience.* Ithaca, NY: Cornell University Press, 2015.

———. "Wittgenstein on Consciousness and Language: A Challenge to Derridean Literary Theory." *Modern Language Notes* 91, no. 6 (1976): 1397–1423.

Anscombe, G. E. M. *Intention.* Cambridge: Harvard University Press, 1957.

"Archie and the Bowling Team." *All in the Family* (CBS TV series). First broadcast on December 16, 1972. With Carroll O'Connor and Jean Stapleton. Directed by Bob La Hendro and John Rich. https://www.youtube.com/watch?v=ITOzrIVV6nY (accessed January 15, 2016).

Arendt, Hannah. *Eichmann in Jerusalem: A Report on the Banality of Evil.* 1963; New York: Penguin, 2006.

———. *Lectures on Kant's Political Philosophy.* Chicago: University of Chicago Press, 1989.

Austin, J. L. *How to Do Things with Words.* Cambridge: Harvard University Press, 1975.

———. "Other Minds." In *Philosophical Papers*, 3rd ed., 76–116. Oxford: Oxford University Press, 1979.

———. "A Plea for Excuses." In *Philosophical Papers*, 3rd ed., 175–204. Oxford: Oxford University Press, 1979.

———. *Sense and Sensibilia.* Reconstructed from the manuscript notes by G. J. Warnock. Oxford: Oxford University Press, 1964.

Baker, G. P., and P. M. S. Hacker. *Wittgenstein: Understanding and Meaning; Part I: Essays.* Volume 1 of *An Analytical Commentary on the "Philosophical Investigations."* 2nd extensively rev. ed. Edited by P. M. S. Hacker. Oxford: Blackwell Publishing, 2005.

Bakhtin, Mikhail Mikhaïlovitch. "Discourse in the Novel." In *The Dialogic Imagination*, edited by Michael Holquist, 259–422. Austin: University of Texas Press, 1981.

Barad, Karen. "Posthumanist Performativity: Toward an Understanding of How Matter Comes to Matter." *Signs* 28, no. 3 (2003): 801–31.

Barthes, Roland. "The Death of the Author." In *The Rustle of Language*, 49–55. Oxford: Basil Blackwell, 1986.

Bartolovich, Crystal. "Humanities of Scale: Marxism, Surface Reading—and Milton." *PMLA* 127, no. 1 (2012): 115–21.

Bauer, Nancy. *Simone de Beauvoir, Philosophy, and Feminism.* New York: Columbia, 2001.

———. "What Philosophy Can't Teach Us about Sexual Objectification." In *How to Do Things with Pornography*, 21–37. Cambridge: Harvard University Press, 2015.

Bauer, Nancy, Sarah Beckwith, Alice Crary, Sandra Laugier, Toril Moi, and Linda Zer-illi. "Introduction." *New Literary History* 46, no. 2 (Spring 2015): v–xiii.

Bearn, Gordon C. F. "The Possibility of Puns: A Defense of Derrida." *Philosophy and Literature* 19, no. 2 (1995): 330–35.

Beauvoir, Simone de. *L'Existentialisme et la sagesse des nations.* Paris: Nagel, 1948.

———. "Literature and Metaphysics." In *Philosophical Writings*, edited by Margaret A. Simons, Marybeth Timmermann, and Mary Beth Mader, translated by Véronique Zaytzeff, 263–77. Urbana: University of Illinois Press, 2004. Originally published as "Littérature et métaphysique" in *L'existentialisme et la sagesse des nations*, 103–24. Paris: Nagel, 1948.

———. "Pyrrhus and Cineas." In *Philosophical Writings*, edited by Margaret A. Simons, Marybeth Timmermann, and Mary Beth Mader, translated by Marybeth Timmer-mann, 89–149. Urbana: University of Illinois Press, 2004. Originally published as *Pyrrhus et Cinéas.* Paris: Gallimard, 1944.

———. "Que peut la littérature?" In *Que peut la littérature?* edited by Yves Berger, 73–92. Paris: Union Générale d'Editions, 1965.

———. *The Second Sex.* Translated by Constance Borde and Sheila Malovany-Chevallier. New York: Knopf, 2010. Originally published as *Le Deuxième sexe.* 2 vols. Paris: Gallimard, 1949.

Beckwith, Sarah. "Are There Any Women in Shakespeare's Plays? Fiction, Represen-tation, and Reality in Feminist Criticism." *New Literary History* 46, no. 2 (2015): 241–60.

———. *Shakespeare and the Grammar of Forgiveness.* Ithaca, NY: Cornell University Press, 2011.

Belsey, Catherine. *Critical Practice.* London: Routledge, 1980.

Bennington, Geoffrey. *Frontiers: Kant, Hegel, Frege, Wittgenstein.* Self-published pdf. 500 pages. 2003. ISBN (pdf format) 0-9754996-0-2.

Benveniste, Emile. "L'appareil formel de l'énonciation." In *Problèmes de linguistique générale*, 79–88. Paris: Gallimard (Coll. Tel), 1974.

———. "The Nature of the Linguistic Sign." Translated by Mary Elizabeth Meek. In *Problems in General Linguistics*, 43–48. Coral Gables, FL: University of Miami Press, 1971. Originally published as "Nature du signe linguistique" in *Problèmes de linguis-tique générale*, 49–55. Paris: Gallimard (Coll. Tel), 1966.

Best, Stephen, and Sharon Marcus. "Surface Reading: An Introduction." *Representations* no. 108 (2009): 1–21.

Borchgrevink, Aage Storm. *A Norwegian Tragedy: Anders Behring Breivik and the Mas-sacre on Utøya.* Translated by Guy Puzey. Cambridge: Polity Press, 2013. Originally published as *En norsk tragedie: Anders Behring Breivik og veiene til Utøya.* Oslo: Gyl-dendal, 2012.

Bourdieu, Pierre. *Distinction: A Social Critique of the Judgment of Taste.* Translated by Richard Nice. London: Routledge Kegan Paul, 1980.

Bradley, Arthur. *Derrida's "Of Grammatology."* Bloomington: Indiana University Press, 2008.

Brooks, Cleanth. *The Well Wrought Urn: Studies in the Structure of Poetry.* New York: Harcourt, Brace and World, 1947.

Brooks, Peter. "The Strange Case of Paul de Man." *New York Review of Books*, April 3, 2014, 44–47.

Butler, Judith. "A 'Bad Writer' Bites Back." *New York Times*, March 20, 1999. http://query.nytimes.com/gst/fullpage.html?res=950CE5D61531F933A15750C0A96F958260

———. "Exacting Solidarities (Letter to the Editor)." *London Review of Books*, July 1, 1999. http://www.lrb.co.uk/v21/n13/letters#letter5.

———. *Excitable Speech: A Politics of the Performative*. New York: Routledge, 1997.

———. *Gender Trouble: Feminism and the Subversion of Identity*. 10th anniversary ed. New York: Routledge, 1999.

Carastathis, Anna. "Identity Categories as Potential Coalitions." *Signs* 38, no. 4 (2013): 941–65.

———. "The Invisibility of Privilege: A Critique of Intersectional Models of Identity." *Les Ateliers de l'éthique* (La Revue du CREUM) 3, no. 2 (2008): 23–38.

Carbado, Devon W., Kimberlé Williams Crenshaw, Vickie M. Mays, and Barbara Tomlinson. "Intersectionality." *Du Bois Review: Social Science Research on Race* 10, no. 2 (2013): 303–12.

Cavell, Stanley. "Aesthetic Problems of Modern Philosophy." In Cavell, *Must We Mean What We Say?*, 73–96.

———. "The Argument of the Ordinary: Scenes of Instruction in Wittgenstein and in Kripke." In *Conditions Handsome and Unhandsome: The Constitution of Emersonian Perfectionism*, 64–100. Chicago: University of Chicago Press, 1990.

———. "Austin at Criticism." In Cavell, *Must We Mean What We Say?*, 97–114.

———. "The Availability of Wittgenstein's Later Philosophy." In Cavell, *Must We Mean What We Say?*, 44–72.

———. "The Avoidance of Love: A Reading of *King Lear*." In Cavell, *Must We Mean What We Say?*, 267–353.

———. *The Claim of Reason: Wittgenstein, Skepticism, Morality, and Tragedy*. 1979; New York: Oxford University Press, 1999.

———. *Contesting Tears: The Hollywood Melodrama of the Unknown Woman*. Chicago: University of Chicago Press, 1996.

———. "Counter-Philosophy and the Pawn of Voice." In *A Pitch of Philosophy: Autobiographical Exercises*, 53–127. Cambridge: Harvard University Press, 1994.

———. *Disowning Knowledge: In Seven Plays by Shakespeare*. Cambridge: Cambridge University Press, 2003.

———. "The Division of Talent." *Critical Inquiry* 11, no. 4 (1985): 519–38.

———. "Excursus on Wittgenstein's Vision of Language." In *The Claim of Reason: Wittgenstein, Skepticism, Morality, and Tragedy*, 168–90. New York: Oxford University Press, 1999.

———. "Existentialism and Analytical Philosophy." *Daedalus* 93, no. 3 (1964): 946–74.

———. *In Quest of the Ordinary: Lines of Skepticism and Romanticism*. Chicago: University of Chicago Press, 1988.

———. "Knowing and Acknowledging." In Cavell, *Must We Mean What We Say?*, 238–66.

———. *Little Did I Know: Excerpts from Memory*. Palo Alto, CA: Stanford University Press, 2010.

———. "A Matter of Meaning It." In Cavell, *Must We Mean What We Say?*, 213–37.

———. "Must We Mean What We Say?" In Cavell, *Must We Mean What We Say?*, 1–43.

———. *Must We Mean What We Say? A Book of Essays.* 1969; Cambridge: Cambridge University Press, 2002.

———. "Notes and Afterthoughts on the Opening of Wittgenstein's *Investigations.*" In *Philosophical Passages: Wittgenstein, Emerson, Austin, Derrida*, 125–86. Cambridge, MA: Blackwell, 1995.

———. "Performative and Passionate Utterances." In *Philosophy the Day after Tomorrow*, 155–91. Cambridge: Harvard University Press, 2005.

———. *Philosophical Passages: Wittgenstein, Emerson, Austin, Derrida.* Cambridge, MA: Blackwell, 1995. 45.

———. *A Pitch of Philosophy: Autobiographical Exercises.* Cambridge: Harvard University Press, 1994.

———. "The Politics of Interpretation (Politics as Opposed to What?)." In *Themes Out of School: Effects and Causes*, 27–59. Chicago: University of Chicago Press, 1988. Originally published as "The Politics of Interpretation (Politics as Opposed to What?)," *Critical Inquiry* 9, no. 1 (September 1982): 157–78.

———. *Pursuits of Happiness: The Hollywood Comedy of Remarriage.* Cambridge: Harvard University Press, 1981.

———. "Seminar on 'What Did Derrida Want of Austin?'" In *Philosophical Passages: Wittgenstein, Emerson, Austin, Derrida*, 66–90. Cambridge, MA: Blackwell, 1995.

———. *The Senses of Walden.* Chicago: University of Chicago Press, 1981.

———. *This New Yet Unapproachable America: Lectures after Emerson after Wittgenstein.* Albuquerque, NM: Living Batch Press, 1989.

———. "What Did Derrida Want of Austin?" In *Philosophical Passages: Wittgenstein, Emerson, Austin, Derrida*, 42–65. Cambridge, MA: Blackwell, 1995.

———. "What Is the Scandal of Skepticism?" In *Philosophy the Day after Tomorrow*, 132–54. Cambridge: Harvard University Press, 2005.

Cohen, Ted. *Jokes: Philosophical Thoughts on Joking Matters.* Chicago: University of Chicago Press, 1999.

Colbert, Stephen. "The Word—Truthiness." Segment of *The Colbert Report.* Broadcast on Comedy Central, October 17, 2005.

Collins, Patricia Hill. "Looking Back, Moving Ahead: Scholarship in Service to Social Justice." *Gender and Society* 26, no. 14 (2012): 14–22.

Coltart, Nina. *Slouching Towards Bethlehem ... And Further Psychoanalytic Explorations.* London: Free Association Books, 1993.

Conant, James. "Elucidation and Nonsense in Frege and Early Wittgenstein." In *The New Wittgenstein*, edited by Alice Crary and Rupert Read, 174–217. London: Routledge, 2000.

———. "Must We Show What We Cannot Say?" In *The Senses of Stanley Cavell*, edited by Richard Fleming and Michael Payne, 242–83. Lewisburg, PA: Bucknell University Press, 1989.

———. "Wittgenstein on Meaning and Use." *Philosophical Investigations* 21, no. 3 (1998): 222–50.

Cortázar, Julio. *A Certain Lucas.* Translated by Gregory Rabassa. New York: Alfred A. Knopf, 1984. Originally published as *Un tal Lucas.* Buenos Aires: Punto de Lectura, 2008.

Crary, Alice. "Introduction." In *The New Wittgenstein*, edited by Alice Crary and Rupert Read. London: Routledge, 2000.

Crary, Alice, and Sanford Shieh, eds. *Reading Cavell.* New York: Routledge, 2006.

Crenshaw, Kimberlé. "Demarginalizing the Intersection of Race and Sex: A Black Feminist Critique of Antidiscrimination Doctrine, Feminist Theory and Antiracist Politics." *University of Chicago Legal Forum* (1989): 139–67.

Critchley, Simon. *Very Little ... Almost Nothing: Death, Philosophy and Literature.* London: Routledge, 1997.

Culler, Jonathan. "The Call of the Phoneme: Introduction." In *On Puns: The Foundation of Letters*, 1–16. Oxford: Basil Blackwell, 1988.

———. *Ferdinand de Saussure.* Rev. ed. Ithaca, NY: Cornell University Press, 1986.

———. *On Deconstruction: Theory and Criticism after Structuralism.* Ithaca, NY: Cornell University Press, 1982.

Culler, Jonathan, and Kevin Lamb, eds. *Just Being Difficult? Academic Writing in the Public Arena.* Stanford, CA: Stanford University Press, 2003.

Danner, Mark. "Words in a Time of War." *The Nation*, May 31, 2007. http://www.thenation.com/article/words-time-war/.

Davenport, Guy. "The Geography of the Imagination." In *The Geography of the Imagination*, 3–15. Jaffrey, NH: Nonpareil Books, David R. Godine Publisher, 1997.

Davidson, Arnold I. *The Emergence of Sexuality: Historical Epistemology and the Formation of Concepts.* Cambridge: Harvard University Press, 2001.

———, ed. *Foucault and His Interlocutors.* Chicago: University of Chicago Press, 1997.

Davis, Kathy. "Intersectionality as Buzzword: A Sociology of Science Perspective on What Makes a Feminist Theory Successful." *Feminist Theory* 9, no. 1 (2008): 67–85.

Davis, Norbert. *The Mouse in the Mountain [Rendez-vous with Fear].* 1943. *The Essential Works of Norbert Davis.* N.p.: Golgotha Press, 2010. Kindle edition.

de la Mare, Walter. "Ducks." In *The Complete Poems of Walter de la Mare*, 816–17. London: Faber, 1969.

de Man, Paul. "Semiology and Rhetoric." In *Allegories of Reading: Figural Language in Rousseau, Nietzsche, Rilke and Proust*, 3–19. New Haven, CT: Yale University Press, 1979. Originally published as "Semiology and Rhetoric," *Diacritics* 3, no. 3 (Autumn 1973): 27–33.

Deleuze, Gilles. *Gilles Deleuze from A to Z.* Interview with Claire Parnet. Directed by Pierre-André Boutang. DVD. Cambridge, MA: MIT Press, 2011.

Deleuze, Gilles, and Félix Guattari. *Qu'est-ce que la philosophie?* 1991; Paris: Minuit, 2005.

Derrida, Jacques. "Afterword." In *Limited Inc*, 111–60. Evanston, IL: Northwestern University Press, 1988.

———. "Derrida's Response to Mulhall." *Ratio* 13, no. 4 (2000): 415–18.

———. *Of Grammatology.* Translated by Gayatri Chakravorty Spivak. Baltimore, MD: Johns Hopkins University Press, 1976. Originally published as *De la Grammatologie.* Paris: Editions de Minuit, 1967.

———. "Signature Event Context." In *Limited Inc*, 1–23. Evanston, IL: Northwestern University Press, 1988.

Descartes, René. *A Discourse on the Method.* Translated by Ian Maclean. Oxford: Oxford University Press, 2006.

———. *Les Passions de l'ame.* Paris: Vrin, 1970.

Diamond, Arlyn, and Lee R. Edwards, eds. *The Authority of Experience: Essays in Feminist Criticism.* Amherst: University of Massachusetts Press, 1977.

Diamond, Cora. "Criss-Cross Philosophy." In *Wittgenstein at Work: Method in the Philosophical Investigations*, edited by Erich Ammereller and Eugen Fischer, 201–20. New York: Routledge, 2004.

———. "The Difficulty of Reality and the Difficulty of Philosophy." In Stanley Cavell, Cora Diamond, John McDowell, Ian Hacking, and Cary Wolfe, *Philosophy and Animal Life*, 43–89. New York: Columbia University Press, 2008.

———. "Ethics, Imagination and the Method of Wittgenstein's *Tractatus*." In *The New Wittgenstein*, edited by Alice Crary and Rupert Read, 149–73. London: Routledge, 2000.

———. "Losing Your Concepts." *Ethics* 98, no. 2 (1988): 255–77.

———. "Missing the Adventure: Reply to Martha Nussbaum." In *The Realistic Spirit: Wittgenstein, Philosophy, and the Mind*, 309–18. Cambridge, MA: MIT Press, 1995.

———. "Murdoch the Explorer." *Philosophical Topics* 38, no. 1 (2010): 51–85.

———. *The Realistic Spirit: Wittgenstein, Philosophy, and the Mind*. Cambridge, MA: MIT Press, 1995.

———. "Rules: Looking in the Right Place." In *Wittgenstein: Attention to Particulars. Essays in Honour of Rush Rhees (1905–89)*, edited by D. Z. Phillips and Peter Winch, 12–34. New York: St. Martin's Press, 1989.

———. "What Nonsense Might Be." In *The Realistic Spirit: Wittgenstein, Philosophy, and the Mind*, 95–114. Cambridge, MA: MIT Press, 1995.

Dolphijn, Rick, and Iris van der Tuin. *New Materialism: Interviews and Cartographies*. Ann Arbor: Open Humanities Press, University of Michigan Library, 2012. http://www.openhumanitiespress.org/books/titles/new-materialism/

Drury, Maurice O'Connor. "Conversations with Wittgenstein." In *Ludwig Wittgenstein: Personal Recollections*, edited by Rush Rhees, 112–89. Totowa, NJ: Rowman and Littlefield, 1981.

———. *The Danger of Words*. New York: Humanities Press, 1973.

Dutton, Denis. "The Bad Writing Contest: Press Releases, 1996–1998." http://denisdutton.com/bad_writing.htm.

———. "Language Crimes: A Lesson in How Not to Write, Courtesy of the Professoriat." *Wall Street Journal*, February 5, 1999. http://denisdutton.com/language_crimes.htm.

Eldridge, Richard. *Literature, Life, and Modernity*. New York: Columbia University Press, 2008.

———, ed. *Stanley Cavell*. Cambridge: Cambridge University Press, 2003.

Ellis, John M. *Against Deconstruction*. Princeton, NJ: Princeton University Press, 1989.

———. *The Theory of Literary Criticism: A Logical Analysis*. Berkeley: University of California Press, 1974.

Everett, Daniel L. *Don't Sleep, There Are Snakes: Life and Language in the Amazonian Jungle*. New York: Vintage Books, 2008.

Farsethås, Ane. *Herfra til virkeligheten: Lesninger i oo-tallets litteratur*. Oslo: Cappelen Damm, 2012.

Felman, Shoshana. *The Scandal of the Speaking Body: Don Juan with J. L. Austin, or Seduction in Two Languages*. Foreword by Stanley Cavell. Stanford, CA: Stanford University Press, 2002.

Felski, Rita. "After Suspicion." *Profession* (2009): 28–35.

———. "Context Stinks!" *New Literary History* 42, no. 4 (2011): 573–91.

———. "Critique and the Hermeneutics of Suspicion." *M/C Journal* 15, no. 1 (2012). http://journal.media-culture.org.au/index.php/mcjournal/article/view/431.

———. "From Literary Theory to Critical Method." *Profession* (2008): 108–16.

————. *The Limits of Critique*. Chicago: University of Chicago Press, 2015.

————. "Nothing to Declare: Identity, Shame, and the Lower Middle Class." *PMLA* 115, no. 1 (2000): 33–45.

————. "Suspicious Minds." *Poetics Today* 32, no. 2 (2011): 215–34.

————. *The Uses of Literature*. Malden, MA: Blackwell, 2008.

Finkelstein, David H. *Expression and the Inner*. Cambridge: Harvard University Press, 2003.

Fischer, Michael. *Stanley Cavell and Literary Skepticism*. Chicago: University of Chicago Press, 1989.

Fish, Stanley. *Doing What Comes Naturally: Change, Rhetoric, and the Practice of Theory in Literary and Legal Studies*. Durham, NC: Duke University Press, 1989.

————. "How Ordinary Is Ordinary Language?" In *Is There a Text in This Class? The Authority of Interpretive Communities*, 97–111. Cambridge, MA: Harvard University Press, 1980.

————. "Intentional Neglect." *New York Times*, July 19, 2005. http://www.nytimes.com /2005/07/19/opinion/intentional-neglect.html?_r=0.

————. "Introduction, or How I Stopped Worrying and Learned to Love Interpretation." In *Is There a Text in This Class? The Authority of Interpretive Communities*, 1–17. Cambridge, MA: Harvard University Press, 1980.

Fleming, Richard. *Evil and Silence*. Boulder, CO: Paradigm Publishers, 2010.

————. *First Word Philosophy: Wittgenstein–Austin–Cavell; Writings on Ordinary Language Philosophy*. Lewisburg, PA: Bucknell University Press, 2004.

————. "Listening to Cage: Nonintentional Philosophy and Music." *Cogent Arts and Humanities* 3. Posted January 14, 2016. http://cogentoa.tandfonline.com/doi/full/10 .1080/23311983.2015.1088733.

————. "Ordinary Language Philosophy." Entry in *A Dictionary of Cultural and Critical Theory*, edited by Michael Payne and Jessica Rae Butto, 516–20. Oxford: Wiley Blackwell, 2010.

————. *The State of Philosophy: An Invitation to a Reading in Three Parts of Stanley Cavell's The Claim of Reason*. Lewisburg, PA: Bucknell University Press, 1993.

Fleming, Richard, and Michael Payne, eds. *The Senses of Stanley Cavell*. Lewisburg, PA: Bucknell University Press, 1989.

Foer, Joshua. *Moonwalking with Einstein: The Art and Science of Remembering Everything*. New York: Penguin, 2011.

Foucault, Michel. "What Is an Author?" In *Language, Counter-Memory, Practice: Selected Essays and Interviews*, edited by Donald F. Bouchard, 113–38. Ithaca, NY: Cornell University Press, 1977.

Frege, Gottlob. *The Frege Reader*. Oxford: Blackwell, 1997.

Freud, Sigmund. "Fragment of an Analysis of a Case of Hysteria [Dora]." 1905. In *The Standard Edition of the Complete Psychological Works*, edited and translated by James Strachey, 7:1–122. London: The Hogarth Press, 1953–74.

————. "The Method of Interpreting Dreams: An Analysis of a Specimen Dream." 1899. In *The Interpretation of Dreams. The Standard Edition of the Complete Psychological Works*, edited and translated by James Strachey, 4:96–121. London: The Hogarth Press, 1953–74.

Fried, Michael. *Absorption and Theatricality: Painting and Beholder in the Age of Diderot*. Chicago: University of Chicago Press, 1980.

——. *Courbet's Realism*. Chicago: University of Chicago Press, 1990.

——. *Manet's Modernism or, The Face of Painting in the 1860s*. Chicago: University of Chicago Press, 1996.

Friedman, Susan Stanford. *Mappings: Feminism and the Cultural Geographies of Encounter*. Princeton, NJ: Princeton University Press, 1998.

Fry, Paul. "Deconstruction II." Lecture 11 in ENGL 300: "Introduction to Theory of Literature." http://oyc.yale.edu/english/engl-300/lecture-11.

Frye, Marilyn. *The Politics of Reality: Essays in Feminist Theory*. Berkeley, CA: Crossing Press, 1983.

Garner, Bryan A., and David Foster Wallace. *Quack This Way: David Foster Wallace and Bryan A. Garner Talk Language and Writing*. Dallas, TX: RosePen Books, 2013.

Gee, James Paul, and Michael Handford. "Introduction." In *The Routledge Handbook of Discourse Analysis*, edited by James Paul Gee and Michael Handford, 1–6. London: Routledge, 2012.

Gellner, Ernest. *Words and Things: An Examination of, and an Attack on, Linguistic Philosophy*. 1959; London: Routledge, 2005.

Gibson, John. *Fiction and the Weave of Life*. New York: Oxford University Press, 2007.

Ginzburg, Carlo. "Clues: Roots of an Evidential Paradigm." In *Clues, Myths, and the Historical Method*, 96–125. Baltimore, MD: Johns Hopkins University Press, 1992.

Glendinning, Simon. "Inheriting 'Philosophy': The Case of Austin and Derrida Revisited." *Ratio* 13, no. 4 (2000): 307–31.

——. *On Being with Others: Heidegger–Derrida–Wittgenstein*. London: Routledge, 1998.

——. "Preface: Arguing with Derrida." *Ratio* 13, no. 4 (2000): 299–306.

——. "Wittgenstein's Apocalyptic Library." In *Wittgenstein and the Future of Philosophy: A Reassessment after 50 Years*. Proceedings of the 24th International Wittgenstein-Symposium, August 12–18, 2001, Kirchberg Am Wechsel (Austria), edited by Rudolf Haller and Klaus Phul, 61–70. Vienna: ÖBV + HPT, 2002.

——. "Wittgenstein's Nomadism." In *What Philosophy Is: Contemporary Philosophy in Action*, edited by Havi Carel and David Gomez, 155–67. London: Continuum, 2004.

Gorman, David. "The Use and Abuse of Speech-Act Theory in Criticism." *Poetics Today* 20, no. 1 (1999): 93–119.

Gould, Timothy. *Hearing Things: Voice and Method in the Writing of Stanley Cavell*. Chicago: University of Chicago Press, 1998.

——. "The Unhappy Performative." In *Performativity and Performance: Essays from the English Institute*, edited by Andrew Parker and Eve Kosofsky Sedgwick, 17–44. New York: Routledge, 1995.

Graff, Gerald. "Editor's Foreword." In Jacques Derrida, *Limited Inc*, vii–viii. Evanston, IL: Northwestern University Press, 1988.

——. "Scholars and Sound Bites: The Myth of Academic Difficulty." *PMLA* 115, no. 5 (2000): 1041–52.

Grosz, Elizabeth. "The Practice of Feminist Theory." *Differences* 21, no. 1 (2010): 94–108.

Hacker, P. M. S. *Wittgenstein: Comparisons and Context*. Oxford: Oxford University Press, 2013.

Hacking, Ian. *The Social Construction of What?* Cambridge: Harvard University Press, 1999.

Hammer, Espen. *Stanley Cavell: Skepticism, Subjectivity and the Ordinary*. Cambridge: Polity Press, 2002.

Hankivsky, Olena. "Rethinking Care Ethics: On the Promise and Potential of an Inter-sectional Analysis." *American Political Science Review* 108, no. 2 (2014): 252–64.

Hansen, Nat. "Contemporary Ordinary Language Philosophy." *Philosophy Compass* 9, no. 8 (August 2014): 556–69. doi: 10.1111/phc3.12152.

Harris, Roy. *Saussure and His Interpreters*. Edinburgh: Edinburgh University Press, 2001.

Harrison, Bernard. *What Is Fiction For? Literary Humanism Restored*. Bloomington: Indiana University Press, 2015.

Hartman, Geoffrey H. *Beyond Formalism: Literary Essays, 1958–1970*. New Haven, CT: Yale University Press, 1970.

Hekman, Susan. *The Material of Knowledge: Feminist Disclosures*. Bloomington: Indiana University Press, 2010.

Hirsch, E. D., Jr. "Against Theory?" In *Against Theory: Literary Studies and the New Pragmatism*, edited by W. J. T. Mitchell, 48–52. Chicago: University of Chicago Press, 1985.

———. *Validity in Interpretation*. New Haven, CT: Yale University Press, 1967.

Hirschkop, Ken. *Mikhail Bakhtin: An Aesthetic for Democracy*. Oxford: Oxford University Press, 1999.

Hjorth, Vigdis. *Leve posthornet!* Oslo: Cappelen Damm, 2012.

Hoffman, Josef. "Hard-boiled Wit: Ludwig Wittgenstein and Norbert Davis." *Mysteryfile.com* (2006). http://www.mysteryfile.com/NDavis/Wit.html.

Huemer, Wolfgang. "Introduction: Wittgenstein, Language and Philosophy of Literature." In *The Literary Wittgenstein*, edited by John Gibson and Wolfgang Huemer, 1–13. London: Routledge, 2004.

Ibsen, Henrik. *Lille Eyolf*. 1896. *Hundreårsutgaven: Henrik Ibsens samlede verker* 12. Edited by Francis Bull, Halvdan Koht, and Didrik Arup Seip, 195–268. Oslo: Gyldendal, 1928–57.

Jakobson, Roman. "Closing Statement: Linguistics and Poetics." In *Style in Language*, edited by Thomas A. Sebeok, 350–77. Cambridge, MA: MIT Press, 1960.

James, Henry. "The Art of Fiction." *Longman's Magazine* 4 (1884): 502–21.

Jameson, Fredric. "Imaginary and Symbolic in Lacan: Marxism, Psychoanalytic Criticism, and the Problem of the Subject." *Yale French Studies* 55–56 (1977): 338–95.

———. *The Political Unconscious: Narrative as a Socially Symbolic Act*. Ithaca, NY: Cornell University Press, 1981.

———. *The Prison-House of Language: A Critical Account of Structuralism and Russian Formalism*. Princeton, NJ: Princeton University Press, 1972.

Jamison, Leslie. *The Empathy Exams: Essays*. Minneapolis, MN: Graywolf Press, 2014. Kindle edition.

Johansen, Anders. "Virkelighetssjokk." *Prosa* 18, no. 5 (2012): 17–23.

Jost, Walter, and Kenneth Dauber, eds. *Ordinary Language Criticism: Literary Thinking after Cavell after Wittgenstein*. Evanston, IL: Northwestern University Press, 2003.

Juhl, P. D. *Interpretation: An Essay in the Philosophy of Literary Criticism*. Princeton, NJ: Princeton University Press, 1980.

Kahneman, Daniel. *Thinking, Fast and Slow*. New York: Farrar, Straus and Giroux, 2011.

Kamuf, Peggy. "Floating Authorship." *Diacritics* 16, no. 4 (1986): 3–13.

Kant, Immanuel. *Critique of the Power of Judgment*. 1790. Translated by Paul Guyer. Cambridge: Cambridge University Press, 2000.

Kates, Joshua. "A Transcendental Sense of Death? Derrida and the Philosophy of Language." *Modern Language Notes* 120, no. 5 (2005): 1009–43.

Kierkegaard, Søren. *Fear and Trembling. Repetition.* 1849. Translated by Howard V. Hong and Edna H. Hong. Princeton, NJ: Princeton University Press, 1983.

Kirby, Vicki. *Telling Flesh: The Substance of the Corporeal.* New York: Routledge, 1997.

Kitching, Gavin, and Nigel Pleasants, eds. *Marx and Wittgenstein: Knowledge, Morality and Politics.* London: Routledge, 2002.

Klinkenborg, Verlyn. *Several Short Sentences about Writing.* New York: Vintage Books, 2013.

Klüger, Ruth. *Still Alive: A Holocaust Girlhood Remembered.* New York: The Feminist Press at CUNY, 2001.

Knapp, Steven, and Walter Benn Michaels. "Against Theory." In *Against Theory: Literary Studies and the New Pragmatism,* edited by W. J. T. Mitchell, 11–30. Chicago: University of Chicago Press, 1985. Originally published as "Against Theory," *Critical Inquiry* 8, no. 4 (Summer 1982): 723–42.

Kompridis, Nikolas. "Recognition and Receptivity: Forms of Normative Response in the Lives of the Animals We Are." *New Literary History* 44, no. 1 (2013): 1–24.

Kripke, Saul. *Wittgenstein on Rules and Private Language.* Cambridge: Cambridge University Press, 1982.

Kristeva, Julia. *Revolution in Poetic Language.* Translated by Margaret Waller. New York: Columbia University Press, 1984. Originally published as *Révolution du langage poétique.* Paris: Seuil, 1974.

———. "The System and the Speaking Subject." In *The Kristeva Reader,* edited by Toril Moi, 24–33. Oxford: Blackwell, 1986.

———. "Word, Dialogue, and Novel." In *The Kristeva Reader,* edited by Toril Moi, translated by Alice Jardine, Thomas Gora and Léon S. Roudiez, 34–61. Oxford: Blackwell, 1986.

Kuhn, Thomas S. *The Structure of Scientific Revolutions.* Chicago: University of Chicago Press, 1970.

Landy, Joshua. *How to Do Things with Fictions.* New York: Oxford University Press, 2012.

Latour, Bruno. "Why Has Critique Run Out of Steam? From Matters of Fact to Matters of Concern." *Critical Inquiry* 30 (2004): 225–48.

Laugier, Sandra. *Why We Need Ordinary Language Philosophy.* Translated by Daniela Ginsburg. Chicago: University of Chicago Press, 2013.

Lesjak, Carolyn. "Reading Dialectically." *Criticism* 55, no. 2 (2013): 233–77.

Lewis, Gail. "Unsafe Travel: Experiencing Intersectionality and Feminist Displacements." *Signs* 38, no. 4 (2013): 869–92.

Löfgren, Ingeborg. *Interpretive Skepticism: Stanley Cavell, New Criticism, and Literary Interpretation.* Acta Universitatis Upsaliensis 47. Uppsala: Litteraturvetenskapliga Institutionen, 2015.

Love, Heather. "Close But Not Deep: Literary Ethics and the Descriptive Turn." *New Literary History* 41, no. 2 (2010): 371–91.

———. "Close Reading and Thin Description." *Public Culture* 25, no. 3 (2013): 401–34.

Macé, Marielle. "Ways of Reading, Modes of Being." *New Literary History* 44, no. 2 (Spring 2013): 213–29. Originally published in *Façons de lire, manières d'être.* Paris: Gallimard, 2011.

Marcus, Sharon. *Between Women: Friendship, Desire, and Marriage in Victorian England.* Princeton, NJ: Princeton University Press, 2007.

Marcuse, Herbert. *One-Dimensional Man: Studies in the Ideology of Advanced Industrial Society.* Boston: Beacon Press, 1964.

Mauro, Tullio de. "Sur F. de Saussure." In *Cours de linguistique générale*, edited by Tullio de Mauro, 319–89. Paris: Payot, 1980.

McCall, Leslie. "The Complexity of Intersectionality." *Signs: Journal of Women in Culture and Society* 30, no. 3 (2005): 1771–1800.

Meisel, Perry, and Haun Saussy. "Saussure and His Contexts." Introduction to Ferdinand de Saussure, *Course in General Linguistics*, xv–xlviii. New York: Columbia University Press, 2011.

Merleau-Ponty, Maurice. *Phenomenology of Perception*. Translated by Colin Smith. London: Routledge, 1962.

Michaels, Walter Benn. *The Shape of the Signifier*. Princeton, NJ: Princeton University Press, 2004.

Miller, J. Hillis. *Speech Acts in Literature*. Stanford, CA: Stanford University Press, 2001.

Miller, James. "Is Bad Writing Necessary? George Orwell, Theodor Adorno and the Politics of Literature." *Lingua Franca* 9 (December/January 2000). http://linguafranca.mirror.theinfo.org/9912/writing.html. Republished in *Quick Studies: The Best of Lingua Franca*, edited by Alexander Star, 75–93. New York: Farrar, Straus and Giroux, 2002.

Millett, Kate. *Sexual Politics*. Garden City, NY: Doubleday, 1970.

Mitchell, W. J. T., ed. *Against Theory: Literary Studies and the New Pragmatism*. Chicago: University of Chicago Press, 1985.

Modleski, Tania. *Feminism without Women: Culture and Criticism in a "Postfeminist" Age*. New York: Routledge, 1991.

Moi, Toril. "The Adventure of Reading: Literature and Philosophy, Cavell and Beauvoir." *Literature and Theology* 25, no. 2 (2011): 125–40. Republished in *Stanley Cavell and Literary Studies: Consequences of Skepticism*, edited by Richard Eldridge and Bernard Rhie, 17–29. New York: Continuum, 2011.

———. "Appropriating Bourdieu: Feminist Theory and Pierre Bourdieu's Sociology of Culture." *New Literary History* 22, no. 4 (1991): 1017–49.

———. "Fem røde epler: Fra navn til bruk; En kommentar til § 1 i Wittgensteins *Filosofiske undersøkelser*." *Edda* 101, no. 4 (2014): 348–53.

———. "From Femininity to Finitude: Freud, Lacan and Feminism, Again." *Signs: Journal of Women in Culture and Society* 29, no. 3 (2004): 841–78.

———. "Hedda's Silences: Beauty and Despair in *Hedda Gabler*." *Modern Drama* 56, no. 4 (2013): 434–56.

———. *Henrik Ibsen and the Birth of Modernism: Art, Theater, Philosophy*. Oxford: Oxford University Press, 2006.

———. "'I Am Not a Woman Writer': About Women, Literature and Feminist Theory Today." *Feminist Theory* 9, no. 3 (2008): 259–71.

———. "Markedslogikk og kulturkritikk: Om Breivik og ubehaget i den postmoderne kulturen." *Samtiden* no. 3 (2012): 20–30.

———. "Meaning What We Say: The 'Politics of Theory' and the Responsibility of Intellectuals." In *The Philosophical Legacy of Simone de Beauvoir*, edited by Emily R. Grosholz, 139–60. Oxford: Clarendon Press, 2004.

———. *Sex, Gender, and the Body: The Student Edition of "What Is a Woman?"* Oxford: Oxford University Press, 2005.

———. "'Something That Might Resemble a Kind of Love': Fantasy and Realism in Henrik Ibsen's *Little Eyolf*." In *Understanding Love: Philosophy, Film, and Fiction*, edited by Susan Wolf and Christopher Grau, 185–208. New York: Oxford University Press, 2014.

———. *Språk og oppmerksomhet.* Stemmer 1. Oslo: Aschehoug, 2013.

———. "Språkets tvangstrøye: Om poststrukturalistisk språkteori og queer teori." In *Når heteroseksualiteten må forklare seg,* edited by Trine Annfelt, Britt Andersen, and Agnes Bolsø, 223–41. Trondheim: Tapir Akademisk Forlag, 2007.

———. "'They Practice Their Trades in Different Worlds': Concepts in Poststructuralism and Ordinary Language Philosophy." *New Literary History* 40, no. 4 (2009): 801–24.

———. *What Is a Woman? And Other Essays.* Oxford: Oxford University Press, 1999.

———. "'What's the Difference?': Om Stanley Cavells lesning av Paul de Man." In *Perifraser: Til Per Buvik på 50-årsdagen fra venner og kolleger ved Litteraturvitenskapelig Institutt,* 142–76. Bergen: Litteraturvitenskapelig Institutt, 1995.

———. "A Woman's Desire to Be Known: Expressivity and Silence in *Corinne.*" In *Untrodden Regions of the Mind: Romanticism and Psychoanalysis,* edited by Ghislaine McDayter, 143–75. Lewisburg, PA: Bucknell University Press, 2002.

Moretti, Franco. "Conjectures on World Literature." *New Left Review,* no. 1 (2000): 54–68.

Morris, Errol, dir. *The Unknown Known.* Documentary, 2014.

Mukařovský, Jan. "Standard Language and Poetic Language." In *The Routledge Language and Cultural Theory Reader,* edited by Lucy Burke, Tony Crowley, and Alan Girvin, 225–30. London: Routledge, 2000.

Mulhall, Stephen. "The Givenness of Grammar: A Reply to Steven Affeldt." *European Journal of Philosophy* 6, no. 1 (1998): 32–44.

———. *Stanley Cavell: Philosophy's Recounting of the Ordinary.* Oxford: Oxford University Press, 1994.

Murdoch, Iris. *The Bell.* 1958; New York: Penguin, 1987.

———. *The Sovereignty of Good.* London: Routledge, 2001.

———. "Symposium: Vision and Choice in Morality." *Proceedings of the Aristotelian Society,* Supplementary Volumes 30 (1956): 32–58.

Nagl, Ludwig, and Chantal Mouffe, eds. *The Legacy of Wittgenstein: Pragmatism or Deconstruction.* Frankfurt am Main: Peter Lang, 2001.

Nash, Jennifer C. "Re-Thinking Intersectionality." *Feminist Review* 89 (2008): 1–15.

Nehamas, Alexander. "What an Author Is." *Journal of Philosophy* 83, no. 11 (1983): 685–91.

Noggle, James. "The Wittgensteinian Sublime." *New Literary History* 27, no. 4 (1996): 605–19.

Nussbaum, Martha C. *Not for Profit: Why Democracy Needs the Humanities.* Princeton, NJ: Princeton University Press, 2010.

Ogden, C. K., and I. A. Richards. *The Meaning of Meaning: A Study of the Influence of Language upon Thought and of the Science of Symbolism.* New York: Harcourt, Brace and World, 1946.

Orupabo, Julia. "Interseksjonalitet i praksis: Utfordringer med å anvende et interseksjonalitetsperspektiv i empirisk forskning." *Sosiologisk tidsskrift* 22, no. 4 (2014): 329–51.

Orwell, George. "Politics and the English Language." In *A Collection of Essays,* 156–71. New York: Harcourt, 1981.

Panagia, Davide. "The Shape of the Signifier or, The Ontology of Argument." *Theory and Event* 8, no. 2 (2005). doi 10.1353/tae.2005.0033.

Perloff, Marjorie. *Wittgenstein's Ladder: Poetic Language and the Strangeness of the Ordinary.* Chicago: University of Chicago Press, 1996.

Pinker, Steven. *The Sense of Style: The Thinking Person's Guide to Writing in the 21st Century.* New York: Viking, 2014.

Plato. *Theaetetus.* Translated by Robin A. H. Waterfield. London: Penguin Classics, 2004.

Potter, Jonathan. "Wittgenstein and Austin." In *Discourse Theory and Practice: A Reader,* edited by Margaret Wetherell, Stephanie Taylor, and Simeon J. Yates, 39–46. London: Sage Publications, 2001.

Pratt, Mary Louise. *Toward a Speech Act Theory of Literary Discourse.* Bloomington: Indiana University Press, 1977.

Quigley, Austin E. "Wittgenstein's Philosophizing and Literary Theorizing." *New Literary History* 19, no. 2 (1988): 209–37.

Read, Rupert. "Marx and Wittgenstein on Vampires and Parasites: A Critique of Capital and Metaphysics." In *Marx and Wittgenstein: Knowledge, Morality and Politics,* edited by Gavin Kitching and Nigel Pleasants, 254–81. London: Routledge, 2002.

———. "Ordinary/Everyday Language." In *Wittgenstein: Key Concepts,* edited by Kelly Dean Jolley, 63–80. Durham, England: Acumen, 2010.

Redfield, Marc. "Introduction." In *Legacies of Paul de Man,* edited by Marc Redfield, 1–16. New York: Fordham University Press, 2007.

———. *Theory at Yale: The Strange Case of Deconstruction in America.* New York: Fordham University Press, 2016.

Rhees, Rush. *Discussions of Wittgenstein.* London: Routledge and Kegan Paul, 1970.

Rhie, Bernie. "Wittgenstein on the Face of a Work of Art." *Nonsite.org,* no. 3 (2011). http://nonsite.org/article/wittgenstein-on-the-face-of-a-work-of-art.

Rhu, Lawrence F. *Stanley Cavell's American Dream: Shakespeare, Philosophy, and Hollywood Movies.* New York: Fordham University Press, 2006.

Ricoeur, Paul. *Freud and Philosophy.* Translated by Denis Savage. New Haven, CT: Yale University Press, 1970.

———. "Husserl and Wittgenstein." In *Phenomenology and Existentialism,* edited by Edward N. Lee and Maurice Mandelbaum, 207–18. Baltimore: Johns Hopkins Press, 1967.

———. "The Model of the Text: Meaningful Action Considered as a Text." *New Literary History* 5, no. 1 (1973): 91–117.

Rilke, Rainer Maria. *The Notebooks of Malte Laurids Brigge.* Translated by Michael Hulse. London: Penguin, 2009.

Robertson, David. *George Mallory.* London: Faber and Faber, 1969.

Rooney, Ellen. "Live Free or Describe: The Reading Effect and the Persistence of Form." *Differences* 21, no. 3 (2010): 112–39.

Rorty, Richard. "Philosophy without Principles." In *Against Theory: Literary Studies and the New Pragmatism,* edited by W. J. T. Mitchell, 132–38. Chicago: University of Chicago Press, 1985.

Roth, Marco. "I Don't Want Your Revolution." Review of Jonathan Lethem, *Dissident Garden. London Review of Books* (February 20, 2014): 24–25.

Rudrum, David. *Stanley Cavell and the Claim of Literature.* Baltimore, MD: Johns Hopkins University Press, 2013.

Sartre, Jean-Paul. *Being and Nothingness.* Translated by Hazel E. Barnes. New York: Washington Square Press, 1992.

———. "What Is Literature?" In *"What Is Literature?" And Other Essays,* edited by Steven Ungar, 21–238. Cambridge: Harvard University Press, 1988.

Saussure, Ferdinand de. *Cours de linguistique générale*. Published by Charles Bally and
    Albert Séchehaye, with the assistance of Albert Riedlinger. Critical edition by Tullio
    de Mauro. Paris: Payot, 1980.
———. *Course in General Linguistics*. Translated by Wade Baskin. Edited by Perry Mei-
    sel and Haun Saussy. New York: Columbia University Press, 2011.
———. "Lettres de Ferdinand de Saussure à Antoine Meillet." *Cahiers Ferdinand de
    Saussure* 21 (1964): 89–130.
———. *Writings in General Linguistics*. Edited by Simon Bouquet and Rudolf Engler.
    Translated by Carol Sanders, Matthew Pires, and Peter Figueroa. Oxford: Oxford
    University Press, 2006.
Schalkwyk, David. *Literature and the Touch of the Real*. Newark: University of Delaware
    Press, 2004.
Scott, Joan Wallach. "The Evidence of Experience." *Critical Inquiry* 17, no. 4 (1991):
    773–97.
Searle, John R. "Reiterating the Differences: A Reply to Derrida." *Glyph* 2 (1977):
    198–208.
———. "The Word Turned Upside Down." Review of Jonathan Culler, *On Deconstruc-
    tion*. *New York Review of Books* (October 27, 1983): 74–79.
Sedgwick, Eve Kosofsky. "Paranoid Reading and Reparative Reading, Or, You're So Par-
    anoid, You Probably Think This Essay Is about You." In *Touching Feeling: Affect, Ped-
    agogy, Performativity*, 123–51. Durham, NC: Duke University Press, 2003.
Segerdal, Pär. "Gender, Language and Philosophical Reconciliation: What Does Ju-
    dith Butler Destabilise?" In *Ethics and the Philosophy of Culture: Wittgensteinian Ap-
    proaches*, edited by Ylva Gustafsson, Camilla Kronqvist, and Hannes Nykänen, 172–
    211. Newcastle: Cambridge Scholars Publishing, 2013.
Seierstad, Åsne. *One of Us: The Story of Anders Breivik and the Massacre in Norway*.
    Translated by Sarah Death. New York: Farrar, Straus and Giroux, 2015. Originally
    published as *En av oss: En fortelling om Norge*. Oslo: Kagge, 2013.
Sherlock. BBC TV-Series. "A Study in Pink." Season 1, episode 1. First broadcast July 25,
    2010. With Benedict Cumberbatch and Martin Freeman. Written by Steven Moffat.
    Directed by Paul McGuigan. DVD.
Shklovsky, Viktor. "Art as Device." In *Theory of Prose*, 1–14. Champaign: Dalkey Archive
    Press, 1990.
Søndergaard, Dorte Marie. "Poststructuralist Approaches to Empirical Analysis." *Quali-
    tative Studies in Education* 15, no. 2 (2002): 187–204.
Spivak, Gayatri Chakravorty. "Criticism, Feminism and the Institution." Interview with
    Elizabeth Gross. In *Intellectuals: Aesthetics, Politics, Academics*, edited by Bruce Rob-
    bins, 153–71. Minneapolis: University of Minnesota Press, 1990.
Staten, Henry. Review of Walter Benn Michaels, *The Shape of the Signifier*. *Modernism/
    Modernity* 12, no. 2 (2005): 362–64.
———. *Wittgenstein and Derrida*. Lincoln: University of Nebraska Press, 1984.
———. "Wittgenstein's Deconstructive Legacy." In *The Legacy of Wittgenstein: Pragma-
    tism or Deconstruction*, edited by Ludwig Nagl and Chantal Mouffe, 43–62. Frankfurt
    am Main: Peter Lang, 2001.
Steedman, Carolyn. *Landscape for a Good Woman: A Story of Two Lives*. New Bruns-
    wick, NJ: Rutgers University Press, 1987.
Stone, Martin. "On the Old Saw, 'Every Reading of a Text Is an Interpretation': Some

Remarks." In *The Literary Wittgenstein*, edited by John Gibson and Wolfgang Huemer, 186–208. London: Routledge, 2004.

———. "Wittgenstein on Deconstruction." In *The New Wittgenstein*, edited by Alice Crary and Rupert Read, 83–117. London: Routledge, 2000.

Straub, Kristina. "The Suspicious Reader Surprised, Or, What I Learned from "Surface Reading." *The Eighteenth Century* 54, no. 1 (2013): 139–43.

Suskind, Ron. "Faith, Certainty and the Presidency of George W. Bush." *New York Times Magazine*, October 17, 2004. http://www.nytimes.com/2004/10/17 /magazine/17BUSH.html?_r=0.

Sword, Helen. *Stylish Academic Writing*. Cambridge: Harvard University Press, 2012.

Symons, Arthur. *The Symbolist Movement in Literature*. 1899. Revised and enlarged edition. New York: E. P. Dutton and Company, 1919.

Terada, Rei. "Philosophical Self-Denial: Wittgenstein and the Fear of Public Language." *Common Knowledge* 8, no. 3 (2002): 464–81.

Tomlinson, Barbara. "To Tell the Truth and Not Get Trapped: Desire, Distance, and Intersectionality at the Scene of Argument." *Signs* 38, no. 4 (2013): 993–1017.

Uschanov, T. P. "Ernest Gellner's Criticisms of Wittgenstein and Ordinary Language Philosophy." In *Marx and Wittgenstein: Knowledge, Morality and Politics*, edited by Gavin Kitching and Nigel Pleasants, 23–46. London: Routledge, 2002.

VG-Nett. "22/7-rettssaken: Ord-for-ord—dag 38 (torsdag 14. juni)." *VG-Nett*, June 15, 2012. Corrected June 17, 2012. http://www.vg.no/nyheter/innenriks/terrorangrepet -22-juli-rettssaken/ord-for-ord-dag-38/a/10058131/.

Vidal, Joaquín. "Faena cumbre de El Viti en Salamanca." *El País*, September 17, 1979. http://elpais.com/diario/1978/09/17/cultura/274831203_850215.html.

Vinten, Robert. "Eagleton's Wittgenstein." *Critique: Journal of Socialist Theory* 43, no. 2 (2015): 261–76.

———. "Leave Everything as It Is – A Critique of Marxist Interpretations of Wittgenstein." *Critique: Journal of Socialist Theory* 41, no. 1 (2013): 9–22.

Wallace, David Foster. *A Supposedly Fun Thing I'll Never Do Again*. New York: Little, Brown, 1997.

Wang, Orrin N. C. "Against Theory Beside Romanticism: The Sensation of the Signifier." *Diacritics* 35, no. 2 (2005): 3–29.

Ware, Ben. *Dialectic of the Ladder: Wittgenstein, the "Tractatus" and Modernism*. London: Bloomsbury Academic, 2015.

Warner, Michael. "Styles of Intellectual Publics." In *Just Being Difficult: Academic Writing in the Public Arena*, edited by Jonathan Culler and Kevin Lamb, 106–25. Stanford, CA: Stanford University Press, 2003.

Weil, Simone. "Reflections on the Right Use of School Studies with a View to the Love of God." Translated by Emma Crawford. In *Waiting for God*, 105–16. New York: Harper Colophon, 1973. For the original, see "Réflexions sur le bon usage des études scolaires en vue de l'amour de Dieu," in *Écrits de Marseille (1940–42): Philosophie, science, religion, questions politiques et sociales*, edited by Florence de Lussy, 255–62. Paris: Gallimard, 2008.

Wetherell, Margaret, Stephanie Taylor, and Simeon J. Yates. "Introduction." In *Discourse Theory and Practice: A Reader*, edited by Margaret Wetherell, Stephanie Taylor, and Simeon J. Yates, 1–8. London: Sage Publications, 2001.

Wetzel, James. "Wittgenstein's Augustine: The Inauguration of the Later Philosophy." In

Augustine and Philosophy, edited by Philip Cary, John Doody, and Kim Paffenroth, 219–42. Lanham, MD: Lexington Books, 2010.

Williams, Joseph M. *Style: Toward Clarity and Grace*. With two chapters coauthored by Gregory G. Colomb. Chicago: University of Chicago Press, 1990.

Wilson, George M. "Again, Theory: On Speaker's Meaning, Linguistic Meaning, and the Meaning of a Text." *Critical Inquiry* 19, no. 1 (1992): 164–85.

Wimsatt, W. K., Jr., and Monroe C. Beardsley. "The Intentional Fallacy." In Wimsatt, *The Verbal Icon: Studies in the Meaning of Poetry*, 3–18. Lexington: University Press of Kentucky, 1954.

Witherspoon, Edward. "Conceptions of Nonsense in Carnap and Wittgenstein." In *The New Wittgenstein*, edited by Alice Crary and Rupert Read, 315–49. London: Routledge, 2000.

Wittgenstein, Ludwig. *The Blue and Brown Books: Preliminary Studies for the "Philosophical Investigations."* 1958; New York: Harper Torchbooks, 1965.

———. *Culture and Value*. Translated by Peter Winch. Chicago: University of Chicago Press, 1980.

———. *On Certainty*. Translated by Denis Paul and G. E. M. Anscombe. Oxford: Blackwell, 1975.

———. *Philosophical Investigations*. The German text, with an English translation. 1953. Rev. 4th ed., translated by G. E. M. Anscombe, P. M. S. Hacker, and Joachim Schulte, edited by P. M. S. Hacker and Joachim Schulte. Oxford: Wiley-Blackwell, 2009.

———. "Philosophy." [Sections 86–93 of the so-called Big Typescript.] In *Philosophical Occasions 1912–1951*, edited by James Klagge and Alfred Nordmann, 160–99. Indianapolis, IN: Hackett, 1993.

———. "Philosophy of Psychology—A Fragment." [Previously known as "Part II."] In *Philosophical Investigations*. The German text, with an English translation. 1953. Rev. 4th ed., translated by G. E. M. Anscombe, P. M. S. Hacker, and Joachim Schulte, edited by P. M. S. Hacker and Joachim Schulte, 182–243. Oxford: Wiley-Blackwell, 2009.

———. *Remarks on the Foundations of Mathematics*. Translated by G. E. M. Anscombe. Cambridge, MA: MIT Press, 1978.

———. *Tractatus Logico-Philosophicus*. 1922. Translated by D. F. Pears and B. F. McGuinness. London: Routledge, 1994.

Woolf, Virginia. *A Room of One's Own*. 1929; New York: Harcourt, 2005.

Yu, Timothy. "Wittgenstein, Pedagogy, and Literary Criticism." *New Literary History* 44, no. 3 (2013): 361–78.

Zerilli, Linda. *A Democratic Theory of Judgment*. Chicago: University of Chicago Press, 2016.

———. *Signifying Woman: Culture and Chaos in Rousseau, Burke, and Mill*. Ithaca, NY: Cornell University Press, 1994.

Ziarek, Ewa Płonowska. *The Rhetoric of Failure: Deconstruction of Skepticism, Reinvention of Modernism*. Albany: State University of New York Press, 1996.

Žižek, Slavoj. *In Defense of Lost Causes*. London: Verso, 2008.

Index

Ingram Content Group UK Ltd.
Milton Keynes UK
UKHW012010130323
418508UK00005B/476